HUMAN RIGHTS IN

We work with leading authors to develop the
strongest educational materials in Law, bringing
cutting-edge thinking and best
learning practice to a global market.

Under a range of well-known imprints, including
Longman, we craft high quality print and
electronic publications which help readers to understand
and apply their content, whether studying or at work.

To find out more about the complete range of our
publishing, please visit us on the World Wide Web at:
www.pearsoneduc.com

HUMAN RIGHTS IN THE UK

A GENERAL INTRODUCTION TO THE HUMAN RIGHTS ACT 1998

David Hoffman
MA (Oxon), BCL, Barrister

John Rowe Q.C.
MA (Oxon), Barrister

PEARSON
Longman

Harlow, England • London • New York • Boston • San Francisco • Toronto
Sydney • Tokyo • Singapore • Hong Kong • Seoul • Taipei • New Delhi
Cape Town • Madrid • Mexico City • Amsterdam • Munich • Paris • Milan

Pearson Education Limited
Edinburgh Gate
Harlow
Essex CM20 2JE
England

and Associated Companies throughout the world

Visit us on the World Wide Web at:
www.pearsoneduc.com

First edition 2003

© Pearson Education Limited 2003

British Library Cataloguing-in-Publication Data
A catalogue record for this book is
available from the British Library

Library of Congress Cataloging-in-Publication Data
Hoffman, David, 1971–
Human rights in the UK : a general introduction to the Human Rights Act 1998 / David
Hoffman, John Rowe.
p. cm.
Includes bibliographical references and index.
ISBN 0-582-47323-3 (alk. paper)
1. Human rights—Great Britain. 2. Civil rights—Great Britain. I. Rowe, John (John)
Jermyn), 1936– II. Title.

KD4080.H64 2003
342.41′085—dc21

2002193198

10 9 8 7 6 5 4 3 2 1
08 07 06 05 04 03

Typeset in 10/12.5pt Sabon by 35
Printed in Great Britain by Henry Ling Ltd., at the Dorset Press, Dorchester, Dorset.

The publisher's policy is to use paper manufactured from sustainable forests.

BRIEF CONTENTS

CONTENTS

FOREWORD

Following the election of the Labour Party in 1997, one of the first announcements by the new Government was of its intention to give people in the United Kingdom direct access to the rights contained in the European Convention on Human Rights. To say that this was a radical idea, considering the established assumption that people in the UK were adequately protected by the common law, and therefore had no need of these 'foreign' rights, is perhaps too mild a description. The keen debate that accompanied the passage of the Human Rights Bill through Parliament, in which I was involved as a Minister, then at the Home Office – the sponsor Department for the Bill, reflected the constitutional significance of the measure. Few were unmoved.

When the Human Rights Act 1998 came into effect on 2 October 2000, it was accompanied by a great deal of publicity, and a good many publications. There is no doubt that the Act presented a considerable challenge, and one that was for lawyers and the courts to deal with in the first instance. However, there was little in the wealth of new literature on the Act that was readily accessible to the interested non-lawyer. Therefore, this book will be very welcome, for not only is it very readable – owing much to the good sense and considerable experience of its authors – it is also comprehensive in its scope.

The reader will find an excellent account of the development of international protection for human rights, the unique constitutional position of the United Kingdom, including the Parliamentary process, and the history of the European Convention. Ordinarily, all of this would be enough for one book, but here it is succinctly and judiciously presented and lays the ground for the main thrust of the book which is, as the name says, *Human Rights in the UK*.

The appearance of this book some two and a half years since the Act came into force, together with all of the contextual material I have just referred to, provides the reader with a sense of perspective, as well as a ready understanding of his or her rights. Clearly, the operation of the Human Rights Act is central to this, and the book presents a balanced analysis, with useful questions at the end of each chapter for the reader to consider against what they have just read. The sections dealing with the relationship between Parliament, the Judiciary and the Executive described by the Act are as good an example as can be found anywhere.

I have no doubt that this book will contribute to the wider development of the human rights culture in the UK.

Lord Williams Of Mostyn QC
Lord Privy Seal and Leader of the House of Lords

ACKNOWLEDGEMENTS

We are grateful to the following for permission to reproduce copyright material:

Image of Magna Carta in Chapter 3 from *The Book of Magna Carta*, by Hindley, G. (Guild Publishing: 1990); Image of the European Court of Human Rights in Chapter 5 reproduced courtesy of EPA/PA Photos; Image of classroom in Chapter 7 reproduced courtesy of Michael Stephens/PA Photos; Image of the Rock of Gibraltar in Chapter 8 reproduced courtesy of the Gibraltar Tourist Board; Image of Molesworth in Chapter 9 copyright Ronald Searle, 1956 from *Molesworth*, by Geoffery Willans and Ronald Searle by kind permission of the artist and The Sayle Literary Agency; Image of Slave Notice in Chapter 10 from *National Geographic* (August, 2002), reproduced courtesy of the Library of Congress; Image of Mayday Protestors being detained on Oxford Street by Police in Chapter 11 reproduced courtesy of Mirrorpix, the online picture library from The Mirror Group and Partners (www.mirrorpix.com); Image in watercolours of the Courtroom in Chapter 12 reproduced courtesy of Lancaster Castle and the Duchy of Lancaster; Image of Catherine Zeta-Jones and Michael Douglas in Chapter 14 reproduced courtesy of Mirrorpix, the online picture library from The Mirror Group and Partners (www.mirrorpix.com); Image of man at Speaker's Corner, London in Chapter 16 reproduced courtesy of Aaron Robson/PA Photos; Image of the 1984 Miner's Strike in Chapter 17 reproduced courtesy of The People's History Museum, with thanks to Phil Dunn; Image of fox hunt in Chapter 19 reproduced courtesy of Getty Images (www.gettyimages.com); Image of the World Trade Center on 11th September 2001 in Chapter 21 reproduced courtesy of Susan Meiselas/Magnum Photos.

In some instances we have been unable to trace the owners of copyright material, and we would appreciate any information that would enable us to do so.

TABLE OF CASES

TABLE OF INTERNATIONAL TREATIES

TABLE OF STATUTES

UK LEGISLATION

EUROPEAN LEGISLATION

OTHER LEGISLATION
FRANCE:

US:

TABLE OF STATUTORY INSTRUMENTS

Chapter 1

INTRODUCTION

'What is the use of a book,' thought Alice, 'without pictures or conversations?' (Lewis Carroll, Alice's Adventures in Wonderland, 1865).

Human rights are those fundamental freedoms and entitlements that each person possesses by virtue of nothing more than their status as a human being. To say that there is a right to life is to say that each person, man or woman, boy or girl, of whatever race or colour, religion or background, has the same basic entitlement to be allowed to live as every other person. Adding the word 'human' stresses that these rights are based on the basic equality of all people. They are all rights that everyone shares – for example, no-one is born with more of a right to life than anybody else.

What rights we include in a list of human rights is not an easy question, and different people throughout the centuries have come up with different lists. Some basic rights are likely to be included in any list we would make today – for example, the right to life, freedom from torture or slavery, freedom of speech. Even these have not always been recognised as basic rights to which all people are entitled – for example, slavery was quite common for much of human history, and still exists in some parts of the world today. Our list should include those rights which protect the values that we hold to be most important.

This book is about a recent Act of Parliament, the Human Rights Act 1998 (hereafter, 'the Act'), which brings the European Convention on Human Rights into the domestic law of the United Kingdom. The European Convention is a treaty which came into being in 1950, but it has not, until now, been directly a part of our law. The treaty contains a particular list of human rights, and it is these which we shall be considering, together with the legal framework for enforcing them created by the new Act. This list, which most European countries, including the United Kingdom, have long recognised as being important, should accord with our view of what basic rights we should have. If it does not, then we can criticise the law for failing to protect all those rights which should be protected.

It is also important to stress at the outset that the Human Rights Act 1998 is one of the most important statutes ever passed in the United Kingdom. It has the scope to change the way we think about our identity as citizens of our country, in a way that only a few laws have in the past. In that sense, it can be termed a piece of constitutional legislation, which joins other significant pieces of law in making up a large part of our Constitution: for example, Magna Carta (1215), the Bill of Rights (1688), which set up our Constitutional Monarchy, the Acts of Union with Scotland (1706–7) and Ireland (1800), the European Communities Act (1972), or the Acts granting Irish independence or a measure of devolution to Scotland or Wales.[1]

The Human Rights Act has constitutional significance not just because it sets out clearly and in an organised manner those basic rights which must be respected, even by Parliament, but also because it applies to all law already existing and to all law that Parliament makes in the future. It therefore has great scope for remodelling many parts of our law if they do not accord proper protection to people's rights. So for the first time in the United Kingdom there is one standard for the protection of rights by which all laws are considered. This can be contrasted with the traditional approach of, for example, the English common law, which is that a citizen of the United Kingdom has the freedom to do anything which is not specifically banned, but which has never set out comprehensively what rights he or she positively possesses. Although our law has provided a fair measure of protection for a large number of basic rights, there is now scope for it to provide more such protection. Thus, our law will inevitably be more focused on the perspective of individual rights than it has been previously – and this has the potential to lead to a major shift in how we see each other as citizens of our country.

We hope that the discussion in this book will provoke thought about human rights in general and their protection in English law in particular. We will consider first the background to the Convention and the Act and to set both in their political context; then the scheme of the Act and how it implements the European Convention; finally we will discuss in more detail the particular rights which the Act embodies, together with practical examples.

The examples we use have been mostly taken from cases decided in the United Kingdom or in Strasbourg, designed to show how the Convention works in practice. We hope that non-lawyers will not be put off by the references to British or European cases: the way one understands legislation is by considering how it works in practical situations, in particular in cases that the Courts have decided. Those who are not studying or practising law should not need to look up any of the cases cited to understand the point that is being made, but full case references have been included for any readers who would like to research particular areas or cases further.

We hope that the cases and other examples will help to show some of the ways in which the Human Rights Act and the implementation of the Convention rights into United Kingdom law will affect us in some surprisingly common and everyday situations and that the use of examples will help our readers to understand the full scope of this important piece of legislation. It should also be understood at the outset that it is not the aim of this book to provide a comprehensive treatment of the case law: we have used those cases which seem to us to be most interesting, or most significant, or most useful in the understanding of the Convention right under discussion.

This book is aimed, broadly, at the undergraduate, or non-lawyer looking for an introduction to the subject. We also hope that it is of use for other students, or for

---

[1] Government of Ireland Act 1920, Anglo-Irish Treaty Act 1922, etc.; Scotland Act 1998, Government of Wales Act 1998; Northern Ireland Act 1998.

those teaching other students, as well as of interest to anyone who would like to know more about this significant legal landmark. We should also introduce the questions at the end of most of the chapters. These are there to provoke thought, and hopefully discussion, whether the reader is a student or not; they are there to highlight some of the issues raised by the chapter; they are not intended as any form of a test on the chapter. We hope that this book will encourage the reader to think about this Act and the rights it protects, and the questions are part of that aspiration. The occasional illustration will serve, we hope, the same purpose.

The Act applies throughout the United Kingdom of Great Britain and Northern Ireland. Although it is one country, the United Kingdom contains three separate legal systems – those of England and Wales, Scotland and Northern Ireland. Our discussion will deal with the law of England and Wales, but we hope that the general discussion of the Act will be of interest and use to readers in the other jurisdictions.

The law is as at 1 November 2002, although some later matters have been able to insinuate themselves into the text at the proof stage.

ACKNOWLEDGEMENTS

This is a convenient point for the authors to acknowledge the invaluable help and assistance of the following, for proof-reading, discussion, reaction and encouragement: Professor Matthew Butcher, Katharine Edgar, the Rt. Hon. Lady Justice Hale OBE, John Hoffman, Anna Short, Owain Thomas, Dave Wilkinson; for research assistance, Jenny Kumeta; and, those who helped to steer this volume towards fruition at Pearson: Pat Bond, Beth Barber, Michelle Gallagher and David Cox. As with all such acknowledgements, any faults or errors which remain are the responsibility of the authors.

ABBREVIATIONS

Throughout this book we will be using the following:

'The Act'	The Human Rights Act 1998. The full text is to be found in Appendix 1.
'The Convention'	The European Convention on Human Rights. The full text is to be found in Appendix 2.
'The European Court'	The European Court of Human Rights, which sits in Strasbourg (not to be confused with the European Court of Justice of the European Union which sits in Luxembourg). This is an international court and may be contrasted with the national or domestic courts of the United Kingdom or other state.
'The Commission'	The European Commission on Human Rights (and again not the Commission of the European Communities / European Union).
'The Convention rights'	The rights which are protected by the Convention and which are included in schedule 1 of the Act.

GLOSSARY OF LEGAL TERMS

The names of legal cases are by the names of the parties, *Smith versus (v) Jones*, where Smith is bringing the case against Jones. Sometime a case is referred to as 'in *re*', which is Latin for 'in the matter of', where the object of the case, such as a will or a piece of land, is an easy shorthand for the case. Where the name of a case includes an initial such as X or Y, this means that the identity of that person is being kept confidential.

Where the name of a case starts with *R*, this will usually be a criminal case, since *R* represents the crown: it stands for *Regina* (the Queen) or *Rex* (the King), in whose name all criminal prosecutions are brought.

Judicial review cases are brought as: *R versus Minister, ex parte Smith*, meaning that Smith is reviewing the decision of the Minister (*ex parte* is Latin for 'on the application of'), or for more recent cases *R (on the application of Smith) v Minister*, or just *R (Smith) v Minister*.

The following terms are used to describe the parties in a case:

Prosecution	person bringing a criminal charge at trial
Defendant	person accused of a crime in a criminal prosecution
Complainant	person against whom a crime is committed
Plaintiff / claimant / applicant	person bringing a civil action or claim
Defendant	person against whom a civil action has been brought
Appellant	person bringing an appeal (civil or criminal)
Respondent	person against whom an application or appeal is brought

Case names sometimes also include the following acting on behalf of the state:

Attorney General (AG): the minister who is ultimately responsible for prosecutions or bringing other legal actions on behalf of the government.
Director of Public Prosecutions (DPP): the head of the Crown Prosecution Service (CPS) in whose name some prosecutions or appeals are brought.

The different judges in the courts of England and Wales (introduced in Chapter 4) are titled as follows:

The most senior judge is the Lord Chancellor (abbreviated to LC).
Judges in the most senior court, the House of Lords, are referred to as Lord or Lady so-and-so, and collectively as the Law Lords. The Law Lords also sit as the Judicial Committee of the Privy Council on some appeals.

Judges in the Court of Appeal are titled Lord or Lady Justice so-and-so (abbreviated to LJ or LJJ in the plural). The senior judges are the Lord Chief Justice (LCJ), the Master of the Rolls (MR), the Vice-Chancellor (VC) and President of the Family Division (P).

In the lower courts, High Court Judges are referred to as Mr or Mrs Justice so-and-so (J or JJ) and County Court or Circuit Judges are referred to as His or Her Honour Judge so-and-so. Below them are Masters and District Judges (DJ). A reference to the Justices of a place refers to a panel of Magistrates.

There are occasional references to the Court of Session. This is the Scottish equivalent of the High Court and Court of Appeal, and is the final court for appeals in Scotland, except that devolution questions (which includes human rights questions) can be appealed to the Privy Council. The Scottish criminal judges of first instance are the sheriffs (equivalent to district judges).

A list of abbreviations used for law reports and other citations can be found in 'Further reading' below, p. 352.

Chapter 2

THE IDEA OF HUMAN RIGHTS

right, *noun*, ... That which is due to anyone by law, tradition or nature; a just or legal claim or title. (*Reader's Digest Illustrated Dictionary*)

THE NATURE OF HUMAN RIGHTS

Before we begin our discussion in detail of the *content* of rights, and specifically the rights guaranteed by the Human Rights Act 1998, it is important to have some idea as to what we actually *mean* by rights. That is the purpose of this chapter: to set out our view on the meaning and importance of the idea of **rights** and introducing some important concepts associated with rights and human rights which will be relevant to consideration of the Act and the Convention rights.

To begin with, it is appropriate to consider what is meant by rights, because when we refer to a right we could in fact be referring to one of several types of entitlement. We could mean:

(i)   a **claim to** something (which someone else has a duty to do or provide)
        for example: an owner's right (claim) to the return of property which has been stolen (and that person has a duty to return it); *or*
(ii)   a **freedom to do** something
        for example: the right to freedom of speech;
        (which is supported by other rights which are claims that other persons do not interfere with the exercise of that freedom); *or*
(iii)   a **power to do** something which affects other people
        for example: a judge's right to decide a case, which affects the rights of the parties involved in the case; *or*
(iv)   an **immunity from** challenge in doing something
        for example: a judge's right not to be sued for the results of a judicial decision.

When we are considering the law, and what its contents should be, there is a particular benefit which comes from concentrating on rights. A focus on rights ensures that we consider the position of **individuals** under the law, as opposed to **collective interests**; and what is due to them in a positive way, as against simply the prohibition of harmful conduct.

When we talk about **human** rights, we are talking about a particular sort of right. We each have a variety of legal rights, for example rights under various laws to a state education or to social security benefits. However, when we talk about our human rights, we mean by this something more fundamental and more general than just those legal rights which are granted by a particular legal system. We can contrast human rights with other legal rights because of their **universality**: they are propositions as to people's general rights which they have in all situations. So, for example, a right to own property is a general right. This does not answer all specific questions about my particular rights, such as what property I in fact own, and the list of my personal property rights and the attributes and consequences of that ownership would be a very detailed one. As we move from the specific to the general, it may be that we can frame more general propositions about property rights. For example, if I own a hedge, I am entitled to trim it. We can phrase that more generally as: all owners of hedges have the right to trim them, but it is still a statement which covers a very specific situation. It may be that we can generalise further, and say that all owners of all property have the right to damage or destroy it: this is approaching a more universal proposition.

However, we would not necessarily say that the right to damage our own property is a human right. This is because human rights have a further quality in addition to their universal application, which is their **importance**. A right should be added to a list of what we consider to be *human* rights if it is important, if it protects something which is fundamental to the basic entitlements that we all possess as human beings. It is because of this that the idea of universality of application is a very important one in setting out moral principles or rights, because theories of morality derive much of their justification from whether or not they can be applied to all people in all situations. When we talk about human rights, we should mean something that is so important that it applies to all people all the time.

Thus whether or not a right really can be said to be universal in application is an important part of whether any particular list of moral or human rights is in fact correctly drawn up – and note that a right can be universal even if it is sometimes subject to exceptions or limitations. Put another way, it is a valid criticism of the inclusion of an entry in a list of human rights if it is not of universal application. Of course, that raises a very big question as to what the list of fundamental and universal rights really is, and that question will be answered differently by different people from different backgrounds. Some rights are generally agreed to be human rights, such as the protection of life and the basic freedom and security of the person. Once lists of human rights move away from these sorts of rights and start to consider social or economic rights such as the right to education, the right to withhold labour (that is, to go on strike) or a right to social security, there is less agreement about whether such rights should appropriately be considered *human* rights. Economic rights, especially those which relate to work or involve the spending of money, such as social security or paying for education, tend to be viewed in a much more culturally relative manner – a right to withhold labour would make no sense in a culture where people don't work for each other – and therefore their universality is less clear.

RIGHTS UNLIMITED?

What *gives* human rights this universality is that these are rights which we consider people have from the simple fact that they are human beings, and all human beings are equally worthy of basic respect. So, a right to life is a human right because it is a fundamental part of all people's existence. However, we must be aware that whilst everyone has rights which deserve respect, this does not necessarily mean that the rights of one individual deserve more respect than the rights of any other individual. To say that I have a right to something, or freedom to do something, does not mean that I have an *unlimited* right to do that or that I should *not* respect other people's rights. This comes from the same equality which grounds the right in the first place: because all human beings are equal and therefore have equal human rights, there is no legitimate basis for distinguishing between persons in respect of their basic entitlements. Thus there is an inherent scope for conflict in rights where different individuals wish to exercise their rights in ways which conflict with each other.

However, it is important to distinguish **limitations on the scope** of rights from an **interference with** that right. A limitation on a right is inherent in the proper definition of those rights, which is to say that a right may not extend to all situations or may not justify an unlimited scope for action. So, for example, freedom to associate does not extend to freedom to have a riot. This is a part of the right, as properly understood.

There is another sort of limitation on the scope of a right which will be far less easy to justify: that is where the *persons* to whom those rights apply has been limited in a particular society. If human rights are not applied equally to all people within a society, those denied equal treatment are being denied the respect due to them *as* human beings. This means that, effectively, society, or some dominant group within it, considers the group denied equal treatment as inferior, as less than fully human. That will commonly be a minority group, for example Gypsies or Jews in Nazi Germany, but can be a majority group, such as blacks in South Africa under apartheid. This is therefore not a legitimate way to limit rights, since it contradicts the equality which underlies those rights.

In addition to rights being limited in scope because of direct conflict with other individual rights, it is important that certain interests are protected for the benefit of the whole community. An example would be the physical environment we live in, whether one is thinking of rules preserving open space, wildlife, and greenery or planning controls to preserve the character or amenities of an area. This is not to say that these are somehow more or less important than the rights of individuals. On the contrary, they are the same thing: to refer to the benefit of 'the whole community' means that something benefits all the people who make up that community. So, for example, limiting the right of a person to build a factory in a residential area, or discharge chemicals into a river, by citing the common interest in a pleasant environment: this is another way of saying that the right of *all* the people in that community to live in a pleasant environment is considered sufficiently important to justify limiting the right of the property owner to build freely on his property.

To take another example, if we say that a right is limited in the interests of national security, the same calculation is going on. Here the community is broader than just a neighbourhood, it extends to the whole country. But it is still a set of individual rights,

albeit a very large set, which means that we can talk about identifiable collective interests. In a community of this size, there may well be more disagreement about what
those interests are. But one can say that each of us has a right to live in a safe and
secure environment, and one can use the phrase 'national security' as a shorthand for
the protection of this right of all those living in a particular country. Whilst we may
disagree about precisely how this right should best be protected, and how it should be
weighed against other rights that people have, there is a reasonable consensus that this
phrase represents a proper collective interest, that is, a set of individual rights, which
deserves some protection.

But this collective interest has to justify itself in the face of any other individual right
it wishes to over-rule. The very need for this justification reminds us that we should
not ignore the interests of people whose rights conflict with a course of action, even
though we may think that this course of action is in the best interests of the whole
community. An interference with rights *always* needs to be justified. To use the earlier
example, the factory builder's right to support himself by starting a business may not,
in the end, justify building a factory, but his right still deserves some respect. That is
why he is allowed to apply to build a factory and have an opportunity to make a case
for being allowed to do so, which must be rejected for good reasons, and not just on
a whim.

So one of the benefits of having a law like the Human Rights Act is that it plants a
clear marker for the attention of those making laws as to which basic rights they will
always have to justify interfering with, even when they are acting in the common interest in doing so. A law of this sort helps to ensure that debate on particular issues, which
involve possible infringements or limitations of rights, is properly focused, and does
not *ignore* individual rights just because they conflict with a collective interest. In particular, in a political system which does not provide much opportunity for individuals
to have a say in the process of making political decisions at a national level – which
is inevitable in any country of any size – an Act to enforce rights acts as a counter-
weight to political desires to implement policies that may benefit one part of the community over another. Such desires are not necessarily bad – for example, benefiting the
poor or sick by taxing those who can afford it – but they should never be allowed to
prevent consideration being given to those who are being affected by the decisions, or
laws, that result from such policies.

Thus resolving questions about rights involves a **balancing** act – in most difficult situations where we are considering the exercise of rights we will have to consider not just
the rights of *one* person, but how to resolve the issue where the rights of two or more
persons come into conflict. We may have to consider which of these rights takes
priority over the other and which interference we should allow: there are very few rights
which can *never* justifiably be interfered with. In fact, the reason that the situation is
a difficult one may well be *because* of this conflict and the consequent need to **balance**
the different rights under consideration. This difficulty is there because it can be a hard
decision as to how a particular right should be exercised or protected, and how that
will affect other people and *their* rights. We have to decide which, or whose, rights are
more important, and what weight we give to the different rights involved. There are
some rights which we can rarely justify infringing – the right to life, for example – and
some which more commonly come into conflict with other rights – for example, freedom

of speech. Determining what should be done where different rights come into conflict involves considering the different rights which could apply to the situation, looking at the importance of the interests protected by the different rights and then judging which right has most weight.

This idea of balancing rights is so important to the analysis of rights we will be undertaking in this book that it is worth considering a particularly difficult case where rights came into conflict: the case of the conjoined (Siamese) twins, Jodie and Mary. In this case, there were Siamese twins, Jodie and Mary, who shared one heart. If left joined, they were both going to die. Their parents had firm religious convictions that nature should be allowed to take its course. The doctors treating the twins wanted to separate them, because they hoped that this would allow the stronger twin, Jodie, to survive, even though it would mean the death of the weaker twin, Mary.

The case came before the Court of Appeal, who had to decide what the doctors should do, to protect the doctors from any complaint afterwards. The Court decided that the twins should be separated: Mary was going to die in any event and was incapable of independent existence, but the separation was without significant risk for Jodie who should survive the operation. The Court took into account the parents' sincere religious belief that it was God's will that the twins be born as they were and that they should be left to live their lives joined together for as long as that might be. But the Court also took into account the rights of the two twins and the views of the hospital that where one life could be saved it should be. The Court had to **balance** the welfare of each child against the other and decided that Mary could have no independent existence but Jodie could. Since Mary was only alive because she was relying on the use of Jodie's organs, removing Mary would effectively be acting in Jodie's defence, to remove a threat of fatal harm. The Court also referred to the right of each of the twins to bodily integrity and human dignity which neither of them could enjoy as they were.[1]

An example of a series of permissible limitations on a right can be found by considering freedom of speech. If you think about freedom of speech, you will quickly realise that there are a large numbers of ways in which we are *not* free to say whatever we like.

So, for example, we are not allowed to say, write, print or broadcast things which:

- make other people afraid they will be harmed (assault by threats)
- falsely insult people or harm their reputation (libel and slander)
- cause or provoke other people to commit a crime (incitement)
- are sexually or racially abusive or insulting (sex or race discrimination)
- reveal matters which are secret or confidential or infringe national security (breach of confidence and official secrets)
- infringe certain standards as to showing sex or violence (obscenity and limits on printing or showing pornography)
- invade other people's privacy without some justification.[2]

---

[1] [2001] 2 WLR 480; we will consider this case further at p. 102 below.
[2] For more detailed discussion of freedom of speech, see Chapter 16 below.

You will probably broadly agree that there are good reasons for most if not all of these limitations, which is to say that they protect other rights or interests which are more important than the right of the person wishing to say or write whatever they want. Thus it is not true to say that freedom of speech is an unlimited right: it has limits where the process of balancing that right and another right leads to the conclusion that there is something more important than allowing unlimited self-expression.

THE INDIVIDUAL AND THE STATE

We have talked about human rights being founded in equality, but the discussion of limiting rights in collective interests also points to another of the key features of human rights: the content of human rights is focused on the relationship between the **individual** and society, or more precisely the **state**. A state is the highest level of organisation in a society with the ability to control the lives of the members of that society. For present purposes, the state can also be used as a shorthand for the social order and government of a society. So, the United Kingdom is a state and our laws have the ultimate say as to what we are or are not allowed to do. The constitution of a state is that area of its law which defines how the state is structured and how the organs of the state – Parliament, government departments, the police, etc. – relate to individual citizens. Any list of basic rights will therefore have *constitutional* significance since it sets out rights with which the *state* is not allowed to interfere, or the basis and extent to which interference with such rights is permissible.

Of course, the very existence of an organised society is itself a benefit to the individuals living within that society. There is a need for individuals living in a community of any size – even a modern city, let alone a country – to have some form of government. Individuals are entitled to what we might call moral autonomy, that is, their own space in which to pursue their life goals, raise a family, pursue education, a career, the enjoyment of interests, sports, hobbies, pastimes, and so on. But individuals can rarely achieve such goals by themselves. The need to have some form of government arises because cooperation between individuals is often required.

One could divide the main functions which government should perform into three broad categories. The first is to organise cooperation between individuals for their common protection and defence; this may be from each other, from other countries and from natural threats such as floods. The second is to resolve questions about how to allocate limited resources, and that includes deciding or prioritising the use of limited natural resources, such as land or water. A decision may need to be taken where these are required for different and conflicting purposes. The question of the use of resources also includes questions about if and how taxation should be used to redistribute resources. The third is to resolve disputes between individuals to prevent them resorting to force, including dealing with situations where individuals have been wronged, or where their interests or activities have come into conflict.

One of the ways in which states typically perform these functions is by having the power to use force, or other forms of coercion, to enforce resolutions to problems. Usually a state will prevent the use of force by all other persons except those authorised by the state and limit the use of force by those authorised to very specific situations. So, it is a crime to hit someone else, unless, for example, you are a police officer who is allowed to restrain someone who is committing a crime. This use of force by states does mean, however, that it is important to define clearly the situations in which the state may use its power and resources, including coercion or force, against its citizens, to ensure that such use of force is limited to that which is strictly necessary in the circumstances. Thus a consideration of the law of human rights will be a discussion of the relationship between the individual and the state, as well as the rights of individuals against each other.

These powers which a state has for the common good – using that term broadly – for defence, allocation of resources and resolution of disputes are also open to abuse. These powers are morally justified, which is to say a morally good thing, because they are to be used for the common welfare. Once these powers are directed, to a greater or lesser extent, in favour of one group and/or against the interests of another for arbitrary, irrational or immoral reasons – for example, because one group is a different colour or sex – the use of such a power is no longer morally justified and the citizens against whom the power of the state is then applied may require the protection of the law. Thus, being ruled within the law is important because it ensures that society is not governed by the whim of those in power; and the recognition of human rights is important because it limits the ability of those in power to infringe certain basic freedoms. The consequence of both of these is that there should be a law above those in power or authority which guarantees certain basic rights and freedoms to individuals, allowing them a degree of moral autonomy. This is made explicit in a piece of legislation such as the Human Rights Act.

Of course, we might expect that in a modern, democratic society there would be no need for such protection. However, no society is ideal, and one of the key lessons of the history of the twentieth century, especially of the actions of totalitarian states like Nazi Germany or the Communist USSR, is that even states which start off as, or claim to be, democracies may be subverted for repressive or discriminatory purposes. One of the results of such events has been a greater recognition of the need to institutionalise protection of basic liberties, as we shall see when we look at the history of the European Convention itself.[3] However, it is also relevant to consider that there has been a growing tendency, especially in the last century, to recognise that those in authority may not always be correct and therefore should have limits placed on their power. This is not a new consideration – after all, the Magna Carta, signed by King John in 1215, was expressly aimed at limiting the King's powers. But it has gained momentum from the world events of the last hundred years, as well as from other factors, such as the greater availability of information to challenge 'official' versions of events. There has also been the increase in participation in elections and in government – for example, in the UK, full voting rights being extended to women in 1928 – which has tended to reduce the influence of any one class or group in government. In a democracy with no clear ruling group, those in government are likely one day to be no longer in government and therefore they may also wish to seek the benefit of rights they allow to their fellow citizens against the state.

---

[3] Chapter 3 below.

THE RULE OF LAW

We have touched on the principle that society should be governed by law and not by arbitrary action. This expresses the important constitutional doctrine known as the **rule of law** and it is worth exploring further. One aspect of this is that the government (and any sovereign) are subject to the same law as everybody else. This is a further consequence of the principle of equality, that the law should treat its subjects equally. The law should also treat its subjects with respect: so the rule of law requires that the law should be capable of being known, understood, and obeyed by its subjects, and should be applied clearly, publicly and consistently by impartial courts.

The ideas contained in the principle of the rule of law are therefore very important; and they are a manifestation of the same ideas which lead us to consider human rights to be important. It could be said that the principle of the rule of law expresses from the point of view of the *institution* of law ideas which could equally well be expressed as individual rights. So, one could say that individuals have the right to be treated equally, to be made subject only to laws that they can know about and which are capable of being obeyed, and so on. It should therefore come as no surprise that these are ideas which will crop up in discussions of several of the Convention rights, in particular the rights under Article 6 to a fair trial, and under Article 7 to freedom from retrospective legislation. Article 7 in particular is an embodiment of an important idea which stems directly from the rule of law: that people should not be punished for something which they did which was legal when they did it. This is an aspect of being able to obey laws: you cannot obey a law which criminalises something you have already done. Article 7 also includes the important ideas of certainty and clarity in the law, which, as we shall see, are applied throughout the Convention rights.

On the other hand, the principle of equality before the law also contains duties. So, for example, there is the principle that 'ignorance of the law is no excuse' – what is meant by this is, in general terms, that illegal or wrongful conduct is not excused just because the actor did not know that what he or she was doing was wrong. This is an expression of equality because it makes the equal assumption that all citizens know what the law is, and an expression of fairness because all citizens should be able to rely on the law for protection. To that extent, the rule of law also imposes (or at least assumes) the duty on the part of citizens to follow the law if they can, as well as imposing duties on those who administer or uphold the law to do so fairly, publicly, consistently, and so on.

The rule of law may be contrasted with legal systems or states or governments which allow arbitrary exercises of power, based on whim or caprice, or power being exercised in private or on the basis of laws which cannot be known or followed. In that sense, the adherence by the state to the doctrine of the rule of law is a morally good thing, because it enforces and encourages respect for its subjects. However, the rule of law does not guarantee that the law itself will be just or right; it does not guarantee more substantive rights such as the right to life or freedom of speech. Nonetheless, the rule of law is an important idea, particularly in the context of human rights, since it is tied directly into certain of those rights.

QUESTIONS

1   What rights do you think are human rights? Why? What values do they protect
    that you consider to be fundamental?
2   Do you consider that animals have rights? Why/why not? If yes, are their rights the
    same as those of human beings?

Magna Carta 1215 (as reissued in 1225 under the seal of Henry III): one of the first English legal statements of a series of rights (discussed opposite).

(*Source:* 'The Book of Magna Carta' by Hindley, G., reproduced courtesy of the British Library.)

Chapter 3

THE HISTORY OF HUMAN RIGHTS AND THE CONVENTION

We hold these truths to be self-evident, that all men are created equal, that they are endowed by their Creator with certain unalienable rights, that among these are life, liberty and the pursuit of happiness. (American Declaration of Independence, 4 July 1776)

Any law which violates the inalienable rights of man is essentially unjust and tyrannical; it is not a law at all. (Maximilien Robespierre, *Declaration of the Rights of Man*, 1789)

Prior to the Human Rights Act 1998, British law had, over the centuries, no single document which contained a comprehensive statement of individual, fundamental rights. Indeed the phrase 'human rights' was only coined in the eighteenth century: it was first used in English by the radical writer Tom Paine in 1791 in his book *The Rights of Man*, in part in translating the revolutionary French National Assembly's *Declaration of the Rights of Man*. The idea which it embodied, that each person is born with 'natural rights', was one that had only developed in those express terms in the previous century or so.

But there have still been some fundamental legal statements which have confirmed or granted individual rights. The earliest, and one of the most significant, was Magna Carta (which means 'the Great Charter'), first issued in 1215 by King John, which contains a number of important rights. Indeed, Chapter 29 of Magna Carta is still in force and states that there should be no punishment without a lawful judgment or by the law of the land, which is what we would today call a declaration of the rule of law. Likewise it states that the King will 'sell to no man [. . . and will] not deny or defer to any man either justice or right', which is a guarantee of a fair and prompt judicial process.

It is important to bear in mind that the intention behind Magna Carta was not to make a grand statement about the equality of individuals in society. On the contrary, it was meant to protect the interests of the barons who had revolted against King John and forced him to grant the Charter, and only incidentally benefited everyone else. Nonetheless, the theme of Magna Carta is that of limiting the power of the King, which is an important statement of the idea behind the rule of law, that is, that there should be government according to the law and not according to the arbitrary wishes of the ruler.

By the end of the thirteenth century, Magna Carta was recognised as an important statement of such limitations on royal power and was reissued by Henry III and Edward I to confirm its provisions. Much of Magna Carta is not relevant today because it remains rooted in the legal system of the thirteenth century. However, its general significance was not lost to later political debate, based as it is on the principle of government according to law, as opposed to unfettered royal power. It gained importance again in the early seventeenth century, when the high-handed exercise of royal power by Charles I ultimately led to the English Civil War (1642–49). The relevance of Magna Carta was brought to the fore by Chief Justice Coke, who used it as part of the political justification for the courts to try to confine royal powers.

This principle of limiting arbitrary rule also lay behind the Bill of Rights of 1688, the constitutional settlement which resulted in the modern constitutional monarchy. This governed the relationship between Parliament and the Crown, confirming the privileges of Parliament on the accession of William III and Mary after the overthrow of James II (the 'Glorious Revolution'). This guarantees such rights as free elections and the immunity of what is said in debates or proceedings in Parliament from being impeached or questioned in any court outside Parliament; it prohibits taxation without the authority of Parliament; and it removed the power which had been claimed by some previous monarchs to suspend or dispense the application of statutes. Again, therefore, there are important aspects of the Bill of Rights which support the rights of the individual, as well as rights which are still considered a basic part of having a free, democratic Parliament.

It was at this time that the idea was propounded that all people possess certain basic rights, especially by John Locke. Locke was a prominent thinker among the supporters of William III. Locke's key contribution to the theory of rights was the idea that, in particular, people have a right to that property which is the product of their labour. This later became a crucial idea in the American Revolution, because it has the corollary that government should not be able to remove property, by way of taxes, without some form of consent on the part of those being governed – or in the phrase which the Americans settlers took to heart, no taxation without representation.

There were also by this stage in English law a number of important and well-established legal protections for what we would today think of as fundamental liberties. One important example is the remedy provided by the writ of *habeas corpus*, which allows an aggrieved party to ask a court to review the reason for an imprisonment, providing some protection against arbitrary detention by ensuring some judicial supervision. This again was a remedy which was developed significantly by Chief Justice Coke and others against the exercise of arbitrary power by Charles I, and its scope has further expanded since then and remains part of our law's protection against arbitrary or unlawful detention.[1]

Even as the idea of basic rights developed among philosophers in the seventeenth and eighteenth centuries, there was no great demand for a statement of all basic rights to be included in English law. This was in a large part because of the view of the leading English legal theorists of the day that the English common law did protect the rights of its citizens without the need for such a statement. The state of English law was defended by, in particular, William Blackstone, in his summary of English law, *Commentaries on the Laws of England* (1765–69). Blackstone considered that the law as it was did protect the rights of the citizens, especially from arbitrary government, and that all the

---

[1] Discussed below in the context of Article 5, p. 146.

rights which needed to be set out in a grand statement were contained within Magna Carta, the Bill of Rights, together with the Petition of Right of 1628 and Act of Settlement 1701 which further specified the limits of constitutional monarchy.

Not everyone agreed with this. We have already referred to Tom Paine, who set out views, radical by the standard of the day, as to the basic rights all men enjoy, and it was Mary Wollstonecroft who pointed out that women also enjoy these rights in her pioneering *Vindication of the Rights of Women* in 1792. Even more so elsewhere, in places where many of those governed did not consider that their rights were being properly protected, which led to influential statements of basic rights. The most notable example was the American Declaration of Independence of 1776, composed primarily by Thomas Jefferson. Individual liberty was a key idea in the Declaration of Independence, as can be seen from its opening words, quoted at the start of this chapter. This was an important goal of the American War of Independence of 1775–83: the American colonists considered that they were fighting against a despotic government which did not respect their rights. The ideas embodied in the Declaration, and then in the Bill of Rights which the United States of America adopted in 1789, were founded on the ideas of individual rights and liberties talked about by Locke and Blackstone and the importance of limitations on arbitrary government in the tradition of Magna Carta.

France likewise, following the 1789 revolution, adopted the Declaration of the Rights of Man. This influenced the French Civil Code, which was later propagated throughout various European countries by Napoleon. However, the declaration of such rights did not guarantee that they were respected: the revolutionary leader Robespierre presided over the Reign of Terror which followed the French Revolution, one of history's more tyrannical and bloody regimes.

In the United States of America, their Bill of Rights was given great weight, in particular after the United States Supreme Court made the landmark decision that it was empowered to declare legislation invalid if it infringed provisions of the Constitution, including the Bill of Rights, which was the first time that there was the potential for considerations of basic rights to defeat legislation.[2] However, important as it was, this Bill of Rights only protected a contemporary understanding of rights, and by today's standards there were some clear omissions in the law it created. So, for example, women did not in fact enjoy equal rights to men for well over a century after the Bill of Rights was adopted; and slavery was still permitted in many states, which we would now consider a fundamental infringement of basic rights, especially taken with the appalling treatment many slaves endured. It was almost one hundred years after the Declaration before the United States abolished slavery,[3] and nearly two hundred years before the Constitution was used by the American Supreme Court to strike down racist laws in individual states.[4]

In Britain, though, the ideas of those such as Blackstone remained influential – the view that there was no need for any further statutory declaration of rights, since the

---

[2] *Marbury v Madison* 5 US 137 (1803).
[3] 13th Amendment to the US Constitution, 1865, which followed the American Civil War.
[4] The leading case was *Brown v Board of Education of Topeka* [1954] 347 US 483.

English common law guaranteed the rights of the individual. Additionally, any form of declaration of rights or code of law smacked of revolution and associations with the continental systems, especially those influenced or imposed by Napoleon, and so was unpopular for that very reason. Thus in A.V. Dicey's influential work on constitutional law of 1885, *Introduction to the Study of the Law of the Constitution*, the British constitution was defended as being opposed to the arbitrary exercises of power which Dicey considered took place in continental Europe.

Even in 1950, when the European Convention on Human Rights was signed, there was no political pressure in Britain for some form of statement of basic rights to be enacted. However, as we shall discuss below, there was pressure for such a document in mainland Europe, especially because of the experience, not shared by the British, of Nazi rule or occupation, and its abuses of governmental power and repression of the liberty of individual citizens. This was why it was not those responsible for British domestic law who were involved in the European Convention, but the Foreign Office. The reason why Britain took a leading role in the formation of the European Convention was because of the perceived importance for our relations with other countries, especially in Europe, of helping to put such an instrument into place. It is relevant therefore to consider the background to this, which is the history, such as it is, of the international protection of human rights.

INTERNATIONAL PROTECTION OF HUMAN RIGHTS

Before the Second World War there had been very little in the way of international protection of human rights. This lack of protection arose out of the nature of international law, the rules which govern relations between states. International law was traditionally considered to be law which governs only the relations between states and not individuals, and therefore as having no role in the protection of individual rights. It is based largely on treaties, which is to say agreements between states, traditionally dealing with such matters as settling disputes over borders or territories and ending wars.

However, from the mid-nineteenth century, there had been some interest in international law making provision for humanitarian matters – that is, a basic level of protection from ill-treatment. The movement for there to be international humanitarian provisions started in the 1860s and produced the founding of the International Committee of the Red Cross in 1863[5] and the Geneva Convention of 1864.[6] This also led to the Hague Conventions on the treatment of prisoners of war,[7] which set out 'rules of war' under which states agreed that they would not permit certain conduct even in wartime. These were still viewed as matters between states, and not matters for complaint by individuals, although the benefit was not to the state itself but to its

---

[5] Originally the International Committee for Aid to Wounded Soldiers; one of the key figures in its founding was Henry Dunant, who was influenced by witnessing the particularly brutal consequences of the Battle of Solferino in 1859.

[6] Geneva Convention for the Amelioration of the Condition of the Wounded in Armies in the Field, 22 August 1864, signed by 12 states; now see the 1949 Geneva Conventions.

[7] Hague Conventions of 1899 and 1907.

citizens. Likewise, although there was a movement against slavery during the nineteenth century, this was primarily due to the actions of individual states, in particular the Royal Navy, which played a part in confiscating slave ships.[8] The increasing recognition of the immorality of slavery did, however, lead to the Slavery Convention of 1926.

There was also a tradition of treaties settling territorial disputes or wars including guarantees of minority rights. This might include one or more states taking a role as protectors of minorities – for example, a Catholic state such as the Austrian Empire or France acting as notional protector for communities of Christians living in the Ottoman Turkish Empire by treaties in the seventeenth and eighteenth centuries or in the nineteenth-century treaties which saw the creation or re-emergence of a number of European states, such as Bulgaria, Romania or Greece. However, this protection was always somewhat theoretical and rarely involved practical action, since there were no institutions to monitor compliance, nor did individuals have any rights to complain.[9]

In the same tradition, the treaties which followed the First World War (1914–18) contained provisions for the protection of minorities, with reference to some individual rights, typically to freedom of life, liberty and equality before the law and non-discrimination. These were secured, in theory, by the new League of Nations and International Court of Justice, founded after the First World War to try to improve international relations. Again, although a system was devised for bringing complaints informally before the League of Nations, these provisions had very little practical effect. Only the system set up by the 1921 treaty relating to Upper Silesia, partitioned between Poland and Germany, had some effect, because it included bodies to deal with individual complaints, although without power to enforce decisions or negotiated compromises. There was one successful use of the treaty in 1933 to provide some (temporary) protection for the Jews of Upper Silesia from the discriminatory laws of Nazi Germany; the treaty lapsed in 1937. Likewise the provisions under which some territories were governed after 1918 under League of Nations Mandates often had some right of individual or group petition, but not much use was made of these, although there were some investigations by commissioners of the League of Nations.

One final strand which involved individuals was the idea of international crimes. The first crime to be recognised as one where there was universal jurisdiction – which means that any state can prosecute any person for such a crime – was piracy, because of the international importance of unimpeded shipping. There were some attempts to extend the idea of individual international criminal responsibility in the First World War peace treaties, specifically in the Treaty of Versailles for the trial of German war criminals, but this did not have much real effect. The first real application of this concept in an international tribunal was after the Second World War with the International Military Tribunal at Nuremberg, which involved prosecutions for war crimes and crimes against humanity.

---

[8] The Royal Navy was supported by the approach of the English courts since the eighteenth century and the formal abolition of slavery in British colonies in 1838.
[9] The first treaty which allowed for individual complaint was the Convention for the Establishment of a Central American Court of Justice which was set up in 1907 and lapsed in 1918; none of the ten individual petitions brought were declared admissible.

THE BACKGROUND TO THE CONVENTION: THE SECOND WORLD WAR AND THE UNITED NATIONS

The European Convention has to be set principally in the historical context of the aftermath of the Second World War (1939–45) and the atrocities committed by, in particular, Nazi Germany, which brutally tortured and murdered millions of people, including several million of its own citizens, such as Jews, Gypsies, blacks, homosexuals, the disabled and political dissidents. There was widespread shock, when the full scale of the Nazi genocide machine became known, that such a course of action could have been implemented in a supposedly civilised society. It was also clear that the traditional approach of international law, that how a state treated its own citizens was a domestic matter and not one in which other states should interfere, could no longer remain unchallenged, since this approach would not allow other states to prevent a repetition of such events.

It was for these reasons that protection of human rights became part of the Allied Powers' war aims in the Second World War. The first key mention of this idea was the reference by American President Franklin Roosevelt in his State of the Union address to Congress on 6 January 1941 to four freedoms – freedom of speech and expression, freedom of religion, freedom from want, and freedom from fear by reduction of armaments. He also referred to human rights, which helped to popularise the phrase. This was still, however, a general idea, and not a call for any form of specific scheme to protect human rights. As a general aim of the Allies, it was supported by the British government, and mentioned in the statement of war aims contained in the Atlantic Charter of 14 August 1941, although there the main focus was on freedom from want through a better economic system. So too in the United Nations Declaration of 1 January 1942 there is a mention of human rights in the preamble, but this was incidental to the main purpose of the declaration which was about the military alliance against Germany and Japan.

However, on the basis of these statements, as the war progressed, interest grew in having protection of human rights as a specific war aim, and various documents on the subject were issued by governments and individuals in America, Britain and Europe. For those writing in occupied Europe, the protection of human rights was part of the movement for European integration, and both human rights protection and European integration were seen as part of the protection which should be put in place for European citizens against their own governments. By 1944 there was therefore widespread interest that protection of human rights against government misconduct should be part of the new world order, especially once the full scale of atrocities perpetrated by Nazi Germany became apparent. This fed into the plans being discussed for a new international organisation to replace the League of Nations, now discredited because of its failure to prevent the Second World War, and to provide greater international security once the war was over. However, in discussions on the shape of a permanent United Nations, there was still widespread concern that such an organisation should not be able to interfere in domestic disputes between a citizen and their own government.

The United Nations Conference on International Organisation was held in June 1945 in San Francisco. At the conclusion of this conference, on 26 June 1945, the Charter of the United Nations was signed by 50 nations. The Charter and the International Court of Justice replaced the old League of Nations machinery entirely. The Charter set up the institutions of the United Nations Organisation, in particular the General Assembly and the Security Council, which has 15 members, with the United States, the United Kingdom, Russia, France and China as permanent members; and also the statute constituting the International Court of Justice, which has jurisdiction to decide any dispute between countries which those countries agree to refer to it.

The United Nations Charter includes some prominent references to human rights, as can be seen in the following extract from the Preamble to the Charter:

We the Peoples of the United Nations determined to save succeeding generations from the scourge of war, which twice in our lifetime has brought untold sorrow to mankind, and to reaffirm faith in fundamental human rights, in the dignity and worth of the human person, in the equal rights of men and women and of nations large and small, and to establish conditions under which justice and respect for the obligations arising from treaties and other sources of international law can be maintained, and to promote social progress and better standards of life in larger freedom [. . .] have resolved to combine our efforts to accomplish these aims.

The United Nations Charter then sets out its main aims in Article 1:

The Purposes of the United Nations are:
1. To maintain international peace and security, and to that end: to take effective collective measures for the prevention and removal of threats to the peace, and for the suppression of acts of aggression or other breaches of the peace, and to bring about by peaceful means, and in conformity with the principles of justice and international law, adjustment or settlement of international disputes or situations which might lead to a breach of the peace;
2. To develop friendly relations among nations based on respect for the principle of equal rights and self-determination of peoples, and to take other appropriate measures to strengthen universal peace;
3. To achieve international cooperation in solving international problems of an economic, social, cultural, or humanitarian character, and in promoting and encouraging respect for human rights and for fundamental freedoms for all without distinction as to race, sex, language, or religion; and
4. To be a center for harmonizing the actions of nations in the attainment of these common ends.

The United Nations Economic and Social Council (ECOSOC) established a Human Rights Commission in early 1946, which was under the chairmanship of Eleanor Roosevelt, the former American First Lady, until 1951. The full Commission met in 1947, and its main initial activity was to draw up an international Bill of Rights, which eventually became the Universal Declaration of Human Rights. This was the result of much work by the members of the Commission, in particular in compromising between different views about the form which the eventual document should take. The view of the British government was that a fairly precise document was appropriate, in accordance with the British legal tradition of precise drafting, and would have meant that the result was a treaty imposing binding obligations. The American view was that something rather more general and declaratory should be adopted. It was in order to resolve this difference of opinion that the more detailed provisions, appropriate for a treaty rather than a declaration, became the International Covenants on Civil and Political

Rights and on Economic and Social Rights: this allowed a more general declaration to be agreed sooner rather than later. A draft declaration was produced in May 1948 and was adopted by the General Assembly on 10 December 1948 as the Universal Declaration of Human Rights. The following is an extract from its preamble:

> Whereas recognition of the inherent dignity and of the equal and inalienable rights of all members of the human family is the foundation of freedom, justice and peace in the world,
> Whereas disregard and contempt for human rights have resulted in barbarous acts, which have outraged the conscience of mankind, and the advent of a world in which human beings shall enjoy freedom of speech and belief and freedom from fear and want has been proclaimed as the highest aspiration of the common people.
> Whereas it is essential, if man is not to be compelled to have recourse, as a last resort, to rebellion against tyranny and oppression, that human rights should be protected by the rule of law . . .[10]

By this time it was clear that there would be difficulties in agreeing meaningful treaties to implement a detailed protection of human rights. There were differences of opinion over such issues as how these covenants should relate to states' colonies, how they would apply in federal countries, especially the United States, where there is a constitutional balance between the individual states and the federal government, and there were Soviet objections to a system which promoted the protection of citizens against their own government. The scope for there to be any form of cooperation in the United Nations was also becoming a casualty of the growing antipathy between the Soviet Union and the United States which was becoming the Cold War. For reasons such as these, negotiations over the covenants became bogged down by the end of the 1940s and interest in effective human rights protection for Western Europe had shifted to a more regional approach. In the end the United Nations covenants were not finalised until 1966 and did not come into force until 1976.

THE BACKGROUND TO THE CONVENTION: THE COUNCIL OF EUROPE

By the end of 1945, Eastern Europe had effectively fallen under the control of the Soviet Union. By 1949 it was clear, because of the international situation, that the United Nations was not going to be successful in providing effective human rights protection, or indeed collective security. The new reality of a Europe split between a communist East and a democratic West was recognised most famously by Winston Churchill in a speech given at Fulton, Missouri on 5 March 1946 when he said 'an iron curtain has descended across the Continent'. The reality of this became clear over the next few years, especially with the division of Germany into two halves, the blockade of the West German parts of Berlin in 1948–49 and the setting up of the Berlin Wall. There was therefore a need for Western Europe to provide for its own security outside the United Nations, and this resulted in the North Atlantic Treaty of April 1949, which set up NATO. The economic wellbeing of Europe was supported by the United States' provision of economic aid, based on the Marshall Plan of 1947, aiming to prevent further communist

---

[10] The full text can be found in Appendix 4.

expansion in Europe, which led to the creation of the Organisation for European Economic Cooperation in 1948.

Politically, there was a movement within Europe in favour of a federal European state, to promote greater peace and security, and prevent a resurgence of a militarily strong Germany. Part of this movement was for the protection of human rights, especially from those with the experience of being oppressed by their own governments. A non-governmental body, the European Federalist Movement, held a Congress in August 1947 where it adopted a proposal for a European Parliamentary Assembly, and for a European Charter of Human Rights.

The British Foreign Office, under Foreign Secretary Ernest Bevin, was a prime mover in the development of regional protection of human rights within Europe, although it was not in favour of a federal Europe. The international protection of human rights was seen as part of foreign policy because it was an important part of the security of Britain and dealings with the United Nations. It was not seen as primarily a domestic issue, since there was a general opinion within the civil service that British law adequately protected human rights. It is worth noting that the whole question of entering a human rights treaty was a matter of some debate within the government. In particular, the British Colonial Office, which at that time administered the various dominions which comprised the British empire, was opposed to the possibility of international interference in the government of dominions. The Home Office, which administers prisons and the police, also had concerns about a human rights treaty, when this finally loomed as a realistic prospect, as did the Lord Chancellor, who is responsible for the law courts. The Foreign Office, however, saw British participation in human rights discussions, at the United Nations and in Europe, as essential to promote a stable Europe and the formation of a coherent West European bloc, including limiting the scope for Soviet interference in European affairs.[11]

As a result of international negotiations in late 1948 and 1949, it was decided that a new organisation would be created to foster relations in spheres other than the economic or the military, with a committee of ministers from member governments and a consultative assembly, the latter being a compromise to the demands of the Federalist movement. This was what became the Council of Europe, whose Statute was signed on 5 May 1949 in London. The following is an extract which sets out the aims behind the Council of Europe:

Article 1: (a) The aim of the Council of Europe is to achieve a greater unity between its members for the purpose of safeguarding and realising the ideals and principles which are their common heritage and facilitating their economic and social progress.

(b) This aim shall be pursued through the organs of the Council by discussion of questions of common concern and by agreements and common action in economic, social, cultural, scientific, legal and administrative matters and in the maintenance and further realisation of human rights and fundamental freedoms.

---

[11] For a more detailed discussion of international and British internal politics surrounding the genesis of the Convention we highly recommend Professor A.W.B. Simpson's *Human Rights and the End of Empire* (Oxford, 2001).

(c) Participation in the Council of Europe shall not affect the collaboration of its members in the work of the United Nations and of other international organisations or unions to which they are parties.

(d) Matters relating to national defence do not fall within the scope of the Council of Europe.

Article 3: Every member of the Council of Europe must accept the principles of the rule of law and of the enjoyment by all persons within its jurisdiction of human rights and fundamental freedoms, and collaborate sincerely and effectively in the realisation of the aim of the Council as specified in [Article] 1.

The treaty which became the European Convention on Human Rights was negotiated between August 1949 and September 1950. Initially the Council of Europe's Committee of Ministers were not particularly enthusiastic about the prospect of a human rights convention, but the Council's Consultative Assembly pressured the ministers into allowing this onto the agenda for the Assembly's session in August 1949. The Assembly adopted a proposal for a treaty supported by a commission and a court in September 1949.

The British government took the view that it should support the negotiations for a convention. It was opposed to the institution of a court in any event, so it was not initially intended that a treaty would lead to an international body judging British domestic law. However, its over-riding concern was that there would be great political damage if negotiations for a convention failed, especially as the British government and Foreign Secretary Bevin had been largely responsible for the Council of Europe coming into the existence in the first place: it would be very embarrassing if the Council of Europe's first major undertaking collapsed.

Again there was a difference of approach within the bodies which debated the drafting of a convention, in particular between the precise drafting typical of the English common law tradition and the civil tradition of European states which tended towards more generalised statements of principle. The difficulty was establishing a list of rights which the various countries, with their different traditions, could all sign up to as representing the basic minimum of human rights. There were also issues about the application of a convention to colonial territories.

There was also a difference of views about whether or not there should be a court of human rights. The compromise on the question of a court was that there should be a human rights court but with optional jurisdiction, which is to say that states signing up to the treaty could choose whether or not to submit to the jurisdiction of the court. There would also be a commission to act as a preliminary filter on complaints. Again by way of compromise, it was decided that it would be open to states to choose whether or not to allow individual citizens, as opposed to another state, the right to bring a complaint.

Eventually, on 4 November 1950, the European Convention for the Protection of Human Rights and Fundamental Freedoms was signed in Rome. An issue about whether or not rights relating to property, education and democratic participation should be included was resolved by continuing the negotiations about the inclusion of these rights and putting them in a separate document, the First Protocol, which was eventually signed in Paris on 20 March 1952. The United Kingdom was, however, the first country to ratify the Convention on 8 March 1951. The Convention came into force on 3 September 1953, and the European Court came into being in 1959.

The Convention was an extremely radical innovation. Never before had there been a system of international law which held states accountable to some superior court in respect of its actions against its own citizens: previous international courts and tribunals were constituted solely to settle disputes between states or, in the case of the Nuremberg Tribunal, to try individuals for their own criminal responsibility.

The system set up by the Convention has proven to have a great political attraction, especially for those countries which are keen to prove their democratic credentials. Thus, the Council of Europe has grown gradually to include most European states, and their signing up to the Convention has been treated as a prerequisite of membership of the Council. So, for example, Greece, which left in 1966, rejoined in 1974 when democracy was restored after eight years of dictatorship; Portugal joined in 1976, following the removal of its dictatorship in 1974; Spain joined in 1977, following the death of General Franco in 1975.

However, the most dramatic period of growth has been in the last 10 years or so. After the countries of Eastern Europe rebelled against communist rule in the early 1990s in an extraordinary series of popular revolutions, many of them joined the Convention system within the next few years, particularly because one of the main complaints that the citizens of those countries had against those who governed them was the lack of respect that was paid to their rights. There are now 41 countries who have signed up to the Convention.[12]

THE CONVENTION AND THE UNITED KINGDOM

The history of the Convention does not explain why it has only recently been incorporated into United Kingdom law. The significance of this is that under British constitutional law, until a treaty has been incorporated into domestic law by an Act of Parliament, it cannot be relied on directly in national courts by those who claim that it has been infringed by their government.

As we have seen, in 1950 the United Kingdom was opposed to giving the European Court jurisdiction over complaints from British individuals. In addition, it was not thought particularly necessary to increase human rights protection in the United Kingdom, because it was thought at that time that the law of the United Kingdom adequately protected the rights of its citizens. Indeed, the British involvement in the drafting of the Convention supported the government's view that the European Convention itself reflected the standards of protection provided by the tradition of English common law.

Britain was, however, the first country to ratify the Convention, although it did not sign up to the optional provisions, namely, submission to the jurisdiction of the European Court and the right of individual petition, which allowed individuals to complain directly to the Commission or the Court. Britain also extended the effect of the Convention (but not the First Protocol) to most of its colonies on 23 October 1953, although during the following decades before most of the colonies gained their independence a number of derogations[13] were entered in various emergency situations.

---

[12] See Appendix 3 for a full list of signatories.
[13] Derogations are formal statements that a provision of a treaty is to be departed from; they are discussed in more detail below at p. 85.

Ironically, since it was largely responsible for the Convention coming into existence, Britain was also the subject of the first inter-state case to be brought under the Convention, which was a complaint to the Commission by Greece regarding the situation in Cyprus, brought in May 1956.[14] The complaint related to British actions taken and regulations imposed in response to the actions of the Greek–Cypriot group EOKA. Greece alleged that there had been breaches of a number of articles, especially Article 3 (freedom from torture) in relation to corporal punishment and treatment of detainees and Article 5 (prohibition of arbitrary detention). After a number of hearings and a visit to Cyprus by some of the Commission members in January 1958, the Commission reported in September 1958 into the regulations and systems in place in Cyprus.[15] The report found no human rights infringements by the United Kingdom, but did made some criticisms. Between the making of the complaint and the report being produced, some laws which might have infringed the Convention had also been repealed as a result of political pressure to avoid a finding by the Commission of a breach of human rights. The Commission report was notable for introducing into the Convention jurisprudence the idea of the margin of appreciation, which is the important principle that states have some leeway to deal with, in particular, emergency situations, before they breach the Convention.[16]

The Cyprus cases did not encourage the British government to be enthusiastic to sign up to the optional provisions relating to the Court and the right of individual petition. The Colonial Office, which administered the various British territories, had always taken the view that the Convention might cause difficulties if there were too close an examination of the various legal systems in place in some of the colonies. In its view, signing up to a right of individual petition and the jurisdiction of the Court would only encourage complaints by agitators, especially those who wished to encourage the independence of the colony in question. In the early 1960s there were a number of formal derogations from the Convention in place in respect of various colonies, which is to say formal statements that the Convention was being disapplied in certain instances, precisely to cover various legislative provisions designed to allow systems of administration which might not conform to the requirements of the Convention but which were thought necessary to deal with various situations.

However, during the early 1960s, Britain was dismantling its empire in a fairly comprehensive way, and by 1964 most of the larger colonies had been granted independence. There was also some political pressure for signing up to the optional clauses; the issue was raised with the government, in particular by Lord McNair, the first British Judge on the European Court, and also the first President of the Court. There was a change of government in 1964 and the new Lord Chancellor, Lord Gardiner, supported signing up to the optional clauses. By late 1965 there were even fewer colonies – the Colonial Office ceased to exist in 1966, replaced by the Commonwealth Office – and

---

[14] Application 176/1956.

[15] Greece brought a second application in July 1957, which raised 49 *individual* cases of alleged torture or mistreatment. This application was overtaken by events, because there was a settlement over Cyprus in February 1959 between Greece and Turkey, so none of the complaints proceeded to a hearing by the Commission.

[16] For a more detailed discussion of the margin of appreciation see p. 45 below.

in December 1965, the Prime Minister, Harold Wilson, announced that Britain would sign up to the optional clauses, which was done in January 1966.

At this stage there was no political pressure for the Convention to be directly incorporated into United Kingdom law. This was something which developed during the 1980s and 1990s, particularly after there had been a number of findings of infringements by the United Kingdom. These put paid to the view that United Kingdom law provided adequate human rights protection without the need for the Convention. However, the European Convention was not high on the political agenda, and it was only when it was made a matter of policy by the Labour Party, in opposition, in the mid-1990s that it gained any real political relevance. The key event here was the delivery by John Smith QC, then leader of the Labour Party, of a lecture entitled 'A Citizen's Democracy' in March 1993. The Labour Party then published a consultation paper in December 1996 and then, after the Labour Party became the government, it published the White Paper 'Rights Brought Home':[17] this was the start of the legislative process which resulted in the Human Rights Act 1998.

The arguments put forward for incorporation, both in the White Paper and by the government in Parliament, were based partly on the practical considerations of the cost and delay involved in taking a case to the European Court at Strasbourg, in the absence of a remedy in the local courts for an infringement of the Convention. But they were also based on the principled reason that it would allow the rights guaranteed by the Convention to more fully enter British law, in so far as they were not already protected. And it showed an acceptance that the argument used in the past, that in no situation did United Kingdom law require the assistance of the Convention to protect people's rights, could no longer be sustained, especially in view of the number of times where the provisions or application of United Kingdom law had been held by the European Court to involve a breach of the Convention rights.

Incorporating the Convention into our law would also allow our judges to contribute to the jurisprudence of the Convention, since there would now be domestic decisions on the Convention rights which could be cited before the European Court or other courts in Europe which had to consider questions of human rights. Further, it would limit the need for findings that a particular law infringed the Convention to be made by the European Court, since it would impose on our courts the duty to interpret our law in a way which is consistent with the Convention, and allow any laws which do not comply to be amended by Parliament. This should limit the number of cases taken to the European Court, and therefore the number of judgments against the United Kingdom, which will limit the political embarrassment such a judgment can cause.

Thus, after being passed by Parliament, the Human Rights Act received Royal Assent on 9 November 1998 and thereby became part of the law of the United Kingdom, 48 years after the United Kingdom signed up to the Convention. The Convention rights are now, for the first time, an integral part of our law, and the Act is sufficiently important to be considered part of our constitution, together with earlier declarations of rights such as Magna Carta and the Bill of Rights. Precisely how it fits into our constitution is the topic we shall consider in the next chapter.

---

[17] Cmd 3782, October 1997.

A CONVENTION CHRONOLOGY

6 January 1941	Four Freedoms speech establishes human rights as a war aim of the Second World War
26 June 1945	United Nations Charter signed in San Francisco
August 1945	Second World War ends after use of nuclear weapons on Hiroshima and Nagasaki
5 March 1946	Winston Churchill speaks of an Iron Curtain descending across Europe
4 March 1947	Britain and France sign Treaty of Dunkirk for mutual defence against Germany
12 March 1947	Truman doctrine pronounced: US economic support for reconstruction in Europe, backed by Marshall Plan in June 1947
January 1948	British Foreign Secretary Bevin refers to a 'spiritual union' for Europe in the House of Commons
17 March 1948	Brussels Treaty signed between UK, France, Holland, Belgium and Luxembourg aimed at strengthening economic, social and cultural ties and includes a reference to human rights
16 April 1948	Organisation for European Economic Cooperation established
June 1948–May 1949	Berlin Blockade
9 December 1948	Genocide Convention adopted by UN General Assembly
10 December 1948	Universal Declaration of Human Rights adopted by UN General Assembly
5 May 1949	Council of Europe established
25 July 1949	North Atlantic Treaty signed, setting up NATO
4 November 1950	European Convention on Human Rights signed in Rome
8 March 1951	United Kingdom ratifies Convention
18 April 1951	European Coal and Steel Community (ECSC) formed
20 March 1952	First Protocol to Convention signed
3 September 1953	Convention comes into force
23 October 1953	UK extends Convention to 42 British dependencies
1954	European Commission for Human Rights begins to operate
1 January 1958	European Economic Community (EEC) and European Atomic Energy Community (Euratom) come into operation
18 September 1959	European Court of Human Rights established
16 September 1963	Fourth Protocol to Convention signed
13 January 1966	UK accepts jurisdiction of European court and right of individual petition
16 December 1966	United Nation Covenants signed (International Covenant on Economic, Social and Cultural Rights, entered into force 3 January 1976, and International Covenant on Civil and Political Rights, entered into force 23 March 1976)
1 July 1967	Merger of EEC with ECSC and Euratom
January 1973	UK joins EEC

21 February 1975	*Golder v UK*:[18] first finding of breach of Convention by UK
28 April 1983	Sixth Protocol to Convention signed
22 November 1984	Seventh Protocol to Convention signed
1 March 1993	John Smith QC delivers lecture 'A Citizen's Democracy'
1 November 1993	European Union replaces EEC when Maastricht Treaty comes into force
11 May 1994	Eleventh Protocol: reforms Convention machinery and Court (repeals or replaces Protocols which did not contain substantive rights)
October 1997	Labour government publishes the White Paper 'Rights Brought Home'; Human Rights Bill introduced into Parliament
1 November 1998	Single permanent European Court of Human Rights comes into being (replaces previous institutions)
9 November 1998	Human Rights Act 1998 passed
2 October 2000	Human Rights Act 1998 comes into force
4 November 2000	Twelfth Protocol opened for signature
3 May 2002	Thirteenth Protocol opened for signature
1 July 2002	International Criminal Court comes into existence (based on 1998 International Criminal Court Treaty)

---

[18] (1979–80) 1 EHRR 524.

The Palace of Westminster, the home of the Houses of Parliament.

Chapter 4

CONSTITUTIONAL CONSIDERATIONS

'constitution: The system of fundamental laws and principles that prescribes the nature, functions, and limits of a government or other institution; the document in which this system is recorded.' (*Reader's Digest Illustrated Dictionary*)

INTRODUCTION TO THE UNITED KINGDOM LEGAL SYSTEM

In order to fully understand how the Act works, it is necessary to understand the structure of the United Kingdom's constitution and legal system. This is because the Act has **constitutional** significance: it has an effect on the way Parliament passes legislation and on the relationship between the various parts of the government and machinery of the state. This section therefore contains an introduction to the key institutions of the state and the relationship between them, primarily for the benefit of those who are unfamiliar with our legal system and constitutional structure. This is because it is important to understand how, if at all, the Act modifies the interaction between different parts of the state machinery, and also how the Act applies to the different parts of the state.

Those who are unfamiliar with the United Kingdom's constitution or with constitutional law may be surprised that we do not have a *written* constitution. However, we do still have a constitution, as defined in the quote above, a system of laws and principles which sets out the nature, function and limits of the different elements of the state. Our constitution is very well established and, even though it is not contained in any one document which can be described as 'the Constitution', it can be found in the constitutional law contained in a combination of statutes, judicial case law, and custom, especially customs known as constitutional conventions, which are treated as effectively binding customary rules and limitations.

The United Kingdom has a constitutional structure which is conventionally categorised in three parts: **legislative** (Parliament), **executive** (government, civil service and other parts of the administration of the country), and **judicial** (courts).

PARLIAMENT

First, **Parliament,** which is the United Kingdom's **legislature** and creates or changes the law by passing **Acts** of Parliament, also known as statutes. Parliament, which sits in the Palace of Westminster, is composed of two houses: the House of Commons, which is made up of elected Members of Parliament; and the House of Lords, which is made up of a mixture of appointed peers (known as life peers) and some hereditary peers. Acts of Parliament also have to be given Royal Consent, although in the modern political system, once an Act has been approved by both Houses in accordance with the proper procedure, Royal Consent is something of a formality.

Under British constitutional law, Parliament is superior to other branches of the state; this is the idea known as **Parliamentary sovereignty**. Sovereignty has two sides to it: not only is Parliament the supreme law-making body within the United Kingdom, which means that measures passed by it (legislation) take precedence over what is decided by the courts or by the executive, but it is supreme in the sense that it is not subject to any other national or international body. In that sense the United Kingdom is a sovereign state.

Another aspect of the traditional theory of Parliamentary sovereignty which is relevant to the Act is the question of whether a future Parliament could repeal the Act. It is often said to be part of Parliament's sovereignty that one Parliament cannot bind its successors, since to do so would be to limit the sovereignty of that later Parliament. It was for this reason that the Act contains no attempt at what is known as entrenchment, that is some form of device to make the Act difficult to repeal, such as the need for a greater than usual majority. It was felt that any sort of entrenchment would not be in keeping with our constitutional tradition.[1] This preserves the constitutional position that Parliament could, in principle, withdraw from the Convention and repeal the Act. It should be said, though, that this would be politically unlikely, since it would amount to Parliament expressing the view that it did not respect human rights. In any event, as we will see, the Act preserves Parliament's sovereignty, even if an Act of Parliament should infringe the Convention.

THE EXECUTIVE

The highest level of the **executive** branch of the state is the **government**, made up of the leading members of whichever political party has a majority in the House of Commons. The government is led by the Prime Minister, who is the leader of the majority party. The Prime Minister appoints the other Ministers, in particular the senior Ministers, who make up the Cabinet. Each of the senior Ministers is responsible for a department of state, such as the Chancellor of the Exchequer who is in charge of the Treasury, the Foreign Secretary who is in charge of the Ministry of Foreign and Commonwealth Affairs, and so on. Each ministry includes other Members of Parliament, or Members of the House of Lords, who act as junior Ministers or Parliamentary Secretaries. The staff of the ministries are then filled out by civil servants. Each ministry's senior civil servant is its Permanent Secretary; and the most senior civil servant is the Cabinet Secretary.

Therefore, for a political party, the result of winning a general election and being the party with the most Members of Parliament is that that party becomes the government and has the opportunity to organise the running of the country until the next election. By having a majority in the House of Commons, the government is usually

---

[1] White Paper Cmd 3782, 'Rights Brought Home'.

also able to pass whatever legislation it chooses, since the organisation of political parties is designed to ensure that its MPs support the party line in votes. A government with a large majority, such as Tony Blair's Labour government which was voted into office in 1997, need not be concerned by a small number of dissenters on a given issue. A government with a small majority may be severely hampered in progressing legislation; an example would be John Major's Conservative government of 1992 to 1997.

The government is then able to determine what political policies will be followed in the running of the country, both through the introduction of legislation into Parliament and in the exercise of the variety of discretionary powers which the various Ministers and their departments have. Such powers are drawn from legislation or sources based on common law, in particular the **royal prerogative**. This is the name for those powers which were recognised in times past by the common law as attaching to the Crown, that is, being exercised by the ruling monarch. These are now exercised by Ministers of state and include powers such as the capacity to represent the state in foreign affairs or the organisation of national defence.

The executive also includes all those organisations which actually run the machinery of the state: the civil service, local government and government agencies, running institutions as diverse as the health service, the armed forces and emergency services, state schools, social services and social security, the transport infrastructure of roads and airports, and so on. Constitutionally, the executive at this level carries out the wishes of Parliament, as expressed in legislation, as to how the state should be run, and where Parliament leaves a discretion or choice as to how particular matters should be decided or institutions run, this is regulated by the wishes of the government. Some matters are not regulated by Parliament at all, except in a supervisory sense. For example, sending armed forces abroad to act as peacekeepers is a decision of the government which must be politically justified in Parliament but need not be approved by it. Local government is also considered part of the executive: although those running local government are elected, local councils do not actually legislate, they implement Parliament's legislation, or act in accordance with discretion granted by Parliament.

Because the government is the same as the majority in Parliament, it might be thought that the role of Parliament is limited to passing legislation in accordance with the government's wishes. However, this is not the case. Even leaving aside the occasional situation where legislation is passed against the wishes of the government, or introduced by Members of Parliament who are not part of the government (Private Member's Bills), Parliament also provides scrutiny of proposed legislation and generally of the conduct of the government and the executive. In particular, this is a major function of the House of Lords. It is also done through a series of Parliamentary Committees, which meet regularly to consider different areas of the practical government of the country. One such committee is the Joint Committee on Human Rights, which considers matters relating to human rights and matters relating to the Human Rights Act.

It is because of this supervisory role performed by Parliament that, when one is trying to understand a statute that is not entirely clear, it is sometimes relevant to consider what was said in Parliament when the wording of the statute was debated. This may help to clarify the intention behind the wording used. Statements made in

Parliament can be referred to in court, if they assist in the interpretation of the statute.[2] This will only be if the statute is ambiguous, since the starting point for the interpretation of all statutes is the ordinary meaning of the words used, allowing for any definitions provided for by the statute being considered, or the definitions of any words with technical meanings.

THE COURTS

The third branch of the state machinery is the **judiciary**, the judges, courts and court services, who administer justice on behalf of the state for the resolution of disputes (civil law) and the trial of those accused of crimes (criminal law) (see Figure 4.1). In England and Wales there are criminal courts, Crown Courts and Magistrates' Courts, which deal with the trials of those accused of criminal offences, on the basis of prosecutions brought primarily by the Crown Prosecution Service, and which impose punishments on those found guilty. Then there are civil courts, the High Court and County Courts, which deal mainly with actions to resolve disputes between individuals, companies or other bodies and award appropriate remedies for wrongs done, predominantly monetary compensation.

If a party considers that a court has decided a matter incorrectly, there is some scope for appealing the decision, especially on the ground that the law has been wrongly applied. This is done by bringing an appeal to the Court of Appeal, which sits primarily at the Royal Courts of Justice at the Strand in London; the Divisional Court is an equivalent court for certain sorts of appeal. There is then a final level of appeal to the House of Lords – more precisely to the Judicial Committee of the House of Lords, since those members of the House of Lords which sit on legal appeals are specifically appointed for that purpose and not drawn from the main body of members of the House of Lords. These Lords are titled Lords of Appeal in Ordinary, informally known as the Law Lords, and are generally appointed from among the appeal judges from the courts of England and Wales, Scotland and Northern Ireland, and other senior judges who hold a peerage. The Law Lords also sit as the Judicial Committee of the Privy Council, which is a body that hears appeals from jurisdictions other than the courts of England and Wales, including some appeals from Scotland and Northern Ireland. The Privy Council also remains the final court of appeal for some former colonial countries, for example a number of Caribbean countries such as Jamaica and Barbados.

It is an important constitutional principle that the judiciary is independent of the government. This is grounded in considerations of legality and the rule of law, that the law is administered by people who are impartial and who are independent of those who made the law.[3] Some countries have a strict separation between the various branches of the state, known as the separation of powers. The United Kingdom has some overlaps between the different sections of the state – for example, the senior judges, the Law Lords, are able to sit in the House of Lords in its legislative capacity, and the most senior judge, the Lord Chancellor, is a member of the Cabinet, and therefore a

---

[2] *Pepper v Hart* [1993] AC 593.
[3] Discussed above, pp. 13–14.

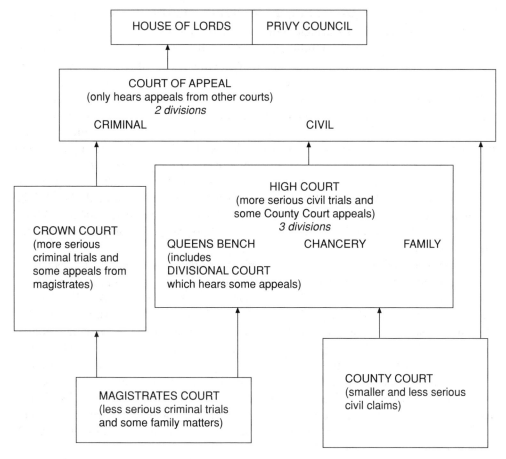

Figure 4.1   Flow chart of the court system of England and Wales

political appointment. However, the independence of the judiciary is nonetheless strictly protected, for example, by the provision that judges can only be removed from office if they commit some impropriety (such as being convicted of a crime) or by the decision of both Houses of Parliament.[4] This ensures that the government cannot sack a judge just because they issue a decision against the government or with which the government disagrees.

JUDICIAL REVIEW

The High Court also has a jurisdiction to supervise the acts of the executive. As mentioned above, the executive has to act in accordance with the powers granted to it, usually by Parliament, and always in accordance with the law, which means,

---

[4] Supreme Court Act 1981 section 11(3).

for example, not deciding to do something illegal or which it is not authorised to do. This again is part of the principle of the rule of law, that not only should discretionary powers be exercised lawfully and properly, but also that the courts should be able to supervise such exercises and that there should be a remedy in respect of any unlawful decisions made or acts done.

When a decision is taken which is for any reason improper, this can be brought before a judge by an action called a **judicial review**. The result of such an action is typically not an award of money, but an order that the decision is unlawful or improper and therefore invalid. This is a type of remedy which is likely to be of great importance in actions under the Human Rights Act, since one of the consequences of the Act is that decisions taken by government ministers or officials will have to take proper account of people's Convention rights. If they do not do so, the decision can be declared to be unlawful and of no effect by the courts. This is particularly important if the decision affects someone in a situation where money would not properly compensate them for the breach of their rights.

The institution of judicial review is an important one and is a significant element of the relationship between the courts and Parliament. The principle applied in a judicial review is that what is being reviewed is a decision which should be taken by a person appointed to take that decision. This will involve the exercise of a **discretion**, that is, that the decision-maker is given at least some degree of choice in what decision to make. This discretion has been granted to the person being challenged and in principle it is not for the courts to supplant that person's discretion by taking the decision themselves. The role of the courts is rather in policing the decision-making process. Thus a judicial review case does not involve the courts deciding whether a decision or action which is taken by a public or governmental body or person is right or wrong, but whether or not it is properly within the scope of the authority or discretion which is being exercised.

Most of the time the discretion in question is provided by a statute, but judicial review principles apply equally to non-statutory discretions exercised by servants of the state, such as the powers which are part of the royal prerogative, mentioned above. Thus the courts consider whether the decision under review is within the powers of the person making that decision. The courts also consider any allegations such as that the decision is arbitrary or unfounded, that the decision-maker is biased or that he or she has not allowed all relevant parties to put their case before a decision is taken. This is where the Act comes in: a decision which infringes someone's Convention rights will be unlawful and therefore one which that person has no authority to make. It will therefore be liable to be challenged and quashed on a judicial review hearing.

In one respect the Act extends the role of the court in a judicial review hearing. The traditional view of judicial review is that what is being considered is the legality and procedural propriety of the decision, to ensure that the decision falls within the scope of the statutory discretion, to ensure that it is not an improper decision because the decision-maker was biased or took into account irrelevant considerations, etc, and to ensure that all appropriate procedural steps have been followed. Under the Act, however, the courts may well have to consider whether the substance of the decision infringes a Convention right, especially if there is a question about whether a decision which would appear to interfere with a right can be justified. As we will be discussing later, a key idea in the question of justification is proportionality, and judging whether or not a decision is a proportionate interference with a right involves a consideration of the substantive basis of the decision, and not just the process by which it was reached.

A helpful statement of this change in approach can be found in the speech of Lord Steyn in the case of *Daly*:[5]

> The intensity of review is somewhat greater under the proportionality approach. [The] doctrine of proportionality may require the reviewing Court to assess the balance which the decision maker has struck, not merely whether it is within the range of rational or reasonable decisions. Secondly the proportionality test may go further than the traditional grounds of review in as much as it may require attention to be directed to the relative weight accorded to interests and considerations.

THE ACT AND PARLIAMENTARY SOVEREIGNTY

One general question which should be considered in respect of many of the individual cases that we will be discussing is the extent to which particular issues as to rights should be, and are, determined by the judges or by Parliament. The Act specifically preserves the sovereignty of Parliament: it does not allow the courts to declare that any statute passed by Parliament is unlawful and so of no effect. Thus it does not change the constitutional relationship between Parliament and the courts or give the courts the powers that, for example, the Supreme Court of the United States has to declare legislation to be invalid if it is unconstitutional. The courts can only declare that the provisions of the statute are incompatible with the Act – that is, one or more provisions of the statute in question infringe the human rights of some person or persons.

The Act therefore does not, in principle, infringe the sovereignty of Parliament – it does not interfere with democratic process, or prevent a government being able to pursue the policies it was elected to pursue, nor does it allow judges to over-rule Parliament. This is important in principle. The justification for this limitation on the scope of the Act is that judges are not elected – they are appointed on the basis of ability and experience – and therefore they are not accountable to the general population. They cannot be elected out of office as politicians can be. It is quite appropriate, and indeed desirable, to have judges decide **legal disputes**, questions about what the law says in a particular area, or how the law should deal with a difficult case, since the resolution of such questions is based on expertise in the law. Considerations of general principles of morality and justice apply only in so far as there is any doubt as to what the law is or any question as to what the law should be, which only occurs in rare cases. Usually the dispute in a case being heard is about what the facts in dispute are, and how the law applies to those facts; it is rare for the facts to be clear but the law to be vague, and it is only in those situations that the judges may have to decide what the right answer *should* be.

However, questions of human rights may well involve **political questions** of the sort which should be decided as a matter of policy by Parliament. Members of Parliament are elected on the basis of their, or their party's, political views on which policies should

[5] *R v Secretary of State for the Home Department (Daly)* [2001] 2 AC 532 at 547.

be adopted on a variety of important issues. They therefore have a democratic mandate to put forward certain views on contentious issues, and are accountable to the electorate for the way in which they present those views.

Thus questions such as how much money should be spent by the government in different areas such as defence or social security or whether the government should pursue a policy of building roads or railways to assist with transport are political, rather than legal. This is because these are questions on which there are a range of possible answers, where general principles of right and wrong do not lead to conclusions on the detail, and where the question is not what the law says (if anything), but what it ought to say. So, it may be a worthy general principle that we should all contribute to the funding of public transport, but that does not answer the political question as to how much money should be allocated to different areas.

In addition, political questions are not usually appropriate to the type of process used in judicial decision-making. This is because judges are there to decide the questions that relate to the dispute between the two parties before them: the right answer for that case on those facts. The sort of matters that we think of as political questions are typically ones where a more general approach is required, since there are invariably more than two different views on the right answer, and more than two parties or groups who will be affected by the solution chosen. They will also often be questions where getting to the best answer will involve much specialist or expert input. Courts have to rely on the expert evidence put before them by the parties to the dispute, whereas politicians and civil servants can be more proactive in seeking relevant information and have access to a wider variety of sources of information, not just those arguments put before them by the parties interested in any given issue.

There is, of course, often no clear distinction between legal and political questions and many questions will be one of degree. For example, where the law is not clear and there is a discretion to be exercised by the judges deciding a case, because the existing cases would support more than one answer, the judges may find themselves making a 'political' decision as to what the right answer should be. This will be especially so if the law is being challenged in the highest court, the House of Lords, where it may effectively be argued that the law should be changed: the Lords will then have to consider the more general implications of the decision they are making, and the policy which they would be implementing by taking a particular view. In such cases there may well be a difference of opinion precisely on whether such a decision should be made by the courts or by Parliament, and whether or not it is appropriate for the courts to be making that sort of decision.

An example of a situation where the courts expressly considered that a policy decision was being taken, and also an example of judicial review under the Act, is the case of *Alconbury*.[6] Here, what was being challenged was a ministerial decision under statutory powers to decide a question as to whether or not planning permission should be given for a number of proposed developments. What was being argued was that the Environment Secretary was not an independent and impartial

---

[6] R *(Alconbury Developments Limited) v Secretary of State for the Environment, Transport and the Regions* [2001] 2 WLR 1389.

tribunal within the meaning of Article 6(1) and therefore his power to decide these questions was incompatible with the Convention.

The House of Lords rejected this argument. The role of the Secretary of State was quite appropriate since the decision at issue was one of administrative policy under the planning legislation. It would be undemocratic for the courts to determine planning questions themselves, since that was not the scheme of the legislation adopted by Parliament: the constitutional role of the Secretary of State was not a judicial role to which Article 6 applies, but involved a political, policy decision. However, overall Article 6 was complied with because the decision of the Secretary of State could be judicially reviewed, to ensure that he complied with the relevant statute, that he had followed the necessary procedural steps, and so on. There was therefore protection to ensure that the decision was *legal* and procedurally proper; but it was not for the court to say whether it was *correct*.

Questions of basic rights raised by the application of the Human Rights Act will often include what are here termed political questions – questions about what solution society should adopt to a particular problem. This means that the question of whether a particular rule infringes someone's rights is not an isolated question. We will see in our discussion of the various Articles of the Convention that most of them make allowances for situations where rights can be legitimately interfered with in the general interest. The way that the Act brings the Convention into our law ensures that where Parliament has adopted a particular position on a political issue, the judges will have to apply the law as Parliament has set it out, even if they consider that this statute infringes one or more Convention rights of parties affected by the legislation.

However, the fact that Parliament can pass legislation which does not conform to the Convention rights does not mean that having the Act as part of our law serves no useful purpose. On the contrary, it does ensure that Parliament must at least expressly consider the possible effects of its legislation on individual rights. Thus there will be political pressure on the government and Parliament not to propose or pass laws which infringe rights and to change those that do. It means that Parliament, in passing legislation, has to focus directly on any issues as to potential infringements of rights which arise. The preservation of Parliamentary sovereignty has been one of the main reasons why incorporating the Convention into domestic law has been politically contentious over the years. The method adopted by the Act, that Parliament is free if it wishes to disregard the Act's provisions, preserves the existing constitutional balance between Parliament and the courts. The Act has constitutional significance; it is not a new constitution.

DEVOLUTION

Another aspect of the constitution which is relevant to how the Act affects the law is how it applies in the different parts of the United Kingdom. The United Kingdom of Great Britain and Northern Ireland consists of four main constituent parts: England, Wales, Scotland and Northern Ireland. These have three different legal systems – one in England and Wales, one in Scotland and one in Northern Ireland. Whilst there are areas of the law which apply in the same way in all three systems, there are also areas which are different. There are also distinct legal systems in the Isle of Man and the

Channel Islands. The reasons for the separate legal systems are historical: in particular, the English and Scottish legal systems were entirely separate before these two countries were united by the Acts of Union.[7]

In the last few years more autonomy from the Parliament at Westminster has been granted to Scotland and Wales; this has been part of the same political interest in constitutional matters on the part of the Labour government which led to the Act being passed. The Scotland Act 1998 set up the Scottish Parliament, which sits in Edinburgh, and is empowered to pass legislation for Scotland. The Government of Wales Act 1998 set up the Welsh National Assembly which sits in Cardiff and creates subordinate legislation. An Assembly has also been set up in Northern Ireland as part of the peace process there by the Northern Ireland Act 1998, although it has not operated continuously since its creation for political reasons. The Northern Ireland Act 1998 also set up the Northern Ireland Human Rights Commission to review the adequacy and effectiveness in Northern Ireland of law and practice relating to the protection of human rights.[8]

Each of these devolved legislative bodies has been given the power to legislate on a variety of areas. The cumulative effect of these provisions is potentially quite a significant decentralisation of power, certainly in those areas which have been devolved, although these vary between the different institutions. However, all of them are subject to the provisions of the Human Rights Act 1998, and any legislation passed by them which infringes the Convention rights can be declared void and of no effect.[9] In this respect, they do not have the authority that the national Parliament does to overrule the Act. Thus in each case, legislation passed by them is open to challenge on the basis that such legislation is in conflict with one of the Convention rights. The court which will ultimately hear any such challenge is the Judicial Committee of the Privy Council, made up of a panel of Law Lords, and there have already been a number of such cases, mainly from Scotland. This ensures that there is some consistency between the application of the Act in the legal systems of Scotland, Northern Ireland, and England and Wales.

THE EUROPEAN CONVENTION IN ENGLISH LAW

As part of the background to understanding the way that the European Convention operates, it is worth explaining here what is meant by an **international treaty**, of which the Convention is one example, and how it relates to domestic British law. The body of law known as public international law sets out the rules that apply to relationships between states. Under international law, a state, such as the United Kingdom, can take on obligations to other states by means of a treaty, which just means a formal and

---

[7] Union with Scotland Act 1706 and Union with England Act 1707, now subject to the Scotland Act 1998.

[8] Northern Ireland Act 1998 section 68-9.

[9] Scotland Act 1998 section 29 and section 57(2) limits the Scottish Executive; Government of Wales Act 1998 section 107(1); Northern Ireland Act 1998 section 6(2).

binding agreement between states. Other examples of treaties apart from the European Convention itself are the treaties setting up the European Union or the United Nations Charter. There are a host of other treaties to which the United Kingdom is a party, for example the Hague and Geneva Conventions, peace treaties, and treaties that regulate international matters ranging from diplomacy between states to the status of outer space.

By entering into a treaty, confirmed if necessary by Parliament in a statute, the United Kingdom government can grant other institutions powers to make decisions about the law in the United Kingdom. So, by being a signatory to the European Convention, the United Kingdom agrees that the European Court has the authority to decide whether or not the United Kingdom has fulfilled its obligations under the Convention or not in particular cases; that is, whether or not it protects the rights of its citizens. In a similar manner, by signing up to the various treaties relating to the European Union, the United Kingdom has consented to grant certain powers to European Union institutions, such as the European Court of Justice.

However, just because the United Kingdom has signed up to a treaty, this does not mean that the treaty can be used to challenge the law which is laid down in an Act of Parliament. Under our constitutional law, treaties entered into with other countries have no effect in our national law unless and until they are passed as a law by Parliament. That is, individuals cannot use treaty obligations as the basis for bringing a legal action until Parliament has passed a law creating individual rights. This again is an aspect of Parliamentary sovereignty: the government cannot simply create law by signing a treaty other than by going through the usual Parliamentary law-making process.

This limitation on the effect of treaties applied equally to the European Convention until the Human Rights Act was passed in 1998, even though the United Kingdom has been a party to the Convention since it was first signed in 1950. Until then, as with any treaty, it could be referred to in a particular dispute, but did not actually dictate how that dispute should be decided.

Thus, before the Act came into force, there were only limited ways in which the Convention could be relied on in a court case in the United Kingdom. It was certainly referred to in a number of cases which raised issues as to fundamental rights, such as freedom of speech or freedom of religion, but could only be used in limited circumstances to assist the court. The main circumstances where the Convention was used in a decision were:

•   As an aid to construction of ambiguous legislation, since the courts should prefer an interpretation which allows the UK to fulfil its international obligations.

For example, in the case of *Brind*,[10] which was about a statutory provision that allowed members of terrorist organisations to be seen but not heard on television, the Convention was referred to, although the court in the end considered that there was no ambiguity in the statute.

---

[10]   *R v Home Secretary, ex parte Brind* [1991] 1 AC 696.

- To assist with an ambiguity in the judge-made part of the common law.

For example, in the case of *Derbyshire County Council v Times Newspapers*,[11] which concerned the question of whether or not a local authority could sue for libel, it was held that it could not, because this would be a restriction on freedom of speech. The Court of Appeal considered that the common law was ambiguous and relied on the Convention; the House of Lords considered that there was no ambiguity in the common law, but considered that the common law was in line with the Convention in any event.

- To assist in the exercise of judicial discretion, again to ensure that the courts uphold rather than deviate from the Convention where there is scope to do so.

For example, regarding the application by the government for an injunction, which is a discretionary remedy, to restrain the publication of extracts of the book *Spycatcher*, members of the House of Lords made reference to the Convention and considered that it was not violated by continuing the injunctions which had been granted.[12]

THE MACHINERY OF THE EUROPEAN CONVENTION

The European Convention itself contains a machinery for the resolution of human rights disputes and allegations of infringements, including provisions to allow an individual to bring a case to the European Court to complain if the law of the country they live in does not properly protect the rights which the Convention sets out. Since 1966, individuals in the United Kingdom have been able to bring such a complaint about any alleged breach of their human rights, and therefore this has been effectively part of the way in which an individual can seek a remedy against the state for some complaint, in addition to suing in our national courts.

Until 1998, the Convention mechanism consisted of the European Commission and the European Court. The system was that the Commission ascertained the facts of a particular case, decided whether or not it was admissible and gave an opinion on its merits. The Court then gave a final judgment, and ordered any 'satisfaction' or remedy by way of the payment of compensation. The Council of Europe's Committee of Ministers had an overseeing role.

From 1 November 1998, the Commission was abolished, as was the judicial function of the Ministers. The present system is that the Court sits full-time, decides the facts and any questions of admissibility, and then gives judgment. The Court may sit as a Committee of three judges, or a Chamber of seven, or a Grand Chamber of seventeen. A party who is dissatisfied with a judgment of a Chamber may ask for a re-hearing before a Grand Chamber, if a serious issue is raised of general importance or concerning the interpretation of the Convention.

---

[11] *Derbyshire County Council v Times Newspapers* [1992] 1 QB 770, Court of Appeal; [1993] AC 534, House of Lords.
[12] *Attorney General v Guardian Newspapers* [1987] 1 WLR 1287, e.g. per Lord Templeman at p. 1296.

As was the case before the Act came into force, it still remains open for a party who wishes to complain about a breach of their Convention rights to take a case to the European Court. However, in order to be allowed to do so, they must first exhaust the scope for challenging the alleged infringement in the national courts. Thus, the number of cases going from the United Kingdom to the European Court is likely to be greatly reduced, since allegations of infringement are likely to be dealt with, one way or another, before they get that far. This is one of the practical advantages of the Act: the European Court is now a final appeal, a last resort, and not a first stop for such complaints.

THE MARGIN OF APPRECIATION

The **margin of appreciation** is an important concept in the European Court's approach to deciding cases and an important part of the European Court's view of the relationship between it and the national state authorities and state courts. The central idea of the margin of appreciation is that there are some areas where different states may take different approaches to particular rights. This is based on the principle that individual states have a certain measure of autonomy under the Convention ('appreciation' here is used in the sense of allowing a measure of understanding or leeway). This is thought appropriate because the states that are bound by the Convention cover the whole of Europe and have different cultures and histories, different dominant religions, different traditions about how people should behave and when and to what extent state interference is justified. In some areas there may be no general consensus across Europe about what should be tolerated and what should not, and that would suggest to the judges of the European Court that states should be given some scope for expressing the popular feelings of their citizens about a particular issue.

The European Court in this way accepts that different people may have different views on moral issues which are not necessarily 'right' or 'wrong'. Another way of putting this is that it is based on the principle of subsidiarity, that matters should be decided at the most local level appropriate. The principle of a margin of appreciation recognises that national courts may be best placed to make an initial assessment of the needs and standards of their own societies; or in some cases, that different countries have evolved different solutions to similar problems, especially on social and moral issues. But it should be emphasised that states will not be given a margin of appreciation on all issues, only where the European Court considers that there is a genuine difference of opinion across Europe and the right in question is one which permits different interpretations to be applied. There is no margin of appreciation to allow torture or slavery, for example, in breach of Articles 3 and 4. It is only on difficult moral issues that states may have a margin of appreciation.

One example is abortion: this is a difficult moral question on which people from different cultures and religions take different views. Under the Convention, the right to life contained in Article 2 is not qualified. However, different states have different laws about abortion. Some states prohibit abortion altogether, for example Ireland because of its predominantly Roman Catholic population; others, like the United Kingdom, allow abortion up to a certain stage of pregnancy. If the European Court was asked to consider whether abortion was an interference with the right to life or whether

banning abortion was an interference with the rights of the mother, this is an area where an application of the margin of appreciation is likely, because there is no European consensus as to what
is morally acceptable and what is not. This question has been considered by the European
Commission, who have taken broadly this approach: they have taken the view that an unborn child
does have some rights, but these are bound up with the rights of the mother.[13]

The principle also reflects an important aspect of the function of the European Court.
The European Court will only consider whether or not the judgments of the national
courts, and the decisions of the national governments and officials, are in accordance
with the principles of the Convention. If a judgment or decision causes a citizen to
suffer a breach of his or her human rights, then the court will step in, by declaring that
there has been a breach. But the European Court will not substitute its judgment for
that of the national court on the application of national law, so it will not reach a decision as to whether or not the national law has been applied correctly. Nor will it review
the admissibility or relevance of the evidence adduced in the national court. It is in this
sense a supervisory jurisdiction.

In the case of *Handyside v UK*,[14] the European Court was asked to consider the bringing of a prosecution in England for obscenity arising out of the publication of *The Little Red Schoolbook*, a
book which was aimed at children and was prosecuted for its frank discussions of sexual matters.
The publisher complained that his rights to freedom of expression under Article 10 had been infringed.
The United Kingdom argued that any infringement was justified in the interest of the protection of
morals.

The European Court decided that, although the book had not been prosecuted in some other
European countries where it had been published, it was within the margin of appreciation allowed
to the United Kingdom authorities to consider that this book was unlawful in Britain. In particular,
there was no uniform European conception of morals and on this ground of justification, state authorities were better placed than the European Court to give an opinion. The Court stated that the
protection established by the Convention is in that sense subsidiary to the national systems safeguarding human rights. The Court stressed, however, that allowing a margin of appreciation goes
hand in hand with European overall supervision, in particular the limiting requirement of proportionality between the infringement of the right and its justification.

It should also be noted that the European Court has developed its ideas over time
as the popular morality of Europe has changed. This is because the European Court
treats the Convention as a developing instrument. This has affected what issues are
considered to be ones where states have a margin of appreciation at any one time.

A recent example of the European Court developing the margin of appreciation is in the Court's
consideration of the rights of transsexuals, that is, people who undergo a sex-change operation.
In the case of *Goodwin v UK*[15] the Court decided that there had been violations of Articles 8 (privacy)
and 12 (right to marriage) in respect of two transsexuals. The Court recognised an international
trend towards increased social acceptance of transsexuals and increased legal recognition of their

---

[13] Discussed further below, p. 103.
[14] (1979–80) 1 EHRR 737.
[15] *Goodwin v UK* (2002) 35 EHRR 18. Also below, p. 246 in the context of Article 12.

new sexual identity, and came to the view that this could no longer be regarded as a matter of controversy. It was therefore no longer open to the United Kingdom to claim that their treatment of transsexuals fell within the margin of appreciation. This was particularly so given the lack of review which appeared to have been undertaken by the United Kingdom government since previous European Court decisions on the subject, notwithstanding changes in attitudes in society. The United Kingdom did however retain a margin of appreciation as to how the rights of transsexuals should be recognised and what changes to domestic law were required as a result.

DEFERENCE TO THE LEGISLATURE

It is, however, important to realise that the margin of appreciation, although an important principle for the European Court, has no direct application when a case is being decided by a national court. So, for example, if a Scottish court were asked to decide whether or not an interference with freedom of association is justified by considerations of public safety, it will not apply a margin of appreciation, since it will have to either accept or reject the justification: it will have to decide whether or not there is an infringement of the right to freedom of association. Unlike the European Court, it is not being asked to consider whether it is appropriate for there to be different answers to the question in different legal systems across Europe, but what the correct answer is under Scottish law. This difference arises out of the different roles of the national courts and the European Court.

However, the domestic courts are still likely to give some discretion as to action to those they are reviewing, although this is not strictly speaking a margin of appreciation. This will apply where, for example, the court considers that Parliament in passing a statute or a decision-maker making the decision under review is better placed to reach a proper conclusion about the matter being considered. Another aspect which the courts will have to consider is to what extent the decision being made is based on a democratic mandate, for example in considering legislation passed by the devolved assemblies: the very fact that these are bodies elected to decide certain matters may have an effect on how much margin the courts allow them in choosing solutions to difficult questions. Comments to this effect have already been made by the House of Lords in a number of cases.

For example, in the case of *Kebilene*,[16] Lord Hope recognised that the United Kingdom courts will not expressly apply the margin of appreciation as used by the European Court. However, the rights provided by the Convention are expressions of fundamental principles, and not just a set of rules. Therefore, where there are competing interests:

> In some circumstances it will be appropriate for the courts to recognise that there is an area of judgment within which the judiciary will defer, on democratic grounds, to the considered opinion of the elected body or person whose act or decision is said to be incompatible with the Convention [. . .] It will be easier for it to be recognised where the issues involve questions of social or economic policy, much less so where the rights are of high constitutional importance or are of a kind where the courts are especially well placed to assess the need for protection.

---

[16] *R v Kebilene* [2000] 2 AC 326, at p. 381, discussed further below, p. 161.

This was also referred to in the case of *Brown v Stott*.[17] This concerned the question of whether a statutory obligation on the owner of a vehicle, to provide information about who was driving the vehicle when an offence was committed, infringes the Article 6 protection against self-incrimination, and if so, whether any infringement is justified. The justification would be based on addressing the social problem of reducing traffic accidents, part of which involves ensuring that those responsible for accidents are prosecuted, which requires identification of the person driving the car. The Privy Council here held that there was no infringement of Article 6. One of the factors referred to by Lord Steyn was that Parliament was in as good a position as a court to assess the gravity of the problem and the public interest in addressing it, in requiring the identity of the driver to be disclosed.

Again in a different context altogether: in the case of *Poplar Housing v Donoghue*,[18] the court had to consider the statutory scheme for providing social housing. The Court of Appeal considered that:

> The court has to pay considerable attention to the fact that Parliament intended [. . .] to give preference to the needs of those dependent on social housing *as a whole* over those in the position of the defendant. The economic and other implications of any policy in this area are extremely complex and far-reaching. This is an area where, in our judgment, the courts must treat the decisions of Parliament as to what is in the public interest with particular deference. The limited role given to the court [. . .] is a legislative policy decision. The correctness of this decision is more appropriate for Parliament than the courts and the Human Rights Act 1998 does not require the courts to disregard the decisions of Parliament in relation to situations of this sort when deciding whether there has been a breach of the Convention.

It is important that in complex areas, requiring political decisions as to the best of a range of permissible solutions, the courts do give weight to the decision of Parliament. However, it will also be important for the courts to ensure that they do not defer to Parliament too much. Deference to Parliament should not prevent the courts from intervening in situations where Parliament has gone beyond the boundaries of what is permitted by the Convention rights.

QUESTIONS

1   Consider the role of judges: can you suggest the sort of matters which you think are suitable or unsuitable for being decided by a court?
2   Do you consider that the Act strikes the right balance between Parliament and the courts? Does the Act go far enough? Should the judges be allowed to overturn Acts of Parliament if they infringe human rights?

---

[17] [2001] 2 WLR 817, Privy Council, discussed further below, p. 152.
[18] *Poplar Housing and Regeneration Community Association Ltd v Donoghue* [2001] 3 WLR 183 at 202; see also below, p. 56.

The home of the European Court of Human Rights at Strasbourg. The European Court's case law is now effectively part of our law, by section 2 of the Act.

(*Source:* EPA/PA Photos.)

Chapter 5

THE SCHEME OF THE HUMAN RIGHTS ACT 1998

'It is now plain that the incorporation of the European Convention on Human Rights into our domestic law will subject the entire legal system to a fundamental process of review and, where necessary, reform by the judiciary.' (Lord Hope of Craighead, *R v DPP ex p. Kebilene*,[1] 2000)

The main scheme of the Act, the way in which the Convention rights are given force, is as follows:

- The decisions of the European Court and Commission are made relevant to all decisions about Convention rights (section 2).
- All United Kingdom legislation, whenever passed, must, if possible, be interpreted so as to be compatible with the Convention (section 3).
- It is made unlawful for a public authority to act in a way which is incompatible with a Convention right (section 6).
- The courts are given the power to award remedies for breaches of Convention rights (section 8).

Before the Act was passed, a citizen of the United Kingdom who felt aggrieved by a breach of their human rights could only bring a legal action in respect of such a breach directly in the European Court.[2] After 2 October 2000, United Kingdom citizens are able to rely on the Convention rights in the United Kingdom courts directly. We will consider in this chapter how and to what extent the Act brings the Convention into our law, and in the next chapter what remedies there are for breaches of the Convention rights and the practicalities of seeking such a remedy.

---

[1] [2000] 2 AC 326 at 375.
[2] See p. 44 above for discussion of the limited ways in which the Convention could be used.

IMPORTING THE DECISIONS OF THE EUROPEAN COURT

Section 2 (1)   A court or tribunal determining a question which has arisen in connection with a Convention right must take into account any: judgment,
decision, declaration or advisory opinion of the European Court of
Human Rights, opinion or decision of the Commission, or decision of
the Committee of Ministers, whenever made or given, so far as, in the
opinion of the court or tribunal, it is relevant to the proceedings in which
that question has arisen.

Section 2 means that the law and interpretation which has been built up by the European Court and other bodies set up by the Convention must be 'taken into account'
by the United Kingdom courts in deciding points under the Act. This should ensure
that the way the United Kingdom courts develop the Act is consistent with the way
the Convention is applied throughout the rest of Europe and by the European Court.
This is important for two main reasons. The first is that having cases decided consistently is an important principle of justice – that like cases are treated alike, that
rights of people in equivalent circumstances are given the same degree of respect. The
second is that it should help to prevent cases having to go to Strasbourg, because the
European Court law will be applied in full. This was one of the key practical reasons
for bringing the Convention directly into British law. However, the consequence of
this provision is to import into domestic United Kingdom law a body of case law with
which lawyers will have to become familiar, as will anyone else who wants to know
what the effect of the Convention will be.

   Note also that the wording in the Act is 'take into account'. This suggests that the
European case law will not be binding on the court that is considering it. The court is
still likely to give any relevant European Court case law very serious consideration and
in practice is likely to follow a decision of the European Court which applies to the
situation it is considering. But the fact that the European case law is not strictly binding is important because European Court cases are decided in relation to a wide variety
of situations arising in many different countries. The European Court also includes a
wide variety of judges from different cultures and backgrounds, especially with the expansion of the Council of Europe over the last ten years or so.[3] Thus a case decided on
the law in another part of Europe may not reach a result which the British court thinks
is correct, even if the facts look similar to a local case. So, although European Court
case law will usually be followed and given great weight, there is the opportunity for
British judges to choose not to follow a particular case if there are good reasons to do
so.

   The other reason why it is helpful that European Court cases are not made strictly
binding is that, in interpreting the Convention, one of the principles which the European Court applies is that the scope and meaning of the Convention can develop over
time. Thus, there are changes and developments in moral standards, and considerations of what is generally thought of as right and wrong, or acceptable or not, and the

---

[3] A table of members showing when each joined can be found in Appendix 3.

European Court may change its views as to how to apply the Convention in particular situations.[4]

This also ties in with the way the Convention is drafted, as a series of general rights, which are open to interpretation. Since the European Court does not consider that it is strictly bound by the results it has reached in an earlier case, it is appropriate that our judges should not be bound by such a decision. If a British court decides not to follow a particular European Court decision, and the British decision is challenged so that the matter goes back before the European Court, it would be open to the European Court to prefer the British court's view to the earlier view of the European Court. Thus, the British courts can make an express contribution to the decisions of the European Court; indeed, this was seen as one of the benefits of having cases on the Convention decided in the British courts. The scope of this provision means that a judge is not limited by a European Court decision: it would be open to the local court to go beyond the European decision, and find that there was, for example, an infringement of a Convention right, even though in a similar case the European Court had found none.

There is one other issue raised by this provision, which is in the following situation. A domestic court, such as the Court of Appeal, could decide, on a particular set of facts, that there is no infringement of a Convention right. The European Court might disagree with that decision, in an appeal on that case, or in a later, separate case, and find that there was an infringement. This raises an issue about whether our courts should prefer the decision of the Court of Appeal or the European Court. Under our usual doctrine of precedence of cases, a Court of Appeal case should be followed in a later case being decided by a less senior court. And, strictly speaking, the European Court decision will not over-rule the earlier case, since section 2 does not make European Court cases binding. However, the courts may have to reconsider the usual doctrine of precedence in order properly to take into account the European Court decision. This will be especially so, if what is being considered is not the precise decision on the facts but a general statement of principle, or the approach to be taken to a particular situation. If the European Court's view is inconsistent with the national case, to follow the Court of Appeal case without question may lead to further infringements of the Convention.

THE ACT AND OTHER LEGISLATION

Section 3 (1) So far as it is possible to do so, primary legislation and subordinate legislation must be read and given effect in a way which is compatible with the Convention rights.

(2) This section –
  (a) applies to primary legislation and subordinate legislation whenever enacted;
  (b) does not affect the validity, continuing operation or enforcement of any incompatible primary legislation; and
  (c) does not affect the validity, continuing operation or enforcement of any incompatible subordinate legislation if (disregarding any possibility of revocation) primary legislation prevents removal of the incompatibility.

---

[4] This comes across especially in the idea of the margin of appreciation, discussed above at p. 45.

This section is perhaps the most far-reaching in the whole Act. The consequence of section 3 is that all past and future Acts of Parliament must be made compatible with the Convention rights – that is, if a Court possibly can, it must read any statute passed by Parliament so that it protects the rights granted by the Act, even if that protection does not appear on the face of the statute in question.

Even before the Act, there were cases which considered that there are some fundamental rights which can only be interfered with by Parliament on the basis of express words, which is a similar idea to section 3. This view was summarised by Lord Hoffmann in the case of *Simms*,[5] a case decided after the Act was passed, but on facts which took place before it came into force:

> Parliamentary sovereignty means that Parliament can, if it chooses, legislate contrary to fundamental principles of human rights. The Human Rights Act 1998 will not detract from this power. The constraints upon its exercise by Parliament are ultimately political, not legal. But the principle of legality means that Parliament must squarely confront what it is doing and accept the political cost. Fundamental rights cannot be overridden by general or ambiguous words. This is because there is too great a risk that the full implications of their unqualified meaning may have passed unnoticed in the democratic process. In the absence of express language or necessary implication to the contrary, the courts therefore presume that even the most general words were intended to be subject to the basic rights of the individual.

Section 3(2)(a) makes it clear that the sweeping statement in 3(1) applies to *all* legislation, whenever enacted – so it would apply to a law passed in 1750 or one passed in 2050. This is different from almost all other legislation. Most statutes are subject to what is called the doctrine of implied repeal: this is the principle that if a later statute is inconsistent with an earlier statute, then the later statute prevails. The implication is that the later statute has repealed – revoked and replaced – the earlier statute to the extent that the two are inconsistent. This principle will not apply to this Act: if a later statute is not consistent with a provision of the Act or a Convention right, there will be no implied repeal of the Act or the Convention right. This means that the Act, or any part of it, can only be repealed by the express provisions of a later Act – Parliament would have to want to repeal it and say so.

Section 3 is complemented by section 11, which states that a person's reliance on a Convention right does not restrict any other right or freedom conferred on them by any other law or limit any claims or remedies they can pursue apart from the remedies provided by the Act. Thus the Act can only extend people's rights, and not limit rights which they already have. But it is worth noting that some such limitations may be inevitable, since any increase in the rights of a person claiming under the Act has the scope to limit the rights of a person they are claiming against – for example, Article 8 has increased rights of privacy, which may correspondingly limit a freedom that existed prior to the Act, for example, to publish material that did in fact breach someone's privacy.

---

[5] *R (Simms) v Home Secretary, ex parte Simms* [2000] 2 AC 115 at 131, discussed in the context of Article 10 below at p. 224.

Under section 3, the courts are obliged to 'read and give effect' to the Convention rights. So where a statute may, or may not, be compatible, the courts will be required to interpret the statute being considered in such a way as to give effect to the Convention rights. They must do this 'wherever possible', which is to say that if there is more than one possible interpretation, one that complies with the Act must be chosen.

TECHNIQUES OF INTERPRETATION

There are in particular, three techniques which can be used to interpret statutes in a way which makes them compatible with the Convention rights; they are important in understanding how the courts approach their duty under section 3, so we shall consider them in some detail. They may be referred to as reading in, reading out and reading down: **reading in** refers to adding words to the statute, **reading out** refers to removing words from a statute, and **reading down** refers to narrowing words with potentially broad meanings so that their effect is in accordance with the Convention rights.

Reading in would refer to a situation where words needed to be added to give effect to the relevant right. The courts already do this in the context of statutes which implement European Union law. This takes priority over domestic United Kingdom law, so if the statute being considered has failed properly to implement the relevant European legislation, it may be necessary to add words to the reading of the statute which should have been included. Likewise, **reading out,** that is, effectively removing words from a statute. Both of these methods of interpretation will certainly apply to subordinate legislation (discussed below). However, there may be difficulties with applying these extensively to primary legislation because the courts are to read and give effect to the Convention rights 'so far as is possible'. It could be argued that if words have to be added or removed to give effect to the Convention right that this is not within the bounds of what is *possible* on the basis of the words of the statute as passed by Parliament: if Parliament wanted qualifying words to be included or excluded, then they would have been. On the other hand, the Lord Chancellor, in the Parliamentary debates on section 3, expressed the view that the courts would have this power: and the courts do appear to have interpreted section 3 so as to allow them to read words in where necessary to allow them to preserve statutes, without having to find that the statute is not consistent with the Convention rights.

An example of reading words into a statute is the case of A,[6] which was a rape trial. Here the House of Lords had to consider the interpretation of section 41 of the Youth Justice and Criminal Evidence Act 1999. This concerns the situation where a person accused of a sexual offence, such as rape, wishes to cross-examine the alleged victim of the offence (the complainant). Very often in such cases, the issue is not whether or not the accused and the complainant had sexual intercourse, but whether or not the complainant consented to sex. The parties' previous sexual history *may* be relevant to this issue. The purpose of section 41 is to limit the circumstances where this can be explored in court, to prevent defendants having too much leeway to go into the detailed sexual history of complainants, since this was being abused to cause unnecessary embarrassment or humiliation of complainants. In the present case, the trial judge ruled that section 41 prevented

---

[6] *R v A (No. 2)* [2001] 2 WLR 1546.

him allowing the defendant to cross-examine the complainant about their previous sexual history. The defendant argued that this was inconsistent with his rights under Article 6 to a fair trial, since that required that he be allowed to rely on all relevant evidence.

The House of Lords' starting point was that section 41 served an entirely proper and legitimate purpose, and was not *by itself* incompatible with Article 6. But in some situations, the application of the limitations contained within section 41 *might* infringe the right to a fair trial since the section might require the exclusion of relevant evidence so as to lead to an unjust conviction. However, the House of Lords applied the interpretative obligation in section 3, and construed section 41 in the light of Article 6 as being subject to the *implied provision* that evidence or questioning of a witness which is required to ensure a fair trial under Article 6 should be allowed by the trial judge. By reading this implied provision into the statute, the House of Lords extended the discretion given to a trial judge so that it was clear it should be exercised in a way which is compatible with Article 6, as well as with the purpose of the statute. This would ensure that the discretion in section 41 would not infringe Article 6, even though this altered the effect of the statutory provision. The House then sent the matter back to the trial judge to reconsider in the light of their view of the law.

One case where the Court of Appeal has declined to read words into a statute was *Poplar Housing v Donoghue.*[7] The statutory provision in question was section 21(4) of the Housing Act 1988, which provides a procedure for bringing to an end a particular sort of lease of property, an assured short-hold tenancy, by service of a notice. The tenant argued that the making of an eviction order would infringe her rights under Article 8. The Court of Appeal agreed with the trial judge that any infringement of Article 8 was justified and there was no need to re-interpret the statute to comply with Article 8. The Court was invited to add the words 'if it is reasonable to do so' into section 21 but declined to do so, since this would defeat Parliament's objective of allowing tenancies to be brought to an end in certain circumstances.

The Court considered how it should approach the exercise of interpretation under section 3 of the Human Rights Act. One factor would be that section 3 is limited to interpretation: the court has to bear in mind that it is still applying the statute passed by Parliament, and that it is not there to approach the matter afresh, which would be an exercise in legislation. If, in order to read the statute under consideration, it would be necessary to alter radically the effect of the statutory provision, that would suggest that what is required to reach that conclusion would be going beyond simple interpretation. In the present case, as well as not being necessary to comply with Article 8, the addition of the words suggested would effectively involve legislating, because it would involve coming to a different view to Parliament about the right way to deal with a particular situation.

Reading down is a slightly different technique, where a word or phrase which could have a wide range of meanings is read so as to prefer a meaning which is in accordance with the Act. Put another way, it involves limiting the possible meanings of a statute to one which is compatible with the Convention rights. There have already been cases where the courts have had to consider questions of interpretation to enable statutes to be read so as to be compatible with the Act.

One particular situation is where a statute imposes a burden of proof on a defendant in a criminal case to prove a defence.[8] This has now been considered in a number of cases. The question arises because of the presumption of innocence in Article 6(2), which is already part of our law, but which

---

[7] *Poplar Housing Association Ltd v Donoghue* [2001] 3 WLR 183, see also below, p. 62.
[8] Discussed further in the context of Article 6, below, p. 160.

has in some situations been given a wider application by the European Court. One question which arises is whether the statutory defence imposes an *evidential* or *persuasive* burden. If it is an evidential burden, the defendant need only provide evidence to raise the statutory defence, whereupon the burden of disproving the defence is on the prosecution so that if the jury is not satisfied that the defence is disproved, the defendant should be acquitted. A persuasive burden is where the onus is on the defendant not just to raise the issue, but to satisfy the jury that the defence is made out on the balance of probabilities.

This was first considered in the case of *Kebilene*,[9] where the House of Lords took the view that the imposition of a persuasive burden *might* infringe Article 6, depending on the basis for the statute and whether or not it was a disproportionate interference with Article 6(2).

Then in the case of *R v Lambert*,[10] the House of Lords did in fact *read down* the statute being considered: their Lordships considered that to read the statute as imposing a persuasive burden would be an unjustified interference with Article 6(2), but that the statute could be read as merely imposing an evidential burden, which would not infringe Article 6(2). The statute was therefore read so as to be compatible with Article 6.

Not all burdens on a defendant must be read down as an evidential burden only: whether or not the statutory words should be read down or not will depend on the subject matter of the statutory provision in question. So in the case of *Drummond*,[11] which concerned the offence of driving while over the limit for consumption of alcohol. In such a case, if the defendant wishes to contend that they consumed alcohol after the alleged offence was committed, but before providing a specimen for testing, there is a burden on the defendant to prove this. The Court of Appeal decided that this was a persuasive burden which was justified and no greater than necessary. For an accused to drink after an event, which might have been a criminal offence, should be discouraged, because it would be likely to interfere with any possibility of a scientific test of blood alcohol level as it was previously, so that it could be determined whether or not an offence took place. In any event the relevant evidence to prove that alcohol was consumed before the test was done is within the knowledge of the accused and not the police.

On the other hand, in the case of *R v Carass*,[12] which concerned an offence of concealing a debt with an intention to defraud under the Insolvency Act 1986, the Court of Appeal held that a provision which required a defendant to 'prove' a defence should be read down as meaning 'adduce sufficient evidence', that is, as an evidential and not persuasive burden, since the Court did not accept an argument that the higher burden could be justified.

COMPATIBILITY AND PARLIAMENTARY SOVEREIGNTY

The limitation in section 3(2)(b) is also very important: the fact that the courts, national or European, decide that a particular statutory provision breaches, or permits a breach of, someone's Convention rights does not stop that statute being valid or enforceable. This preserves the existing constitutional position discussed earlier[13] that Parliament is superior to the courts, and the courts cannot declare an Act of Parliament to be void or of no effect. So if it is not possible for an Act of Parliament to be read in a way which is compatible with the Convention rights, then the courts must

---

[9] *R v DPP, ex parte Kebilene* [2000] 2 AC 226, see further below pp. 160–1.
[10] [2001] 3 WLR 206.
[11] [2002] 2 CAR 25.
[12] [2002] 1 AC 45.
[13] Chapter 4 above, p. 39.

still apply that Act, notwithstanding the breach of Convention rights. This may be contrasted with, for example, the Supreme Court in the United States of America, which *does* have the power to invalidate legislation if it is unconstitutional, for example if it infringes the Bill of Rights in the United States Constitution.

The House of Lords has confirmed that the Act does not affect the sovereignty of Parliament in the case of *R v Lyons*.[14] Here it had been decided by the European Court that compelling persons to give answers to questions in particular circumstances infringed the Article 6 right against self-incrimination. However, the procedures used had been expressly permitted by Parliament in the relevant statute. The Court of Appeal stated that this meant that it could not be said that the evidence obtained in breach of Article 6 should have been excluded at trial. Notwithstanding that the decision of the European Court meant that the relevant legislative provision was in breach of the Convention, the Human Rights Act 1998 does not allow the courts to avoid giving effect to an express statutory provision. Thus, the courts have no discretion to exclude evidence obtained in a way which may be in breach of the Convention rights, if an Act of Parliament expressly permits the use of such evidence.

But our courts would not be entirely powerless in such a situation. Although they cannot refuse to enforce the offending legislation, they can make a **declaration of incompatibility,** provided for by section 4 of the Act. By doing so, the courts make clear that the legislation being considered does not comply with the European Convention: in effect, such a declaration tells Parliament that it has acted in breach of the human rights of its subjects.

One example where a declaration of incompatibility has been made is the case of *Wilson v First County Trust*.[15] Here the case concerned section 127(3) of the Consumer Credit Act 1974. This provides that if certain formalities are not complied with in an agreement covered by this Act, then the agreement is not enforceable. The Court of Appeal held that this blanket ban on enforcement was incompatible with Article 6, the right to a fair trial, since there was no scope for the exercise of judicial discretion, and Article 1 of the First Protocol, the right to security of property, since the effect was that the person making the loan was unable to recover even the main amount loaned. The Court of Appeal also considered that a declaration of incompatibility would be appropriate, since it was not possible to read the section in a way which gave effect to those rights.[16]

It should be noted, however, that a declaration of incompatibility does not invalidate the offending legislation any more than the fact of incompatibility does; it is not even binding on the parties who are before the court (section 4(6)). The remedy for such a breach is thus purely political, not legal – that is, it can only be remedied by persuading Parliament to change the law, not by bringing an action before the courts.

Nonetheless, the Act and those proposing it clearly envisage that such breaches will be remedied by Parliament.[17] In particular, section 10 and schedule 2 of the Act set up

---

[14] [2002] 3 WLR 1562, affirming the Court of Appeal.

[15] *Wilson v First County Trust Limited (No. 2)* [2001] 3 WLR 42, discussed also below, p. 252.

[16] This case has not gone before Parliament by way of remedial order since it is being appealed to the House of Lords (at the time of writing).

[17] This may be the Scottish Parliament if it relates to a devolved matter: schedule 2, paragraph 7.

a fast-track procedure for remedying legislation which is incompatible with Convention rights: a Minister who considers there are compelling reasons, 'may by order make such amendments to the legislation as he considers necessary to remove the incompatibility' (section 10 (2)). There is no definition as to what amounts to compelling reasons. An order has to be put before Parliament, but this does not require the full process of passing a statute, so that the matter can, in principle, be remedied fairly speedily.

There was some criticism of this procedure when the Act was debated in Parliament for allowing amendments to be made by a summary process to legislation passed after full Parliamentary debate. On the other hand, the concerns which led to the inclusion of the provisions for remedial orders were largely based precisely on the time it would take for the full Parliamentary process to be followed, and on the practical difficulties of enacting legislation to remedy any incompatibility. It is the case nowadays that governments tend to have substantial programmes of legislation, and Parliamentary sessions do not usually have time to deal with all of that, let alone further proposed legislation on matters which might be wholly unrelated to anything currently being considered. The making of a remedial order does not deprive Parliament of the opportunity to consider the matter because the order is still subject to being approved by Parliament before it can become law (schedule 2, paragraph 2). The only exception to this is where the matter is considered to require urgent action (paragraph 2(b)), and in such a case, the order still has to be approved by Parliament within 120 days, or else the order will cease to have effect (paragraph 4(4)).

Further, since the subject of the remedial order will also have been the subject of a declaration of incompatibility or a judgment of the European Court, there will already have been detailed legal arguments, and one or more judgments. To ensure that a remedial order is not made prematurely, an order can only be made where no further appeal or court proceedings are being brought (section 10(1)). The court's consideration of the matter should also have identified very precisely the incompatibility, which will define the scope of the remedial order, which can *only* be made to remove an incompatibility.

One further safeguard is introduced to try to prevent this situation arising: Members of Parliament, usually Ministers, who place legislation before Parliament for consideration and approval at its second reading must make a **statement of compatibility**, which states that the person proposing believes that the proposal does not infringe anyone's human rights – or if it does, that the government still intends to proceed (section 19). The purpose of this is to ensure that attention is at least focused on whether any particular legislation is going to protect people's rights, and that Parliament is made aware if it is specifically proposed that it should infringe anyone's rights.

One would hope that such proposals would be rare, and that in such an event there would be political pressure not to proceed. However, there may well be cases where there is debate about whether or not the proposed legislation really is compatible with the Convention rights. One particularly contentious example was the Anti-Terrorism, Crime and Security Act 2001. This contains a number of provisions which potentially raised questions about their compatibility with Convention rights, and indeed a derogation was entered in respect of one such detention provision, because it was recognised that it could be used in a way which would not be compatible with the Convention.[18]

---

[18] The derogation and the Anti-Terrorism Act are discussed further in Chapter 21.

A statement of compatibility in other respects was still made, but it has since been held that a power to detain foreign nationals in circumstances where British nationals cannot be detained is discriminatory and breaches Article 14 of the Convention, although this was reversed on appeal.[19] Thus, the fact that a statement has been made in Parliament will not guarantee that the statement is correct, especially if the case is a difficult one and there is political pressure for the statute to be passed. On the other hand, the making of the statement at least ensures some scrutiny of the proposed legislation in the light of the Convention.

SUBORDINATE LEGISLATION

A note on **subordinate legislation**: this refers to regulations or statutory instruments made by Ministers under powers given to them by a statute to provide further detailed provisions dealing with the precise implementation of that statute, which is known in this context as the primary or enabling Act. So, for example, an Act setting up a government agency on health may allow the Secretary of State for Health to make regulations which set out how that agency operates. Another example of subordinate legislation is the order a Minister is empowered to make by section 10(2) of the Act for remedying a statutory incompatibility with the Convention rights, as discussed above.

Subordinate legislation does not have the same superiority as primary legislation, and the courts may strike down such regulations if they are in breach of the Convention. This itself is a very wide-ranging power as very much more of the business of government is conducted by passing subordinate legislation than by passing primary legislation. This assumes, of course, that the subordinate legislation cannot be interpreted in a way which gives effect to the Convention rights: there will be no need to strike down the subordinate legislation if it can be read in a way which is compatible with the Convention rights, even if one or more decisions made under the subordinate legislation is declared invalid. It is clear that the courts have this power even without the Act: where possible, the exercise of a power under subordinate legislation should be interpreted in such a way as to make them subject to fundamental rights.[20]

The only exception to the court's power to strike down subordinate legislation under the Act is where the wording of the primary legislation prevents removal of the incompatibility. In such a case, the court may only make a declaration of incompatibility (section 4(4)). However, in such a case, the power of a Minister to make a remedial order also applies, even though the challenge was not directly to the primary legislation itself (section 10(3) and (4)). There is a list of what sorts of provisions are to be treated as primary and secondary legislation for the purposes of the Act in section 21.[21]

---

[19] *A v Secretary of State for the Home Department* [2002] LTL 1.8.02; [2002] further below, p. 284.

[20] *R v Home Secretary, ex parte Simms* [2000] 2 AC 115, referred to further above, p. 54, and below, p. 224.

[21] Set out in Appendix 1.

THE UNLAWFULNESS OF INFRINGING CONVENTION RIGHTS

> **Section 6** (1) It is unlawful for a public authority to act in a way which is incompatible with a Convention right.
>
> (6) 'An act' includes a failure to act [. . .]

This is the provision of the Act which has most practical force: it means that it is unlawful for any public authority to act in a way which infringes any of the rights protected by the Convention. However, the use of the word 'unlawful' does not mean that an infringement of the Act is a crime: by section 7(8), nothing in the Act creates a criminal offence. This means that the remedy for an infringement of a Convention right is not a prosecution in the criminal courts but an action in the civil courts. Such an action would result in a decision that the act was unlawful and, if appropriate, an award of compensation. So the next question is, what bodies are covered by this obligation – what are public authorities?

DEFINITION OF PUBLIC AUTHORITIES

> **Section 6** (3) In this section 'public authority' includes –
>
> (a) a court or tribunal, and
>
> (b) any person certain of whose functions are functions of a public nature [. . .]
>
> (5) In relation to a particular act, a person is not a public authority by virtue only of subsection (3)(b) if the nature of the act is private.

As you can see, there is no complete definition of what a **public authority** is, although sometimes this will be self-evident. So, for example, a government department or ministry or a local authority are quite clearly public authorities because that is their whole purpose: their existence is as a part of the state machinery of government. This would also include any body to which a minister's powers were delegated: it is clear from European Court law that a state remains responsible for such delegated actions. Section 6(3)(a) makes it clear that a law court or tribunal is also a public authority.

The meaning of public authority is then expanded by section 6(3)(b) to include any person 'certain of whose functions are of a public nature', but section 6(5) limits this by stating that such a person is not acting as a public authority if the nature of the act is private. So it might depend what the person is doing as to whether or not they are a public authority. 'Person' in this context does not just mean an individual: for the purposes of interpreting statutes, there is a wide definition of person, which includes not just 'real' people, but also entities that have what is called legal personality, such as companies, as well as local councils and government departments. Thus, sometimes a person, company or body is obviously a public authority, and will be so for all purposes. Sometimes it is not, such as a private individual or a private company running a small business. However, there is a middle ground under section 6(3)(b), where the question of whether or not a person or body is a public authority will turn on whether or not a public function is being exercised.

In such a situation, one source for guidance for the interpretation of statutes is to look at the Parliamentary debate on the Act to see what the intention of Parliament was in respect of this section. The main intention behind using a general definition was to ensure that bodies which are treated in the Act as public authorities are much the same as those which would be treated by the European Court as liable for a breach of the Convention on behalf of the state – that is, bodies for which the state is responsible. The aim of this is to mirror those bodies or institutions for which the United Kingdom government would be answerable to the European Court. This achieves the practical objective of ensuring that there is no need for a claim to be brought before the European Court only because the definition of public authority is too narrow for it to be brought domestically.

There were also a number of specific examples given during the Parliamentary debates.[22] So, for example, a privatised utility company could well be a public authority when exercising public functions, although it may not count as a public authority all the time. A company such as Network Rail, which maintains the railway network, will be considered a public authority in so far as it performs an important public function in regulating the safety of the railway network; but it may be involved in a different activity, such as developing new offices, which would be a private function.

Other examples of public authorities are likely to be:

- the armed forces, police forces and other emergency services, including, for example, the Royal National Lifeboat Institution, in discharging its public function of running the lifeboat service;
- prison and immigration officers and authorities, who will all be public authorities since they act on behalf of the state, but a private security firm would only be a public authority if it was being employed to secure or patrol a public institution, such as a prison;
- the BBC and Channel 4, which are publicly funded broadcasters, but not ITV or Five, which are privately funded, although the Commission which regulates them would be a public authority;
- the National Health Service and NHS hospitals, but not private hospitals, which may mean that a doctor is a public authority when doing NHS work but not when being paid privately;
- education authorities and state-funded schools will be public authorities, although private schools will not;
- housing associations which assist local authorities in providing housing may well be public authorities, certainly when they are discharging public functions on behalf of a local authority;[23]
- there are bodies which do not have statutory foundations but which perform public functions in regulating certain industries or services, and these are likely to be public authorities. This will be especially so where the function is one which the

---

[22] The main debates referred to here were the House of Commons Second Reading debate (HC Vol. 306, cols 776–778, 16 February 1998) and Committee Debate (HC Vol. 314, cols 406–433, 24 June 1998).

[23] *Poplar Housing Association Ltd v Donoghue* [2001] 3 WLR 183.

state would be likely to have to perform if there were no private body to do it. Examples include the Press Complaints Commission, the City Takeover Panel (which regulates company takeovers), the Advertising Standards Authority and the British Board of Film Classification.

THE COURT AS A PUBLIC AUTHORITY

However, the difference in applying the Act as between public and private authorities in many contexts may not make a great deal of practical difference. As noted above, the courts are also public authorities, as are other tribunals which decide disputes, such as an employment tribunal. This means that they have to apply the Act in reaching their decisions. Since the courts' decisions are for the purpose of resolving disputes whether or not either party is a public authority, this means that disputes between private individuals must be determined in accordance with the Act and giving effect to the Convention rights. This means that, in practice, there will be many areas where the standards applied to public authorities directly, and to private persons via the application of the Act by the courts, are much the same.

This will have far-reaching consequences. Much of the law applied by the courts is not to be found in Acts of Parliament, but in case law, which is the previous decisions of the courts over the years – in some cases, centuries. This is because of the doctrine of precedent, which means that decisions of judges bind future judges. Precedence also includes a hierarchy, whereby, for example, the House of Lords binds, but is not bound by, all other courts; the Court of Appeal is bound by the House of Lords and its own decisions but not by decisions of lower courts; lower courts are bound by both the Court of Appeal and House of Lords, and so on. All of this case law which has built up must be applied, where necessary, to give effect to the Convention rights. There are many areas of law which are not likely to be significantly affected by this, but, as we will see in our discussion later of individual rights, there are some important areas where changes have already been made, even though the law being discussed is not contained in an Act of Parliament, and so was not directly altered by the Human Rights Act.

One example is the law on personal privacy. As we will see in our discussion of Article 8,[24] the general law on privacy and preventing invasions of privacy before the Act did not provide much protection for individuals from the intrusion of others, and especially the press. Because the courts have had to apply Article 8 and the standards provided for by the cases decided by the European Court, the protection provided by the law has been expanded. Thus the courts have used their obligation as a public authority to 'give effect' to the Convention rights to ensure that individuals' rights of privacy are protected, even where the person or company against whom the complaint of invasion of privacy is being made is not itself a public authority. Certainly in the leading case on this point, *Douglas v Hello!*, Lord Justice Sedley considered that in this area at least the courts were obliged to apply the Convention rights as between the parties to the case.[25] This is sometimes referred to as giving the Articles **horizontal effect**, for

---

[24] Below, Chapter 14.
[25] [2001] 2 WLR 992 at 1027, paragraph 133.

example in the *Douglas* case, since in the eyes of the law all citizens are on the same level; as opposed to applying rights as between the citizen and the state, referred to as giving them **vertical** effect, since the state is metaphorically considered to be 'above' the citizen.

PARLIAMENT AS A PUBLIC AUTHORITY

Section 6 (2) Subsection (1) does not apply to an act if –
   (a) as the result of one or more provisions of primary legislation, the authority could not have acted differently; or
   (b) in the case of one or more provisions of, or made under, primary legislation which cannot be read or given effect in a way which is compatible with the Convention rights, the authority was acting so as to give effect to or enforce those provisions.
(3) In this section 'public authority' . . . does not include either House of Parliament or a person exercising functions in connection with proceedings in Parliament.
(4) In subsection (3) 'Parliament' does not include the House of Lords in its judicial capacity.
(6) 'An act' includes a failure to act but does not include a failure to –
   (a) introduce in, or lay before, Parliament a proposal for legislation; or
   (b) make any primary legislation or remedial order.

Section 6 has several provisions which tie in with the limitations we noted in the discussion of section 3, that the courts have no power to strike down or fail to enforce Acts of Parliament. By section 6(2), a public authority which implements legislation which is incompatible with the Convention is not acting unlawfully, so long as 'it could not have acted differently' – that is, it will have to show that the statute being implemented cannot be put into effect in a way which does not breach the Convention. This argument will fail if the statute can be read in more than one way, or if the court interprets the statute by reading words into it, as discussed above.

Section 6 also prevents proceedings in Parliament being criticised by or made the subject of legal action in the courts. This again is in line with our existing constitutional position, known as Parliamentary privilege, which states that proceedings in Parliament cannot be made the subject of a court action, because the courts have no jurisdiction over Parliament – instead Parliament regulates its own affairs. So, for example, a Member of Parliament speaking in a debate in the House of Commons cannot be sued for slander for anything they say which may defame some person, although he may be disciplined by the House if that was appropriate. By section 6(3), the Member of Parliament could not be sued for a breach of the Convention rights if what he says or does or proposes as legislation should infringe someone's rights, nor can Parliament itself be sued for implementing legislation which infringes Convention rights, whether that is known at the time or not. Not only can Members of Parliament (in either House) not be sued for proposing legislation, but also by section 6(6), a Member of Parliament cannot be sued for failing to propose legislation, for example, to correct a law which infringes a person's rights. You should note, though, that the House of Lords, when sitting as a court, is excluded from this: this is because its functions are not legislative but judicial, and the judiciary (the courts) are included in the scope of the Act.

QUESTIONS

1   Do you agree with the reasons for not making the decisions of the European Court binding on our courts?

2   Consider the definition of public authorities: can you think of further examples of bodies that are public or private, or which may be either depending on the function it is performing? Do you think that the Act gives sufficient guidance on which bodies are covered? Do you think it should be broader or narrower, and if so why?

The Royal Courts of Justice in the Strand, London, home of the Court of Appeal and the Central Registry of the High Court.

Chapter 6

REMEDIES UNDER THE HUMAN RIGHTS ACT

'Money is coined liberty, and so it is ten times dearer to a man who is deprived of freedom. If money is jingling in his pocket, he is half consoled, even though he cannot spend it.' (Fedor Dostoevsky, *House of the Dead*, 1862)

In this chapter we shall be considering what remedies are available to a person who considers that their rights have been infringed. We will not be covering the detail of the procedures for bringing an action, but will be considering the specific requirements of the Human Rights Act and other relevant provisions which affect who can bring such a claim, how they go about it and what remedies are available if a Convention right has been infringed.

WHO CAN COMPLAIN ABOUT INFRINGEMENT?

Section 7 (1) A person who claims that a public authority has acted (or proposes to act) in a way which is made unlawful by section 6(1) may –
   (a) bring proceedings against the authority under this Act in the appropriate court or tribunal, or
   (b) rely on the Convention right or rights concerned in any legal proceedings,
   but only if he is (or would be) a victim of the unlawful act. [. . .]

(3) If the proceedings are brought on an application for judicial review, the applicant is to be taken to have a sufficient interest in relation to the unlawful act only if he is, or would be, a victim of that act. [. . .]

(7) For the purposes of this section, a person is a victim of an unlawful act only if he would be a victim for the purposes of Article 34 of the Convention if proceedings were brought in the European Court of Human Rights in respect of that act.

Article 34 The court may receive applications from any person, non-governmental organisation or group of individuals claiming to be the victim of a violation by one of the High Contracting Parties of the rights set forth in the Convention or the protocols thereto. The High Contracting Parties undertake not to hinder in any way the effective exercise of this right.

Anyone who claims that a public authority has acted or proposes to act in a way which is incompatible with Convention rights can bring proceedings against that authority, so long as he is a 'victim' within the meaning of section 7(7); this is the effect of section 7(1)(a). Alternatively, anyone may rely on Convention rights in any legal proceedings brought by others: for example, as part of a defence to criminal or civil proceedings (section 7(1)(b)). The relevance of being a person who would be a victim is either in proceedings which aim to prevent a Convention right infringement which has been threatened but has not actually happened yet, or in defending a claim, where a breach of a Convention right would occur if the claim, or prosecution, were successful. Section 7(3) ensures that in judicial review proceedings,[1] the test for who can bring those sorts of proceedings, which enable the courts to grant particular sorts of remedies, is the same as for other proceedings.[2]

A **victim** is defined by reference to Article 34 of the Convention, which is the definition used by the European Court. The Convention and the Act should therefore be consistent in their effect. Article 34 in turn grants a remedy to 'any person, non-governmental organisation or group of individuals claiming to be the victim of a violation by one of the High Contracting Parties' of the Convention rights. In the context of United Kingdom law, this would include any person, non-governmental organisation or group of individuals who claimed that their Convention rights had been infringed by a public authority. However, a governmental body cannot be a 'victim' under Article 34, so will not be able to sue under the Act either.

Article 34 has been discussed by the European Court in a number of cases which have clarified how it should be applied. In particular there has to have been an *actual* violation: it is not enough for a person to allege that a particular statute or law could in theory be used to infringe his or her rights. However, it is sufficient to show that there is a *threatened* violation, or that the person is at risk of being directly affected by the measure: for example, where something a person does regularly is made illegal even though they have not in fact been prosecuted for it. The victim could also be closely connected to the person who is directly affected: for example, a husband, wife or child, especially where the complaint relates to the death of the person whose rights were infringed.

Victims can be companies or other groups of people as long as it is that company or group that is affected: a trade union could not claim to be a victim because one of its members' rights are infringed, only if it is the rights of the trade union itself which have been infringed. This does not prevent an interest group, such as a trade union, charity or campaigning organisation, from supporting a complainant, either with help bringing the claim, with funding or the provision of legal representation, or by applying to appear in its own right to assist the court with the issues before it, particularly if the decision will be one which decides a new or important point.

---

[1] Introduced at p. 38 above.
[2] Section 7(4) is the equivalent provision for Scotland.

WHAT CAN THE COURT DO?

Section 7 (1) A person who claims that a public authority has acted (or proposes to act) in a way which is made unlawful by section 6(1) may –
(a) bring proceedings against the authority under this Act in the appropriate court or tribunal, or
(b) rely on the Convention right or rights concerned in any legal proceedings [. . .]
(6) In subsection (1)(b) 'legal proceedings' includes –
(a) proceedings brought by or at the instigation of a public authority; and
(b) an appeal against the decision of a court or tribunal.

Once it has been established that a person has the right to bring a complaint before the courts because they are a victim of a breach of their Convention rights, they can do so in two ways. They can bring their own legal action under section 7(1)(a), or they can rely on their Convention rights as a defence in any legal proceedings under section 7(1)(b). By section 7(6), relying on a Convention right in legal proceedings includes relying on that right as a defence to an action brought by a public authority, which will include a criminal prosecution, or in an appeal from the decision of a court or tribunal.

If the claim that a right has been infringed is established, there are then a number of ways in which the courts can deal with the matter to ensure that a proper remedy is granted. The starting point for this is section 8, which specifies that the court may grant such relief as it considers 'just and appropriate'. The courts are therefore given a very broad discretion.

The courts have a number of remedies or forms of relief which they can grant and all of these will be available, where appropriate, in cases of human rights infringements. In particular, the court can:

- order the payment of damages, which is the term for compensation for a legal wrong, in this case the infringement of the Convention right;
- grant an injunction, which is an order to prevent an ongoing or threatened infringement;
- allow the Convention rights to provide a defence to a claim or a criminal prosecution;
- refuse to allow a party to rely on evidence obtained in breach of a Convention right;
- order that a governmental decision or subordinate legislation which infringes a person's rights is invalid and not to be relied on; or
- make a declaration of incompatibility.

We have already introduced the last two remedies, judicial review and declarations of incompatibility.[3] Judicial review will usually result in an order that a decision be quashed, meaning that it has to be made again, although there are other orders open to a court, for example, an order prohibiting a person or body from taking a particular course of action. Declarations of incompatibility are a new remedy provided by section 4 of the Act where a statute is incompatible with a Convention right, and cannot be interpreted

[3] Above, pp. 38 and 58.

in a way which makes it compatible. The Act does not allow the court to refuse to enforce the incompatible statute, but the court can then make a declaration of incompatibility, which will indicate to Parliament that there is a potential injustice to be corrected and will allow the Parliamentary procedure for a remedial order to be implemented.

Allowing a Convention right to be used as a defence is a straightforward idea. In a criminal case, this could mean an argument that the criminal charge that is being prosecuted is in breach of the Convention for some reason. In a civil case, this would mean that what was being suggested was that the party bringing a claim was not entitled to a remedy because this would infringe the defendant's rights. In each case, the use of the Convention as a defence will depend on the substance of the law which is being argued. There are no special rules about using Convention rights in this way which are distinct from raising any other legal argument in the course of a trial.

The courts have a well-established discretion to refuse to admit evidence which has been obtained wrongfully, and this will include refusing to admit evidence obtained in breach of a Convention right.[4] This will allow the courts, for example, to decide that the prosecution cannot rely on evidence which was obtained by infringing the defendant's right to privacy, where evidence was obtained without the proper authorisation or statutory authority. This can also apply to evidence being relied on in a civil case: for example, in a personal injury action where the defence wished to rely on video surveillance evidence which invaded someone's privacy.

The most important remedies, though, will be those available where the person complaining of an infringement is bringing their own legal action, which will be for **damages**, which is monetary compensation, or an **injunction**, an order to prevent a threatened or ongoing breach.

DAMAGES

Section 8 (1) In relation to any act (or proposed act) of a public authority which the court finds is (or would be) unlawful, it may grant such relief or remedy, or make such order, within its powers as it considers just and appropriate.

(3) No award of damages is to be made unless, taking account of all the circumstances of the case, including –

(a) any other relief or remedy granted, or order made, in relation to the act in question (by that or any other court), and

(b) the consequences of any decision (of that or any other court) in respect of that act,

the court is satisfied that the award is necessary to afford just satisfaction to the person in whose favour it is made.

(4) In determining (a) whether to award damages, or (b) the amount of an award, the court must take into account the principles applied by the European Court of Human Rights in relation to the award of compensation under Article 41 of the Convention.

---

[4] The most important discretion is that under section 78 of the Police and Criminal Evidence Act 1984; there is further discussion on excluding evidence in the context of Article 6, below, pp. 163–5.

Article 41	If the [European] court finds that there has been a violation of the Convention or the Protocols thereto, and if the internal law of the High Contracting Party concerned allows only partial reparation to be made, the court shall, if necessary, afford just satisfaction to the injured party.

Where damages are referred to in section 8, this means specifically damages for an unlawful act of a public authority (section 8(6)). Such damages are assessed on the principles set out in sections 8(1), (3) and (4). These are as follows:

First, the award of compensation has to be 'just and appropriate', which is not further defined.

Second, the award has to be 'necessary to afford just satisfaction' to the person whose rights have been infringed, bearing in mind any other remedies granted to that person. So, for example, if a person complains of a breach of a Convention right, but on the same facts also complains of an assault, and is awarded damages for that assault, it will not be necessary to award damages for the breach of the Convention right, since the claimant will already have been compensated. Section 11 of the Act makes clear that the Act does not limit any rights that a person may have to bring a legal action or claim or bring any proceedings which they could make or bring apart from the specific remedies provided by the Act.

Third, the court must also bear in mind the consequences of deciding to grant any remedy in respect of the infringement. This is because the courts have to act in a way which is consistent – this is a fundamental requirement of justice and the rule of law, that like cases are treated alike, that if one person is compensated for a particular complaint, so will another who has the same complaint. Therefore, if the courts create a new remedy in a particular case by awarding damages for a particular infringement, any other infringement of the same sort will attract the same remedy, and that might have consequences which the court has to take into account before making the award in the first place. For example, it might be feared that allowing compensation in a particular case will lead to a flood of other cases, although such fears usually turn out to be misplaced.

Finally, the court must bear in mind the principles applied by the European Court in relation to the award of compensation under Article 41 of the Convention. Of course, the courts are already obliged to apply European Court law by section 2 of the Act, but the reference here should specifically ensure that compensation is likely to be awarded by our courts to the same extent as by the European Court. This will help to prevent cases having to go to the European Court: there would be a breach of the Convention if a national court could not award an adequate remedy, where a Convention right is infringed. The principles developed by the European Court in exercising its power to award compensation under Article 41 therefore have to be considered by the court in deciding whether an award would be just and appropriate.

The basic principle applied by the European Court in awarding damages is that the injured party should be restored to the position they should have been in if the breach of the Convention had not taken place. This is the same basic principle which the United Kingdom courts already apply to claims concerning a wrong done by one person to another.

The European Court has not developed clear guidelines or principles as to how much will be awarded, but prefers to approach decisions on damages on a case by case basis. In some cases, therefore, there are inconsistencies between different cases. To this extent, there are limits on how much use the European cases will be in this area, since our courts will have to work out more definite principles for dealing with questions of quantifying losses.

Some principles do emerge from the European Court cases. In particular, it is clear that in many cases, the fact that the court has found a violation of the Convention may be a sufficient remedy to provide 'just satisfaction'. This may be particularly so if the violation is not particularly serious or if it is not clear that it has caused any loss or damage of any sort, or if a remedy has been or can be provided in some other way, such as by a retrial or a pardon. This may also be appropriate if the conduct of the person bringing the claim is not very meritorious: for example, if there is a successful claim of a breach of the right to a fair trial in a criminal matter, but that does not affect the fact that the person would have been convicted anyway, it may not be just to award them monetary compensation. An example is the case of *McCann*,[5] which concerned the circumstances under which three suspected IRA terrorists were shot in Gibraltar. Although the European Court decided that there was a breach of Article 2, no compensation was awarded, since the Court was satisfied that the persons shot were planning a terrorist attack, so compensation would have been inappropriate.

This may particularly apply to cases brought under Articles 5 and 6, where there is a breach of someone's rights when they were arrested or tried, but where there is no challenge to their conviction for the crime for which they were arrested and tried. In such cases, unless the infringement is particularly serious, it may be considered that they have a sufficient remedy in the finding that their rights were infringed.

On the other hand, if there is a real loss, and the violation is sufficiently serious, damages may be awarded. The European Court will also take into account the conduct of the state, for example if it has behaved particularly unpleasantly. So damages have been awarded to compensate for medical expenses incurred, loss of earnings or pension rights and property which has been unlawfully expropriated. The Court has also awarded damages for non-pecuniary losses, which is to say losses that cannot be easily assessed in terms of money, such as damages for injuries, to compensate for pain and suffering caused, as well as for distress caused, injury to feelings and loss of reputation.

In any case where damages are claimed under the Act, the burden of satisfying the court that there has been an interference with a Convention right is on the person bringing the claim. Once an interference has been proven, if it is being argued that the interference is justified, the burden of satisfying the court of this is on the state. If it is demonstrated that the interference is without justification, and amounts to a breach of a Convention right, the burden is then on the claimant to prove to the court the amount of their losses for the purposes of compensation, or that some other remedy is justified. Where there is a claim for damages, it is also necessary for the claimant to satisfy the court that any losses suffered were *caused* by the infringement of rights which has been alleged.

---

[5] Considered below, p. 107.

This question of **causation** applies to any legal claim: the point is that one should only make someone who has done something wrong pay compensation for the consequences that they have *caused*. Thus damages will not be awarded for matters which would have happened anyway, or which were caused by the person bringing the case, or by someone or something else altogether. Thus it will be important to address the question of what consequences have been caused by the breach of a right. In some cases, the relevant question will be how much *worse* were matters with the breach than without it. So, for example, a delay in bringing an accused to trial may breach Article 6, but if the person is convicted and the delay has not affected the validity of that conviction, the delay may not have *caused* that person any loss beyond the consequences of their own criminal conduct. The European Court takes a reasonably strict approach to causation, and in many cases has made no monetary award because it is not satisfied that the losses were caused by the infringement.

There is also in the European Court's decisions a limited scope for **waiver** of a right: that is, a situation where a person has agreed that they will not rely on a Convention right. However, this will only apply where there is the clearest indication that a right is being waived, so that the waiver is unequivocal, and where the waiver does not run counter to an important public interest.

In the Scottish case of *Millar*,[6] the Privy Council had to consider a situation where it was claimed that four defendants had waived their rights to rely on Article 6. They were all tried before temporary sheriffs; but it had since been decided that the use of temporary sheriffs infringed Article 6.[7] However, the Privy Council considered that the fact that the accused did not take a point on this at their trial was not a waiver of their rights under Article 6. The accused and their representatives were unaware of their right to challenge the sheriffs, which prevented a right being waived, since what was reasonably understood to be the law at the time did not suggest that there was any right to be waived. Further, a waiver must be made in an unequivocal manner, demonstrating that there was a deliberate intention not to take a point. That would usually have to be express, and for a right to be waived by not saying anything, as was suggested here, could only be inferred where the point was obvious and well-known, so that it was clear that the failure to rely on it was a conscious choice. That could not apply here, where no-one realised there was a point to be taken. The public interest in the right being considered was also relevant: the more important the right, the less likely the court is to accept that it has been waived.

Thus, in cases under the Convention, our courts will consider what is just and appropriate, and necessary to give just satisfaction; and our courts will also consider the principles of causation, taking account only of the losses caused by the infringement, and the conduct of all parties. These will not be very different from the principles applied by our courts in any event: they already apply a test of compensation, and consider questions of causation. It is already an established principle that a declaration may in some circumstances be a sufficient remedy if there is no loss suffered. The courts also have the ability to award interest on awards of damages, which compensates a person who suffered a monetary loss for the period of time they have had to wait for compensation.[8]

---

[6] *Millar v Dickson* [2002] 1 WLR 1615.
[7] *Starrs v Ruxton* [2002] UKHRR 78, considered below, p. 158.
[8] Supreme Court Act 1981 section 35A and County Courts Act 1984 section 69.

The principles for awarding an injunction will be similar. The general principle is that the courts will order an injunction where damages would not be an adequate remedy. So, if someone threatens to invade someone else's privacy, for example because they intend to publish pictures which are intrusive, then the courts may consider that the breach of privacy would not be something which could be properly assessed in monetary terms.

In all cases, a successful party may also be awarded their costs of bringing the claim, or defending the claim if the claim was unsuccessful. The courts already have a general discretion as to costs.[9] This will allow them to make whatever award is considered appropriate. It will also allow the courts to deal with questions such as who should pay the costs of a party which intervenes, such as the Crown in a case where there is a declaration of incompatibility.

WHEN MUST PROCEEDINGS BE BROUGHT?

> **Section 7** (5) Proceedings under subsection (1)(a) must be brought before the end of –
> (a)   the period of one year beginning with the date on which the act complained of took place; or
> (b)   such longer period as the court or tribunal considers equitable having regard to all the circumstances,
> but that is subject to any rule imposing a stricter time limit in relation to the procedure in question.

All legal proceedings are subject to **limitation** provisions. That is, there is a time limit within which legal proceedings have to be started after the occurrence of time of the action being complained of. Limitation periods serve the purpose of ensuring that claims do not relate to matters which are so long ago that the parties involved have no proper recollection or records of them, where it would be unfair for them to have to deal with a claim. They also provide a measure of certainty and finality, so that people do not have to be concerned about claims hanging over them indefinitely; so, for example, insurance against claims for business or professional liability need not be continued indefinitely. There are exceptions where the matter which is being complained of cannot be discovered at the time and only comes to light later. Limitation periods are acceptable under the Convention for these reasons, and their existence is not a breach of the Article 6 right to a fair trial, so long as the period of the limitation is reasonably proportionate to its purpose or it does not restrict or reduce a person's access to a court to such an extent that the very essence of the right of access to a court is impaired; in this respect, states enjoy a certain margin of appreciation.[10]

Under section 7(5), there is a one-year limitation period for claims for a breach of a human right, but with a discretion in (b) for the court to extend that period if there

---

[9] Primarily by section 51(3) of the Supreme Court Act 1981 for civil cases and sections 16 and 17 of the Prosecution of Offences Act 1985 for criminal cases.

[10] See, for example, *Stubbings v UK* (1997) 23 EHRR 213; *Perez de Rada Cavanilles v Spain* (2000) 29 EHRR 109.

are good reasons for doing so. This might apply if, for example, the breach of human rights was not found out about until after the year was up. The proviso at the end of the section means that if the remedy being sought has in general a shorter time limit then that shorter time limit applies – for example, judicial review claims usually have to be brought within three months of the making of the decision which is being challenged.

Note, however, that this limitation period does not apply to reliance on the Act or the Convention rights in legal proceedings which are not directly for a claim under the Act under section 7(1)(b). So if the claim that is being brought is a claim for trespass or assault, where the Act is relied on but not as the main cause of action, the usual limitation period for that type of claim will apply and not the one-year limitation period for a claim under the Act.

It is also necessary that the claim was in respect of something which happened after the Act came into force on 2 October 2000. The only limited exception to this is that section 22(4) of the Act applied section 7(1)(b) to proceedings begun before that date. That is, it allowed the Act to be used as a defence to proceedings brought by, or at the instigation of, a public authority, whenever the act or omission in question took place, even where the breach of those rights occurred before the Act came into force. This is stated to include appeals from courts and tribunals.

However, the scope of this section has been interpreted restrictively by the decisions of the House of Lords in *Lambert*[11] and *Kansal*.[12] In those cases, the House of Lords held that this section does not apply to an appeal from a conviction where the trial occurred before the Act came into force, if what is being said is that the court in reaching its decision at that trial failed to give effect to the Convention. Thus it would appear that it cannot be used to *bring* an appeal in respect of a trial which took place before 2 October 2000, only to *defend* an appeal by a public authority from a trial before that date. This distinction is not a happy one, as recognised by the House in *Kansal*, where a majority of the judges considered that the decision in *Lambert* was not correct but the House declined to reverse it.

BRINGING A CLAIM UNDER THE ACT

Section 8 (2)   Damages may be awarded only by a court [or tribunal] which has power to award damages, or to order the payment of compensation, in civil proceedings.

Section 9 (1)   Proceedings under section 7(1)(a) in respect of a judicial act may be brought only
(a)   by exercising a right of appeal;
(b)   on an application (in Scotland a petition) for judicial review; or
(c)   in such other forum as may be prescribed by rules. [. . .]

(3)   In proceedings under this Act in respect of a judicial act done in good faith, damages may not be awarded otherwise than to compensate a person to the extent required by Article 5(5) of the Convention.

---

[11] *R v Lambert* [2001] 3 WLR 206.
[12] *R v Kansal* [2001] 3 WLR 1562.

If someone who considers that their rights have been infringed launches a legal action, this would be an example of a civil claim, as opposed to a criminal prosecution. This is confirmed by section 8(2), that damages can only be awarded by a court which will normally make an award of that sort. The effect of this is that damages cannot be awarded by a court hearing a criminal prosecution, since criminal courts do not normally make awards of damages.

The procedure for bringing a claim under the Act is generally the same as for any other civil claim, although there are some special provisions contained in the various court rules which apply to civil and family cases.[13] The main provisions about bringing civil claims are as follows:

- there are limitations on which judges are to hear claims under the Act: actions are to be heard by High Court judges or circuit judges or recorders (who sit in the County Courts).[14] Claims under the Act arising out of anything done in court or by a judge are to be tried only in the High Court.[15] By section 4(5) of the Act, only the High Court, Court of Appeal, House of Lords and Privy Council may grant a declaration of incompatibility.
- proper notice must be given that a point under the Act is going to be raised: if a claim under the Act is to be brought it must be clearly set out when the claim is brought; cases being relied on must be provided in good time for the hearing; and if a Human Rights Act point is being relied on in an appeal it must also be clearly set out in the Notice of Appeal.[16]
- there must also be proper notice (21 days or such period as the court directs) to the government if a statute is challenged as being incompatible with the Act or if a remedy is being sought in respect of a judicial act, to allow the government to make representations in defence of the statute or act being considered, and an appropriate government representative is entitled to be joined as a party.[17] If the question of a declaration of incompatibility arises during the course of proceedings, the Crown must still be given notice that this is being considered.[18]

---

[13] The Civil Procedure Rules 1998 ('CPR') and Family Proceedings Rules 1991 ('FPR'), which are the rules referred to in sections 7(2) and 9(1)(c) of the Act.

[14] Civil cases: CPR Practice Direction 2B, Paragraph 7A; Family cases: President's Direction 24.7.00 [2000] 2 FLR 429, High Court and circuit judges only.

[15] Section 7(2); CPR Rule 7.11.

[16] CPR Practice Direction to Part 16 Paragraph 16.1 (inclusion in statements of claim), Practice Direction to Part 39 Paragraph 8.1 (authorities to be provided 3 days before hearing), Practice Direction to Part 52 (Notices of Appeal raising new HRA point); FPR Rule 10.26(2) (inclusion in originating document), President's Direction 24.7.00 [2000] 2 FLR 429 (provision of authorities).

[17] Sections 5(1), (2) and 9(4); CPR Rule 19.4A; FPR Rule 10.26 (4) to (21). The appropriate government representative who is entitled to be joined will be a relevant Minister of the Crown, member of the Scottish Executive, Northern Ireland Minister or department, or the Welsh Assembly: section 5(2) and National Assembly for Wales (Transfer of Functions) (No 2) Order 2000, SI 2000/1830.

[18] Section 5(3).

- in addition to the courts' usual duty to give reasons for its decision and to state whether or not there has been an infringement where that is the subject of the claim before it, a court should also state expressly if it finds that there has been an infringement of the Act or Convention rights in proceedings where the court orders a release from prison in an appeal from a committal to prison for breach of a court order or contempt of court, an application for habeas corpus, or release of a secure accommodation order for a child.[19]
- where the court makes a decision that the claimant's Convention rights have been infringed, but the claimant is still not satisfied with the result, the court hearing the further complaint, which will usually be an appeal court, need not rehear the case, but may accept the finding of the court which heard the original complaint that there was an infringement.[20] This enables the court hearing the matter on the further complaint not to have to insist on the original claim being heard again.

These provisions do not apply to criminal cases, although it will still be usual for notice to be given that human rights points are going to be taken. That will allow any legal argument to be dealt with in the most efficient manner, for example, by holding a preliminary hearing to consider any human rights point that is being taken. There are equivalent provisions on giving notice to the government where the Court of Appeal is being invited to make a declaration of incompatibility in a criminal appeal.[21]

Where the act being complained of is a decision of a judge in court, the procedure to be used to complain about an infringement of Convention rights will be to appeal the decision which is alleged to infringe the human rights of the party: section 9(1). This is in accordance with the way the law works generally: if a party considers that a judge has decided a case in a way which is wrong, their remedy is to appeal that decision. This is a perfectly adequate remedy since the appeal court has power to decide that the result of the case should be different so that it does not infringe the party's rights, including quashing a criminal conviction. The only circumstance where this is not a sufficient remedy is that envisaged by section 9(3), where as a result of the decision which is being appealed, a person has been detained in prison in contravention of Article 5. In this case, the state will pay compensation for the wrongful detention (section 9(4)).

Section 12 of the Act provides some additional procedural requirements where a court is considering whether to grant any relief which might affect the exercise of the Convention right to freedom of expression under Article 10. This will apply most obviously in cases where a party seeks an injunction to prevent publication of something which is alleged to be, for example, a breach of privacy or confidentiality. In particular:

- in cases of urgency, it is possible to apply for an injunction in the absence of the person against whom it is being made. However, where section 12 applies, such an injunction is not to be granted unless the court is satisfied that all practicable steps

---

[19] CPR Practice Direction 40B Paragraph 14.4; FPR Rule 10.26 (22).
[20] CPR Rule 33.9.
[21] Criminal Appeal Rules 1968, rules 2(aa) and (ab) and 14A, as amended by the Criminal Appeal (Amendment) Rules 2000 (SI 2000 No. 2036).

have been taken to notify that person or that there are compelling reasons why notice should not be given (section 12(2));

- an injunction to prevent publication before there has been a trial of the issues unless the court is satisfied that the person seeking the injunction is likely to establish that publication should not be allowed (section 12(3)); and
- for journalistic, literary or artistic material, the court must have particular regard to the extent to which the material is, or is about to be, available to the public in any event, the public interest in publication of the material, and any relevant privacy code (section 12(4)).

One case in which the effect of this section has been considered is *A v B*,[22] which stressed the importance of establishing that an injunction is likely to be granted after a full hearing, since the granting of an injunction to prevent publication may well determine the outcome of the whole case; if there is no publication, there may be no point in further litigation. On the other hand, if the injunction is not granted, and the material is published, if it is then decided that publication should not have been allowed, it will effectively be too late; the damage may be done. Thus the standard required before an injunction should be granted is the high standard set by section 12(3)[23]: it is not just a question of who is more likely to win at trial – the party seeking the injunction must show that they have a real prospect of succeeding at trial before they will be granted an injunction to prevent publication pending a full hearing of their allegations.

We will consider this further in the context of Article 10.[24]

---

[22] *A v B (a company)* [2002] 3 WLR 542, discussed further in the context of Article 8, p. 117.
[23] *Cream Holdings Ltd v Banerjee* (2003) LTL 14.2.03, a defamation case where the Court of Appeal agreed that the Claimant did have a real prospect of success, so the High Court was right to grant an injunction preventing publication.
[24] Below, pp. 229–30.

Discrimination between children with different language backgrounds in their access to education in their own language was considered in the Belgian Linguistics, discussed in the context of Article 14 (see p. 92).

(*Source:* Michael Stephens/PA Photos.)

Chapter 7

INTRODUCTION TO THE CONVENTION RIGHTS

'We should not say that human rights, or their exercise, are subject to the common good. [. . .] On the other hand, we can appropriately say that most human rights are subject to or limited by each other and by other *aspects* of the common good.' (John Finnis, *Natural Law and Natural Rights*)

WHAT RIGHTS ARE PROTECTED BY THE ACT?

Section 1 (1) In this Act 'the Convention rights' means the rights and fundamental freedoms set out in –
(a) Articles 2 to 12 and 14 of the Convention,
(b) Articles 1 to 3 of the First Protocol, and
(c) Articles 1 and 2 of the Sixth Protocol,
as read with Articles 16 to 18 of the Convention.

The Convention rights brought into our law by the Act are those provided for by the following Articles of the Convention, which are set out in full in schedule 1 of the Act:

- Article 2, the right to life;
- Article 3, freedom from torture, and inhuman or degrading treatment or punishment;
- Article 4, freedom from slavery and forced or compulsory labour;
- Article 5, the right to personal liberty;
- Article 6, the right to a fair trial;
- Article 7, freedom from retrospective criminal law;
- Article 8, the right to respect for private and family life, home and correspondence;
- Article 9, freedom of thought, conscience and religion;
- Article 10, freedom of expression;
- Article 11, freedom of peaceful assembly and association;
- Article 12, the right to marry and found a family;
- First Protocol, Article 1, protection of property;
- First Protocol, Article 2, right to education;
- First Protocol, Article 3, right to free elections; and
- Sixth Protocol, Article 1, abolition of the death penalty.

We will be discussing these rights in detail in the following chapters. In each case, we will be considering what situations it covers, whether it is absolute or can be interfered with in some circumstances, and what the addition of the Convention right adds to our existing law. In this chapter we will be discussing certain general matters which apply to all or many of the Articles, as well as a number of general provisions contained within the European Convention which relate to all the rights. As well as the Articles listed above, Articles 14, 16, 17 and 18 are included within the Act. We will discuss these later in this chapter: as we will see, these are all of an ancillary nature and do not create free-standing rights.

OMISSION OF ARTICLES 1 AND 13 FROM THE ACT

ARTICLE 1: OBLIGATION TO RESPECT HUMAN RIGHTS
The High Contracting Parties shall secure to everyone within their jurisdiction the rights and freedoms defined in Section I of this Convention.

ARTICLE 13: RIGHT TO AN EFFECTIVE REMEDY
Everyone whose rights and freedoms as set forth in this Convention are violated shall have an effective remedy before a national authority notwithstanding that the violation has been committed by persons acting in an official capacity.

It was not thought necessary to include Articles 1 and 13 in the list of rights protected by the Act. In the case of Article 1, this sets out the obligation of the state to protect the Convention rights, and this is being done by the passing of the Act itself. In the case of Article 13, this is the article which secures a remedy for violations of the Convention rights. It was considered by those who drafted the Act, and by the government in Parliament[1] in proposing it, that an effective remedy is provided by section 8 of the Act, which gives the courts a general ability to provide a remedy for any breach of the Convention rights. Thus it was concluded that there was no need to have a specific separate right to an effective remedy by enacting Article 13: to include Article 13 would be a duplication.

THE PROTOCOLS

The basic list of rights drawn up in the original Convention in 1950 has been supplemented by a number of protocols. We will consider here those protocols which set out additional rights; there were also a number of protocols which amended the powers and procedures for bringing a complaint under the Convention, and these have all now been replaced by the Eleventh Protocol, which is incorporated into the current text of the Convention.[2] As regards the protocols which contain additional rights, states may choose whether or not they accept these, and are therefore free to decide whether or not to sign up to any particular protocol.[3] The United Kingdom signed up to the First Protocol in 1952, and it is therefore included in the Act.

---

[1] For example, by the Lord Chancellor (HL Vol. 583, col. 475, 18 November 1997) and the Home Secretary, Jack Straw (HC Vol. 312, col. 981, 20 May 1998).
[2] The text of the Convention, including the Eleventh Protocol, can be found in Appendix 2, p. 320; the current court structure under the Convention is discussed above at p. 44.
[3] These additional protocols are included in Appendix 2 and a table showing which states have signed up to which protocols may be found in Appendix 3, p. 346.

The Sixth Protocol prohibits the death penalty for criminal offences, with a limited exception in wartime included within the Protocol. The death penalty was largely abolished in 1965,[4] and was abolished for treason and piracy in 1998.[5] The Sixth Protocol was included in the Act as a result of an amendment to the Act during its passage through Parliament in 1998. There was a free vote, which is to say that the Members of Parliament were free to vote without the political parties taking a view, and the vote was in favour of including this Protocol. As a result, it was included in the Act and the Sixth Protocol was signed by the United Kingdom in January 1999 and ratified in May 1999.

There are some further protocols which contain substantive rights. The Fourth Protocol contains four rights:

- the prohibition of imprisonment for debt;
- freedom of movement for a state's nationals within and between countries;
- prohibition of expulsion of people from their own country and on refusing entry to a country's own citizens; and
- the prohibition of the collective expulsion of aliens (aliens here means people who are not citizens of the country doing the expelling).

The Seventh Protocol contains five rights:

- Procedural safeguards in the case of expulsion of non-nationals
- Right of appeal in criminal cases
- Right to compensation for wrongful conviction
- Right not to be tried or punished twice for the same offence
- Equality of rights and responsibilities between spouses

The United Kingdom has not signed up to the Fourth and Seventh Protocols, and so they are not included in the rights protected by the Act. The rights contained within these protocols are considered to be largely, but not entirely, consistent with the equivalent provisions in British law. However, the government has chosen not to sign up to these protocols until the inconsistencies have been removed, so they were not included in the Act. The government's White Paper, which set out its proposals for the Act, suggested that they would be kept under review, with a view to signing up to the protocols when the inconsistencies had been removed, in particular for the Seventh Protocol.[6] Of course, the protocols can still be used as standards with which our law should seek to comply, in which case our current law can be criticised if it is inconsistent with them.

So, for example, there is already in our law a right of appeal in criminal cases and a right not to be punished twice for the same offence. On the other hand, one of the concerns about signing up to the Fourth Protocol is that there are a number of categories of British citizens, which have arisen from, for example, the de-colonisation of the British Empire, or the status of people who come from the remaining Dependent Territories. Not all the people in these categories have full rights to enter the United Kingdom itself as they wish. This was one of the areas where it was therefore thought

---

[4] Murder (Abolition of Death Penalty) Act 1965.
[5] Prevention of Crime and Disorder Act 1998 section 36.
[6] HC Vol. 312, col. 1006, Mr O'Brien, Home Office Minister.

that there could well be a problem in agreeing to the Protocol, if our current law does not comply with it.

Since the Act was passed, two more protocols have been drawn up. The Twelfth Protocol contains a general prohibition of discrimination in respect of any legal right on the ground of sex, race, colour, language, religion, political or other opinion, national or social origin, association with a national minority, property, birth or other status. This is a more extensive protection against discrimination than the existing Article 14 of the Treaty which only prohibits discrimination in respect of the Convention rights themselves. However, at the time of writing, this protocol is not in force yet, since it has not been agreed to by the minimum number of states required before it becomes effective. Likewise, the Thirteenth Protocol, which expands the prohibition on the death penalty to all circumstances, including in time of war, has been opened for signature, but has not come into effect yet.

However, although these other protocols are not included in the rights protected by the Act, the Act does specifically provide for these to be added to the Act at a later date, in section 1:

> **Section 1 (4)** The Lord Chancellor may by order make such amendments to this Act as he considers appropriate to reflect the effect, in relation to the United Kingdom, of a protocol.
> (5) In subsection (4) 'protocol' means a protocol to the Convention –
>   (a) which the United Kingdom has ratified; or
>   (b) which the United Kingdom has signed with a view to ratification.
> (6) No amendment may be made by an order under subsection (4) so as to come into force before the protocol concerned is in force in relation to the United Kingdom.

Thus, under this provision, by a statutory instrument put before Parliament, rights can be added to the Act to expand the list of Convention rights where the United Kingdom ratifies a protocol; and this also applies where a protocol has been signed but not ratified. The only proviso is that the protocol has to be 'in force': this means that, for example, if a protocol needs to be ratified by 10 countries before it is effective, it is not binding until this has been done. So until then, even if the United Kingdom has ratified it, it would not be in force and so could not be added to the Act.

DEROGATIONS AND RESERVATIONS

> **Section 1 (2)** Those Articles [specifying the Convention rights] are to have effect for the purposes of this Act subject to any designated derogation or reservation.
>
> *ARTICLE 57: RESERVATIONS*
> (1) Any State may, when signing this Convention or when depositing its instrument of ratification, make a reservation in respect of any particular provision of the Convention to the extent that any law then in force in its territory is not in conformity with the provision. Reservations of a general character shall not be permitted under this article.

(2) Any reservation made under this article shall contain a brief statement of the law concerned.

ARTICLE 15: DEROGATION IN TIME OF EMERGENCY

(1) In time of war or other public emergency threatening the life of the nation any High Contracting Party may take measures derogating from its obligations under this Convention to the extent strictly required by the exigencies of the situation, provided that such measures are not inconsistent with its other obligations under international law.

(2) No derogation from Article 2, except in respect of deaths resulting from lawful acts of war, or from Articles 3, 4 (paragraph 1) and 7 shall be made under this provision.

(3) Any High Contracting Party availing itself of this right of derogation shall keep the Secretary General of the Council of Europe fully informed of the measures which it has taken and the reasons therefor. It shall also inform the Secretary General of the Council of Europe when such measures have ceased to operate and the provisions of the Convention are again being fully executed.

A **reservation** is a declaration which allows a state to agree to a treaty, such as the Convention, where there is a particular law in force in the territory of that state which is not in conformity with the provision, which the state does not wish to alter in order to conform with the Convention. The reservation has to be very specific, and cannot be a general exception to one of the articles: it has to be a specific point which does not substantially detract from the protection of the article. A reservation is lodged prior to ratification of the treaty, so a state cannot add a reservation later.

A **derogation** allows for limited non-compliance with the Convention in the event of war or public emergency threatening the life of the nation. However, the derogation must only be to the extent *strictly* required by the situation and must not be inconsistent with the state's other obligations under international law – so cannot permit a law which mandated actions which would amount to war crimes or crimes against humanity. If a derogation is considered necessary, a declaration must be lodged with the Secretary General of the Council of Europe, who must also be kept informed as to when the measures requiring the derogation have ceased to operate and the provisions of the Convention are again being fully executed.

There are some articles which contain rights which are so important that no derogation from them is permissible. These are the right to life contained in Article 2, except in respect of deaths resulting from lawful acts of war, freedom from torture (Article 3), freedom from slavery (Article 4(1)) and freedom from retrospective criminal penalty (Article 7). In addition, there can be no derogation or reservation from the abolition of the death penalty in the Sixth Protocol, although Article 2 of this Protocol does provide a limited exception permitting the death penalty in time of war.

Under the Act, the Convention rights have effect subject to any designated derogation or reservation. This means that if the United Kingdom has entered a derogation or reservation in respect of a particular statutory position, although there may appear to be an incompatibility between that statute and the Convention rights, there is no infringement of the Convention.

'Designated reservation' for the purposes of the Act is defined in section 15. This refers at present only to the reservation to Article 2 of the First Protocol which was

entered into in 1952, which is currently the only United Kingdom reservation.[7] The
section also allows for the possibility that the United Kingdom might enter a reservation
in the future, by permitting an order to be made by the relevant government Minister[8]
designating the reservation for the purposes of the Act. Since a reservation must be
entered when a treaty is signed, this could only happen if, for example, a new protocol
was ratified subject to a reservation.

The details of what is meant by a designated derogation is set out in section 14, which
provides that any derogation may be designated by an order by the relevant government Minister.[8] When the Act was passed it included the derogation from Article 5(3),
which was then in force. That derogation has now been withdrawn, since the law to
which it relates was replaced.[9] However, since then, a new derogation has been entered
to Article 5(1) in relation to powers to detain suspected terrorists or illegal immigrants
pending deportation, and that has now been included in the Act, based on the public
emergency caused by the terrorist attacks on New York in September 2001.[10] This is
currently the only designated derogation under the Act.[11]

If a derogation is amended or replaced it ceases to be a designated derogation, and a
new order is required to (re)designate the new or amended derogation. By section 16,
all designations of derogations expire after five years, but may be extended for a further five years; this ensures that no derogation simply continues without being reconsidered periodically. Section 17 requires that the appropriate minister must review it
and report to Parliament before the designation expires, so that Parliament can make
an informed decision on any proposed order to renew the designation.

LIMITATIONS ON RIGHTS: QUALIFIED RIGHTS

Many rights set out in the Convention contain express or implied **qualifications**. This
means that there are circumstances where an action which might *appear* to be an infringement of the right is *not* an infringement because the right, as properly understood, allows
for exceptions. Put another way, the drafting of the Convention expressly recognises
that most human rights are not absolute: there are circumstances when it is justified
to limit their application, because there is a need to protect the rights of others, where
there is a conflict between the rights of different people, or because there is some common interest which requires protection, using the terms 'common interest' here as a
shorthand for the general rights of others. This is what we referred to in our discussion
of the nature of rights as **balancing** rights, where we considered some examples of
situations where there is a need to resolve a conflict between different rights.[12]

---

[7] Discussed in the context of the right to education, p. 220; the text can be found in Appendix 1.
[8] The designation of reservations and derogations is currently the responsibility of the Lord
Chancellor: The Transfer of Functions (Miscellaneous) Order 2001 (SI 2001 No. 3500).
[9] Human Rights Act 1998 (Amendment) Order 2001 (SI 2001 No. 1216).
[10] Human Rights Act 1998 (Designated Derogation) Order 2001 (SI 2001 No. 3644); Human
Rights Act 1998 (Amendment No. 2) Order 2001 (SI 2001 No. 4032); we will consider this
in more detail below, p. 279.
[11] The full text of the derogation can be found in Appendix 1.
[12] Above, Chapter 2, p. 10.

In a very large number of the cases we will be considering, there is one party asserting a right, and a state attempting to justify an interference with it. What we will be considering here is the general approach which should be taken to such a situation, applying the European Convention, and also the guidance and principles developed by the European Court.

The European Court has developed its own way of approaching all limitations on the Convention rights. First, the rights themselves are construed in a broad and purposive way, while the limitations are construed narrowly. Thus, first the right is applied to the facts of a particular case on the basis that it is intended to provide a right in those circumstances. Second, however, where the state seeks to limit the particular right, by relying on the second paragraph of the Article, the state must prove strictly that the circumstances fall within the exceptions set out there which are construed narrowly. Thus, if the complaint is one of breach of the right to privacy under Article 8, it is for the applicant to satisfy the court that Article 8 applies to the situation and that it appears to be infringed; it is then for the government to establish, if it can, that what appears to be an infringement is justified in the interests of one of the grounds set out in Article 8(2).

In addition, the European Court has developed the principles that in order to justify an interference, it must be in **accordance with the law, necessary** in a democratic society and **proportionate** to the reason for what would otherwise be an infringement. We will consider the specific circumstances where one applies a particular qualification in the discussion of the individual articles. The purpose of this discussion is to consider this general approach.

'IN ACCORDANCE WITH THE LAW'

This is an important requirement to ensure that the rule of law is upheld: if there are to be circumstances where what would appear to be an infringement of a right is permitted, it must be one which is clearly defined and set out by the law of the country in question. This applies equally to the phrase 'in accordance with the law' in Articles 8 to 11 or the references to 'the law' or being 'prescribed by law', for example, in Articles 2, 5 and 6.

There are two aspects to this idea. First, there must be some basis in the national law for the provision being relied on, and second, the national law must be accessible and precise. As to the first, in most cases this is present; it is uncommon for there to be a complete absence of legal basis for official action in any of the states who are parties to the Convention. It is also not common in the European Court cases that there was a breach of national law, because if there is such a breach, there is usually a remedy under the national law; and it is necessary to exhaust the local court process before seeking a remedy from the European Court. Thus if a police officer acts in breach of the law on how to arrest someone, there will be a liability for wrongful arrest without the need to rely on any breach of Article 5 which may also have been committed. It is usually only if the national law has been complied with that there is a need to criticise it for infringing human rights.

One example where it was held that there was *no* relevant law is the *Halford*[13] case. Alison Halford was the Assistant Chief Constable of Merseyside. She complained that calls which she had made from her office and home telephones were intercepted by the police in order to gather information for use against her in sex discrimination proceedings, in breach of Article 8. At the time there was an Act of Parliament in force (the Interception of Communications Act 1985) which aimed at providing a statutory framework to ensure that the interception of communications on public systems would be authorised and controlled in a manner commanding public confidence. But it did not apply to internal communications systems operated by public authorities, such as that at Merseyside Police Headquarters, and there was no other provision in domestic law to regulate interceptions of telephone calls made on such systems. Thus it could not be said that the interference in her case was 'in accordance with the law', since there was no relevant legal framework to regulate interferences with the right to respect for privacy.

The more usual contention, on the part of the individual who is complaining of a violation, is the second one, that the national law is uncertain or gives too wide a discretion to officials. This is described by the European Court as meaning that there must be a 'quality of law', the law must be precise and accessible. Again, usually these criteria will be fulfilled in our law: usually Acts of Parliament are relatively clear in their meaning, and the judgments of the courts are couched in careful and precise language. However, this is still important, because all citizens are presumed to know the law, so that all are treated fairly by the courts: this is why it is sometimes said that ignorance of the law is no excuse for breaking it. It means that the ordinary citizen should be able to ascertain, albeit with legal advice if necessary, what the law is which applies to a particular situation. This does not mean that they have to be able to know what legal powers *are* being exercised, but what *could* be exercised.

To continue with the example of tapping a telephone, consider a situation where the police wish to tap a telephone line to prevent or detect criminal activity. Clearly it would defeat that purpose if the police were obliged to inform the citizen that their telephone conversations were being monitored. As soon as the person being monitored found out about the surveillance, they would stop using the telephone for any criminal purposes. However, in general terms, everyone is entitled to know under what circumstances it is possible or likely that an order can be made permitting the police to tap their telephone; and further, they should be able to know what safeguards exist to prevent unwarranted invasions of this privacy.

So in the case of *Malone*,[14] the applicant was prosecuted for offences related to the dishonest handling of stolen goods; during the trial it emerged that his telephone had been tapped by the police acting on the authority of a warrant issued by the Home Secretary. He was acquitted and sought to establish that the tapping had been unlawful, complaining of a breach of Article 8. The European Court decided that the English law did not indicate with sufficient clarity the scope and manner of exercise of the relevant discretion conferred on public authorities in the field of interception of communications. To that extent the minimum degree of legal protection to which citizens were entitled under the rule of law in a democratic society was lacking. The law should be sufficiently clear in its terms to give citizens an adequate indication as to the circumstance in which and the conditions on which public authorities are empowered to resort to their secret and potentially dangerous interference with the right to respect for privacy.[15]

---

[13] (1997) 24 EHRR 523.
[14] (1985) 7 EHRR 14.
[15] There are some further examples in the discussion of Article 5 below, p. 134.

'NECESSARY IN A DEMOCRATIC SOCIETY'

In Articles 8 to 11, this is the second element which must be proved by the state in order to justify the interference with the right or freedom; but the idea of necessity is found in cases on other Articles. The key idea is that the particular legal provision or official activity on the part of the state, which has caused the interference with the right or freedom, must go no further than is necessary. This is not the same as 'reasonable', 'ordinary' or 'desirable'. In accordance with the doctrine of the margin of appreciation, it will usually be for the national authority to make the initial assessment of whether there is a pressing social need which the measure is addressing.[16] But the European Court will still review this assessment, and has established that there are three distinct matters which must be addressed. As well as answering a **pressing social need,** the measure must pursue one of the **legitimate aims** set out in the relevant Article, if it contains grounds which justify interference; and there must be a reasonable relationship of **proportionality** between the means employed and the aim which is being pursued.

One example where the European Court considered whether a restriction was 'necessary in a democratic society' was the case of *Chassagnou v France*.[17] This case concerned a French law which compelled certain landowners to join a hunting association and allow hunting across their land. In deciding that this was in breach of the Article 11 right to freedom of association, the European Court stated that:

> The Court reiterates that in assessing the necessity of a given measure a number of principles must be observed. The term 'necessary' does not have the flexibility of such expressions as 'useful' or 'desirable'. In addition, pluralism, tolerance and broadmindedness are hallmarks of a 'democratic society'. Although individual interests must on occasion be subordinated to those of a group, democracy does not simply mean that the views of a majority must always prevail: a balance must be achieved which ensures the fair and proper treatment of minorities and avoids any abuse of a dominant position. Lastly, any restriction imposed on a Convention right must be proportionate to the legitimate aim pursued.
>
> In the present case the only aim invoked by the Government to justify the interference complained of was 'protection of the rights and freedoms of others'. Where these 'rights and freedoms' are themselves among those guaranteed by the Convention or its Protocols, it must be accepted that the need to protect them may lead States to restrict other rights or freedoms likewise set forth in the Convention. It is precisely this constant search for a balance between the fundamental rights of each individual which constitutes the foundation of a 'democratic society'.

In this case, the aim invoked by the French government was the protection of the rights of others; but the right relied on was a right to hunt, which is not one of the Convention rights. The Court considered that in such a case only 'indisputable imperatives can justify interference with a Convention right'. The ethical objections of the applicants to hunting were sufficiently cogent and important to be worthy of respect in a democratic society. It could therefore not be said that it was *necessary*, in a democratic society, to interfere with them, and so the compulsory obligation to join a hunting society was in breach of Article 11.

PROPORTIONALITY

The idea of proportionality is an important one in all cases where there is a proviso to a right or where the European Court has had to consider any argument that an

---

[16] *Handyside v UK* (1979–80) 1 EHRR 737; the margin of appreciation is discussed above, p. 45.
[17] (2000) 29 EHRR 615; the property aspect of the case is considered below, p. 256.

interference with a right is justified. The idea is that such interference should be proportionate: the extent of the interference covers only the purpose which justifies it, and does not go beyond it. So, for example, an interference with the right to privacy which consists of asking people questions about where they are going may be a proportionate response to a terrorist threat where arresting them without reasonable suspicion might not be. This is important because there is a point beyond which an interference with a right cannot be justified.

In considering a question of proportionality, the court must ensure that the measure is carefully designed to meet the objective in question; that it is not arbitrary, unfair or based on irrational considerations; that the limitation impairs the right as little as possible; and whether, even if these criteria are met, the interference is so severe in effect that it outweighs the objective for which it would otherwise be permitted. One example of a case where the European Court considered that the interference with the Convention right met the criteria of being a legitimate aim, but what prevented the interference being necessary in a democratic society was that it was disproportionate, was *Vogt v Germany*.[18]

Here Mrs Vogt had been dismissed from her job as a teacher for being a member of the German Communist Party, which the German tribunal considered stood for anti-constitutional aims, meaning that Mrs Vogt was infringing her duty of political loyalty as a civil servant.

The European Court considered that there was an interference with the Article 10 right to freedom of expression, which was for a legitimate aim, namely, the obligation on civil servants to actively uphold Germany's free and democratic constitution, especially given Germany's history and desire to prevent a repeat of 'the nightmare of Nazism'.

However, the Court considered that the justification put forward by the German government was not sufficient to establish that it was necessary to dismiss Mrs Vogt from her job, which was a disproportionate consequence. In particular, there were no complaints about Mrs Vogt's performance at her job, there was no evidence that Mrs Vogt had actually made any anti-constitutional statements or personally adopted an anti-constitutional stance. Nor had the Communist Party been banned.

A very large number of the cases we will be discussing in the context of the different articles turn on the question of proportionality, which will vary from situation to situation, and will depend also on the right in question. There may well be differences of opinion as to what measure of response is proportionate to a particular need. To this extent, our courts will have some regard for the solution that Parliament adopts for a particular problem, although the margin of appreciation does not apply as such to the decision of United Kingdom courts.[19] However, this measure of deference should not prevent the courts from deciding that a particular provision is a disproportionate response if the court considers that it goes beyond what is justified.

WHICH RIGHTS ARE QUALIFIED?

Whether or not there are exceptions to a Convention right varies from article to article. The rights provided for by Articles 3 (freedom from torture), 4(1) (prohibition

---

[18] (1996) 21 EHRR 205.
[19] Discussed above, p. 47.

of slavery) and 7 (no punishment without law) contain no exceptions and these are rights where there is no legitimate justification for an infringement. The right to life in Article 2 has some very specific and narrowly drawn exceptions for self-defence and capital punishment. Articles 4(2) (prohibition of forced labour) and Article 5 (personal liberty) contain some specific exceptions. The right to a trial in public, which is part of Article 6(1), contains express exceptions; some of the other rights within the Article 6 rights to a fair trial, which have no express qualifications, are examples of where the European Court has held that some limited qualifications should be implied.

A number of the Convention rights are qualified by the express words of an article. Thus Articles 8, 9, 10 and 11 each have a first paragraph which sets out the right in question and then a second paragraph which sets out express qualifications to that right. The qualifications set out the circumstances in which the state may interfere with the right or freedom. The right to property in Article 1 of the First Protocol also has express qualifications.

The same principles are applied to an *implied* limitation as are applied to articles where there are express qualifications, in particular, the principle that there must be proportionality between the extent of the infringement and the interest which justifies the infringement. Thus in the case of Article 2, in respect of the very limited exceptions to the right to life, in each case it must be shown that the action being criticised was not only justified, but absolutely necessary, which sets a very high standard on the state seeking to justify the infringement. Likewise for Article 5, for the circumstances where personal liberty may be infringed, although there is no express reference in the article to the standard of justification, the principle of proportionality applies. Again with Article 6, although most of the rights set out there contain no express qualification, they are not all treated as absolute, but any attempt to limit them must be strictly proportionate to a justifiable interest.

The qualifications for each right are not identical. One must bear in mind the different objectives of each article and the nature of the right being protected, so some of the qualifications are specific to their context. However, all of those with express qualifications do state that any limitations must be prescribed by law. So, the second paragraph of each of Articles 8 to 11 refers to this requirement and then states that limitations must be necessary in a democratic society to protect certain specified common interests. Some of these interests are common to all of these four articles: public safety, the protection of public order or prevention of disorder, the protection of health or morals, and the protection of rights of others. The first three of these are key functions of the state. The fourth expresses the point we considered above, that rights can be limited where they conflict with the rights of others, since there are many situations where two parties' rights conflict and they cannot both exercise their rights to the fullest possible extent. Other protected interests appear in most of these articles, namely national security and the prevention of crime. Article 10 has some additional limitations which relate specifically to freedom of speech. Similar ideas appear in the Article 6 right to a public trial.

Thus one must look specifically at the words of the article before one can be sure which qualifications apply. But the critical point is that, whichever article we are considering, the general principles we have set out above will apply.

NON-DISCRIMINATION

ARTICLE 14: PROHIBITION OF DISCRIMINATION
The enjoyment of the rights and freedoms set forth in this Convention shall be secured without discrimination on any ground such as sex, race, colour, language, religion, political or other opinion, national or social origin, association with a national minority, property, birth or other status.

One further general restriction on interferences with Convention rights is that contained in Article 14. This prohibits discrimination, but only in relation to the exercise of the other Convention rights. Thus, one could imagine a case in which there was a limitation on one of the other rights, for example the Article 10 right to freedom of speech. It might be that this limitation did not infringe Article 10, if the state could show that it was reasonably necessary and proportionate. However, if the limitation was applied differently to different groups without any justification – for example, if men and women were treated differently in its application, for no good reason – although there was no breach of Article 10, there would be a breach of Article 10 taken together with Article 14. However, if *none* of the other rights are engaged, then there can be no breach of Article 14 simply because there is discriminatory conduct.

The question then is, what amounts to **discrimination**? The European Court has held that Article 14 does not prevent *all* differential treatment. What it prohibits is differential treatment which is not objectively and reasonably justified, which is to say that there is a legitimate aim for the discrimination and the treatment is proportionate to that legitimate aim. This was the view stated by the European Court in the *Belgian Linguistics* case.[20]

Here, the Court was asked to consider the provision for the education of the children of French speakers in Belgium, which has two main languages, French and Flemish. The Court found no violation of the right to education contained in Article 2 of the First Protocol as such. The Court then looked at this right taken together with Article 14, and found that the lack of provision of education in French was not unjustified discriminatory conduct, but that there was a breach of Article 2 read together with Article 14 in so far as certain children were prevented from having access to French-language schools, solely on the basis of where their parents lived. There was no good reason for using this as a criterion for discriminating between some prospective students and others.

The way to decide whether there is discrimination is firstly, to compare the treatment of two different groups. The applicant will have to show that they are being treated less favourably than people who are in a comparable group. The treatment will be discriminatory if it is because of one of the factors listed in the Article – sex, race, colour, language, religion, political or other opinion, national or social origin, association with a national minority, property, birth or other status. There may also be similar factors which are considered unjustifiable, as examples of 'other status'. So, for example, in the case of *Chassagnou v France*,[21] which we considered earlier, the European Court found a

---

[20] (1979–80) 1 EHRR 241 & 252.
[21] (2000) 29 EHRR 615; above, p. 89; below, p. 256.

violation of Article 14, as well as Article 11, because the law discriminated between owners of small pieces of property, who were not allowed to object to hunting, and owners of large areas of land, who were. Other factors which have been held by the European Court not to justify differential treatment are sexual orientation, illegitimacy of birth, being a prisoner, being a conscientious objector to military service, or disability.

On the other hand, the difference in treatment does have to be *because of* the characteristic which is said to be the basis for the discrimination. If there is a real, objective difference between the two groups which are being compared, then there will not be discriminatory treatment, since there is a proper reason for treating them differently. So, for example, treating a juvenile prisoner and an adult prisoner differently is not discriminatory;[22] nor is treating a prisoner who is a serious security risk differently from one who does not pose a security risk.[23] However, where the factor is one such as sex, race or religion, the European Court has made it quite clear that the task of showing that this factor justifies differential treatment will be a difficult one.

Further examples of the application of Article 14 will be found in the discussions of some of the other articles. It is also important to note in this context that the lack of protection provided by Article 14, where there is no other Convention right involved, does not necessarily mean that a victim of discriminatory conduct in such a case would have *no* legal remedy: our law already contains various provisions prohibiting discrimination on the grounds of sex, race or disability[24] in a wide variety of situations, whether or not there is a breach of any other right.

GENERAL PROVISIONS: ARTICLES 16–18

These articles of the Convention all also have general application. As with Article 14, none of them create any free-standing rights. Instead they assist in the interpretation and application of the other articles which do create rights.

> *ARTICLE 16: RESTRICTIONS ON POLITICAL ACTIVITY OF ALIENS*
> Nothing in Articles 10, 11 and 14 shall be regarded as preventing the High Contracting Parties from imposing restrictions on the political activity of aliens.

By 'aliens', what is meant is foreign nationals. Article 16 has barely been referred to in cases under the Convention. The reason for this is because it is one provision which, although considered important when the Convention was drafted in 1950, no longer reflects contemporary attitudes to aliens, as can be seen from the provisions for the protection of aliens in the Fourth Protocol, for example. Nowadays, there is little demand to restrict the political activities of specifically foreign nationals: so long as they are allowed to enter the country, it is generally considered appropriate for their rights to freedom of expression and freedom of assembly to be the same as British nationals.

---

[22] *Nelson v UK* (1986) 49 DR 170.
[23] *X v UK* (9 December 1992), European Commission.
[24] The main legislative provisions are the Sex Discrimination Act 1975, the Race Relations Act 1976 and the Disability Discrimination Act 1995.

In the case of *Farrakhan*,[25] there was a challenge to the decision of the Home Secretary to refuse entry to the country to Louis Farrakhan, an American black Muslim activist, because of his expression of racist and anti-Semitic views. The Court of Appeal's decision was that Article 10 was engaged by this decision, but that it was justified under Article 10(2) as an informed assessment of the risk of disorder posed by Mr Farrakhan's presence. Article 16 was referred to, but the court considered the Article to be 'something of an anachronism, half a century after the agreement of the Convention'.

As well as the massive growth in international travel during the past 50 years, making it far more common for people to be visitors in other countries, one of the most significant reasons for this is the existence and growth of the European Union. It is contrary to European Union law to refuse to allow entry to, or discriminate (for most purposes) between, citizens of different countries who are members of the European Union. So, for example, the seizure of cars from people crossing from France has been held to be disproportionate, and therefore unlawful, under European Union law, in the absence of reasonable grounds for stopping the owner or for the owner to challenge the seizure.[26] The European Court has also considered whether a citizen of the European Union qualifies as a 'foreign' national: they do not, but it is relevant.

In *Piermont v France*,[27] the European Court had little hesitation in holding that France could not rely on Article 16 in limiting the rights of Mrs Piermont to freedom of expression under Article 10. Mrs Piermont was a German citizen and a Member of the European Parliament (MEP). The Court considered that her Article 10 rights had been infringed in limitations placed on her when travelling to French Polynesia, and that France could not rely on Article 16 since not only was she a European citizen, but also an MEP, and therefore a member of a political body relevant to French Polynesia.

ARTICLE 17: PROHIBITION OF ABUSE OF RIGHTS
Nothing in this Convention may be interpreted as implying for any State, group or person any right to engage in any activity or perform any act aimed at the destruction of any of the rights and freedoms set forth herein or at their limitation to a greater extent than is provided for in the Convention.

Article 17 is also of relatively limited application. The purpose of Article 17 is to prevent those with extreme political views taking advantage of the Convention rights for protection, where those views are *so* extreme that they are aimed at the *destruction*, or substantial limitation, of the basic rights and freedoms set out in the Convention. It will comparatively rare therefore that this article will apply. It can only apply to those rights that can be *used* to make a political point – for example, freedom of expression and freedom of assembly – and not those rights which solely exist to protect the individual – such as personal liberty and freedom from torture. Article 17 is effectively a further general limitation on some of the other articles, and as with any other limitation,

---

[25] R *(Farrakhan) v Secretary of State for the Home Department* [2002] 3 WLR 481.
[26] R *(Hoverspeed) v Commissioners of Customs and Excise* [2002] 3 WLR 1219.
[27] (1995) 20 EHRR 301.

in order to rely on it, a state must show that its action is strictly necessary and proportionate to the threat.

One case which refers to Article 17 is the case of *Lawless v Ireland*.[28] Mr Lawless was a member of the Irish Republican Army (IRA), a terrorist organisation. His complaint was that his Article 5 rights had been infringed by a prolonged period of detention. One of the arguments that the Irish government raised was that it was entitled to rely on Article 17: the IRA was banned because its activities were aimed at the destruction of the rights and freedoms set out in the Convention and therefore Mr Lawless could not rely on his rights under Article 5 (or any other article).

The European Court disagreed. The Court considered that the aim of Article 17 was to prevent a person relying on a right to engage in any activity which was aimed at destroying the Convention rights, but did not positively *deprive* that person of the protection of the Convention in respect of their personal rights, such as the rights under Article 5. Whatever the goals of the IRA, in complaining about his detention, Mr Lawless was not relying on his Convention rights to justify acts aimed at destroying the Convention.

A more recent case is that of *Lehideux v France*.[29] In this case, the applicants had been prosecuted for paying for an advertisement which defended Marshal Petain, the governor of France's Vichy government under the Nazi occupation, who had been sentenced to death in 1945 after the Second World War for collusion with Germany.

The European Court considered that there had been a breach of Article 10 and that Article 17 did not prevent that breach. This was because the text did not claim to support the German occupation or Nazi philosophy, but argued for a sympathetic view of the actions of Petain, which the Court considered was, after 40 years, a legitimate subject of historical debate: in a democratic society, views that offend, shock or disturb may still require protection. The Court was, however, very careful to make the distinction between offering a view of the man, Petain, and an apology of Nazism. The Court stated that:

> [this] is part of an ongoing debate among historians about the events in question and their interpretation. As such, it does not belong to the category of clearly established historical facts, such as the Holocaust, whose negation or revision would be removed from the protection of Article 10 by Article 17. [. . .] There is no doubt that, like any other remark directed against the Convention's underlying values, the justification of a pro-Nazi policy could not be allowed to enjoy the protection afforded by Article 10.

ARTICLE 18: LIMITATION ON USE OF RESTRICTIONS ON RIGHTS
The restrictions permitted under this Convention to the said rights and freedoms shall not be applied for any purpose other than those for which they have been prescribed.

Finally, there is Article 18, which again has only rarely been referred to in the cases. This is really not much more than an aid to interpretation, that when considering the application of a restriction to one of the other Convention rights, such a restriction shall only be allowed for the purpose for which it is intended, which is to say that restrictions shall not be imposed hypocritically. A state should not impose a restriction on a right, which may be justifiable, but then use that restriction for some other purpose. Given the degree of scrutiny to which the European Court has in fact subjected any

---

[28] *Lawless v Ireland (No. 3)* (1979–80) 1 EHRR 15.
[29] (2000) 30 EHRR 665; for Article 10.

claim for the justification of an interference with a right, a state which was faced with evidence that it was not using the provision interfering with that right for the reason stated would be likely to lose its case, without reference to Article 18.

QUESTIONS

1   Consider the list of rights which are protected by the Convention and by the Act. Are there any which you consider should be excluded or any other rights which you think should be included? In particular, you may like to consider the rights set out in the protocols, and the rights protected by the Universal Declaration of Human Rights (these can be found in Appendices 2 and 4 respectively).

2   One example is a right of freedom from discrimination. Do you consider that our law should recognise a free-standing right (as in the Twelfth Protocol), as well as the Article 14 right, or do you think that the Article 14 right is sufficient?

3   Do you agree in principle that the definitions of rights should set out in what circumstances they can be interfered with (it would be relevant to consider the text of the articles in Appendix 2)? Do you think that any of the Convention rights should have more extensive descriptions of permissible limitations?

The rock of Gibraltar: three IRA suspects were killed here in 1988 by security forces, which was the subject of the important European Court case of *McCann v UK*, considered in this chapter.

(*Source:* Reproduced courtesy of the Gibraltar Tourist Board.)

Chapter 8

THE RIGHT TO LIFE

'Civilisation is nothing more than the effort to reduce the use of force to the last resort.'
(José Ortega y Gasset, *La Rebelión de la Masas*, 1930)

ARTICLE 2: RIGHT TO LIFE
1   Everyone's right to life shall be protected by law. No one shall be deprived of his life intentionally save in the execution of a sentence of a court following his conviction of a crime for which this penalty is provided by law.
2   Deprivation of life shall not be regarded as inflicted in contravention of this Article when it results from the use of force which is no more than absolutely necessary:
    (a)   in defence of any person from unlawful violence;
    (b)   in order to effect a lawful arrest or to prevent the escape of a person lawfully detained;
    (c)   in action lawfully taken for the purpose of quelling a riot or insurrection.

SIXTH PROTOCOL, ARTICLE 1: ABOLITION OF THE DEATH PENALTY
The death penalty shall be abolished. No one shall be condemned to such penalty or executed.

THE RIGHT TO LIFE

As a provision which not only safeguards the right to life but sets out the circumstances when the deprivation of life may be justified, Article 2 ranks as one of the most fundamental provisions in the Convention – indeed one which, in peace time admits of no derogation under Article 15. Together with Article 3 of the Convention, it also enshrines one of the basic values of the democratic societies making up the Council of Europe. As such, its provisions must be strictly construed.

This statement is part of the European Court's judgment in the case of *McCann,*[1] which we shall consider later. It is hard to argue with the proposition it sets out – the right to life is perhaps the most basic human right, and it is appropriate that it is the first substantive right in the Convention. The very fact that it needed stating in 1950 says something about the appalling treatment, and destruction, of millions of people by various states in the previous decades.

---

[1] *McCann v UK* (1996) 21 EHRR 97, below, p. 107.

However, one might well ask what is the need for this statement of the right to life. In circumstances where death occurs, there are already long-established criminal offences such as murder, manslaughter, and causing death by dangerous driving. And quite apart from the criminal law, there are statutes and regulations providing for health and safety in situations where death might occur. For example, there are provisions to protect employees or visitors in shops and offices, factories and industrial premises; and there are regulations about the supply and use of potentially dangerous substances, both dangerous chemicals and germs, and everyday dangers, such as domestic electricity and gas. Police officers may use force, and sometimes death results, either accidentally or deliberately. But when that happens, the particular officer is subject to the ordinary course of the law, and he may be prosecuted or disciplined for his actions. The law is quite clear, and has been so for many years; he may not use more force than is reasonable in the circumstances, and if he does so he runs the risk of being found negligent or criminally responsible.

So what difference has Article 2 made, what has it added to our law? The answers are to be found in the surprising number of cases that have been decided by our courts which have involved Article 2. They have helped to define the duties of state agents and public authorities where death has occurred, or where there has been a risk of death.

The rights set out in Article 2 have an immediate corresponding duty. The opening words of Article 2 announce the right to life; this is everybody's right, and the state has the obligation to ensure it. There are two aspects to this obligation. First, there is a positive obligation to take steps to **protect life**: and second, there is a negative duty to **refrain from taking life**.

The burden of these duties is on the state, through its agents, officers and departments. In practice this burden of protecting life, and not taking life, will fall most of all on those who make life and death decisions, such as those responsible for security, the police and armed forces, and doctors taking life and death decisions. But this duty also falls on the courts, as a public authority and part of the state.[2] So, where there is a risk to the life of a person, the courts must provide whatever protection they can, by way of court orders to minimise such a risk, or, where death has occurred, by investigating what has occurred and awarding compensation for any breach which has occurred.

THE DUTY TO PROTECT LIFE

Dealing first with the duty to safeguard life, we find from time to time that the court is faced with a situation in which a person is at risk of death, or very serious injury, and the court is asked to order steps which may avert that risk. An example of this is the case of *Thompson and Venables*.[3]

---

[2] See above, p. 63.
[3] *Thompson and Venables v News Group Newspapers Ltd, Associated Newspapers Ltd and MGN Ltd* [2001] 2 WLR 1038; considered further below, pp. 114 and 187.

At the time of the hearing, the claimants were both 18 years of age. In 1993, when they were 10, they killed James Bulger, a two-year-old boy, and later in the same year they were convicted of his murder. The trial judge made injunctions restricting the publication of any details about them, beyond their names and background, without limit of time. In 2001, a number of newspapers sought clarification of the injunctions, or to have them removed, so they could publish those details; and the claimants asked the court to continue the prohibition on publication. The High Court heard evidence of sustained hostility directed at them, so that they were at risk of death or serious injury if they were found. The claimants relied on Article 2, since there was a risk to their life, as well as Article 3, for the risk of serious injury, and Article 8, the right to privacy. The newspapers relied on their Article 10 right to freedom of expression.

Lady Justice Butler-Sloss, President of the Family Division, made the injunctions, so preventing the newspapers from publishing the claimants' details, on the ground that there was a real and serious risk to the claimants, under Articles 2 and 3. Notwithstanding the interference with the Article 10 rights, Article 2 required the imposition of orders to protect the claimants.

THE RIGHT TO DIE?

The converse of this situation is where the court is asked to decide whether a person should be allowed to die, or even *caused* to die. These are cases where there is a certainty of death, and the patient, or his doctors, or his relatives, are asking the court whether particular treatment – doing something or not doing something – which is likely to cause the patient's death, would be a breach of Article 2. There are, of course, important and agonising decisions to be made, by everybody – not least by the judge. The right to protect life has no qualifications or limitations in the words of Article 2; but the proper determination of its scope, how far the state should go to protect life, will require a balancing exercise, a consideration of competing interests, in the individual circumstances of the case. The basic principle of our law is that a patient, who is in possession of their mental faculties, has the right to refuse treatment. The real difficulty arises where the patient does not have all of their mental faculties.

In the case of two patients, *M and H*,[4] two hospitals wished to withdraw treatment from patients in their care, who were in a permanent vegetative state. The High Court's starting point was that their right to life was protected by Article 2, as well as by the same principle in English law, and Article 2 also imposed on the state the duty not to take life. However, to be an infringement of Article 2, there would have to be a positive act, resulting in death, and not simply a discontinuance of treatment. Only where the circumstances were such that there was a *positive obligation* on the state to preserve life would a failure to provide treatment amount to a breach of Article 2. Where a responsible clinical decision was made to withhold treatment because the continuation of treatment was not in the patient's best interests, the state's obligation under Article 2 was discharged. The Court also noted that it was accepted in legal systems across Europe, that there was no continuing obligation to provide treatment to those in a permanent vegetative state.

The other situation where the decision has to be taken for the patient is where the patient is a child, and too young to be asked. In such cases, the need to balance the rights of the various parties may be very acute. One case, which we referred to when

---

[4] *National Health Service Trust A v M* [2001] 2 WLR 942.

introducing the idea of balancing rights,[5] is the case of *A (Children) (Conjoined Twins: Surgical Separation)*.[6]

Jodie and Mary were conjoined twins, and the separation of them would lead to the death of Mary, because her lungs and heart were too deficient to oxygenate and pump blood through her body. Had Mary been born alone, she would have died shortly after birth; she remained alive because a common artery enabled Jodie who was stronger to circulate the blood for both of them. Separation would involve the cutting of the artery. The parents did *not* consent to the operation of separation; they had a parental desire to keep both children alive if possible, and a religious faith in the preservation of life. The doctors, on the other hand, were convinced that if they separated the girls they would save Jodie. Without the operation, Jodie would die in 3 to 6 months; and thereupon, of course, so would Mary. The doctors sought a declaration that the operation might lawfully be carried out; as well as the rights of the children and of the parents, the court also had to consider the rights of the doctors, to exercise their medical skill for the purpose of saving life and to know if, by doing so, they would be acting unlawfully, if they caused the death of Mary.

The Court of Appeal held that the operation would *not* be unlawful. The interests of Jodie had to be preferred to those of Mary, because as they were, neither of them could enjoy a proper or meaningful right to life, and Mary's life could not be saved by any operation. The situation was one where the doctors could act in defence of Jodie's life, and this justified the ending of Mary's life. It was also important that the purpose of the doctors here was to save Jodie: for there to be a violation of Article 2, there would have to be an intention to kill Mary, and that required a purpose to kill, which was not present here.

This case emphasises the overall importance of the right to life in such balancing exercises; it was all the more difficult here because there were two different persons, both of whose right to life was being threatened by the other. But, suppose the person who has the right to life expresses the desire to give up life, and to abandon that right?

AK,[7] a patient aged 19, suffered from motor neurone disease. He requested his doctors to discontinue, two weeks from the date when he should lose his ability to communicate, the artificial ventilation, nutrition, and hydration which was being provided to him. He was able to communicate solely by the movement of one eyelid, but this movement would shortly cease. In communicating his wish by this means to have the ventilator removed, he had been aware that such action would lead to his death. The doctors asked the court to make a declaration that it would be lawful to comply with his wishes.

The court held that it would be lawful to do as he wished, since a patient's refusal to consent to medical treatment had to be observed and complied with, where that patient was an adult of full capacity. It was *not* an *un*lawful termination of life to cease invasive treatment; rather it would be unlawful to treat a patient in the face of a wish *not* to be treated; and there would be no breach of Article 2.

But there is no right to die; this point was made in *Pretty*.[8] Mrs Pretty was suffering pain and degradation as a result of her illness, which was terminal, and she wished to die and to have her husband's assistance in bringing about her death. That would amount to an offence on his part,

---

[5] Above, p. 11.
[6] [2001] 2 WLR 480.
[7] *AK (adult patient) (Medical Treatment: Consent)* [2001] 1 FLR 129.
[8] *R (Pretty) v DPP* [2002] 1 AC 800, see also below, p. 120.

of assisting a suicide. So, Mrs Pretty asked the Director of Public Prosecutions to undertake not to prosecute her husband if he did assist her. The DPP refused to give that undertaking. Mrs Pretty sought judicial review of that refusal, and her argument was that the provisions of the Suicide Act 1961 were in breach of Article 2. The House of Lords held that the right to life could not be read as a right to die, or a right to enlist the help of another in bringing about one's own death. In short, there cannot be a simple abandonment of the right to life.

THE UNBORN CHILD

We have considered the state's duty to safeguard life, and how this applies to those who cannot take decisions for themselves. How does this apply to the unborn child, the foetus, and what rights does it have? The answer is that it has some rights, it must be considered, but it does not have the full right to life under Article 2: the Convention does not prohibit abortion.[9]

In the case of *Paton v UK*,[10] Mr Paton was married to a woman who was eight weeks' pregnant, and she announced that she intended to have an abortion. The Abortion Act 1967 permits termination of a pregnancy on the ground of risk to the life of the mother or injury to the physical or mental health of the mother, and Mrs Paton's doctors certified that there was this risk. The High Court refused to grant Mr Paton an injunction to prevent the abortion, and the abortion was carried out at 10 weeks. Mr Paton applied to the European Commission, asserting that the Abortion Act denied the right to life of the foetus, and thereby violated Article 2.

The Commission declared the application to be inadmissible, and rejected it. The Commission stated that the 'life' of the foetus is intimately connected with the life of the pregnant mother, and it cannot be regarded in isolation from that life. Particular regard was given to the fact that the termination was carried out at 10 weeks, and in order to save the mother, and the Commission concerned itself specifically with whether a right to life should be assumed for the initial stage of the pregnancy. The Commission recognised a wide divergence of opinion in different countries, as to whether the foetus has a right to life, but it did note that laws on abortion have tended towards liberalisation. The Commission considered that to regard a foetus at such a stage as having a right to life would prohibit all abortions, there being no express exception in the article, and this was not a general view across Europe. But the European Commission did not need to reach a decision on the principle of a right to life being protected by Article 2, at stages of pregnancy later than 10 weeks.

THE PROTECTION OF LIFE AT WORK

The examples of cases in the previous section are very graphic: death, or the risk of it, was already in prospect, in one way or another. But suppose that the risk is less obvious; or suppose the risk is caused by the citizen's own doing? In such a situation, the state nonetheless owes a duty to protect life. This may be because there has been a failure to impose a properly ordered system or to manage the situation properly. This comes across in the decision in *Barrett v UK*.[11]

---

[9] See also below, p. 194, in the context of Article 8.
[10] (1980) 19 DR 244.
[11] (1997) 23 EHRR CD 185.

Mr Barrett was a naval serviceman, serving at a naval base in Norway. In one evening in June 1988, he drank 10 units of alcohol in one bar on the base, and then went to another bar and drank a further 12 units and he died from alcoholic poisoning. His widow brought a claim before the European Commission, complaining that the control and supervision of the supply and consumption of alcohol at the base, and the care and attention the deceased received following his collapse, were inadequate and such as to endanger his life in breach of Article 2.

The Commission rejected her claim, but only on the basis that the facts did not support it; the Commission recognised that there is indeed a duty on the state in such circumstances:

> The Commission recognises that the excessive consumption of alcohol may pose a risk to life. Where a state provides facilities for drinking, in circumstances where there is an obvious and substantial risk of excessive consumption, the absence of any measure designed to discourage drinking to excess and, in the event, to secure adequate care and treatment, is likely to raise issues under Article 2 of the Convention.

The Commission found that there were in fact adequate measures in place – orders and regulations – so there was no breach by the state, although the staff had failed to enforce the standards which had been provided.

PRISONERS

Prisoners in jail are usually there because they have committed an offence. But even though they are responsible for their being in prison, that does not mean that they forfeit rights other than their liberty. The state still owes them a duty, just as much as to any other citizen, to ensure that their right to life is protected.

In the case of *Edwards v UK*,[12] Christopher Edwards was a prisoner, being held on remand in Chelmsford Prison, who had shown signs of developing serious mental illness. He was placed in a cell with another prisoner, RL, who had been diagnosed as suffering from schizophrenia or personality disorder. RL attacked Edwards and stamped and kicked him to death, and RL later pleaded guilty to manslaughter by reason of diminished responsibility. Edwards' parents claimed that there had been a violation of Article 2, so far as their son was concerned, in that there was a failure on the part of several agencies – the doctors, police, prosecution and court – to pass on information about RL to the prison authorities, and there had been an inadequate screening of RL when he first arrived at prison.

The European Court agreed. The various agencies were part of the state system, and they had a duty to safeguard the prisoner's life. The Court heard that an inquiry had been held which reported that there had been a systematic collapse of the mechanisms which should have protected vulnerable prisoners.

THE QUALITY OF LIFE

The duty of the state to protect life goes further than cases where literally life or death has been at stake; the ambit of Article 2 is more extensive than that. The right to life has been read as protecting a minimum **quality** of life. This is relevant to situations in which decisions are being taken, or something has happened, which threatens this quality, such as when planning decisions are taken, or where there is an incident of environmental pollution.

---

[12] (2002) 35 EHRR 487.

In the case of *LM & R v Switzerland*,[13] there was a complaint by people living in houses near a railway line. The basis of the complaint was that wagons containing nuclear waste were for a short time standing stationary on the lines nearby, and then were taken past the houses. The residents complained that they were at risk of contamination from nuclear radioactivy, with a consequent risk to health, so that there was a violation of Article 2. The European Commission's decision was that the situation could fall within Article 2, although in the circumstances, the state had taken all necessary precautions.

The decision is useful for the principle which it recognises: Article 2 is relevant to circumstances where health is at risk, and is not confined to cases of death or an immediate risk of death. Then, in the case of *Guerra v Italy*,[14] one of the judges gave a clear indication that Article 2 should apply to situations where the quality of the environment is in question.

Residents near a chemical factory complained of toxic fumes, which caused arsenic poisoning, and 150 people were taken to hospital; they complained of a violation of their rights under Article 2, as well as under Article 8 (respect for private and home life).[15]
The majority of the judges of the European Court did *not* find it necessary to deal with Article 2, having found a violation of Article 8. But a minority of the judges specifically filed opinions, indicating that they considered that a violation of Article 2 was also proved, since there were on the facts real and serious risks to life. Judge Jambek specifically said that it was time for the Court to start developing Article 2 in such a situation.

This last point is an express recognition that there are, within Article 2, aspects to the right to life which may be developed: the categories of protection are not closed.

THE DUTY TO REFRAIN FROM TAKING LIFE

This second duty of the state, to refrain from taking life, means that there must be a system of law to enforce this duty – a police force which prevents criminal acts causing risk to life, and which detects criminals, and a criminal justice system which provides for the trial and punishment of those who take life. Furthermore, where death has occurred as a result of force used by agents of the state, there is an especial requirement that there should be some form of official investigation into the circumstances of the death, and an investigation which is effective.

This duty to hold a proper investigation is important. The reason for insisting on it, in the European jurisprudence, was spelled out in the case of *McCann*,[16] which we quoted at the start of this chapter, and which we consider further below. The European Court said,

A general prohibition of arbitrary killing by the agents of the state would be ineffective, in practice, if there existed no procedure for reviewing the lawfulness of the use of lethal force

---

[13] (1996) 22 EHRR CD 130.
[14] (1998) 26 EHRR 357.
[15] The Court's view on Article 8 is considered below, p. 199.
[16] (1996) 21 EHRR 97.

by state authorities. The obligation to protect the right to life [taken with the state's duty to secure the Convention rights] requires by implication that there should be some form of effective official investigation when individuals have been killed as a result of the use of force by, *inter alia*, agents of the state.

In that case, the European Court found that the inquest proceedings, held in Gibraltar, had satisfied the requirement of an effective investigation. But this principle has now been applied in our law, and in some situations the result has been a fuller investigation than would have taken place prior to the Act. The following case sets out the high standard to be expected of an investigation or inquiry into a death in custody or involving a public authority.

In the case of *Manning*,[17] Mr Manning's brother, who had been remanded in police custody awaiting trial for an offence of violence, died of asphyxia while under restraint following an altercation with two officers. The death was investigated by the police and the papers were referred to the Crown Prosecution Service. At a coroner's inquest the evidence indicated that death had resulted from the manner in which one of the officers had held the deceased's head during the incident, and the jury returned a verdict of unlawful killing. A specialist case worker in the CPS undertook a detailed examination of all the available evidence, including that adduced at the inquest, and in his review note recorded his investigations. He considered a charge of the unlawful act of manslaughter, but concluded that it was only the fatal force to the deceased's neck which could be characterised as excessive, so that the only potential defendant was the officer identified as holding the head. He concluded that there was a prima facie case against that officer, but *no* realistic prospect of the prosecution being able to establish that excessive force had been used deliberately, rather than as the result of an attempt to effect proper restraint. His conclusion was that there should be no prosecution of the police officer.

The Court of Appeal held that there had been a violation of Article 2. It recognised that the right to life is the most fundamental of human rights, and that there is a duty on the state to investigate the death of a person in the state's custody, which resulted from violence inflicted by its agents. The first requirement of such an investigation was met, that the CPS should give reasons for not prosecuting the officer, which had been done. But those reasons failed to address all the specific matters, which the police officer would have to answer about the detailed circumstances of the struggle, to meet what would appear to be a strong case against him. That failure meant that the investigation had not been effective enough.

Another example is the case of *Edwards*,[18] which we have already considered, the case of a death in police custody caused by a fellow prisoner. As well as finding that the system of safeguards had failed to protect the prisoner's life, the European Court also considered that there had been no effective investigation. The other prisoner had been convicted, after which the inquest had been closed, and the prosecuting authorities considered there was insufficient evidence to bring a charge of manslaughter by gross negligence against any of the prison or medical authorities. An inquiry was held, commissioned by the Prison Authority, the County Council, and the Health Authority, from which the deceased prisoner's parents were excluded, except to give evidence; this was a private inquiry with no power to compel witnesses to attend. The European Court considered that these steps were inadequate to ensure an effective investigation.

---

[17] *R v DPP, ex parte Manning* [2001] QB 330.
[18] (2002) 35 EHRR 487.

One further example is another case about the investigation of a death arguably caused by a state authority. This is the case of *Wright*,[19] who was an inmate at Leeds Prison with a long history of serious asthma, and under treatment from the prison medical staff, who were arguably negligent during their treatment of him. Mr Wright suffered an asthma attack and told his cell mate that he needed a nebuliser, but although, after a delay, medical help arrived at the cell, Mr Wright died. An inquest was held, at which the prison service was represented; the family were not. No reference was made at the inquest to any shortcomings in the medical treatment of Mr Wright before the night of his death. The family later read a newspaper article stating that a doctor who had treated him in prison had been guilty of serious professional misconduct, and had been suspended. The family claimed that Mr Wright's treatment had been in breach of Article 2.

   The High Court found that the prison service had been negligent in their medical treatment of Mr Wright, and therefore were arguably in breach of Article 2. Further, the court found that there had not been an adequate official investigation into the death: the inquest did not meet this requirement, as the relevant witness was not called to give evidence, there was no consideration of the shortcomings of the medical treatment of Mr Wright, or of the doctor's disciplinary record, and the family was not represented. The Judge set out the requirements of an adequate investigation: the investigation must be independent, effective, reasonably prompt, having a sufficient element of public scrutiny, and the next of kin must be involved to an appropriate extent.

   This case is a good illustration of the width of the requirements of the Article 2 duty to conduct a full investigation. It is clear from these cases that the usual procedures prior to the Act coming into our law were not sufficient to discharge this duty.

THE USE OF FORCE

Article 2(2) provides limited exceptions to the duty to protect life. These are exhaustive:[20] they are the only situations where the taking of life by the agent or officer of a state is not a violation of Article 2. The situations are where the force is required for self-defence or defence of other persons (but not of property), to carry out an arrest or prevent escape, or to quash a riot or insurrection. Even in such a situation, the force used must be no more than is **absolutely necessary** and must be **strictly proportionate** to the situation. The actions taken must also be in accordance with national law; for example, laws such as those controlling the use of firearms must be properly applied.

   When ascertaining what is 'absolute necessity', there are two questions to be asked. The first is whether the use of force met the test of being strictly proportionate to one of the situations set out in Article 2(2), bearing in mind the danger of the situation. The second is whether the operation was planned and controlled by the authorities so as to minimise, to the greatest extent possible, the use of lethal force. This two-stage test was set out and considered by the European Court in the case of *McCann*,[21] from which we have quoted previously.

In *McCann*, the relatives of three people who were killed in Gibraltar by soldiers of the SAS claimed a violation of Article 2, arising out of their deaths. Information reached the authorities that a unit

---

[19] *R (on the application of Wright) v Secretary of State for the Home Department* [2001] UKHRR 1399; considered further below, p. 117, in the context of Article 3.
[20] *Stewart v UK* (1985) 7 EHRR 453.
[21] (1996) 21 EHRR 97.

of the Provisional IRA was planning a terrorist attack on Gibraltar, and three suspects were known to have entered Gibraltar. SAS soldiers were sent to assist the Gibraltar authorities to arrest the IRA active service unit. The SAS soldiers were faced with an active service unit of the IRA, composed of persons who had been convicted of bombing offences, and a known explosives expert. The soldiers shot the three suspects at very close range, believing that they were about to press remote control devices in order to detonate a bomb. The bodies were examined, and no remote device was found. The suspects' relatives alleged that the killings violated Article 2 of the Convention.

The European Court held that there had indeed been a violation of Article 2. The Court had to judge the actions not only of the soldiers themselves, but also those in charge of the whole operation; and stated the need to consider whether the force used by the soldiers was strictly proportionate to the aim of protecting persons against unlawful violence, and whether the whole operation was planned and controlled by the authorities so as to minimise recourse to lethal force.

The European Court accepted that the soldiers honestly believed in the light of the information which they had been given that it was necessary to shoot the suspects in order to prevent them from detonating a bomb and causing serious loss of life, and the action which they took was perceived by them as absolutely necessary in order to safeguard innocent lives. The actions of the soldiers themselves did not violate Article 2.

However, the Court did consider that there was a breach of Article 2 in the control and planning of the operation. First, there was no evidence about the training or instruction of the soldiers, especially as to whether they were trained to wound rather than kill; the Court expressly considered that a degree of caution in the use of firearms is to be expected from law enforcement personnel in a democratic society. The Court stated that the soldiers' reflex action suggested a lack of instruction, and a lack of care, on the part of the authorities, in the control and organisation of the operation. The authorities had failed in two further ways: they did not stop the suspects from entering Gibraltar; and they did not stop to consider whether the intelligence information, that the suspects had a remote controlled device, might be wrong, since it was this that led to the automatic recourse to lethal force. So the Court was *not* satisfied that the use of force was no more than was absolutely necessary, and therefore those in command had brought about a violation of Article 2(2).

THE DEATH PENALTY

Sixth Protocol:

Article 1: Abolition Of The Death Penalty
The death penalty shall be abolished. No one shall be condemned to such penalty or executed.

Article 2: Death Penalty In Time Of War
A State may make provision in its law for the death penalty in respect of acts committed in time of war or of imminent threat of war; such penalty shall be applied only in the instances laid down in the law and in accordance with its provisions.

Article 3: Prohibition Of Derogation
No derogation from the provisions of this Protocol shall be made under Article 15 of the Convention.

Article 2, as drafted, allows for capital punishment, the death penalty, although it is careful to limit this to the execution of the sentence of a court following conviction for a crime for which this penalty is provided by law. This includes the core Convention values of legality, that there should be a proper trial, and conviction, with the penalty provided by law. However, in the United Kingdom, this has been largely academic, since the death penalty for most offences, most notably murder, was abolished in 1965.[22] It was abolished for treason and piracy in 1998.[23] Following this, the Sixth Protocol was signed by the United Kingdom on 27 January 1999, after a free vote in Parliament. The Minister of State for the Home Office, Lord Williams of Mostyn QC, said that ratification made it impossible for Parliament to reintroduce the death penalty in the future, without denouncing the whole of the Convention.[24]

It is notable that there can be no derogation[25] from Article 1 of the Sixth Protocol: even in times of emergency, states are not allowed to suspend this Article and reintroduce the death penalty. The only exception is that in Article 2 of this Protocol, acts committed in time of war or of imminent threat of war; and even here, the penalty shall only be applied where the law specifies it. This provision would not justify the infliction of a death penalty unless it was prescribed and followed a fair trial. The United Kingdom has not signed the Twelfth Protocol, which outlaws the death penalty in all circumstances.

There will be a breach of Article 1 of the Sixth Protocol where an individual is deported or extradited from the United Kingdom to a country where they are likely to suffer the death penalty.[26] This is clear from the case of *Aylor-Davis v France*.[27]

Joy Aylor-Davis was arrested in France, having false identification papers; it then appeared that she was wanted for murder in Texas, and the United States sought her extradition. She opposed the application, contending that she would suffer the death penalty, if she were to be found guilty in Texas.

France had already abolished the death penalty, and had ratified the Sixth Protocol. The American authorities gave an assurance to the French authorities that if she were to be found guilty, the death penalty would not be carried out. The French courts accepted this, and ordered her extradition. She complained to the European Commission that the extradition was a breach of the Protocol.

The Commission agreed that if indeed there had been a likelihood of her suffering the death penalty, the extradition would have been a violation; but on the facts, there was no such violation, because the French authorities were entitled to accept the assurance.

QUESTIONS

1   Consider the situations of medical treatment, where the courts are being asked whether or not treatment should be continued. Do you think the courts are ever right to allow treatment to be withdrawn? Do you agree or not that the patient's wishes are paramount? Do you think that the law should recognise a right to die?

2   Do you agree with the abolition of the death penalty? If so, do you think that the United Kingdom should sign up to the Twelfth Protocol, or do you agree that it may be justified in times of war?

---

[22] Murder (Abolition of Death Penalty) Act 1965.
[23] Prevention of Crime and Disorder Act 1998 section 36.
[24] *Hansard*, HL Vol. 593, col. 2084; section 21(5) of the Act also implements this decision.
[25] Derogations are explained above, p. 85.
[26] Deportations may also risk breaching Article 3, considered below, p. 121.
[27] Application no. 22742/93.

Kane descend whack gosh oo gosh oo gosh.

'Kane descend whack gosh oo gosh oo gosh': corporal punishment in schools is considered below, p. 115.

(*Source:* Copyright Ronald Searle, 1956 from *Molesworth*, by Geoffery Willans and Ronald Searle by kind permission of the artist and The Sayle Literary Agency.)

Chapter 9

FREEDOM FROM TORTURE

'Is not the pleasure of feeling and exhibiting power over other beings, a principal part of the gratification of cruelty?' (John Foster, *Life and Correspondence*, 1846)

ARTICLE 3: PROHIBITION OF TORTURE
No one shall be subjected to torture or to inhuman or degrading treatment or punishment.

THE IMPORTANCE OF ARTICLE 3

Article 3 makes no provision for exceptions and no derogation from it is permissible under Article 15 in time of war or other national emergency. This absolute prohibition on torture and on inhuman or degrading treatment or punishment under the terms of the Convention shows that Article 3 enshrines one of the fundamental values of the democratic societies making up the Council of Europe. (European Court in *Soering v UK*[1])

In resounding phrases, the European judges have declared the principles of this article. It embodies a fundamental right because the right to freedom from bodily harm is second only to the right to life, based on the right which all people have to be respected as human beings. In particular, once a person has been taken into custody by the state, or is otherwise in the power, or under the control, of the state and its officials, they should be safe from the infliction of deliberate physical harm. Patients in hospital, prisoners in jail, and pupils in a school are all examples of persons in such a position, where they are under the direction of others, and the treatment applied to them – using the word in its broadest sense – engages this article, since physical mistreatment by the state machinery is something which is *never* to be tolerated in a civilised society. Likewise, the rights set out in Article 3 are so important that, as with the right to life, the state effectively has a duty to safeguard them, to protect its citizens from any foreseeable risk of such harm occurring.

That is why the rights embodied by this article may not be infringed by a state, no matter what the justification, and no matter what threat the state may be acting against. In the case of *Chahal*,[2] who was a Sikh separatist leader who was refused asylum, on the ground that he was a terrorist, and was therefore facing deportation to India from the United Kingdom, the European Court said,

---

[1] (1989) 11 EHRR 439.
[2] *Chahal v UK* (1997) 23 EHRR 413.

Article 3 enshrines one of the most fundamental values of democratic society. The Court is well aware of the immense difficulties faced by a state in modern times in protecting their communities from terrorist violence. However, even in these circumstances, the Convention prohibits in absolute terms torture or inhuman or degrading treatment or punishment irrespective of the victim's conduct.

Finally, emphasising the importance of this article, there is the principle that ignorance is no excuse; the state cannot plead that it was unaware of the facts. This was made clear in the case of *Ireland v United Kingdom*,[3] in which the government of the Republic of Ireland complained that the British government had used ill-treatment in the course of the interrogation of prisoners detained under the prevention of terrorism powers. The Court said,

> It is inconceivable that the higher authorities of a State should be, or at least should be entitled to be, unaware of the existence of such a practice. Furthermore, under the Convention those authorities are strictly liable for the conduct of their subordinates; they are under a duty to impose their will on subordinates and cannot shelter behind their inability to ensure that it is respected.

But what difference will Article 3 make to our law? Torture is already an offence in the criminal law, and so are ill treatment and assault, and one would think that those offences would cover the same situation as the words 'inhuman or degrading treatment or punishment'. The answer is that Article 3 covers situations which are not necessarily criminal, and which often have nothing to do with crime. There was no crime being committed against Mr Chahal, who was facing deportation to a place where he might face persecution. And there was no crime being committed against Ms Price, a case which we shall examine later, who had her rights infringed where she was sentenced to 7 days' imprisonment, but, notwithstanding that she was disabled with four-limb deficiency and kidney problems, was kept in police and prison cells which were wholly unsuitable for her physical requirements. But even where there is no crime being committed, Article 3 applies a general minimum standard for the treatment of people by the state, especially in these kinds of situations where the state is in a dominant position.

THE SCOPE OF THE ARTICLE

Article 3 deals with three separate categories of treatment which are prohibited: **torture;** punishment or treatment which is **inhuman;** and punishment or treatment which is **degrading.** One case in which the European Court has considered the definition of all of these was *Ireland v United Kingdom*.[4] This was a case in which the Court had to consider the conduct of security forces in Northern Ireland when interrogating prisoners and it arose out of the exercise by the British government of powers of arrest, detention, and internment.

From 9 August 1971 onwards, numerous people in Northern Ireland were arrested and taken into custody by security forces, acting under emergency powers. Those arrested were interrogated,

---

[3] (1980) 2 EHRR 25.
[4] Ibid.

usually by members of the Royal Ulster Constabulary, in order to determine whether they should be interned, and also to compile information about the IRA. The interrogation took the form of 'interrogation in depth'. The methods used were described as 'disorientation', or 'sensory deprivation' techniques; and the interrogation led to the obtaining of a considerable quantity of intelligence information. These techniques gave rise to allegations of ill treatment, and this was the substance of the complaint by the Irish government before the European Court. There were five particular methods: wall-standing, where for long periods, the detainee was made to stand legs spread apart, on the toes, with fingers high above the head against the wall, and the weight mainly on the fingers; being hooded, with a bag over the head; being subjected to a continuous and loud hissing noise; being deprived of sleep; and being deprived of food and drink.

The European Court examined the three categories of treatment set out in Article 3, and gave the following definitions. 'Torture' the Court defined as an aggravated and deliberate form of cruel, inhuman or degrading treatment or punishment. Ill treatment, the Court held, must attain a minimum level of severity if it is to fall within the scope of Article 3. The assessment of this minimum is in the nature of things relative; it depends on all the circumstances of the case, such as the duration of the treatment, its physical or mental effects and in some cases the sex, age, and state of health of the victim.

In the *Ireland v UK* case itself, the Court held that the techniques did *not*, in the particular circumstances of the case, have the particular intensity and cruelty which the word 'torture' implied. However, the five techniques were applied in combination with premeditation and for several hours at a stretch; they caused, if not actual bodily injury, at least intense physical and mental suffering to the persons subjected thereto and also led to acute psychiatric disturbances during interrogation. They accordingly fell into the category of inhuman treatment within the meaning of Article 3. The Court also said that the techniques were 'degrading', since they were such as to arouse in their victims feelings of fear, anguish, and inferiority, capable of humiliating and debasing the prisoners, and possibly breaking their physical or moral resistance.

It really is a matter of judgement on the facts of a particular situation whether the victim's suffering amounts to a violation of Article 3. As the court said in the *Ireland* case, the treatment of the victim must attain a minimum level of severity before it can be said that there has been a violation. Some cases will be more obvious than others. Our discussion will focus not so much on a consideration of the detail of where torture has been established and where it has not, but on distinct types of situations where Article 3 has been commonly raised. And the sort of situations where Article 3 can apply are indeed surprisingly common.

VIOLENCE AND THE THREAT OF IT

This is almost too obvious, it might be said. Violence, if it is serious, is at least a candidate to qualify as torture, or inhuman or degrading treatment. Furthermore, violence will usually amount to a criminal offence, and so will be likely to be dealt with in the criminal courts, and in that event what is the point of bringing it within the Convention jurisprudence? One particular case provides a good example of where the threat of extreme violence risked a violation of Article 3, and where the English court was able to provide protection for the potential victims. The case is one we have already referred to in the context of Article 2, that of *Thompson and Venables*,[5] in which the two applicants, both young men aged 18, claimed that they could suffer death or serious injury if they were identified.

Thompson and Venables had been convicted of a particular shocking murder, that of the 2-year-old James Bulger. The judge made an order forbidding publication of material which might identify them, and the newspapers sought to have this removed; Thompson and Venables claimed that the order was necessary for their protection. The court heard evidence of serious threats made against them and found that there was a real and serious risk of death or serious injury to the two young men, and therefore there was a risk of violations of Article 3, as well as Article 2. The judgment does not distinguish between the threats under each Article, but it is clear that, if the threats were carried out, if death did not result, very serious harm qualifying as torture, or inhuman or degrading treatment might well do. Thus, the order restraining publication was continued, even though that would interfere with the rights of expression of the newspapers under Article 10.

For the purposes of the present discussion, this emphasises that, where there is a risk of serious physical harm, and the state is in a position to do something about it, Article 3 will be engaged. It will then be for the state to ensure that it does all it can to prevent the harm. In this case, this meant that the court ordered that the relevant information should not be disclosed.

SENTENCING OF CRIMINALS

After a person has been convicted of a crime, they will be sentenced, which may involve the payment of a fine, or some form of community service order, or a prison sentence. The question in the context of Article 3 is whether a sentence can be so excessive that it can amount to an inhuman or degrading punishment.

In our legal system, the sentence imposed in any particular case is based on guidelines developed by the Court of Appeal. Save where the sentence is mandatory – such as life imprisonment for murder – a judge has a discretion as to the type and length of sentence, but if a judge imposes a sentence which is outside the guidelines, or is excessive in the circumstances of the case, the sentence is likely to be reduced by the Court of Appeal.

In all these circumstances, if a judge passes a sentence which is so excessive as to be inhuman or degrading, it is likely anyway to be reduced by the Court of Appeal, as being outside the guidelines, or excessive on the facts. So, in most cases, it will not be necessary to rely on the Convention. But the European Court has had occasion to consider a sentence imposed by an English court in this context in the case of *Weeks v UK*.[6]

Mr Weeks, at the age of 17, entered a pet shop with a starting pistol loaded with blank cartridges, pointed it at the owner and told her to hand over the till. He got 35 pence, which he dropped on the shop floor. Later, he telephoned the police station, to say he would give himself up. Two police

---

[5] *Thompson and Venables v News Group Newspapers* [2001] 2 WLR 1038; above, p. 100; see also below, p. 187 in the context of Article 8.
[6] (1988) 10 EHRR 293.

officers met him in the street, and as they arrested him he took the pistol from his pocket, and in a struggle two blanks were fired, and one officer suffered powder burns to his wrist. He committed the robbery because he owed his mother £3, who had that day told him to find other lodgings. He was convicted of robbery. There was no evidence of mental instability; a probation officer said he was subject to mood fluctuations and was immature; he had an interest in literature of violence and a fascination with guns. A psychiatric report had not been obtained. The trial judge said that the defendant was very dangerous, and that he should be detained indefinitely, and sentenced him to life imprisonment. The Court of Appeal said that life imprisonment was imposed in mercy to the defendant, as he might be released much sooner than if a longer term had been imposed.

The European Court considered Article 3, and stated that having regard to Weeks' age at the time and to the particular facts of the offence he committed, had it not been for the specific reasons advanced for the sentence, one could have serious doubts as to its compatibility with Article 3, as a case of inhuman punishment.

CORPORAL PUNISHMENT

Corporal punishment is no longer allowed in schools,[7] and in the United Kingdom is no longer practised as a punishment for criminals. However, the cases on it still have some relevance for the meaning of what amounts to inhuman or degrading treatment. This is because the European Court has accepted the principle that corporal punishment may be permissible, including in schools, but punishment must not reach the level of being inhuman or degrading. And it will be a matter of taking the particular circumstances of each case and judging whether that level has been reached. This is demonstrated by the case of *Costello-Roberts v UK*[8] where on the facts of the case it was held that there was no violation.

A 7-year-old boy at an independent school received corporal punishment from the headmaster for breaches of the school rules; he had been there only five weeks, he had collected demerit marks, for minor offences, which 'totted up' under the school rules meant that he would be punished; he was told he would get the slipper, and then had to wait three days before the execution of it; he was given three whacks of the slipper on his clothed buttocks.

The European Court reviewed the circumstances: his age, how new he was to the school, the 'totting up' procedure, the three-day wait, and then the humiliation, and the impersonal and automatic way in which the punishment had been administered. Nonetheless, the Court held that in the circumstances of this case it did *not* reach the level of being degrading. In order for punishment to be degrading and in breach of Article 3, the humiliation or debasement involved must attain a particular level of severity, and must in any event be other than that *usual* element of humiliation inherent in any punishment. The Court considered that the reference in Article 3 to the express prohibition of 'inhuman' and 'degrading' punishment, implied a distinction between such punishment and punishment more generally.

This case therefore stands for the proposition that there was no violation simply in administering a punishment. The question of *what* level of violence is permissible before it will be characterised as 'inhuman' or 'degrading' will depend on the precise facts of the case. But looking at *Costello-Roberts*, one might think that the European Court

---

[7] Discussed in the context of Article 9, pp. 209–10.
[8] (1995) 19 EHRR 112; also considered in the context of Article 8, below, p. 189.

requires a high level of severity before the level is reached. One case where the European Court found that the level was attained, where there were particularly unpleasant circumstances, was *Tyrer v UK*.[9]

Mr Tyrer, aged 15, had been sentenced to three strokes of the birch for an assault occasioning actual bodily harm. He had to wait several weeks after the announcement of the sentence. On the day, he had to wait several hours at the police station before it was done. The birching was carried out at the police station, by a police officer, by striking him on his bare backside. Two police officers held him as he bent over a table. The birch rod broke on the first stroke, but the birching continued. His father lost his self-control and tried to attack a police officer, having to be restrained.

The European Court held that this was a violation of Article 3; it was a punishment which was degrading: there was an assault on the boy's dignity and physical integrity: he had to endure the mental anguish of anticipating the violence in the three-week interval, and he had the indignity of the punishment inflicted on the bare posterior; that aggravated the degrading character of the sentence. The Court said that the institutionalised character of the violence was further compounded by the 'aura of official procedure attending the punishment' and by the fact that those inflicting it were total strangers to the offender.

TREATMENT OF PRISONERS

When one person inflicts unlawful or unreasonable violence on another, that is an assault. And most fair-minded people would add this: it makes it worse if the assailant is a custodian and the victim is his prisoner. The one is at the mercy of the other. The European Court has applied this in the approach it takes in Article 3 cases. In principle, such an assault is likely to be inhuman or degrading treatment or punishment. The European Court said this in the case of *Ribitsch v Austria*.[10]

Mr Ribitsch was a prisoner in a police station, and while in custody he was subjected to violence at the hands of police officers. The Court found that he had been treated in such a way that his rights under Article 3 had been breached.

The Court said that any violence to a prisoner is 'in principle' a violation of Article 3. The precise words of the Court are interesting: 'In respect of a person deprived of his liberty, any recourse to physical violence, which has not been made strictly necessary by his own conduct, diminishes human dignity and is in principle an infringement of the right set forth in Article 3 of the Convention. [The Court] reiterates that the requirements of an investigation and the undeniable difficulties inherent in the fight against crime cannot justify placing limits on the protection to be afforded in respect of the physical integrity of individuals.'

In other words, although crime may be prevalent, and although the particular criminal investigation may require an urgent answer, these considerations will not justify violence to a prisoner, however inconvenient it may be that they must be treated properly in accordance with their rights. The courts have developed this approach, of protecting the rights of prisoners, and the cases have gone beyond the standard set out in the *Ribitsch* case of simply forbidding violence. Living conditions, health and comfort are now assessed, and Article 3 is a touchstone of prisoners' rights in all these areas.

---

[9] (1980) 2 EHRR 1.
[10] (1995) 21 EHRR 573.

For example, in the case of *Napier*,[11] the ordinary standard of prison life was challenged. Mr Napier, a prisoner aged 21, was on remand in Barlinnie Prison, Glasgow; his cell was grossly inadequate in living space, lighting, and ventilation, particularly as he shared it with another prisoner; the sanitary arrangements consisted of slopping out, which is urinating and defecating into a vessel in the cell, which had to be emptied two or three times a day; the two prisoners were confined to the cell for excessive lengths of time; and the conditions exacerbated Napier's eczema. The government admitted that the conditions amounted to a violation of Article 3, but contended that it was impracticable to change it, as that would mean altering the conditions for every prisoner. But the Court of Session decided that Napier was entitled to have his case determined on its own merits, and the broader consequences of treating every prisoner in a similar way did not alter the balance in his favour.

This case is authority for several important propositions: first, Article 3 extends to simple living conditions; second, once a violation is proved, inconvenience and cost are irrelevant; and third, normal prison practices are called into question, something which could not have been done without reliance on Article 3 and the Act.

Whatever debate there is about the benefit of sending someone to prison – not a debate we can pursue here – there is no doubt that prison is intended by the state as a punishment. Nonetheless, that punishment must take account of the prisoner's individual weakness, and the prison authorities must consider, monitor, and balance the effect of the prison system on the health of the prisoner, including the effect on him of punishment within the system. That is the effect of the case of *Keenan v UK*.[12]

Mr Keenan was a prisoner serving a short prison sentence; he had mental health problems, and was known to be a suicide risk. He attacked a prison officer, and after a delay of two weeks, he was brought before a prison adjudication board, and an extra 28 days' custody was imposed, 7 days of it to be in solitary confinement. There was no possibility of appeal or review. This extra sentence was imposed 9 days before he was due to be finally released from prison. On the day after the adjudication, he committed suicide.

The European Court found that there had been inadequate monitoring of his mental condition. Further, the combination and timing of the new punishment was to be regarded as inhuman; his physical and moral resistance was threatened, and the way he was treated was not compatible with what was required for a mentally ill person. The whole way in which he was treated amounted to inhuman and degrading treatment.

Again, this is an important case. It is a signal to state authorities that there has to be a close degree of care and control in the administration of institutions such as prisons; the key, after *Keenan,* will be care for the individual. And, following *Napier,* cost and inconvenience will not be an excuse for a failure to meet this standard. The next case is one where there was a failure to monitor the individual prisoner, and also a failure to provide a proper system for ensuring the appropriate treatment of prisoners. The case is *Wright.*[13]

---

[11] *Napier v The Scottish Ministers* [2002] UKHRR 308.
[12] (2001) 33 EHRR 38.
[13] *R (on the application of Wright) v Secretary of State for the Home Department* [2001] UKHRR 1399, also see in the context of Article 2 above, p. 107.

Paul Wright was an inmate in Leeds Prison, with a long history of serious asthma. He had been treated for several months by the prison medical service; but the drug prescription and administration had been seriously deficient, so that his lung function deteriorated. His condition was not properly monitored, and he was given inappropriate medication. By November 1996, because of negligent medical treatment, he was exposed to the risk of a severe asthmatic attack. On the night of 7 November, he was locked in his cell with inadequate medication and inadequate apparatus. No key was available nearby for the purpose of unlocking the cell rapidly. He suffered an asthmatic attack; he told his cell mate that he needed a nebuliser. After a delay, medical help arrived at the cell, but Mr Wright died. The judge held that there were arguably breaches of both Articles 2 and 3: the medical treatment had been negligent; in the minutes leading up to his death he must have endured considerable pain and suffering; and to leave a sick man locked in his cell and exposed to the risk of such pain and suffering may arguably be characterised as inhuman treatment.

On the one hand, it may be said that these cases impose a high burden on the state authorities, because so much attention must be paid to individual ill health or disabilities. On the other, the punishment to which the courts sentence the prisoner is imprisonment, not to imprisonment with risk to life or health. Furthermore, it would be quite wrong not to deal appropriately with people who have some sort of disability: prison is a punishment, but it should not provide more of a danger to people with more particular needs than other prisoners. The next case, that of *Price*,[14] aptly illustrates this. Ms Price was disabled, and was sent to prison; but the premises provided for her custody were quite unsuitable; and the Convention was engaged.

Ms Price, a four-limb-deficient thalidomide victim with numerous health problems including defective kidneys, was committed for contempt of court in civil proceedings, and she was ordered by a judge to be detained for 7 days; she was in fact detained for only 3 nights. In police cells, she had to sleep in her wheelchair, and she could not use the toilet as it was too high; every half-hour she complained of cold, and a doctor who came recorded that the cell was cold and not adapted for her. She could not wash. When she was in prison, the nurse was unable to lift her on to the toilet, and she was obliged to submit to male officers doing so. She had become dangerously cold; there was retention of urine, and she had to be catheterised.

The European Court found that there was a violation here of Article 3. To detain a severely disabled person in these conditions − so cold that it is a danger, risk of sores when the bed is hard or inaccessible, undignified toileting, and no washing − constitutes degrading treatment. The Court also considered *intention* in the context of Article 3, that is, the intention of the person imposing the treatment or punishment. The Court stated that in considering whether treatment is degrading, one of the factors which the court will take into account is the question whether the *object* of the treatment was to humiliate and debase the person. However, there is no requirement for such a purpose, and even when it is absent there may be a finding that a violation has occurred.

There is an important point here, that, for there to be a breach of Article 3, there is no need to prove that there is an *intention* to inflict inhuman or degrading treatment. In *Price* itself, there was no evidence of any positive intention to humiliate or debase the applicant. Nonetheless, since that was the effect of the treatment that she suffered, there was an infringement of Article 3. The *Price* case also illustrates the kind of

---

[14] *Price v UK* (2002) 34 EHRR 53.

situation which may well develop with people with particular physical needs or disabilities. The state authorities must give consideration to the kind of facilities which are required for such situations. The fact that someone can be justifiably restrained or imprisoned does not mean that they can be kept in grossly unsuitable conditions.

ILL TREATMENT OF CHILDREN

Just as the authorities must provide for the prisoner who has a medical condition, especially a condition which may be exacerbated by the regime of prison and its discipline, so they must take account of the youthfulness of a prisoner. The European Court stated thus in the next case, but held that on the particular facts there was no violation of Article 3. The case is *MM v UK*.[15]

M was a juvenile, aged 12, arrested by police in Northern Ireland, on suspicion of car theft and criminal damage. At 5 p.m. he was taken to a police station and interviewed; his solicitor warned that he might do harm to himself, and advised against detaining him overnight; however, he was detained. At midnight he was charged; at 1 a.m., he was taken to a juvenile centre about 72 km away. At 2.30 a.m., he arrived, and was placed in a cell with no furnishings and no floor covering. At 10.30, he was taken to the magistrates' court, and released on bail. The Commission held that the detaining of a child of 12 for eight hours in such a hostile and intimidating environment was cause for concern, but the treatment was *not* sufficiently severe to raise an issue under Article 3.

It is a matter of judgement and impression whether there has been a violation, and the point of this case is that the tenderness of infancy must be a real factor in finding whether there has been inhuman or degrading treatment.

But Article 3 has a wider application than simply the custody of children. In general terms our law has a great deal of protection for the rights of children. There is a range of legislative provisions which provide a child with rights to be cared for or looked after, and in all such cases, the interest of the child is of paramount importance. In such cases, Article 3 adds an extra ground to be considered in making sure that a child's rights are fully protected, and in some cases, an extra remedy.

In the case of *Z v UK*,[16] the European Court had to consider the case of children who had been ill treated by their families. Z and his three siblings had been subjected to severe long-term neglect and abuse, and had sued the relevant local authority for failing in its statutory duty to safeguard them; the House of Lords had rejected the claim. Z complained that the authorities had violated Article 3. The behaviour of the family had been reported to social services on several occasions, yet they had only acted five years after the first complaint, when the children were placed in emergency care at the insistence of their mother.

The European Court held that the social services system had failed to protect the children. While the role of social services was a difficult one, the state had clearly failed in its positive obligation to protect the children from ill treatment of which it had, or ought to have had, knowledge. There was a breach of Article 3.

---

[15] (2002) 8 January, Application 58374/00.
[16] (2002) 34 EHRR 3.

Again, this is an example where the state should be protecting those who cannot protect themselves from mistreatment. The European Court found that the English system for doing so had failed, and therefore the law should have provided a remedy for the children for the invasion of their dignity and integrity.

MEDICAL TREATMENT

What now follows is not a collection of cases where doctors have caused pain or prescribed inhuman treatment. The point here is that sometimes the best treatment and the most skilful surgery may be so harsh that the patient can justifiably say that he or she should not suffer it, and should do without it, even if that brings about death. We see this in the case of *National Health Service Trust v D*.[17]

Here a 19-month-old child was in a poor state of health, with an irreversible and worsening lung disease, which meant a very short expectation of life. The NHS Trust applied to the court for a declaration regarding the future: it was that in the event of future cardiac or respiratory failure, the doctors would be entitled to treat the child *without* resuscitation by artificial ventilation, but *with* full palliative care, allowing the child to die peacefully and with dignity. The doctors asked for the declaration, because a decision might have to be taken as a matter of urgency. The parents opposed the doctors' application, as being premature.

The court granted the declaration, stating that the full palliative treatment, but without artificial ventilation, was in the best interests of the child; and his interests must be considered above all other views, even those of the parents, when deciding whether medical treatment should be given or withheld. The body of medical opinion was of the clear view that artificial ventilation would be an intrusive and painful process, and would not offer any lasting benefit. Provided that the suggested form of care was in the best interests of the child, such a decision could not be said to be in contravention of Article 3, or the Article 2 right to life either. Even though the avoiding of invasive and hurtful treatment would or might lead to death, if this course was in the best interest of the child, that would *not* amount to inhuman treatment.

But it is deceptively easy to say that the court will simply try to avoid imposing degrading treatment. That argument was advanced in the case of *Pretty*,[18] which we have already considered in the context of Article 2, since Mrs Pretty's primary argument was that she had the right to die.

Mrs Pretty was suffering pain and degradation as a result of a terminal illness, and she sought an assurance from the Director of Public Prosecutions that her husband would not be prosecuted for assisting her suicide, which the DPP refused to give.

In deciding that the DPP was entitled not to give such an assurance, the House of Lords examined the relation of Article 2 to Article 3, and stated that in some circumstances the state might be justified, in order to maintain the right to life, in imposing treatment which might be so invasive that it would otherwise be in breach of Article 3. But the House disposed of the Article 3 argument in this case, by pointing out that it was not the DPP's decision which was causing the pain and degradation, but her own illness.

---

[17] (2000) 2 FCR 577.
[18] *R (Pretty) v DPP* [2002] 1 AC 800; above, p. 162.

Thus, the failure of Mrs Pretty's argument was not a failing in her legal rights or a decision of the court that she should be obliged to undergo pain, but because it was her illness that was causing the pain, not the treatment she was being given or anything done or decided by anybody.

DEPORTATION OF IMMIGRANTS

The Act, of course, extends only to the United Kingdom; it does not extend to other nations, or to public authorities of other countries, nor does it bind them. So what is the position when a person is being sent to another country, outside the jurisdiction of our courts, and out of the safety of the Convention? Suppose it is obvious that this person will, in that country, suffer torture, or inhuman or degrading treatment or punishment, whether at the hands of that state's officers, or from some other person?

The answer is that it will be a breach of Article 3 for the United Kingdom authority to send the person there. And this is illustrated in the case of *Soering v UK*,[19] quoted at the start of this chapter.

Mr Soering was the subject of a decision by the Home Secretary to extradite him to the United States to face trial in Virginia on a charge of capital murder; if he were to be convicted, and sentenced to death, he would be exposed to the so-called 'death row phenomenon'. He could expect to spend six to eight years in a stringent custodial regime, with likely attacks by fellow prisoners, and with the 'ever present and mounting anguish of awaiting execution of the death penalty'. Further, at the time of the killing, he was 18 years of age, and of a mental state which impaired his responsibility for his acts. He complained that to extradite him in these circumstances amounted to a violation, on the part of the government of the United Kingdom, of Article 3.

The European Court agreed, and stated, referring to the appeal procedures in the USA,

However well intentioned and even potentially beneficial is the provision of a complex of post sentence procedures, the consequence is that the condemned prisoner has to endure for many years the conditions on death row, and the anguish and mounting tension of living in the ever present shadow of death.

In other words, however fair and careful were the legal procedures in favour of the accused, if the treatment was inhuman or degrading within the meaning of Article 3, there would be a violation of the article to release the person to such treatment.

The inhuman or degrading treatment may come about because the standard of life in the destination country is inferior to the standard of life in the United Kingdom. The point is that the change of standard of life may be so great, *for the particular individual*, that it bears upon him with inhumanity or degradation. And this is particularly so where a medical condition or medical treatment is at the heart of the change. We see this in the case of *D v UK*.[20]

D, who came from St Kitts, arrived at Gatwick Airport in possession of prohibited drugs. He was refused leave to enter the country, and he was subsequently convicted of a drug offence, and imprisoned. While in prison he was diagnosed as suffering from AIDS, and he was treated for this. After serving a term of imprisonment, and when he was due to be released on licence, the immigration

---

[19] (1989) 11 EHRR 439.
[20] (1997) 24 EHRR 423.

authorities gave directions for his removal to St Kitts. D requested leave to remain in the United Kingdom, claiming that his removal would entail the loss of vital medical treatment, and his life would be shortened. His request was refused. He complained to the European Court that to deport him in these circumstances would be in breach of Article 3.

The European Court took account of the fact that he was receiving sophisticated treatment, and the Court was satisfied that the abrupt withdrawal of this would bring about the most dramatic consequences for him, and that his removal to St Kitts would hasten his death. It was held that to deport him would mean a violation of Article 3. But the Court noted that in principle, aliens who serve their prison sentences and are then subject to expulsion cannot claim to remain in the territory of the expelling state in order to continue getting benefit from medical, social or other assistance. There were in this case exceptional and compelling humanitarian considerations to conclude that the removal would involve a violation of Article 3.

SEXUAL DISCRIMINATION AND HARASSMENT

Will the courts hold that sexual discrimination or harassment is capable of amounting to a violation of Article 3? Probably, if the humiliation and indignity suffered by the victim is sufficiently intense. This is important. Public authorities may have procedures which pose intrusive questions; or the state may fail to recognise sexual orientation. A case in the European Court illustrates the relevant principles in this field. It is an example of both discrimination and harassment.

Smith and Grady v UK[21] involved two separate cases where Ms Smith and Mr Grady were discharged from the armed forces for being homosexual. Prior to their discharge, the investigation into their private lives, by service police, was of an exceptionally intrusive character. As soon as the matter was in the hands of the police, Mr Grady was obliged to leave his wife and children in the USA and return to the United Kingdom; in his absence, detailed and intrusive interviews about his private life were held with his wife, a colleague, and others. His accommodation was searched. He was later interviewed, as were Ms Smith and her partner. At the interviews of Ms Smith and Mr Grady, they were each asked detailed questions of an intimate character about their particular sexual practices and preferences; they were asked about their habits, their friends, and in the case of Ms Smith about her relationship with her own foster-daughter. They were each discharged, pursuant to a Ministry of Defence policy of excluding homosexuals from the armed forces. Their discharge had a profound effect on their careers and prospects.

The European Court considered that the investigation, and discharge, together with the Ministry blanket policy, were of a particularly grave nature. And the Court accepted that the kind of treatment experienced by Ms Smith and Mr Grady, grounded on a bias of a heterosexual majority against a homosexual minority, could *in principle* fall within the scope of Article 3. But on the facts, the Court held that there was *no* breach. In short, the actual experience of Ms Smith and Mr Grady did not reach the level of degradation required by the jurisprudence of the Convention. However, the case does demonstrate how intrusion into privacy may amount to inhuman or degrading treatment.

PURSUING A CLAIM UNDER ARTICLE 3

'Fundamental' – that is how the courts regard the right under Article 3. And therefore the state must not obstruct a citizen who claims that a violation has occurred; and indeed

---

[21] (2000) 29 EHRR 493.

the state has an obligation to ensure that an effective investigation takes place. This is confirmed by the case of *Green*.[22]

Mr Green was knocked off his bicycle by an unmarked car in April 1999; the car was driven by a detective sergeant; Mr Green got up, but claimed that he was knocked down again; he sustained severe injuries and he made a claim against the police officer, and this was referred to the Police Complaints Authority (PCA), which investigated the complaints in order to consider the criminal and disciplinary aspects. Mr Green sought disclosure of material from the PCA, which refused to provide it.

The Court of Appeal approved the principle that if there is a situation where there may have been a breach of Article 3, the state has an obligation to ensure that an independent and effective investigation is held. This did not, however, go as far as to entitle a complainant, such as Mr. Green, to see the full details of the evidence before the PCA. A complainant's interests were sufficiently safeguarded by his rights to contribute evidence, to be kept informed of the progress of the investigation and to see the reasoned decision at the end of the investigation. He does not have the right to participate in the investigation itself, especially if there is a possibility that a prosecution may still be brought against police office.

Obviously, each case depends on its own facts, and the Court of Appeal made clear that in some cases, disclosure could be given, if concerns remained after the reasoned decision had been given. Nevertheless, this decision shows the spirit of the Article; the European Court has always said that the rights of the Convention must be effective and not illusory, and that is the principle which our courts will seek to apply.

QUESTIONS

1   How far should states have to go in taking responsibility for protection of the person? (You may like to consider in particular the case of *Thompson and Venables*.)
2   How far should states be responsible for medical treatment?
3   Do you consider that corporal punishment in schools and/or prisons should be allowed? Why/why not?

---

[22] *R (on the application of Green) v Police Complaints Authority* [2002] UKHRR 985.

An eighteenth century advertisement for a slave market in the American colonies.

(*Source:* Reproduced courtesy of the Library of Congress.)

Chapter 10

FREEDOM FROM SLAVERY

Epitaph on a tombstone in the churchyard of the Windermere Parish Church of St Martin:
'In Memory of Rasselas Bellfield, a native of Abyssinia, who departed this life on 16th day
of January 1822, aged 32 years
A slave by birth: I left my native land,
And found my Freedom on Britannia's Strand:
Blest Isle! Thou Glory of the Wise and Free!
Thy Touch alone unbinds the Chains of Slavery.'

ARTICLE 4: PROHIBITION OF SLAVERY AND FORCED LABOUR
1. No one shall be held in slavery or servitude.
2. No one shall be required to perform forced or compulsory labour.
3. For the purpose of this Article the term 'forced or compulsory labour' shall not include:
    (a) any work required to be done in the ordinary course of detention imposed according to the provisions of Article 5 of this Convention or during conditional release from such detention;
    (b) any service of a military character or, in case of conscientious objectors in countries where they are recognised, service exacted instead of compulsory military service;
    (c) any service exacted in case of an emergency or calamity threatening the life or well-being of the community;
    (d) any work or service which forms part of normal civic obligations.

THE RELEVANCE OF ARTICLE 4 TODAY

A great English Judge, Lord Mansfield, Chief Justice, said in 1771 that one man could not own another. This was in the case of *Somersett*[1] and that has remained our law ever since. But the slave trade continued to flourish. It still exists today: there are situations and places where people are held in subjection, where they are treated as the property of someone else.

But this chapter will not deal so much with slavery in this core sense, where one person is treated as being owned by another. Modern European legal systems do not allow people to be treated as property, although there may in fact be situations of this sort in existence, without the sanction of the law. However, Article 4 is also about people who are made to do forced labour, and questions arise about what is meant by forced labour, and whether this extends to work for long hours or for inadequate pay. This is an aspect of the same principle: it is a fundamental part of treating people with the

---

[1] (1771) 20 State Trials 1.

basic dignity which they deserve as human beings, that they should be treated as *people* and not as *property*, or, one could add, work tools or machines.

WHAT IS SLAVERY?

Nonetheless, the starting point must be the more fundamental provisions, those of Article 4(1), and to know what Article 4 is about, we must look at the definitions of the terms of the Article. The words 'slavery' and 'servitude' are not defined in the Convention. However, when studying the European Convention, and its jurisprudence, it can be helpful to look at other Conventions; especially any which were already part of international law in 1950, since they would have been considered by those drafting the European Convention in that year.

One helpful definition is that contained in the Slavery Convention of 1926, which defines **slavery** as 'the status or condition of a person over whom any or all of the powers attaching to the right of ownership are exercised'. This Convention does not define the term **servitude**: it would be fair to say that servitude means something similar to slavery, but with overtones of someone who is obliged to perform services, such as forced labour, as in the phrase 'penal servitude'. The Supplementary Convention on the Abolition of Slavery 1956 does include a definition of 'serfdom', which is a word which comes from the same Latin derivation as servitude. Serfdom is defined here as 'the condition or status of a tenant who is by law, custom or agreement, bound to live and labour on land belonging to another person and to render some determinate service to such other person, whether for reward or not, and is not free to change his status'. The key idea here, which is of use in considering what is meant by servitude, is the obligation to provide a service to someone else, without the freedom to leave that person's service – unlike the usual situation when one provides a service as an employee, where the employee is free to leave their job, even if it is only on certain conditions, such as giving notice.

It is notable, in considering the scope of Article 4, that the 1956 Supplementary Convention on the Abolition of Slavery provides for states who sign it to take all necessary measures to bring about the abolition of a number of conditions analogous to slavery. These include serfdom, as defined above; debt bondage, where a person pledges his personal services as security for a debt, except where the scope of the services is limited to the payment of the debt; children being provided as labour; and situations where women are obliged to marry without right of refusal. Whilst most, if not all, European states do not legally recognise these sorts of arrangements, there are certainly countries, or parts of countries, in the world today which do, and places where such practices continue, even if they are illegal. So, the consideration of the basic meaning of slavery has, sadly, not ceased to be relevant.

Are we really likely, in Europe today, to find any instances of the slavery and servitude aspects of Article 4? One should keep an open mind. There may be situations where an individual is indeed virtually in the ownership of another, or bound to them in some way. This was argued in the case of *Van Droogenbroeck v Belgium*.[2]

A man aged 30 was convicted of theft, and sentenced to 2 years' imprisonment, and the Belgian court also ordered him to 'be placed at the Government's disposal' for 10 years, under a statutory

---

[2] (1982) 4 EHRR 443.

power, since he was regarded as having a persistent tendency to commit crime. He served his sentence of imprisonment, and was then put in 'semi-custodial care', which meant his attending a central heating firm as an apprentice, as well as going to intensive vocational courses on Fridays and Saturdays. He disappeared, but he then committed more offences, and he was detained again, until he had earned sufficient money to enable him to be released and rehabilitated. He complained that this sentence, and especially his being placed at the disposal of the government for 10 years, was a violation of Article 4.

The European Court rejected his claim; it stated that conduct would be regarded as servitude only if it involved a particularly serious form of denial of freedom, and that was not the case here.

The case is instructive: it shows that Article 4 *may* be relevant when one considers the sentence imposed by a court, and the prison and penal system, even though it may be *unlikely* that this will amount to slavery or servitude.

FORCED OR COMPULSORY LABOUR

Forced or compulsory labour is prohibited by Article 4(2). 'Labour' is not limited to physical work; it applies to any kind of work. Once again, some assistance in defining these terms can be found in two other Conventions. The first is the Convention Concerning Forced Labour 1930,[3] which requires the suppression of forced or compulsory labour. This defines **forced labour** as work or service which is extracted under the menace of a penalty, or for which the person has not offered himself voluntarily. The second is the Convention for the Abolition of Forced Labour 1957.[4] This was agreed in the years immediately following the Second World War, and reflects the experiences of the concentration camps, and the use of political imprisonment by totalitarian states. It prohibits forced or compulsory labour as a means of political coercion, or punishment for the expression of political or ideological views, or as a means of labour discipline, or for punishment for participation in strikes, or for racial, social, national or religious discrimination.

The European Court has also considered the definition of what amounts to forced or compulsory labour. The Court has held that for a person to show that they have been subjected to this, they must show that the work was not voluntary, and that it was unjustifiable or oppressive in its nature. This was set out in the case of *Van Der Mussele v Belgium*.[5]

Mr Van Der Mussele was a Belgian lawyer, an *avocat*, in Antwerp. He was enrolled as a trainee *avocat*, and during the course of his training, he was appointed to defend a defendant in a criminal case, and he conducted that case in court. He did so without remuneration; that was in accordance with the traditions and practice of the Belgian Bar to provide legal representation to persons of insufficient means. If he had not done so, he would have run the risk of being struck off the register of *avocats*. He complained of a violation of Article 4.

The European Court rejected his claim. It defined the phrase 'forced or compulsory labour' in the manner set out above: it must be performed against the person's will, and the obligation to perform it must be unjust or oppressive, or its performance must constitute an avoidable hardship. The Court noted that the *avocat's* services did not fall outside the ambit of the normal activities of

---

[3] Treaty No. 29 of the International Labour Organisation.
[4] Treaty No. 105 of the International Labour Organisation.
[5] (1984) 6 EHRR 163.

an *avocat*, and the work did not differ from the usual work of members of the Bar. Furthermore, conducting the case contributed to Mr Van Der Mussele's professional training, and gave him an opportunity to enlarge his experience and to increase his reputation. Then follows a phrase which is important: 'Finally, the burden imposed on the applicant was not disproportionate.'

Those final words are notable. Even in the context of a right as basic as Article 4, the European Court jurisprudence brings into play the principle of proportionality.

The *Van Der Mussele* case is a modern example of how this phrase 'forced or compulsory labour' will be interpreted: it is a somewhat old-fashioned phrase, and certainly it brings to mind a picture of chain-gangs and other such forms of work. But we should remember that the Conventions of 1930 and 1957, especially the latter, define forced or compulsory labour, not by reference to its physical *severity*, but by reference to its *purpose*. The European Court referred to these Conventions in *Van Der Mussele*, stating that it would take them into account, since they are in fact binding on nearly all member states of the Council of Europe.

Cases such as *Van Droogenbroeck* and *Van Der Mussele* could occur in the United Kingdom. Work, or employment, or service, might by its conditions impose a burden on an individual who thereby feels oppressed. In fact there are a whole series of legislative provisions which govern work practices, both in British law alone, and based on European Union Directives, a number of which regulate working practices across the whole of the EU, including health and safety requirements, and conditions of work, as well as specific situations such as maternity leave. Just to give one example, the Working Time Regulations 1998, which implement the European Union's Working Time Directive. These set out minimum health and safety requirements for the organisation of working time; they apply to full-time, part-time, agency and casual workers (with some exceptions), and they provide rules for hours worked, rest breaks, and time off.

PERMISSIBLE LABOUR

Article 4(3) limits the content of the right contained by Article 4(2): it provides that 'forced or compulsory labour' shall not include the activities in (a)–(d). The European Court has made it clear that Article 4(3) should be seen as setting out the scope of Article 4(2); that is, it is an exhaustive list of the only situations where forced labour is permitted, since these are the only situations which are excluded from Article 4(2). Thus Article 4(3) serves as an aid to the interpretation of 4(2). In the case of *Schmidt v Germany*,[6] the European Court said:

> The four subparagraphs of Article 4(3), notwithstanding their diversity, are grounded on the governing ideas of the general interest, social solidarity and what is normal in the ordinary course of affairs.

The activities in those sub-paragraphs reflect situations of general benefit to the whole community, and are examples of what might loosely be called community service. They are all situations where it is considered that there is a public benefit, or public service being provided, which can justify the imposition of an obligation to do the work. Although this is not expressly stated in the article, one would expect, in each case, that the labour should be provided in accordance with the relevant national law, so that it is a clear

---

[6] (1994) 18 EHRR 513.

obligation. Following *Van Der Mussele*, one would also expect that the scale of the labour should be proportionate to the necessary requirements of one of the situations set out in (a) to (d), namely, work which is compulsory in the course of lawful detention in prison, military service, service which is required in the event of an emergency, or any work or service which forms part of normal civic obligations. Work in prison, military service and normal civic obligations all fall within the description of being 'normal in the ordinary course of affairs' as well as being within the 'general interest'. The situation where there is an emergency which threatens the life or wellbeing of the community is a clear example of the general interest being likely to over-ride the freedom of the individual to refuse to help out: where there is a national emergency, one would expect each person to recognise that they have a *duty* to do their part to help.

There have been some cases on the scope of these different categories. One case on Article 4(3)(b) was *Spottl v Austria*.[7]

Thomas Spottl was called for military service in Austria, but he registered as a conscientious objector, one who has moral objections to doing military service. This was accepted, but Austrian law then required him to carry out civilian service instead. He complained that this was forced labour, and was also discriminatory, contrary to Article 14, since women were not obliged to carry out military or civilian service.

The European Commission rejected his claim. The compulsory civilian service was tied to the underlying duty to perform military service, falling within Article 4(3)(b) and women were not required to perform military service. That differential treatment was justified, and many nations, while requiring military or civilian service, did not require women to carry out military service.

Finally, we shall consider the case of *Schmidt v Germany*,[8] which was quoted above. This concerned an obligation within Article 4(3)(d).

Mr Karlheinz Schmidt's complaint was that, under the law of the state in which he lived, it was compulsory for men, but not women, to serve in the fire brigade or pay a financial contribution in lieu of this service. In so far as this fell within Article 4(3)(d), work or service which was part of normal civic obligations, Mr Schmidt's complaint was that it was discriminatory in breach of Article 14.

The European Court agreed that this compulsory fire service was a part of normal civic obligations. The Court did consider that the distinction between imposing it on men and not on women was in breach of Article 14 taken with Article 4(3)(d), especially as in reality there were a sufficient number of volunteers, and so the only real duty was the obligation to pay the financial contribution, in respect of which there was no adequate justification for treating men and women differently.

QUESTIONS

1 It seems to be taken for granted that slavery and forced labour should not be allowed. Do you agree with this? Why? Do you think that the other specific practices covered by the Slavery Conventions should be expressly forbidden? Why?

2 Do you agree that the activities covered by Article 4(3) should not be thought of as prohibited examples of forced or compulsory labour? Put another way, do you agree that there are rights or interests of individuals or society as a whole which justify these exceptions?

---

[7] (1996) 22 EHRR CD 88.
[8] (1994) 18 EHRR 513.

May Day 2001: protesters being detained in Oxford Circus by police.

(*Source:* www.mirrorpix.com)

Chapter 11

PERSONAL LIBERTY

'No free man shall be taken or imprisoned or dispossessed, or outlawed or exiled, or in any way destroyed, nor will we go upon him, nor will we send against him except by the lawful judgment of his peers or by the law of the land.' (Magna Carta, 1215)

ARTICLE 5: THE RIGHT TO LIBERTY AND SECURITY

1. Everyone has the right to liberty and security of person.
   No one shall be deprived of his liberty save in the following cases and in accordance with a procedure prescribed by law:
   (a) the lawful detention of a person after conviction by a competent court;
   (b) the lawful arrest or detention of a person for non-compliance with the lawful order of a court or in order to secure the fulfilment of any obligation prescribed by law;
   (c) the lawful arrest or detention of a person effected for the purpose of bringing him before the competent legal authority on reasonable suspicion of having committed an offence or when it is reasonably considered necessary to prevent his committing an offence or fleeing after having done so;
   (d) the detention of a minor by lawful order for the purpose of educational supervision or his lawful detention for the purpose of bringing him before the competent legal authority;
   (e) the lawful detention of persons for the prevention of the spreading of infectious diseases, of persons of unsound mind, alcoholics or drug addicts or vagrants;
   (f) the lawful arrest or detention of a person to prevent his effecting an unauthorised entry into the country or of a person against whom action is being taken with a view to deportation or extradition.
2. Everyone who is arrested shall be informed promptly, in a language which he understands, of the reasons for his arrest and of any charge against him.
3. Everyone arrested or detained in accordance with the provisions of paragraph 1(c) of this Article shall be brought promptly before a judge or other officer authorised by law to exercise judicial power and shall be entitled to trial within a reasonable time or to release pending trial. Release may be conditioned by guarantees to appear for trial.
4. Everyone who is deprived of his liberty by arrest or detention shall be entitled to take proceedings by which the lawfulness of his detention shall be decided speedily by a court and his release ordered if the detention is not lawful.
5. Everyone who has been the victim of arrest or detention in contravention of the provisions of this Article shall have an enforceable right to compensation.

PERSONAL LIBERTY

Article 5 embodies a fundamental part of what we mean when we say that we are free. After the rights that we should be protected from physical harm, perhaps the next most basic right is freedom of the person, the liberty to go where we please and do as we please, without interference by others or by the state, so long as we do not harm others or infringe their rights. The counterpart to this is that the conditions under which we can be deprived of this personal freedom by the state should be specified and limited, and that is the substance of Article 5. It sets out very strict limits and conditions on the ability of the state to arrest or detain its citizens.

Arrest and detention is a regular occurrence – the police make many hundreds of arrests daily. There are good reasons why an arrest or detention could be required, sometimes to deal with a crime that has been committed, sometimes to protect others from a dangerous person, sometimes to protect a person from others or from themselves. Yet any form of arrest or detention should always be seen as something which requires strict justification.

In 1970, in the case of *De Wilde*,[1] the European Court said that the right to liberty is too important for a person to lose the benefit of the protection of the Convention for the single reason that he gives himself up to go into custody. That is remarkable: even when a man volunteers to be detained, his liberty is protected by the Convention. The European Court there emphasised the importance of liberty itself, and how it should be kept safe by the law.

Our courts have traditionally done the same, and, as we shall see, the basic principles of Article 5 are nothing new to our law. The very strong idea that liberty must be cherished, and that only the law may take it away is one which has been prevalent in our courts for centuries. And especially, our courts have strongly resisted any invasion of liberty without lawful authority, by unauthorised acts of the executive. In the 1931 case of *Eshugbayi Eleko*,[2] it was argued that the court was prohibited from investigating the legality of an order of the Governor of Nigeria ordering Eleko to leave a specified area. The Privy Council rejected this argument, and held that the Governor had no power to make such an order. The great English judge, Lord Atkin, said, 'no member of the executive can interfere with the liberty or property of a British subject except on the condition that he can support the legality of his action before a court of justice'. As we shall see, this principle of legality, having lawful authority for action, is a key part of the application of Article 5.

THE LAW ON ARREST

We must pause a moment to consider what the law of arrest and detention is, so that we may put it in the context of the Convention rights guaranteed by Article 5. The main relevant statute is the Police and Criminal Evidence Act 1984[3] and the Codes of Practice issued under it. The basic power of arrest is straightforward: section 24 of PACE

---

[1] (1979–80) 1 EHRR 373, discussed at p. 136 below.
[2] *Eshugbayi Eleko v Officer Administering the Government of Nigeria* [1931] AC 662 at 670.
[3] We shall use the common abbreviation: PACE.

provides for a power of summary arrest in respect of arrestable offences: 'summary arrest' means arrest without a warrant, and 'arrestable offences' refers to offences for which the sentence is fixed by law, offences for which a person of 21 or over may be sentenced to imprisonment for 5 years, and other specific offences. There must be a reasonable suspicion that the person arrested has committed the offence.

As for detention, the position is that a person must not be kept in a police station for more than 24 hours without being charged, although that period may be extended for 12 hours by a senior police officer, and then further by a magistrate, up to an overall maximum of 96 hours. Codes of Practice are issued under PACE, which provide standards for the treatment of a detained person. Even within that time, as soon as the investigating police officer considers that there is sufficient evidence to successfully prosecute a detained person, he must without delay be brought before a custody officer, who will consider whether or not the detainee should be charged. Then the prisoner must be taken before a magistrate or a judge, who may, depending on the circumstances, allow him to be released on bail. Likewise, if the overall time limit expires, or there are no grounds for continuing detention, the person must be released. There are also legal proceedings which can be taken to challenge detention, such as applications for bail, or using the writ of *habeas corpus*; we will explain these in the context of Article 5(4) below.[4]

So overall, our law provides rules for arrest and detention, and for bringing a suspect before a court, and for release on bail; and police officers, and the courts, must abide by those rules. So the liberty of the subject does appear to be reasonably well protected.

What then does Article 5 add, since the existing law seems to provide fully for the same things? The answer is that Article 5 adds a dimension to the law in requiring that the state exercises its powers compatibly with the Convention and with fairness and proportionality, and not arbitrarily. This means considering not just the existence of the power of arrest, or whether the formal requirements for making an arrest have been complied with, although these remain crucially important. Article 5 requires an overall consideration of the necessity and proportionality of the arrest and the length of detention: even if the rules and procedures are complied with, there is still scope for a breach of Article 5 if the reasons for the arrest and detention cannot be properly justified. Thus, the Article provides for substantive scrutiny of the arrest, and not just a consideration of whether the formal requirements have been complied with.

THE SCHEME OF ARTICLE 5

The opening sentence of Article 5 announces in ringing terms the right to liberty and security of the person, and the second sentence defines the conditions under which a person may be deprived of his liberty. These are the grounds on which the state, or a public authority, may interfere with this right, set out in a list labelled (a) to (f). That list is exhaustive; the European Court said so in the case of *Ireland v United Kingdom*,[5] which involved a challenge to the forceful means of interrogation used by

---

[4] Below, p. 146.
[5] (1980) 2 EHRR 25, discussed above in the context of Article 3, p. 112.

the British security forces in Northern Ireland. The Court noted that the wording of Article 5(1) is 'No one shall be deprived of his liberty *save in the following cases . . .*' followed by the six cases, (a) to (f). The words in italics mean this: there can be interference with liberty *only* in the circumstances set out in (a) to (f). Those circumstances cannot be extended. In addition, the arrest itself must be **lawful**, must conform to the purposes of the relevant sub-paragraph, and must **not** be **arbitrary**, because, for example, it is made in bad faith or is not a proportionate response to the situation.

THE QUALITY OF THE LAW

Pausing first on the second sentence of Article 5(1), we note that the conditions for interfering with the right must be 'in accordance with a procedure prescribed by law'. We have already considered this phrase, the idea behind which appears in a number of the Convention Articles.[6] The same idea applies to the use of the word 'lawful' in 5(1)(a) to (f), applied to the arrest or detention which is in question. As we discussed earlier, the phrases 'lawful', and 'in accordance with a procedure prescribed by law' mean two things: first, lawful according to national law, and second, lawful in the Convention sense of according with the principle of legality. Thus if the arrest or detention is not lawful by the standards of the national law, there will be a breach of Article 5. On the other hand, if the arrest is lawful under the national law, it may still infringe Article 5 if the law under which the arrest is made is not accessible and precise.

These requirements are particularly important in the context of Article 5, since what is being considered is a situation where a person's personal liberty is being infringed. It is one thing where someone is arrested for doing something which they should have realised was criminal. It is quite another where they could not have known that what they were doing was against the law. This may be because the words of a statute are not precise or because the court's own order is unintelligible. To illustrate this are two cases, one where the law passed the test of being precise enough, and in the other it did not.

In *Steel v UK*,[7] the European Court was dealing with several separate incidents. Ms Helen Steel, with about 60 other people, had attempted to obstruct a grouse shoot in Yorkshire, and she was arrested for breach of the peace, when she impeded a member of the shoot by walking in front of him as he lifted his shotgun. She was detained for 44 hours. At court she was convicted of a breach of the peace. She was ordered to be bound over to keep the peace, but she refused and she served a prison sentence. Another protester tried to stop the building of the M11 motorway, and she had broken into the site, and was arrested, for conduct likely to provoke a disturbance of the peace, whilst standing under a mechanical digger. She was detained for about 17 hours and was ordered to be bound over to keep the peace. She refused, and she too served a prison sentence. Both complained of violations of Article 5, saying that the concept of breach of the peace and the power to bind over were not sufficiently clearly defined for their detention to be 'prescribed by law'.

The European Court held that a breach of the peace was an 'offence' within Article 5(1)(c) and therefore there was a lawful arrest on reasonable suspicion of having committed an offence. It also met the requirement of being sufficiently precise to be 'lawful', with foreseeable consequences.

---

[6] It is discussed above, pp. 87–8.

[7] (1999) 28 EHRR 603, see also p. 226 in context of Article 10.

However, in the case of *Hashman and Harrup v UK*,[8] the applicants tried to disturb the Portman hunt, by blowing a horn and hallooing, so that the hounds were distracted and drawn out of the control of the huntsmen and the whippers-in. There was no finding by the Crown Court of a breach of the peace – which distinguishes the case from that of *Steel*. But the Crown Court found that they had behaved *contra bonos mores* (against good behaviour), and bound them over to keep the peace and not to behave *contra bonos mores*.

The European Court held that the finding of being *contra bonos mores* and the decision to bind them over was not a procedure 'prescribed by law' (in this case in breach of Article 10): the phrase *contra bonos mores* had not been defined with precision; it was not clear to the applicants what they had to refrain from doing in the future.

Thus, in the case of *Steel*, the applicants had committed a breach of the peace: there was a crime which could be recognised as being factually clear, as the basis of the decision and the order of the court, and that was what the applicants were being required not to do in the future. In the case of *Hashman* there was no breach of the peace, the language of the charge against the defendants was less than clear, and they were not left in a situation where they could know what they should do or refrain from doing, to avoid repeating the offence.

THE MEANING OF 'ARBITRARY'

Let us turn to the point that the arrest or detention must not be arbitrary. Pausing a moment, we should note that the requirement that an arrest should not be arbitrary is not to be found in the relevant sections of PACE, nor in the Codes of Practice. And this consideration will apply, even where the relevant arrest or detention is lawful, in the sense that it has a lawful basis: the court will still look to see if it is free from the taint of being arbitrary.

There is a good example of how our judges regard Article 5 in the case of *Evans*.[9] Mrs Evans had been convicted of robbery, burglary, and assault, and she was sentenced to 2 years' imprisonment. Before she was sentenced, she had spent various periods in custody following her arrest for each of these offences. Then, nearing the end of her sentence, a dispute arose between herself and the prison governor as to what was her date of release. The governor relied on Home Office Guidelines, which were based on court decisions about the calculation of sentences, but those decisions were erroneous, and she spent 59 days longer in prison than she need have done. She sued for wrongful imprisonment.

The House of Lords held that the Governor – however blameless – was liable to her for damages for wrongful imprisonment. Although the House in fact decided that the detention was unlawful in any event, so there was no need to consider Article 5, the Law Lords referred to it and decided that the Governor had not acted in an arbitrary way. Lord Hope expressly considered the scope for questioning whether:

> . . . assuming that the detention is lawful under domestic law, it is nevertheless open to criticism on the ground that it is arbitrary because, for example, it was resorted to in bad faith or was not proportionate.

Note those words of Lord Hope: they give examples of what may be characterised as 'arbitrary' – bad faith or lack of proportion. They are important; as we have noted,

---

[8] (2000) 30 EHRR 241; see also below, p. 226, in the context of Article 10.
[9] *R v Governor of Brockhill Prison, ex parte Evans (No. 2)* [2000] 3 WLR 843.

our laws of arrest and detention do not refer to bad faith or lack of proportion, so we see these ideas entering our law from the European cases.

Here is another case, which is a good example of where the court was asked to say that the provisions of a statute were disproportionate. The court looked at the surrounding circumstances in order to determine this argument; that is permissible, of course, since the concept of proportionality involves a process of measuring the means and the aim, in a context of a 'pressing social need'. The case is *Anderson, Reid, and Doherty*.[10]

Three men were being held in a state hospital in Scotland as 'restricted patients', meaning that they had been before the courts on charges of the greatest gravity. Anderson had killed a girl of 12, and was convicted of culpable homicide; Doherty had been guilty of the kidnapping and manslaughter of a 12-year-old boy in Northern Ireland, in circumstances which the judge described as 'cruel and macabre'; and Reid had been found guilty of culpable homicide.

Under a previous law, the House of Lords had held, in a case quite unconnected with these men, that if a judge was satisfied that a patient was suffering from a psychopathic personality disorder and could not be treated, he was to discharge the defendant. Parliament thereupon passed the Mental Health Act 1999, which provided that the judge should refuse an appeal if the defendant was suffering from a mental disorder which makes it necessary to protect the public from serious harm, and the defendant would then continue in hospital whether or not for medical treatment. These three men contended that the Mental Health Act was in breach of Article 5.

The Privy Council, on appeal from the Court of Session, held that the Mental Health Act lays down a system, namely, that the patient should be of unsound mind, and it was necessary for the protection of the public that he be detained in hospital; here the judge was satisfied that the men were suffering from a mental disorder, and that it was necessary for the protection of the public to detain each of them. And the fact that they were not susceptible to treatment was not a violation of Article 5; there was nothing arbitrary or disproportionate about the circumstances. The very fact that the protection of the public was necessary was in itself a legitimate reason for detaining a person of unsound mind.

The scope of the requirement that detention should not be arbitrary is broad. We have already referred to the next case, where the detainees actually gave themselves up, although in the circumstances the European Court was satisfied that the detention was not arbitrary.

In *De Wilde v Belgium*,[11] three gentlemen, Mr De Wilde, aged 38, Mr Ooms, aged 32, and Mr Versyp, aged 54, separately presented themselves at police stations in Belgium saying that they were without work or food or lodging, and they were taken into custody and brought before the police courts, who found each was a vagrant and they were detained in different ways and for differing periods. The men complained that they had been detained illegally. The Belgian government contended that by giving themselves up they had forfeited the protection of the Convention.

The European Court said that temporary distress may drive a person to give himself up to be detained. This does not mean that he is in a state of vagrancy; the wishes of the applicant cannot remove the mandatory character of the Belgian court's decision. The right to liberty is too important in a democratic society, within the meaning of the Convention, for a person to lose the benefit of Article 5 for the single reason that he has given himself up to be taken into detention. Detention might

---

[10] [2002] 3 WLR 1460.
[11] (1979–80) 1 EHRR 373.

be arbitrary even though the person concerned might have agreed to it. Scrupulous supervision by the court is necessary. On the facts of these cases, the European Court found that in all the circumstances there had been no irregularity or arbitrariness, as the police court had examined the facts properly.

Another situation where detention must not be arbitrary is detention after conviction of an offence. One would think that, if a criminal court has passed a sentence on a prisoner, especially if the prisoner has been to the Court of Appeal and unsuccessfully challenged the sentence, it would be difficult for him to say that the sentence was an arbitrary one. But that is to leave out of account Article 5, which requires the question to be asked: is the sentence an arbitrary one? We see this in the next case, although the European Court was satisfied in the circumstances that it was not arbitrary. The Court was considering a case of a long sentence which had been imposed on a very young man by the English court, and the question was whether the continuing custody was still connected to the original reasons for the sentence. It is the case of *Weeks v UK*.[12]

Mr Weeks, at the age of 17, entered a pet shop with a starting pistol loaded with blanks, and got 35 pence, which he dropped on the shop floor. He was convicted of robbery, and he was given an indeterminate life sentence. After 10 years in prison, he was released on licence, but then he was recalled to prison after several breaches of the licence; and then he claimed that his detention was no longer lawful.

The European Court said that there had to be a sufficient causal connection between the conviction and the deprivation of liberty, and where the life sentence was imposed by reason of instability and personality disorder, his progress should be monitored, and he should be released when there was no longer a danger. Instability and personality disorder were susceptible to change and Article 5(1)(a) would be violated if a decision to keep him in custody was based on grounds inconsistent with the objectives of the sentence; a detention which had been lawful at the outset would be transferred into a deprivation of liberty that was arbitrary. However, on the facts of the case, it was a correct decision to deny him his release: in the intervals of his release on licence, he had shown that he was unstable, disturbed and aggressive.

The Court of Appeal had rejected his appeal; there was no discussion about whether the sentence was 'arbitrary' – the Act was not then part of our law. The Court of Appeal did consider whether the sentence was excessive, and so in a sense was considering whether the sentence was disproportionate. But that word was not used. What the European Court did was to emphasise that there must be a strict relationship between the offence and the penalty and a strict basis of reasoning for the length of the sentence. And what was being scrutinised – almost under a microscope – was the decision to keep the prisoner in custody. Decisions must not be arbitrary; and decisions which are based on the wrong reasons, or on no reasons, are likely to be arbitrary.

A case of an executive decision based on the wrong reasons, was *Stafford v UK*,[13] where the European Court took the view that the prisoner was being detained unlawfully. It is a good example of the effect of the Convention on English law: before the

---

[12] (1987) 10 EHRR 293, also considered in the context of Article 3 above, p. 114.
[13] (2002) 35 EHRR 32.

incorporation of the Convention, it is likely that the decision would not have been challenged.

Mr Stafford had been convicted in 1967 of murder and sentenced to life imprisonment; the Parole Board recommended his release on life licence, and the Home Secretary agreed, so he was released on licence in 1991. In 1994, however, he was convicted of a cheque fraud, and sentenced to 6 years' imprisonment, and his life licence was revoked by the Home Secretary. In 1996–7, when he would normally have been released from the fraud sentence, the Parole Board recommended his release on life licence, noting his previous successful transition from prison to the community without *violent* re-offending. The Home Secretary rejected the Parole Board's recommendation, on the ground that there was a risk of *non-violent* re-offending. And when Mr Stafford challenged that in court, the House of Lords found, in favour of the Home Secretary, that he had a wide discretion. Mr Stafford was eventually released in 1998.

The European Court held that the Home Secretary's decision was not justified under Article 5(1):

> The Court could not accept that a decision-making power by the executive to detain him on the basis of perceived fears of future non-violent criminal conduct unrelated to his original murder conviction was in the spirit of the Convention, with its emphasis on the rule of law and protection from arbitrariness.

The point is that the Home Secretary's decision was not related to the original conviction of murder, and had no connection with the original sentence. It was simply an executive decision to keep him in custody. Again we see attention being paid to the requirement of Article 5 that a decision is not arbitrary.

TYPES OF PERMISSIBLE DETENTION

We are now ready to examine each paragraph of Article 5, keeping in mind the principles we have discussed; whenever the court considers the case under one of these paragraphs, it will first determine whether the wording of the particular paragraph covers the situation, and second, it will apply the principles of lawfulness and freedom from arbitrariness.

DETENTION AFTER CONVICTION

Article 5(1)(a): the lawful detention of a person after conviction by a competent court;

We have already referred to a number of cases which fall within this category, where there is a conviction for a criminal offence, by a court which has proper jurisdiction in the matter. Our legal system allows for there to be an appeal to a higher court after a conviction by a lower court, and if the appeal succeeds the conviction is quashed and any sentence of imprisonment is brought to an end. The question then arises, does that mean that the conviction was unlawful, and was the imprisonment a violation of Article 5? The answer is that the simple fact that a conviction is quashed on appeal in the domestic court does *not* mean that the conviction is unlawful. The European Court recognised this in the case of *Benham v UK*.[14]

---

[14] (1996) 22 EHRR 293.

Mr Benham had failed to pay his community charge, and he was summonsed to appear before the magistrates. The magistrates found that he was guilty of culpably neglecting to pay, and they imposed a prison sentence on him. He appealed to the High Court, which adjudged that Mr Benham had not been guilty of culpable neglect. Mr Benham complained to the European Court that he had been imprisoned unlawfully, in violation of Article 5, and that the only paragraph which could have justified his period of custody was 5(1)(a), but the High Court had found that his conviction was wrong.

The European Court examined the decision of the High Court and found that it did not necessarily mean that the magistrates' order was unlawful; an order which was erroneous in fact or law was not necessarily unlawful, and the error did not make the decision arbitrary. There was therefore no breach of Article 5.

BREACH OF A COURT ORDER

Article 5(1)(b): the lawful arrest or detention of a person for non-compliance with the lawful order of a court or in order to secure the fulfilment of any obligation prescribed by law;

The main situation where this paragraph will apply is where a court orders a person to do, or not do, something, and the court order is disobeyed. This is the sanction where a court issues an injunction, an order that a person refrain from doing something, such as harassing another, or trespassing on someone else's property: a person who breaches an injunction is liable to be sent to prison for a period of time as a result. This is not quite the same as Article 5(1)(a): they have not acted in a way which amounts to the commission of a criminal offence as such, but they have acted unlawfully in refusing to comply with the order of the court.

The reference to securing the fulfilment of an obligation prescribed by law is intended to cover similar situations. It is not aimed at general legal obligations, which would be covered by 5(1)(a), but specific obligations, such as an obligation to fulfil a contractual duty, which would have to be backed up by a court order if there was a possibility of prison, or a duty to provide information in a specific situation. The lack of application of this provision to general legal obligations was considered by the European Commission in *Lawless v Ireland*.[15]

Mr Lawless, an Irish citizen resident in Dublin, was a member of the IRA, and he was detained for several months without trial in a military detention camp in Ireland, from July to December 1957, by order of the Irish Minister of Justice, under the Offences against the State Act 1939. The Irish government had argued that Article 5(1)(b) applied, on the basis that the detention was 'in order to secure the fulfilment of an obligation prescribed by law'.

The Commission held that the detention of Mr Lawless by order of a Minister of State on suspicion of being engaged in activities prejudicial to the preservation of public peace and order or to the security of the State cannot be deemed to be a measure taken 'in order to fulfil an obligation prescribed by law' and this point was not pursued by the Irish government when the case came before the Court.

---

[15] (1961) 1 EHRR 15; see also above, p. 91 for the case's reference to Article 17.

REASONABLE SUSPICION OF AN OFFENCE

Article 5(1)(c): the lawful arrest or detention of a person effected for the purpose of bringing him before the competent legal authority on reasonable suspicion of having committed an offence or when it is reasonably considered necessary to prevent his committing an offence or fleeing after having done so;

As we noted towards the start of this chapter, the general law on arrests in the United Kingdom usually requires the fulfilment of similar criteria to these. However, the precise application of our law may well be influenced by the way in which this paragraph has been applied by the European Court. *Fox, Campbell and Hartley v UK*[16] is one example of the consideration by the European Court of what amounts to 'reasonable suspicion of having committed an offence'.

Mr Fox and Ms Campbell, who were married to each other but separated, were detained in Northern Ireland for periods of 30 to 44 hours, under an Act which allowed detention of persons suspected of being a terrorist. During their detention, each was questioned about their suspected membership of the Provisional IRA, and about their involvement with that organisation. They were eventually released without charge.

The European Court considered that there was a violation of the Article because *no* facts were put before the Court to show that the suspicion was reasonable. The European Court said:

The reasonableness of the suspicion on which an arrest must be based forms an essential part of the safeguard against arbitrary arrest and detention which is laid down in 5(1)(c). 'Reasonable suspicion' pre-supposed the existence of facts or information which would satisfy an objective observer that the person concerned may have committed the offence. What is 'reasonable suspicion' will depend on all the circumstances.

The key idea is that the reasonableness of the suspicion is a safeguard, and therefore requires some basis. It is not enough that the arresting officer believes it to be reasonable. It is not a subjective test, but an objective one, and the court will judge whether it was reasonable. The suspicion, and the arrest, must be proved objectively to be justified.

Not only that, but also *an offence* must be suspected. It will not be enough that the suspicion is of some vaguely described conduct. The person making the arrest must decide what is the apparent offence that he or she is going to make the basis of the arrest. This was one of the points which arose in the case of *Brogan v UK*.[17]

Mr Brogan was arrested in Northern Ireland and detained for 5 days and 11 hours, then released without having been charged with any offence or taken before a magistrate or judge. In custody, he was questioned about an offence of murder of a police officer, and about suspected membership of the Provisional IRA. Brogan argued before the European Court that he had been deprived of his liberty in breach of Article 5(1)(c) in that he had not been arrested 'for having committed an offence'.

---

[16] (1991) 13 EHRR 157; also referred to at p. 278 below.
[17] (1989) 11 EHRR 117, also considered below, p. 144.

The European Court held that the definition of 'terrorism' – namely 'the use of violence for the purpose of putting the public in fear' – which was given as the basis of the arrest, was well in keeping with the idea of an offence; and in addition, he was questioned about a specific offence. In short, there was *no* violation of Article 5.

DETENTION OF MINORS FOR EDUCATION

Article 5(1)(d): the detention of a minor by lawful order for the purpose of educational supervision or his lawful detention for the purpose of bringing him before the competent legal authority;

You may be surprised that the Convention contains a provision like this; it must be rare that a minor is actually detained for the purpose of making him undergo some educational training. However, the provision is wider than this. The following is an example of where Article 5(1)(d) was considered in an English case, concerning a secure accommodation order.

In *Re K*,[18] K was a 15-year-old boy, who had been convicted of a number of offences. He was diagnosed as having hyperkinetic conduct disorder and as being a serious risk to himself and others. He was made the subject of a secure accommodation order. This was challenged as being in breach of Article 5.

The Court of Appeal held that a secure accommodation order is a deprivation of liberty within Article 5, and Article 5(1)(d) applied, because the case related to the detention of a minor. For the purposes of 5(1)(d), 'educational supervision' did not just refer to a rigid notion of classroom teaching; in the context of local authority supervision, it covered many aspects of a local authority's exercise of parental rights for the benefit and protection of the child. Thus Article 5(1)(d) in principle allowed for the making of a secure accommodation order; it was then a question on the facts of the case as to whether its application in a particular case complied with the Convention right. In the present case K was a serious risk to others and the order was quite proper, and extended.

As usual with these grounds of detention, the key question is whether the detention is reasonable, proportionate, lawful and non-arbitrary. An example is the European Court's decision in *Bouamar v Belgium*.[19]

Naim Bouamar, aged 17, had a disturbed personality due to family problems, and in 1980 he was on several occasions placed in a remand prison for periods of 15 days, on the order of the Juvenile Court, on the ground that it had been shown to be impossible to find an individual or institution which would accept him. The Belgian government's argument to the European Court was that he was detained by lawful order for purposes of educational supervision, and that Article 5(1)(c) covered the situation. But the European Court noted and emphasised that nine placements had been attempted and called it 'fruitless repetition'; they referred to the way he had been shuttled to and fro between prison and his family, and never placed in an appropriate institution, nor under the supervision of educationally trained staff; and the Court held that these circumstances had the effect of making the treatment of Naim less and less lawful.

---

[18] [2001] 2 WLR 1141.
[19] (1989) 11 EHRR 1.

That last word is the key to the case. The European Court will not re-open the question of whether educational supervision is in principle required, as defined by the national court, but it will look at the way in which that court has applied its own definition, judged by the test of proportionality and absence of arbitrariness.

PERSONS OF UNSOUND MIND

Article 5(1)(e):   the lawful detention of persons for the prevention of the spreading of infectious diseases, of persons of unsound mind, alcoholics or drug addicts or vagrants;

Again, under this paragraph, the European Court will not interfere with a domestic definition as to what amounts to 'unsound mind', but it will enquire to see if a decision is objectively justified. So, we have the case of *Ashingdane v UK*.[20]

Mr Leonard Ashingdane was convicted in 1970 of offences of dangerous driving and unlawful possession of firearms; he was then 41 years of age. Medical evidence showed that he suffered from mental illness – paranoid schizophrenia – and his mental disorder was of such a degree as to warrant his detention in a psychiatric hospital, and the court made a hospital order, together with an order restricting his discharge without limit of time. He was placed in a secure special hospital, but in 1978 his condition improved, and the Home Secretary authorised his return to a local psychiatric hospital. However, the local authority for that hospital refused to accept him, because of a dispute with staff, and so the Home Secretary declined to order the transfer to proceed. Mr Ashingdane was eventually, in 1980, transferred to the local hospital, but he complained that the period, from 1978 to 1980, of continued detention in the secure hospital was unlawful.

The European Court held that to justify detention under Article 5(1)(e) the existence of a mental disorder of a sufficient degree had to be established on the basis of objective medical expertise. The disorder had to persist to justify continued detention. There was no reason to doubt the medical evidence here, that it did persist; and Mr A would still have been in detention even if he had been moved earlier to the local hospital.

The courts of the United Kingdom have now had to consider these principles in cases concerning mental health patients. We considered earlier the case of *Anderson, Doherty and Reid*, in the context of non-arbitrary detention; in that case, the justification for the detention was that the persons being detained fell within Article 5(1)(e), and they were being detained under the Mental Health Act as suffering from a mental disorder making detention necessary to protect the public from serious harm. The Privy Council held that this detention was not arbitrary or disproportionate.

ARREST FOR DEPORTATION

Article 5(1)(f):   the lawful arrest or detention of a person to prevent his effecting an unauthorised entry into the country or of a person against whom action is being taken with a view to deportation or extradition.

---

[20] (1985) 7 EHRR 528.

We have seen that the word 'lawful' bears two meanings: lawful according to the law of the domestic state, and lawful according to the jurisprudence of the Convention. In this next case, we see that the Convention jurisprudence is used to enable the English court to read the United Kingdom statute in a way which is lawful. In the case of *Saadi*,[21] the facts were as follows.

Some Turkish Kurds claimed asylum on arrival in Britain, and they were detained at Oakington Reception Centre for up to 10 days to bring about a speedy determination of their asylum applications. This was under a Home Office fast-track procedure to deal with a large influx of applicants for asylum. This involved asylum seekers being detained for short periods of 7 to 10 days, and no longer, to ensure a speedy determination of their case by keeping them available whilst their case was decided. The detention was permitted by the terms of the Immigration Act 1971, 'pending examination and a decision to give or refuse leave to enter the country', although this does not say that this was for the *purpose* of the examination.

The House of Lords held that this detention was lawful and was not an arbitrary detention. It was not irrational to have such a policy since a short period of detention is justifiable to ensure a speedy decision on the claim for asylum, and the length of detention was not disproportionate.

PROMPT REASONS FOR ARREST

Article 5 (2): Everyone who is arrested shall be informed promptly, in a language which he understands, of the reasons for his arrest and of any charge against him.

We now move on to consider the requirements which Article 5 imposes following an arrest. The first is this: that once a person has been arrested, they are told why they have been arrested. This is an additional safeguard against arbitrary arrest: if the person making the arrest cannot say why they are doing so immediately after the arrest has been made, they are unlikely to be able to demonstrate that it is not arbitrary. This duty is already a requirement in our law,[22] that the arrested party should be told on what charge or on suspicion of what crime they are being arrested, and this applies as much to a policeman as to a private person making a citizen's arrest. If this cannot be done on arrest, it must be done at the first reasonable opportunity after the arrest.

PROMPT APPEARANCE BEFORE A COURT

Article 5 (3): Everyone arrested or detained in accordance with the provisions of paragraph 1(c) of this Article shall be brought promptly before a judge or other officer authorised by law to exercise judicial power and shall be entitled to trial within a reasonable time or to release pending trial. Release may be conditioned by guarantees to appear for trial.

---

[21] *R (on the application of Saadi) v The Secretary of State for the Home Department* [2002] 1 WLR 3131.
[22] *Christie v Leachinsky* [1947] AC 573.

There are three rights in this paragraph: judicial review of detention, reasonably speedy trial, and release on bail. We shall look at the second, trial within a reasonable time, in our discussion of Article 6.[23] The other two rights are entirely within the philosophy of Article 5, which is to ensure that detention is not arbitrary. The duty to bring a detainee before a judicial authority means that a court has to authorise the continuance of detention, and the court then has the duty to consider releasing the detainee on bail; that is, releasing them from custody, pending their trial. This is usually on conditions, such as the payment of a sum of money as security; or having to report to a police station, or not leave the country, whilst on bail.

One case which provides an example of the European Court's attitude to the need for prompt judicial review is *Brogan*,[24] which we considered above.

In this case four men had been arrested under the Prevention of Terrorism Act, and they were detained for periods varying from 4 days 6 hours to 6 days $16\frac{1}{2}$ hours, without being charged or brought before a magistrate. The periods of detention had been reviewed and extended by a Minister of State, but not by any judicial officer.

The European Court held that they had not been brought before a judge, promptly or at all, because the person reviewing their detention had been a member of the executive and not a judge. There was therefore a breach of Article 5(3). This provision has now been altered by the Terrorism Act 2000, and detainees are now taken before a judge.

As for bail, the European Court has made it clear that there should be nothing automatic about detention; there should be no rule of the domestic law which provides that bail is unobtainable in the case of specified offences. That would be an arbitrary policy; it would prevent the courts applying proportionality to an individual case; indeed, the converse, it would oblige the courts to refuse bail where it was proportionate to grant it.

This is the general position under United Kingdom law. The Bail Act 1976 provides that a detained person shall be granted bail unless particular circumstances exist. These are set out in the Act, and they are if the defendant might fail to surrender, might commit an offence, might interfere with witnesses or otherwise might obstruct the course of justice. The court has a discretion, with a leaning in favour of granting bail.

But there was until recently a provision in an Act which prevented bail being granted, whatever the particular circumstances of the case. This was section 25 of the Criminal Justice and Public Order Act 1994, and this provided that bail could not be granted to a defendant charged with an offence of homicide or rape, when he had been previously convicted of a similar offence. The discretion of the court was taken away. That provision was held to be a violation of Article 5 in the case of *Caballero v UK*.[25]

Mr Caballero had been convicted in 1987 of manslaughter, and sentenced to a term of imprisonment; he was released in August 1988. In 1996 he was arrested on suspicion of attempted rape, and although he instructed his solicitor to apply for bail, no application was made, because of section 25. He was later convicted of attempted rape, and sentenced to life imprisonment. He complained to the European Court of a violation of Article 5(3) in that he had not been brought before a judge, and indeed could not be, and he could not be released while awaiting trial. The United

---

[23] See below, p. 155.
[24] (1989) 11 EHRR 117, above, p. 140.
[25] (2000) 30 EHRR 643.

Kingdom government agreed that there had been a violation. Between the trial of Mr Caballero and the decision of the European Court, the government amended the law, by the Crime and Disorder Act 1998, so that in such cases the court could grant bail if it found exceptional circumstances justifying bail.

The European Court has paid close attention to bail, and to the circumstances when a court may be justified in refusing it. The Court's approach can be summed up as follows: custody must be strictly justified. For example, see the case of *Letellier v France*.[26]

Mrs Monique Merdy, née Letellier, was a French national residing in France, and she took over a bar restaurant in March 1985. She was separated from her second husband, Mr Merdy, a petrol pump attendant, and she was living with a third man. On 6 July 1985, Mr Merdy was killed by a shot fired from a car. On the same day the police detained a Mr Moysan, who was found to be in possession of a pump-action shotgun. He admitted that he had fired the shot, but he said he had acted on the instructions of Mrs Merdy, and that she had agreed to pay him and a friend – who also accused her – the sum of 40,000 francs for killing her husband and that she had advanced him 2,000 francs for the purchase of the weapon. She denied the accusations, but admitted that she had seen the murder weapon, and she had given her agreement without thinking too much about it. She admitted she gave 2,000 francs to Mr Moysan to buy a car. She was charged with being an accessory to the murder.

On 8 July 1985, the judge remanded her in custody. She was given bail on 24 December 1985, but on 22 January 1986, she was returned to custody, where she remained until her trial on 10 May 1988; she was sentenced to 3 years' imprisonment, and released on 17 May 1988, the pre-trial detention being automatically being deducted from her sentence. The grounds for refusing her bail had been: the risk of pressure on witnesses, but that had diminished and disappeared; the danger of absconding, because of the severity of the likely sentence, but she had complied with her bail conditions in the time of her liberty in 1985–6; and public order, it being a murder of a husband.

The European Court found that Mrs Merdy's detention after 23 December 1986 had ceased to be based on relevant and sufficient grounds, and was a violation of Article 5(3). The European Court said:

> The persistence of reasonable suspicion that the person arrested has committed an offence is a condition *sine qua non* for the validity of the continued detention, but, after a certain lapse of time, it no longer suffices; the court must then establish whether the other grounds cited by the judicial authorities continue to justify the deprivation of liberty. Where such grounds are relevant and sufficient, the court must also ascertain whether the competent national authorities displayed special diligence in the conduct of the proceedings.

The European Court added that when the only remaining reason for continued detention – after dismissing other matters – was a fear that the accused would abscond, release on remand had to be ordered if the accused was in a position to provide adequate guarantees to ensure her appearance at her trial.

SPEEDY REVIEW OF DETENTION

Article 5(4): Everyone who is deprived of his liberty by arrest or detention shall be entitled to take proceedings by which the lawfulness of his detention shall be decided speedily by a court and his release ordered if the detention is not lawful.

---

[26] (1992) 14 EHRR 83.

By this provision the Convention imposes a duty on states to provide a system of reviewing a detainee's custody. These again are provided for in principle by United Kingdom law in the possibility of applying for bail, on the principles we have just discussed. Another way in which detention can be reviewed is by proceedings for **habeas corpus** (literally, 'you shall have the body'). This was originally intended to ensure that the person being detained was physically brought before the court. Habeas corpus is available to anyone who is detained in custody. It calls upon the person keeping the prisoner in custody to justify the detention. The court enquires into whether the detention is lawful or not; the question for the court is whether the reason for the detention, given by the gaoler, is sufficient as a matter of law to justify the detention; but the court does not consider all the detail of the case to see whether the cause given is actually correct. Thus, if a statute should provide particularly wide powers of detention, perhaps without trial or without the need to show reasonable suspicion that an offence has been committed, the protection of habeas corpus will lessen accordingly, since the statute will have widened the scope of lawful detention.

Again, the question of what is a speedy review and whether there has been a proper hearing raise issues which we will be considering in the context of Article 6. Again, although the principle of Article 5(4) is provided for by our law, it will be possible for it to be breached in particular cases, for example, if the review is not sufficiently speedy.

One case where the process of review has been held to infringe Article 5(4) is that of *Noorkoiv*.[27]

This case related to the review of the period of detention to be served by a life prisoner. Where a person is sentenced to detention for life, they may still be released on parole after a minimum period of time fixed by the court which sentenced them. In this case, the parole board did not meet to consider the continued detention of the prisoner until two months after this minimum period had expired. The Court of Appeal considered that this infringed Article 5(4): the parole board should have reviewed the continued detention before the end of the minimum period, since the state was required to release a life prisoner on parole when the minimum period ended unless he constituted a danger to the public.

COMPENSATION FOR WRONGFUL DETENTION

Article 5(5):   Everyone who has been the victim of arrest or detention in contravention of the provisions of this Article shall have an enforceable right to compensation.

Again, this is an important right, but one which is already substantially protected in United Kingdom law. There is already the right to claim compensation, by way of damages awarded by a court, for wrongful arrest and/or for false imprisonment, where the proper procedures for arrest or detention have not been followed; some of the cases we have discussed earlier were of this sort.

[27] *R (Noorkoiv) v Secretary of State for the Home Department and Parole Board* [2002] 1 WLR 3284.

DEROGATION FROM ARTICLE 5

It is appropriate to note here that Article 5 is the one article to which derogations have been entered,[28] on the basis that there were particular provisions of United Kingdom law relating to terrorism which should be retained even though it had been held that they infringed Article 5.

The initial derogation was based on the result in the case of *Brogan*,[29] where it was held by the European Court that extended periods of detention under the Prevention of Terrorism Act were in violation of Article 5(3). This was because the detention was authorised by a government minister and not by a judge or magistrate. A derogation was therefore entered regarding Article 5, on the basis that there was an emergency in Northern Ireland by reason of terrorist activity, and that to bring a suspect before a judge for an extension of custody would oblige the police to disclose the secret or sensitive intelligence which was the reason for the arrest. That derogation has now been lifted since the Prevention of Terrorism Act has now been repealed.

However, a further derogation in respect of Article 5(1)(f) has now been entered in respect of the Anti-terrorism, Crime and Security Act 2001.[30] This Act was passed following the terrorist attacks of 11 September 2001 in the United States. The derogation refers to an extended power to arrest and detain a foreign national where it is intended to remove or deport the person from the United Kingdom because the Secretary of State believes that his presence is a risk to national security and suspects him of being an international terrorist, but where such removal or deportation is not for the time being possible. The derogation is to cover a situation where there may be extended detention which is not consistent with Article 5(1)(f), for example, if there is an extensive delay before the question of whether or not the person can be granted asylum is decided, or if the government would deport the person as being a suspected terrorist but cannot without, for example, breaching Article 3 because there is a risk of that person being ill-treated on arrival in the country to which they would be deported. We will consider the justification for this derogation in more detail in our discussion of terrorism;[31] for the purposes of the present chapter, it is simply something that should be noted, since it is a situation where even if a period of detention does *not* comply with Article 5, our courts would not be able to grant a remedy under the Convention.

QUESTIONS

1   Consider the list of permissible reasons for detention in Article 5(1). Do you agree that these should all be included? Do they all serve a justifiable purpose?
2   Do you consider that Articles 5(2) to (5) provide sufficient safeguards for persons who have been arrested? Are there any other safeguards which should be included?

---

[28] For discussion of derogations, see above, pp. 84–5.
[29] *Brogan v UK* (1989) 11 EHRR 117, above, p. 140.
[30] Human Rights Act 1998 (Amendment no. 2) Order 2001, SI 2001 No. 4032.
[31] Below, Chapter 21.

A trial for kidnapping at Lancaster Castle in 1826; the Castle is still used as a Crown Court today (the standing barrister is Henry Brougham, later Lord Chancellor).

(*Source:* Reproduced courtesy of Lancaster Castle and the Duchy of Lancaster)

Chapter 12

THE RIGHT TO A FAIR TRIAL

'My Lord Hermiston occupied the bench in the red robes of criminal jurisdiction, his face framed in the white wig. Honest all through, he did not affect the virtue of impartiality; this was no case for refinement; there was a man to be hanged, he would have said, and he was hanging him.' (Robert Louis Stevenson, *The Weir of Hermiston*, 1896)

'For many years, the – a – I would say the flower of the Bar, and the – a – I would presume to add, the matured autumnal fruits of the Woolsack – have been lavished upon *Jarndyce and Jarndyce*. If the public have the benefit, and if the country have the adornment, of this great Grasp, it must be paid for in money or money's worth, sir.' 'Mr Kenge,' said Allan . . . 'Do I understand that the whole estate is found to have been absorbed in costs?' 'Hem! I believe so,' returned Mr Kenge. (Charles Dickens, *Bleak House*, 1853)

ARTICLE 6: THE RIGHT TO A FAIR TRIAL
1. In the determination of his civil rights and obligations or of any criminal charge against him, everyone is entitled to a fair and public hearing within a reasonable time by an independent and impartial tribunal established by law.
    Judgment shall be pronounced publicly but the press and public may be excluded from all or part of the trial in the interest of morals, public order or national security in a democratic society, where the interests of juveniles or the protection of the private life of the parties so require, or to the extent strictly necessary in the opinion of the court in special circumstances where publicity would prejudice the interests of justice.
2. Everyone charged with a criminal offence shall be presumed innocent until proved guilty according to law.
3. Everyone charged with a criminal offence has the following minimum rights:
    (a) to be informed promptly, in a language which he understands and in detail, of the nature and cause of the accusation against him;
    (b) to have adequate time and facilities for the preparation of his defence;
    (c) to defend himself in person or through legal assistance of his own choosing or, if he has not sufficient means to pay for legal assistance, to be given it free when the interests of justice so require;
    (d) to examine or have examined witnesses against him and to obtain the attendance and examination of witnesses on his behalf under the same conditions as witnesses against him;
    (e) to have the free assistance of an interpreter if he cannot understand or speak the language used in court.

THE IMPORTANCE OF A FAIR TRIAL

'. . . the object and purpose of Article 6, which, by protecting the right to a fair trial and in particular the right to be presumed innocent, is intended to enshrine the fundamental principle of the rule of law'. So runs the judgment of the European Court in the case of *Salabiaku v France*,[1] where criminal liability was presumed against the accused.

Article 6 contains some of the fundamental principles which underlie the idea of the rule of law, that individuals shall be treated with respect by the state: they shall not be punished unless they have committed a crime, and before they are punished it shall be proven, and not presumed, that they have done something illegal. They should be tried by a fair and impartial court which shall act on the basis of proof and the provisions of the law, and not on the basis simply of an accusation or the wishes of the state. Likewise, in deciding disputes between individuals, it is equally fundamental that the law is applied fairly and impartially, that all parties have equal access to the courts, and equal opportunities to put their case. And trials shall be in public wherever possible, so that justice may not only be done, it may be seen to be done, lending public confidence to the justice system.

The idea of a fair trial is by no means a new one to the British courts. Our law has over the centuries developed rules for the hearing of trials. Magna Carta, drawn up in 1215, includes a guarantee of impartial and speedy legal process. For centuries, it has been the tradition that trials are held in public, so that justice can be seen to be done. Likewise, it has long been part of our law that the burden is on the prosecution of proving that a criminal offence has been committed, with the trial usually heard by a jury. Although it was only in the nineteenth century that a defendant in a criminal case was allowed to give evidence on oath, the right to put the case for the defence is a well- and long-established one, in particular the right to put questions by way of cross-examination of the witnesses for the prosecution, and the right to legal representation. Excluding unreliable evidence, such as hearsay, is also of long standing, as is the right not to answer questions if they will incriminate the witness.

In more recent times, there have been further improvements to our system to maintain fairness, for example rules on the fair use of identification evidence or the conduct of identity parades, or the court's power to exclude evidence obtained improperly. Likewise in civil cases there are detailed rules of procedure to ensure that both parties have an equal opportunity to set out their case and put all relevant evidence before the court.

What, then, does Article 6 add to our law, if the protection of a fair trial is already such an integral part of it? Especially since the British trial tradition was an important influence on how the Article was drafted in the first place, and if our law provides a higher standard of protection than the Convention, that will continue to apply.

The effect of Article 6 will not be to alter fundamentally how trials are conducted, or the basic principles which apply, or the main safeguards for fairness. However, the result of the European Court jurisprudence on Article 6 has been that changes have been made to a number of areas, where our judges have used the European cases to reconsider or review the existing rules or approach of the law and in many cases increase

---

[1] (1991) 13 EHRR 379.

the protection provided to ensure a fair trial. It has not altered the basic principles of our law, but it has changed some of the ways in which these are applied.

And it is not in a narrow field, or in a limited kind of case, that the Convention has been applied. It has been invoked in a wide variety of situations: for example, in the criminal field, imposing a burden of proof on a defendant, drawing inferences from silence, compelling a defendant to answer incriminating questions, tempting a person to commit an offence and not allowing evidence obtained unfairly. In the civil sphere, it has been cited in questions of the conduct of hearings, the use of hearsay evidence, and the imposition of an expert witness on a party.

The addition of Article 6 to our law has therefore required the courts to consider all these areas afresh, asking the general question, is the law, or the way it is applied, fair and proportionate, or arbitrary; how far do our existing provisions do enough to provide a fair trial?

CIVIL AND CRIMINAL CASES

There is a time-honoured division of cases into criminal and civil, because different considerations apply to how the two different categories of case are dealt with by the courts. In a civil case, the key is that both parties, being individuals, are dealt with comparably and therefore fairly by the court, which must be impartial between them until it has heard all the evidence and argument, and then makes a decision.

In a criminal case, however, there is an imbalance from the outset: the prosecution has the resources of the state available to it, both through the police and the Crown Prosecution Service. The result is also more serious for the accused: if found guilty, they will acquire a criminal record and be liable to punishment, which will involve prison in more serious cases. It is for these reasons that the presumption of innocence is so important: before a person is deprived of their good name and liberty, it must be proved beyond reasonable doubt that they are guilty: it should not be for them to prove that they are not guilty. A court should never assume that the fact that someone is accused of something means that for that reason alone they are likely to have done it, a serious mistake too often made in the media.

The wording of Article 6 recognises that there are both civil and criminal cases in its reference to 'the determination of civil rights and obligations or of any criminal charge'. We shall follow this division when examining how the Convention affects English law, because although the general principles are the same in both sorts of trial, the way in which they are applied can be quite different.

IS ARTICLE 6 UNQUALIFIED?

The first question is how much protection does Article 6 provide: is the right provided by Article 6 – the right to a fair trial – an absolute right or is it subject to any qualification? As we have seen, other rights in the Convention are expressly qualified.[2] The only such express qualification in Article 6 is to the right to have a trial in *public*, where the grounds on which this can be limited are set out.

---

[2] For example, Articles 8 to 11; see above, p. 86.

The courts have said that the overall fairness of a trial cannot be limited or qualified. There is no question of allowing a trial to be 'moderately fair' or for one kind of case to have a first-class fairness, and another a second class.

However, that is not the whole picture. Article 6 has express rights; they are expressly set out in its wording. It also has implied rights. The European Court has carried out a process of reading into the words of Article 6 a collection of other rights; they give effect to the fundamental and absolute right to a fair trial. For example, the express right to be presumed innocent includes the right to silence, and the right against self-incrimination. And as to those implied rights there may be implied restrictions.

It will be a matter of judicial interpretation, in the circumstances of the case, whether the words of Article 6 imply a right, and whether there is any qualification of that right. The qualification will be especially gauged by the facts. Let us look at an example. There is a right to be presumed innocent; that is express. Implicit in it, according to the European Court, is the right not to incriminate oneself. But suppose an Act of Parliament permits a police officer to ask questions, and obliges the person to answer in such a way that the answers will incriminate the person being questioned? That would surely be a violation of Article 6 and the right not to incriminate oneself. On the other hand, it is in the public interest that crimes should be prevented or punished, and it may be necessary to make it obligatory to answer these questions. There will be a process of balancing the right of the individual against that of the public; and the limitation on the individual's right to a fair trial must be a proportionate one. This was the scenario in the case of *Brown v Stott*.[3]

Margaret Anderson Brown was at a superstore when the staff suspected that she had stolen a bottle of gin, and they called the police, who noticed that she appeared to have been drinking alcohol; the police asked her how she came to be at the store, and she answered that she had come by car, and she pointed to a car which she said was hers. She was charged with theft, and taken to a police station, where she was *required* to say who was driving the car when she used it to get to the store, and she admitted that she was the driver; she was *required* under the Road Traffic Act 1988, which obliges the keeper of a car to give information as to the identity of the driver at the time of an offence. The Privy Council held that there was no breach of Article 6. Lord Bingham said:

> The jurisprudence of the European Court very clearly establishes that while the overall fairness of a criminal trial cannot be compromised, the constituent rights comprised, whether expressly or implicitly, within Article 6 are not themselves absolute. Limited qualification of these rights is acceptable if reasonably directed by national authorities towards a clear and proper public objective and if representing no greater qualification than the situation calls for. [. . .] *The high incidence of death and injury on the roads caused by the misuse of motor vehicles is a very serious problem common to almost all developed societies. The need to address it in an effective way, for the benefit of the public, cannot be doubted.* [. . .] I do not for my part consider that section 172, properly applied, does represent a disproportionate response to this serious social problem, nor do I think that reliance on the respondent's admission, in the present case, would undermine her right to a fair trial. (emphasis added)

Note the words in italics; the judges took into account the purpose of the legislation, specifically current road conditions, and carried out a balancing exercise. On the one hand, there were the rights of the individual, and on the other, the aim of the statute

---

[3] [2001] 2 WLR 817.

to punish road traffic offences, and they found that the interference with the right was proportionate to what it was trying to achieve.

The same exercise was carried out in a drink-driving case, where the law provided that a particular fact should be presumed against a defendant, and presumed irrebuttably – he should have no right to refute it. That presumption, one may say, is in sharp conflict with another presumption – the presumption of innocence. That case was *Parker v DPP*.[4]

Mr Parker had been convicted by the Magistrates Court of driving whilst over the prescribed limit, contrary to section 5 of the Road Traffic Act 1988; section 15(2) of that Act provided that there was an irrebuttable presumption that the level of alcohol provided at the time of the offence could not be less than the reading given by the specimen he supplied at the police station later. Mr Parker's argument was that the section providing the presumption was incompatible with Article 6, and so should be read as *not* containing the presumption. But the Queen's Bench Divisional Court held that the presumption was reasonable in the context of the road traffic legislation as a whole, having regard to the interest at stake, which was aimed at preventing motorists from consuming alcohol before they took charge of a motor vehicle. Thus the presumption was *not* a violation of Article 6.

Once again, the court referred to the surrounding circumstances, and it undertook a balancing exercise, which took account of the importance to the public of the maintenance of road safety. And the case is a good illustration of the principle which is so important: some rights under Article 6 may be qualified, when the qualification is proportionate to its aim, in the circumstances of the particular case.

A FAIR HEARING

These words are the heart of Article 6. On reading the words the first thing that we are entitled to is a **fair hearing,** and every point that is described in the wording of the remainder of the article is an ingredient of a fair hearing. For example, one aspect of a fair hearing is to be presumed innocent of accusations against you; and another is the right to examine witnesses against you. But even when none of those specific requirements is said to have been infringed, the court may nonetheless consider the fairness of the proceedings; it is not necessary for any of the specific ingredients of Article 6 – express or implied – to be present for the court to judge whether the hearing is fair. The word 'fair' in Article 6 has its own effect, and the courts have held that a trial may be unfair, without referring to any other words of the article. So in the case of *King*,[5] the court examined the circumstances and found that Mr King had been treated unfairly.

Mr King was disabled and had suffered a stroke; he appeared before the Crown Court for failing to carry out works at his property, when required to do so under the Housing Act 1985. At the Crown Court he was kept waiting from 10 in the morning until 4 in the afternoon; he had no legal representation, and he was not allowed to make a closing speech. The High Court held that in all

---

[4] [2001] RTR 240.
[5] *R v King* [2001] EHRLR 14.

these circumstances he had not had a fair trial, in breach of Article 6; and particular reference was made to the guidelines published for all judges, the Equal Treatment Bench Book, as being of assistance in achieving a 'fair' trial.

No reference was made to any specific part of Article 6, but the court had no difficulty in judging fairness without any such reference. The concept of fairness was provided by Article 6, without having to rely on one of its ingredients. And the same goes for this next case, the *International Roth*[6] case, where the court held that the manner in which a penalty was imposed on lorry drivers was unfair. For there to be a fair hearing, there must *be* an actual hearing.

The question arose out of a penalty scheme imposed by the Immigration and Asylum Act 1999. This meant that lorry drivers and owners were liable to a fixed penalty of £2,000 if a person, seeking to enter the country in a clandestine way, was found concealed in such a vehicle; the driver or owner had the right to show that he acted under duress, or that he had a total lack of knowledge, or that he had an effective system to prevent such a stowaway; the vehicle meanwhile was liable to be seized by immigration officials. A group of sixty drivers complained that this was a violation of Article 6.

The Court of Appeal agreed, holding that the scheme was unfair. In particular, although the court recognised that the fixed penalty scheme was intended to deal with a social problem, that of illegal immigration, the court still considered that a substantial fixed penalty could not be reconciled with the important principle that the punishment must fit the crime, since there was no opportunity for the person being penalised to argue that the penalty should be mitigated in the particular circumstances of their case. In principle, the regime infringed the right to have the penalty determined by an independent tribunal.

The Court took into account the aims of the scheme – to prevent illegal immigration, and to promote vigilance on the part of cross-border carriers – and balanced them against the inflexibility of the statute, which imposed a penalty regardless of blameworthiness. This was what was unfair, even though it is not an express or specific requirement of Article 6, and even though there were references to other specific points, such as the burden of proof imposed on the carriers which one judge held constituted a disproportionate and unjustifiable inroad on the right of silence.

A fair hearing also means that the judge should in fact hear what each party has to say, without undue interruption. If a proper hearing is denied to one party, there is a sense of injustice, and justice is not seen to be done. This is illustrated by the case of *CG v UK*.[7]

CG was charged with theft, pleaded not guilty, was tried before a judge and jury and was found guilty. Her complaint was that the trial judge frequently interrupted both her defence counsel – preventing him from testing the evidence – and her own evidence. There were indeed interruptions on almost every page of cross-examination of the key prosecution witness, and on 22 out of 31 pages of her own evidence. The Court of Appeal said that there was some substance in her criticism, but the interruptions were not such as to make the conviction unsafe, and so the appeal was dismissed.

---

[6] *International Roth GmbH v Secretary of State for the Home Department* [2002] 3 WLR 344.
[7] (2002) 34 EHRR 34.

The European Court took account of the fact that the Court of Appeal had examined the case. It made a careful examination of the facts, and found that some interruptions were due to misunderstandings; also, that her defence counsel had not been prevented or deterred from developing the line of defence. The European Court concluded, by a majority, that there was *no* breach of Article 6.

Nonetheless, this illustrates the principle: the way that a judge conducts a particular trial, including their interruptions, may make a trial unfair; even though on the facts of this case, that stage had not been reached.

WITHIN A REASONABLE TIME

We turn now to the next phrase in Article 6(1), that the trial must take place within a **reasonable time**. Here again, the criminal law again has well-established rules to deal with delays in bringing proceedings. A defendant who complains of undue delay in bringing him to trial may apply to the court for an order that the proceedings should be stayed, on the ground that it would be an abuse of process to permit them to continue. It is said that it would be unfair to try the defendant, or that a trial of the defendant would be an unfair one.

The European Court has developed its own approach to complaints of undue delay, and our courts have followed the jurisprudence of the Convention in two areas especially. The first is about the question, from what time does one measure the period of delay? The European Court has held that it is the time when the defendant is first affected by the accusation, by being interviewed, or when an investigation begins. The second area is about prejudice; must the party complaining of delay prove that they have suffered some prejudice from the delay?

The approach in the British courts until recently was that time ran from when the defendant was charged, and that he had to prove prejudice. But in a recent decision, the Privy Council reconsidered these in the light of the cases of the European Court.[8]

The Privy Council had to consider two cases. The first concerned two police officers, Watson and Burrows, who gave evidence at Linlithgow Sheriff Court, in April 1998, on the trial of a man charged with offences of public order, and vandalism, where at the end of the trial the Sheriff in open court announced his opinion that the two officers had committed perjury. However, after enquiries and interviews of the officers, proceedings against them were only commenced in April 2000. The other, which was quite separate, related to a boy, JK, aged 13, who was interviewed by the police in October 1998 about sex offences he was alleged to have committed. The indictment to commence criminal proceedings was served only in January 2001.

Each prosecution was stayed, on the grounds that there had been such a delay in bringing proceedings against the defendants as to breach the reasonable time requirement contained in Article 6. The Crown appealed to the Privy Council, which held that there *should* be a stay in the case of JK, because there had been an unreasonable delay, in a case which was not complex, but which required careful handling, and JK had not been responsible for any aspect of the delay; but there should *not* in the case of the two police officers, where the delay was 20 months, and they were not in custody. The Privy Council regarded time as starting to run in the case of the

---

[8] *Dyer v Watson and Burrows; HM Advocate v JK* [2002] 1 WLR 1488.

police officers when they were detained and interviewed, which is when they were seriously affected by the allegation and investigation.

This case set out the general approach to the requirement of a hearing within a reasonable time. Whilst it will not be easy to show that a case has not been heard in a reasonable time, if the period which has elapsed gives ground for real concern, the court must look into the detailed facts of the particular case; and the prosecution must explain and justify any lapse of time which appears to be excessive. The court must consider the complexity of the case, the conduct of the defendant and the manner in which the case has been dealt with by the administrative and judicial authorities. What is quite clear is that the state cannot blame an unacceptable delay on a lack of resources, whether lack of judges or prosecutors, or a general under-funding of the legal system. The obligation under Article 6 is on the state to organise its legal system to ensure that case are prosecuted and heard within a reasonable time.

Likewise, although the question of whether or not a defendant has been prejudiced by the delay will be relevant, since the risk of prejudice by the delay is at the heart of the requirement for a prompt hearing, it is not necessary for the defendant to show that there has been prejudice to establish that there has been a breach of the requirement for a hearing within a reasonable time.

AN INDEPENDENT COURT

This is a critical requirement of a fair trial. The trial cannot be fair if the court does not approach the case with an open mind. In our law this is usually expressed as comprising two fundamental principles. The first is that a person may not be a judge in his own cause: if they have an **interest in the result** of the case, it cannot be said that they are independent. Second, there must be no **bias**: a judge must not show favour to one side or another, nor have a reason to do so, nor appear to do so.

Judges in the courts of the United Kingdom are conscious of their independence; they do not hear the case if they realise they are connected with the subject matter of the case, or when there is any suggestion that they may have. Even if there is in fact no connection, a possible appearance of it may be enough for the judge to consider not hearing the case. A judge should avoid the *appearance* of partiality or bias, even if it does not actually exist.

AN INTEREST IN THE CASE

The question of whether or not a judge has an interest in the subject matter of the case can be illustrated by the case of the Chilean dictator, *General Pinochet*.[9]

Senator Pinochet was a former Head of State of Chile. A judge in Spain issued warrants of arrest, alleging that Pinochet had committed various crimes against humanity during his period of office.

---

[9] *R v Bow Street Metropolitan Stipendiary Magistrate and others ex parte Pinochet Ugarte (No. 2)* [2000] 1 AC 119.

Pinochet was therefore arrested during a visit to London under a warrant issued under the extradition law. The arrest warrants were contested and quashed in the English courts on the basis that Pinochet had immunity from arrest and extradition as a former Head of State, and the matter was appealed to the House of Lords, who held by a majority that Senator Pinochet did *not* have immunity.

One of the Lords who heard the case was Lord Hoffmann, who was a member of the majority in the decision. Amnesty International, a human rights body, which had campaigned against the Senator, was represented at the hearing before the House of Lords. Subsequently, Senator Pinochet learned that Lord Hoffmann was an unpaid director and chairman of a subsidiary company of Amnesty International. Senator Pinochet applied to the House of Lords to set aside its decision, on the ground not that Lord Hoffmann had any actual bias but that there was *apparent* bias – a real danger or reasonable apprehension or suspicion that Lord Hoffmann *might* have been biased.

The House of Lords agreed. Once Amnesty International had been allowed to intervene, they became a party to the case. Although they were neither prosecutor nor accused, they had an interest in establishing that there was no immunity for former heads of state in relation to crimes against humanity. They therefore had an interest in procuring Pinochet's extradition, albeit a political interest, rather than, for example, a monetary interest, and *that* was an interest in promoting one of the arguments being advanced rather than another. Since Lord Hoffmann was a director of the subsidiary company, he should have been the subject of automatic disqualification: the principle is that where a judge is a party to the action or has a financial or proprietary interest in its outcome, he is automatically disqualified from hearing it, whether or not there is any likelihood or suspicion of actual bias.

BIAS

Bias is rather different. It is partiality, or a lack of objectivity, or the possible appearance of it. The incorporation of the Convention has brought about an even closer scrutiny of the notion of independence. And this appears in a case about the court-martial system, which is where a member of the armed forces is tried for a crime under military law. Although the court-martial procedure had been in existence for a long time, this is one area where our law has been changed,[10] following the decision of the European Court in *Findlay v UK*.[11]

When Lance Sergeant Findlay was tried for a shooting incident, which he blamed on suffering post-traumatic stress disorder, in the then usual way, the court-martial consisted of 5 members of the armed forces. These members were subordinate to the convening officer of the court-martial, who himself played a significant role before the hearing, was central to the prosecution, and he had power to dismiss the court-martial. The decision was confirmed by the convening officer.

The European Court held that the court-martial was not independent within the meaning of the Convention, and therefore there was a violation of Article 6, because of the overlapping roles of the convening officer between prosecution and judge. Critical questions in deciding whether a court is impartial include the manner of appointment of its members and their term of office, the existence of guarantees against outside pressures and the question whether the body presents an appearance of independence. And to be impartial, the court must not only be subjectively free of personal prejudice or bias, it must also be impartial from an objective viewpoint, that is, it must offer sufficient guarantees to exclude any legitimate doubt in this respect.

---

[10] Armed Forces Act 1996.
[11] (1997) 24 EHRR 221.

The House of Lords has confirmed that the courts-martial system now complies with Article 6, because it has permanent presidents, with sufficient safeguards that a fair-minded observer would *not* conclude that the court was not independent or impartial.[12]

It is objective impartiality which is so important: being *seen* to be impartial. The European Court in *Findlay* states clearly the ingredients of it – manner of appointment, term of office, and guarantees of independence from pressures. But those words about independence from pressures were relevant in another case, where until the incorporation of the Convention, no thought had been given to the possibility of bias.

In *Starrs and Chalmers v Ruxton*,[13] in a criminal court, the complainants appeared before a Temporary Sheriff, who was a judge appointed by the Secretary of State; however, the appointment was dependent on the recommendation of the Lord Advocate, and it was he who conducted the prosecution. The office of Temporary Sheriff was the start of a route to higher judicial office. The court held that there was an appearance of lack of objectivity, because of the manner of the appointment, and the lack of tenure of office. In these circumstances there was a violation of Article 6.

Where a judge is appointed by the government to a post which has no security of tenure, there may be an objective appearance of the judge being tempted to give a decision in favour of the government, however much it is known and accepted that the particular judge is a person of complete independence and integrity. And the case of *Findlay* was used by the English court in a case about magistrates in their capacity as licensing justices, when they are carrying out their function of granting or refusing licences to premises for alcohol or entertainment.

The relevance of Article 6 is that when a licensing decision is appealed to the Crown Court, it is heard by a judge and four magistrates, two of whom must be members of the magistrates' bench where the premises are situated which are the subject of the appeal. The idea behind this is presumably that those two magistrates will have knowledge of local conditions in the licensing field. But it means that two of the justices sitting in the Crown Court are hearing an appeal from a decision of their colleagues on the local bench. However independent and scrupulous those two magistrates are, they may be perceived to be seeking to uphold their colleagues' decision.

This was challenged in the case of *The Preston and Lincoln Crown Courts*,[14] where the High Court held that the arrangement – two magistrates sitting on the appeal from their own bench – was a violation of Article 6. The Court pointed out that the two magistrates sit on the Crown Court bench at the invitation of their own clerk, and may be asked to make an order for costs against their colleagues, and there is a danger that they may incline, even unconsciously, to conform with their colleagues.

As well as being an illustration of the way in which a judge may possibly be in a position of partiality, that is, apparent partiality, this is also a prime example of the influence of the Convention on our law. It is the wording and spirit of Article 6 which have made the courts examine again rules and procedures, which have been used over the years without question.

---

[12] *R v Spear* [2002] 3 WLR 437.

[13] [2000] UKHRR 78.

[14] *R (on the application of the Chief Constable of Lancashire) v Preston Crown Court; R (on the application of Smith) v Lincoln Crown Court* [2002] 1 WLR 1332.

The test, to detect possible partiality, is a high one. It is to ask whether the circumstances would lead a fair-minded and informed observer to conclude that there was a real possibility or a real danger that the tribunal was biased. This definition of the test was set out by the Court of Appeal after an examination of the previous English cases and after applying the Convention jurisprudence.[15]

The case in question concerned an application by the Director General of Fair Trading (DGFT) to the Restrictive Practices Court to discharge a 30-year-old order which had exempted branded medicines from the general ban in law on there being minimum prices on the resale of products, since the DGFT argued that this exemption could no longer be justified.

One member of the court was a doctor, and during the course of the hearing she applied to be employed by a firm which was providing expert evidence in the case, although the firm rejected her application. The trade associations defending the exemption applied for this doctor and the rest of the court to withdraw from hearing it, alleging that the court was biased. The court refused. On appeal from this decision, the Court of Appeal held that there was a violation of Article 6. After setting out the test of whether or not there is a real possibility of bias, the Court decided that in this case, a fair-minded observer would be concerned that if the doctor esteemed the firm sufficiently to wish to be employed by them, she might consciously or unconsciously be inclined to consider them a more reliable source of expert opinion than their rivals. Thus there was a real danger that the doctor would be unable to make an objective and impartial appraisal of the expert evidence, and so she and the other members of the court should have withdrawn from the case.

One feature of the case is that the Court of Appeal, having examined the jurisprudence of the European Court, thereupon altered the English approach in cases of bias, from one in which the court decided the likelihood of the lower court being *in fact* biased, to one in which the court asks what the *fair-minded observer* would have thought.

So far we have considered the position of judges; but where there is a jury, the parties in the case have a right to be sure that the jury is also independent. In the normal course of events, a jury is indeed independent. It is composed of individuals who have no connection with the parties, and have no knowledge of the facts of the case before it starts. When a case involves famous or notorious events or personalities, the jury is directed to ignore anything which they may have heard outside the court, and to concentrate on the evidence given in court. From time to time, it is true, efforts are made to make corrupt offers or threats to jurors, which will impair their independence; if that is discovered, the jury are discharged from giving a verdict, and the case starts again with a fresh jury. But leaving aside cases of that kind, lack of independence in a jury may arise in another way, and it has attracted the attention of the European Court. In two cases it came to the notice of the judge that the jury, or a number of them, were harbouring an attitude of racial discrimination.

In *Gregory v UK*,[16] the applicant, who was black, was tried at Manchester Crown Court for robbery. The jury retired to consider their verdict, and nearly two hours after retiring, a note was passed from the jury to the judge, reading, 'Jury showing racial overtones. One member to be excused.' The judge warned the jury to try the case according to the evidence and to put aside any prejudice. The jury

---

[15] *In re Medicaments and Related Classes of Goods (No. 2), DGFT v Proprietary Association of Great Britain and Proprietary Articles Trade Association* [2001] 1 WLR 700.
[16] (1998) 25 EHRR 577.

eventually returned with a majority verdict of guilty. Relying on Articles 6 and 14, the applicant complained to the European Court that he had not had a fair trial, and that he had been discriminated against on the basis of race. The European Court found that the judge had dealt with the note firmly, and that after his direction, to try the case on the evidence, there was no further suggestion from the jury of any racial comment, and so the judge could reasonably consider that the jury had complied with the terms of his direction. He had taken sufficient steps to ensure that the jury was behaving impartially.

However, in the case of *Sander v UK*,[17] there were conflicting notes from the jury, and when the judge attempted to clear up what was being said, there was further contradiction. The judge allowed the jury to continue their deliberations, and they convicted the applicant. He complained that he had suffered a violation of Article 6, and the European Court agreed. The judge had not made sure that the jury were conducting themselves properly, and there remained a doubt about this.

PRESUMPTION OF INNOCENCE

In the courts of the United Kingdom, the prosecution must prove the guilt of the defendant, and there is no burden on the defendant to prove that he is not guilty. This is called the **presumption of innocence,** and it is expressly stated in Article 6(2) – a defendant is presumed to be innocent until he is proved guilty. Since this is already the courts' guiding principle, the question is whether the article has anything to add.

The answer is that it has indeed added something – especially in cases where the law has imposed a **burden of proof** on a defendant. This occurs commonly in statutes, for example where there is a criminal offence to do something or to be in a particular place, but the statute goes on to state that the defendant may prove facts which will give him a defence – that he did not have the requisite knowledge, or that he was acting as an employee and did not have the control of the activity, for example. Modern statutes have created offences and imposed burdens on a defendant with words such as '. . . unless the defendant proves the contrary'. These words are commonly described as 'reverse onus clauses'. In time past the English courts have regarded the burden of proof on the defendant as being 'on a balance of probabilities', which is a burden lower than that resting on the prosecution, who must prove guilt so that the court is sure. It means the prosecution are taken to have proved what is necessary against the defendant, unless he satisfies the jury on a balance of probabilities to the contrary. However, this still imposes what is known as a **persuasive burden,** which is the onus of satisfying the court that the defence is proven, as opposed to an **evidential burden,** a burden simply to provide enough evidence to credibly raise the defence, which the prosecution must then disprove.

But this should now be appraised afresh, because of the influence of the Convention case law on the approach of our courts; this is aptly illustrated in the case of *Kebilene*.[18] There the House of Lords analysed the thinking behind reverse onus clauses, namely, that there may be difficulty in proving the defendant's intention or purpose, or actual possession, especially when the defendant is a terrorist and had been trained in ways of avoiding detection, or has an explanation which is a plausible one.[19] And the

---

[17] (2001) 31 EHRR 44.

[18] *R v DPP, ex parte Kebilene* [2002] 2 AC 326.

[19] For a discussion of the particular problems raised by terrorism, see Chapter 21 below.

speeches show how a balance has to be struck between the rights of the individual, and the interest in general security represented by the state.

In 1997, officers of the anti-terrorist squad arrested Mr Kebilene, Mr Boukemiche, and Mr Souidi, who were Algerian nationals; they were charged with offences of having articles in their possession in circumstances giving rise to a reasonable suspicion that the articles were in their possession for the purposes of terrorism. The articles in this case were chemical containers, radio equipment, manuals, credit cards, and money. The statute under which they were charged provided that the defendant had a *defence* to the charge by proving that the article in question was not in his possession for the purpose of terrorism. But the statute also had a provision which assisted the prosecution to prove possession: it provided that where the prosecution proves that the defendant and the article were both present on the same premises, or the article was on premises occupied by the defendant, *that* would be sufficient evidence of his possessing the article, *unless* the defendant proved that he did not know of the article, or had no control of it.

The defendants contended that, contrary to Article 6, there was in this section no presumption of innocence; as to the two main ingredients of the offence, possession and purpose, the one could be proved by a presumption – as to the presence of the defendant and the article on the same premises – and the other by a reasonable suspicion, which is a burden lower than that normally imposed on the prosecution. After that, the burden was on the defendant.

The trial judge agreed that there was a breach of Article 6, and so did the Divisional Court. But the House of Lords held that the section of the statute did not necessarily violate Article 6 (it reached no final conclusion because it took the view that the decision to prosecute could not be challenged in any event). Much depended on the surrounding facts and circumstances. This was indeed a reverse onus clause, but such clauses had to be analysed. They might impose on the defendant only an evidential burden, the burden of introducing evidence on the point, which is *not* a breach of Article 6, or it might be a persuasive burden, the burden of proving the point on a balance of probabilities, which *might* be a violation, depending on the circumstances. Those circumstances have to be balanced, in this case the protection of the state against terrorism with the right of the individual to a fair trial.

The House of Lords recognised the new attitude the courts must take in the light of the Convention. Some of the relevant factors were set out by Lord Hope:

> In the hands of the national courts[,] the Convention should be seen as an expression of fundamental principles rather than as a set of mere rules. The questions which the courts will have to decide in the application of these principles will involve questions of balance between competing interests and issues of proportionality. [. . .] In considering where the balance lies it may be useful to consider the following questions:
> (1) what does the prosecution have to prove in order to transfer the onus to the defence?
> (2) what is the burden on the accused – does it relate to something which is likely to be difficult for him to prove, or does it relate to something which is likely to be within his knowledge [or] to which he readily has access?
> (3) what is the nature of the threat faced by society which the provision is designed to combat?

This question of reverse burdens is one which must be considered in the context of the statute which imposes the burden, since in each case the balance between the result of the reverse burden and the underlying reason for it may be different. We will consider one more case of this kind to illustrate how the courts are dealing with these situations.[20]

---

[20] Some other examples of reverse burdens are also considered in the context of statutory interpretation, above, pp. 56–7.

In the case of *R v Lambert*,[21] the defendant was arrested in a car park at Runcorn railway station, in possession of a duffel bag; it contained 2 kg of cocaine worth £140,000. He was charged with an offence of having in his possession a class A controlled drug with intent to supply, contrary to section 5(3) of the Misuse of Drugs Act 1971. The defendant relied on section 28(3) of that Act which provides that an accused shall be acquitted if he proves that he neither believed nor suspected nor had reason to suspect that he possessed a substance which is a controlled drug. He said a man in London, for whom he was accustomed to run errands, sent him to Runcorn, with an envelope. He alighted from the train at Runcorn, and met a man he knew, who gave him a bag, saying that it was jewellery.

The question that arose was, is the burden of proof imposed on the accused in the words 'shall be acquitted' an evidential one or the more heavy one of a persuasive burden? There was a difference of opinion in the House of Lords, but the majority view was that it was an evidential burden only and so there was no breach of Article 6. One member of the court, Lord Hutton, considered that this was a persuasive burden, but that even so this was not a violation of Article 6, since the threat of drugs to the wellbeing of the community and the peculiar difficulty of proving knowledge in such cases justifies the imposition of a persuasive burden.

ADVERSE INFERENCES

The presumption of innocence means that the prosecution must prove the guilt of the defendant; he is entitled to remain silent and make the prosecution prove his guilt, if they can. This is usually referred to as the defendant's right of silence. But in English law there is a qualification to this right. By section 34 of the Criminal Justice and Public Order Act 1994, where a defendant, during his interview by police officers, fails to mention something which he later relies on in his defence, the jury may draw from that failure such inferences as appear proper to them; this is usually called 'drawing adverse inferences'.

This has been considered by the European Court in the case of *Condron v UK*.[22] The European Court there held that when an accused has been interviewed by police officers, and maintained a silence when questioned, if the jury is allowed to infer anything adverse to him from that silence, there must be safeguards in place, and the courts have now tailored their directions to juries to meet the European Court's comments. The facts were as follows.

Both applicants were heroin addicts, and they lived at 51 Cubitt House, a large block of council flats in South London. Adjacent to their flat, at 50, lived a Mr James Curtis, and the prosecution alleged that the applicants would prepare wraps of heroin for sale, and pass them to Mr Curtis when he knocked on the back window of their flat. The wraps would be handed from the balcony of 51 to someone leaning out of the window of 50. Mr Curtis would then sell the wrap to a purchaser. When the applicants were arrested, wraps of heroin, and other material, were found in their flat. They were charged with the supply and possession of heroin with intent to supply. At a police station, they were interviewed by police officers, although their solicitor thought that they were unfit to be interviewed, because of drug withdrawal. The interviews were preceded by a warning from the interviewing officer, which stated: 'You do not have to say anything but it may harm your defence if you do not mention when questioned something which you later rely on in court. Anything you say may be given in evidence.' Each applicant said, in answer to the interviewer's questions, 'No comment'.

---

[21] [2001] 3 WLR 206.
[22] (2001) 31 EHRR 1.

At their trial, both applicants gave explanations, which they had not given in interview, saying in evidence that the heroin found in their flat had been for their own personal use, that the package seen being passed between the flats was a quantity of cigarettes, and that they had said 'No comment' acting on the advice of their solicitor, who had grave doubts about their fitness to be interviewed. The solicitor gave evidence to the same effect. The trial judge, in his direction to the jury, left them with the option of drawing an inference, under section 34, which was adverse to the applicants, from their silence in interview. They were convicted; Mr Curtis was acquitted. The applicants complained to the European Court that they were entitled to remain silent at the interviews, and to draw an inference from their silence was unfair, and a violation of Article 6.

The European Court stated that the right to silence is *not an absolute right*; and whether the drawing of an adverse inference from an accused's silence infringes Article 6 is a matter to be determined in the light of all the circumstances of the particular case. But, said the Court, particular caution was required before a court could use an accused's silence against him. The Court held that the jury could draw an inference adverse to the two accused *only* if they, the jury, were satisfied that their silence at the interview must be attributed to their having no answer or none that would stand up to cross-examination. The Court of Appeal had held that it would have been 'desirable' to give that direction. But for the European Court, that was not enough.

AGENTS PROVOCATEURS

In the investigation of crime, police officers have developed a technique of being proactive – of placing temptation in the way of a person, whom they suspect of committing crimes, but whom they cannot catch. When the person succumbs to the temptation, the watching police arrest him. The argument in favour of using this technique is that the secrecy in which some crime is carried out, and the consequent difficulty of detection, makes it necessary. But it is one thing to place an opportunity in the way of a person who is looking for the opportunity, and it is quite another to incite the commission of a crime, or to instigate it. Incitement or instigation will probably be an offence in itself. It is in this situation that the courts have been obliged to deal with the argument, advanced on behalf of the defendant, that the officers have acted as agents provocateurs, in the sense that they have incited the defendant to commit the crime.

Both the European Court and our own courts have grappled with the problem of deciding when such techniques are unfair. They will be unfair if they lead to an abuse of the process of the law. 'It is simply not acceptable that the state through its agents should lure its citizens into committing acts forbidden by the law and then to seek to prosecute them for doing so.' These are the words of Lord Nicholls, in the case of *R v Looseley*, which we are about to examine.

The English courts have dealt with unfairness by using section 78 of the Police and Criminal Evidence Act 1984 (PACE), which enables the court to exclude prosecution evidence if it would be unfair to admit it. And the courts have developed the machinery of a stay of a prosecution as being an abuse of process where they decide that it would be unfair to try the defendant, or where the trial would be unfair. In this next case the House of Lords were expressly asked to consider whether, in a case of a so-called agent provocateur, Article 6 had modified the law relating to section 78 or stay for abuse of process. The case is *R v Looseley*, heard with another case, referred on a point of law where there had been no conviction, *Attorney General's Reference No. 3 of 2000*.[23]

---

[23] [2001] 1 WLR 2060.

In the case of Mr Looseley, a police officer telephoned Mr Looseley and asked for 'a couple of bags'; the officer met him and bought heroin from him on this occasion, and then met him on two more occasions for two more purchases. Mr Looseley was charged with being involved in the supply of heroin. The defendant argued that he had been incited to commit the offence, which was an abuse of the legal process, and unfair. The trial judge disagreed and refused to stay the prosecution, and the House of Lords agreed, saying that the officers had *not* instigated the offence.

In the second case, undercover officers were offering contraband cigarettes for sale on a housing estate. The defendant bought cigarettes from them, and the officers then asked him if he could provide them with heroin; he said he could not get heroin at short notice, and that he was 'not really into heroin', but eventually he obtained heroin from another source, and sold it to the officers. The trial judge granted a stay of the prosecution, as the police had procured the commission of offences which the defendant would not otherwise have committed. The House of Lords agreed, saying that the police had done more than give the defendant an opportunity to commit an offence; they had instigated offences, because they had offered inducements. The House said:

> It would be unfair and an abuse of process if a person had been incited or pressurised by an undercover police officer into committing a crime which he would not otherwise have committed, but it would not be objectionable if the officer, behaving as an ordinary member of the public would, gave a person an unexceptional opportunity to commit a crime, and that person freely took advantage of the opportunity.

And the House stated that Article 6 had *not* modified the English approach on section 78 of PACE, or the staying of a prosecution on the ground of abuse of process.

EVIDENCE OBTAINED BY COVERT MEANS

Police and customs officers use covert and intrusive methods of collecting evidence against suspects; they are obliged to do so, when offenders themselves use care and guile to escape detection. They listen to telephone conversations, use intrusive listening devices and long-range photography, and they adopt disguises in order to mix unobserved with the suspects. Many of these devices will bring about a violation of the suspect's right to respect for a private life, in breach of Article 8.[24] This then raises a question which is relevant to the right to a fair trial: does it make a trial unfair where evidence is relied upon which was obtained in breach of Article 8?

In English law, the fact that evidence is obtained by an underhand or even illegal method, is not necessarily a reason for excluding it. The House of Lords held so in *R v Khan*.[25] The European Court takes the same view; in *Khan v UK*,[26] the European Court held that the admission of evidence obtained by means of a listening device in breach of Article 8 did *not* automatically render the proceedings unfair. There is no absolute requirement that illegally obtained evidence should be excluded, but the use of such evidence may give rise to unfairness in the particular circumstances of a case. There should be a scrutiny of the fairness and proportionality of the circumstances in each case.

---

[24] Considered below, p. 202.
[25] [1997] AC 558.
[26] (2001) 31 EHRR 45; see also below in the context of Article 8, p. 203.

On 17 September 1992, Mr Khan arrived at Manchester Airport on a flight from Pakistan, with his cousin. Both men were searched; the cousin was found to be in possession of £100,000 worth of heroin; but none was found on Mr Khan. About four months later, on 26 January 1993, he visited a friend, B, in Sheffield, who was under police investigation for dealing in heroin. Indeed, a few days before, on 12 January 1993, unknown to Mr Khan or B, the installation of a listening device on B's premises had been authorised, on the grounds that B was suspected of dealing in drugs, and conventional methods of surveillance were unlikely to provide proof. The police thereby obtained a tape recording of a conversation in which Mr Khan admitted that he was a party to the importation of the drugs by his cousin when he arrived in Manchester. Mr Khan was arrested; he was interviewed, but he made no admission. At his trial, he admitted that the voice on the tape recording was his voice. The Crown agreed that a civil trespass had been committed on B's house, with minor damage.

Mr Khan argued that the evidence of the tape conversation was obtained in violation of Article 8 and should be excluded. The trial judge ruled that it was admissible. Mr Khan thereupon pleaded guilty. Mr Khan appealed; the House of Lords held that even if there was a violation of Article 8 the evidence was admissible, and the trial was not unfair.

The European Court held that there had been a violation of Article 8, and that the United Kingdom had not satisfied Article 8(2), since there was no statutory scheme or guideline governing the use of the covert listening device, and so it was not 'in accordance with the law'. However, the European Court found that there was *no* breach of Article 6, on the basis that the surveillance was not actually unlawful, and the defendant had been able to challenge both the authenticity and admissibility of the tape, and he had spoken, in the taped conversation, voluntarily, without inducement; there was no risk, in the circumstances, that the tape was unreliable, and at each stage the court had made an assessment of the fairness of the proceedings. In these circumstances, there was no breach of the right to a fair trial.

The European Court reached a majority decision, and as a statement of principle, it is worth considering the dissenting opinion of Judge Loucaides, who said this:

> I cannot accept that a trial can be 'fair', as required by Article 6, if a person's guilt for any offence is established through evidence obtained in breach of the human rights guaranteed by the Convention. It is my opinion that the term 'fairness', when examined in the context of the European Convention of Human Rights, implies observance of the rule of law and for that matter it presupposes respect of the human rights set out in the Convention. [. . .] If violating Article 8 can be accepted as 'fair' then I cannot see how the police can be effectively deterred from repeating their impermissible conduct.

The Court of Appeal has confirmed that the statutory discretion under section 78 of PACE and an argument under Article 6 will focus on similar considerations:[27] the exercise in both cases is to consider the proportionality and justification for the surveillance.

THE MINIMUM CONTENT OF A FAIR TRIAL

It is worth noting, before we turn from criminal to civil proceedings, that, as well as the general requirement of a fair hearing, Article 6 contains a further list of minimum requirements for fairness in criminal cases. As well as the requirements of Article 6(1) – a fair and public hearing within a reasonable time by an independent and impartial tribunal – and 6(2) – the presumption of innocence – there are also the specific requirements of Article 6(3). These are the rights to be informed promptly, in a language which

---

[27] *R v Mason* [2002] 2 CAR 38.

is understood and in detail, of the nature and cause of the accusation being made; to have adequate time and facilities for the preparation of a defence; to defend oneself in person or through legal assistance, with state help in paying for this if necessary; to cross-examine witnesses; to obtain the attendance and examination of witnesses; and have the free assistance of an interpreter, if the language of the court is not understood or spoken. In broad terms, all of these further, more detailed rights are part of our law already. However, there may be specific situations where the article will add something: for example, the requirements for the state to pay for legal assistance or for an interpreter may in some situations impose a greater burden on the state than presently.

CIVIL PROCEEDINGS: THE SCOPE OF ARTICLE 6

Turning now to consider the effect of Article 6 in civil proceedings, the first question is, how do you determine which are civil and which criminal proceedings? 'Civil rights and obligations' are the words in line 1 of Article 6, and it would be tempting to say that this covers whatever decisions are made which are not about criminal offences. However, not every decision will fall within either category. It will therefore be a question to be determined from case to case, whether the proceedings are criminal or civil in substance.

For example, in the case of *McCann*,[28] where three brothers, aged 13, 15, and 16 years were each made the subject of an anti-social behaviour order, requiring them each to leave a designated area of Manchester on account of their behaviour. The order provided that if the order was breached, the brothers could be brought before the court and dealt with by way of punishment for that breach. The brothers appealed, arguing that the proceedings were criminal, so that the safeguards of Articles 6(2) and 6(3) should be in place.

The House of Lords, agreeing with the Divisional Court, held that the proceedings were not criminal in nature. The obtaining of an order of this sort was merely a restriction on activities to protect the public, and not a punishment as such. There was only a punishment if there was then a breach of the order. Although the making of an order is a serious matter, involving a high standard of proof, it is still a civil proceeding. To apply the criminal standard to the process of the making of the order would defeat the object of the proceedings, which was to deal with the difficulty of persuading people to give evidence of the behaviour complained of, and the civil proceedings made it easier to prove.

If the sanction is dismissal or suspension from the person's employment, trade, profession, or status, that is more likely to be a 'civil' proceeding. And sometimes, they will not fall within either category, where they are, for example, an internal procedure with a sanction falling short of dismissal or suspension from a job. Where proceedings are purely disciplinary, Article 6 may well not apply.

One example is a school disciplinary proceeding for reinstatement to a school, in the case of *B (and others)*.[29] This case concerned complaints regarding the exclusion of a number of pupils from their schools for misbehaviour. The Administrative Court considered that an independent appeal

---

[28] *R (McCann) v Manchester Crown Court* [2001] 1 WLR 1084.
[29] *R v Head Teacher of Alperton Community School ex parte B* [2002] LGR 132.

panel under the provisions of the School Standards and Framework Act 1998 was a disciplinary proceeding under a statute in a specific area and not part of the law applicable to persons generally. The determination of an application for reinstatement did not therefore engage Article 6: it did not involve the consideration of a criminal charge, nor did it determine a question which would affect the pupil's right to enjoy a reputation, since any consequences for reputation were incidental to the question of reinstatement and were not the point of the proceeding, given that there were procedural safeguards in place and the decision could be reviewed by the courts to ensure these were complied with.

Disciplinary proceedings may include professional discipline: the Court of Appeal held in the case of *Fleurose*[30] that disciplinary proceedings conducted against a securities trader for improper conduct, which resulted in his being suspended from trading for 2 years, were not criminal proceedings.

But proceedings which are referred to as disciplinary *may* attract the provisions of Article 6. In the case of *Al-Hasan*[31] the Court of Appeal considered that a prison adjudication for taking a controlled drug while in prison which resulted in the addition of 21 days to Greenfield's sentence was not a criminal proceeding. However, the European Court has since decided in the case of *Ezeh*,[32] which concerned allegations of assault and threats by prisoners, that such proceedings *are* criminal in nature, given the nature of the charges and the nature of the penalties imposed, since they render the person accused liable to an additional prison sentence.

Some decisions may fall outside Article 6 for a slightly different reason: not because they are in some sense internal and not general, but because they are not in any real sense judicial, which is to say made by an independent tribunal which is constituted to find facts and apply the law. However, in many cases, such a decision will attract the protection of Article 6 indirectly, by way of judicial review by the courts.

One illustration of this is the *Alconbury* case,[33] which we considered in the context of the constitutional relationship between Parliament and the courts.[34] Here it was being argued that the Environment Secretary was not an independent and impartial tribunal within the meaning of Article 6(1) and therefore his power to decide these questions was incompatible with the Convention. The House of Lords rejected this argument, deciding that, since the Secretary of State's role in the planning legislation was the determination of policy and not a judicial decision as such, Article 6 did not therefore directly apply to his decision, but Article 6 *was* complied with in the procedure taken as a whole, because the decision of the Secretary of State could be judicially reviewed. There was therefore protection to ensure that the decision was *legal* and procedurally proper; but it was not for the court to say whether it was *correct*. In so far as the decision involved the finding of facts, to which Article 6 could apply, that was something which the court could consider in a judicial review application.

---

[30] *R (on the application of Fleurose) v Securities and Futures Authority Ltd* (2002) IRLR 297.
[31] *R (on the application of Al-Hasan) v Secretary of State for the Home Department* [2001] 1 WLR 345.
[32] (2002) 35 EHRR 691.
[33] *R (Alconbury Developments Limited) v Secretary of State for the Environment, Transport and the Regions* [2001] 2 WLR 1389.
[34] Above, p. 41.

Thus, even where Article 6 does not apply directly, it may have a role in the over-all supervision of the proceedings, indirectly, through the standards applied by the court in reviewing the decision made for a basic application of procedural fairness.

CIVIL PROCEEDINGS: ACCESS TO JUSTICE

There is within Article 6 an implied right of access to court: it is a right to *get* to court, in order to have the fair trial promised by Article 6. This right of access applies particularly to civil proceedings, rather than to criminal cases; after all, in the latter there is no difficulty in getting access to the court, since the person who wishes to rely on Article 6 is usually brought there whether they like it or not. In civil cases, in order to have a *fair* trial, one must actually get to court, which is to say, one must have access to the process which gets one to court, by having the ability to consult a lawyer and issue a claim.

This is nowhere stated in Article 6, which assumes that the person bringing a claim has actually reached court and got as far as a trial. But the European Court has said that there is implicit in Article 6 the right of *access* to a fair trial; the right to a fair trial is of no value if one cannot reach court, and so to give value and substance to the rights expressed in Article 6, there must be implied in Article 6 the right to have access to a court, and to the machinery of the court – the right to consult a solicitor, and to commence proceedings. This was the approach of the European Court in the case of *Golder v UK*.[35]

Mr Sidney Elmer Golder was in October 1969 serving a sentence of 15 years' imprisonment in Parkhurst Prison, Isle of Wight; he was then 46 years of age. On that date a serious disturbance occurred in a recreation area of the prison, where Mr Golder happened to be. A prison officer was attacked by prisoners, and injured, and he at first identified Mr Golder as being one of his assailants. Thereupon Mr Golder was placed in segregation, he was notified that disciplinary proceedings would be brought against him, and his letters to a Member of Parliament and a Chief Constable were stopped. The prison officer then withdrew the allegation against Mr Golder; he was returned to his normal cell, the charges were dropped, and the records were amended; but those records still bore the note about the incident. Mr Golder sought permission to consult a solicitor with a view to commencing libel proceedings against the prison officer, but permission was refused.

The European Court held that by refusing him permission to consult a solicitor, the Home Secretary hindered his right of access to the courts, and there was a violation of Article 6. The Court said:

In civil matters one can scarcely conceive of the rule of law without there being a possibility of having access to the courts. [. . .] Were Article 6(1) to be understood as concerning exclusively the conduct of an action which had already been initiated before a court, [the state] could, without acting in breach of that text, do away with its courts, or take away their jurisdiction to determine certain classes of civil actions and entrust it to organs dependent on the Government. Such assumptions, indissociable from a danger of arbitrary power, would have serious consequences which are repugnant to the aforementioned principles and which the Court cannot overlook. [. . .] It would be inconceivable, in the opinion of the Court, that article 6(1) should describe in detail the procedural guarantees afforded to parties in a pending lawsuit and should not first protect that which alone makes it in fact possible to benefit from such guarantees, that is, access to a court.

---

[35] (1979–80) 1 EHRR 524.

However, in order for this right of access to apply, there has to be a legal right which can found a claim, or about which there is an argument, and a case. If there is no such right, there is nothing to go to court for, and so no-one is being prevented from claiming anything. This was the conclusion in the case of *Matthews v Ministry of Defence*:[36]

Mr Alan Robert Matthews had served in the Royal Navy as an electrical mechanic from 1955 and 1968; he claimed he was exposed to asbestos fibres and dust and as a result he developed asbestos-related injuries, which were not diagnosed until September 1999; he claimed damages on the ground of negligence and breach of statutory duty against the Ministry of Defence. The Ministry took the point that it was immune from liability, under the Crown Proceedings Act 1947, section 10, which deprived servicemen of their civil right to sue in negligence, and substituted an entitlement to a pension, and Mr Matthews claimed that this section prevented him from putting forward his claim, and that this was a breach of Article 6, and was incompatible with it. He was in effect prevented from having access to the court. But the House of Lords held that whether a civil right existed was a matter of substantive law. Since the effect of this Act was to deprive Mr Matthews of any right on which he could sue, there was nothing in respect of which he was being denied a fair trial. Article 6 had no impact on the substantive law; therefore there was no breach of the Article, and no right to complain that he was prevented from asserting a right.

CIVIL PROCEEDINGS: THE EFFECT OF THE CONVENTION

Reading through Article 6 there is a very distinct emphasis on criminal proceedings. Whilst Article 6(1) mentions both civil and criminal proceedings, Articles 6(2) and (3), refer expressly to criminal proceedings and to them alone. And from this the European Court has derived two particular principles. The first is that if a case is a civil one, the citizen is not permitted to rely on the express words of Articles 6(2) and (3); the important rights enshrined in those paragraphs, the presumption of innocence and strict rules of evidence and procedure, are not applicable. However, the second is that Articles 6(2) and (3) must still be applied to civil cases in a broad way, so that the concepts of a fair hearing in adversarial proceedings are applied. The court will look at the wording of Article 6 as a whole and apply the spirit of it to the particular facts. An example is the case of *Dombo Beheer v Netherlands*.[37]

Dombo Beheer was a company registered in Nijmegen, in The Netherlands. Its business included managing several other companies, in commercial activities. One of the managers of the company was Mr van Reijendam. Dombo banked with a Netherlands bank in Nijmegen. In about 1981, a dispute arose between the company and the bank about the credit limitation allowed to Dombo, and (civil) court proceedings took place. Mr van Reijendam was not permitted to give evidence on behalf of Dombo, by reason of a rule of Dutch law; but the bank manager was permitted to do so, and he did give evidence, for the bank. Dombo claimed that this was unfair, and a violation of Article 6. The European Court agreed that it was a violation, saying that Dombo was placed at a substantial disadvantage when compared with the bank. The Court said:

> The requirements inherent in the concept of 'fair hearing' are not necessarily the same in cases concerning the determination of civil rights and obligations as they are in cases concerning the determination of a criminal charge. [. . .] Nevertheless, certain principles concerning the notion of a 'fair trial' in cases

---

[36] (2003) *Times* 14.2.03.
[37] (1994) 18 EHRR 213.

concerning civil rights and obligations emerge from the Court's case law. Most significantly for the present case, it is clear that the requirement of 'equality of arms' in the sense of a 'fair balance' between the parties, applies in principle to such cases as well as to criminal cases. The Court agrees with the Commission that as regards litigation involving opposing private interests, 'equality of arms' implies that each party must be afforded a reasonable opportunity to present his case – including his evidence – under conditions that do not place him at a substantial disadvantage vis-à-vis his opponent.

This case was about the handicap of being unable to call a witness; and the Court defined that point as being a lack of equality of arms. But the actual impediment, of the witness being shut out of court, is reflected in the wording of Article 6(3)(d), 'to obtain the attendance and examination of witnesses on his behalf'. The Court did not refer to Article 6(3)(d), and simply took the benchmark of a 'fair hearing'. However, it is clear that the constituent parts of Article 6 provide guidance for what should be fair, in both a criminal and a civil trial.

In another civil case, the unfairness lay in the fact that one party did not hear all the evidence, and was not given the opportunity of commenting on it. That also is an aspect of 6(3)(d), 'to examine witnesses against him'. Again, the European Court has held that this was, in the circumstances, a breach of Article 6, although the Court did not refer to (3)(d) in the case of *Lobo Machado v Portugal*.[38]

Mr Pedro Lobo Machado was an engineer, living in Lisbon, and he was employed by a petroleum business, which was nationalised by the Portuguese government in 1975. Having retired in 1980, he brought proceedings, against the state, in 1986, claiming that after retirement he had been wrongly classified at a lower grade for pension purposes than his entitlement. This was a civil proceeding. The case reached the Supreme Court, and the Deputy Attorney-General, representing the state, delivered to the Supreme Court an Opinion stating that the case had already been fully considered, and that the case should be dismissed. Mr Lobo Machado did not have any opportunity to see this Opinion, or to make any submissions against it. The European Court said:

> Regard being had, therefore, to what was at stake for the applicant in the proceedings in the Supreme Court and to the nature of the Deputy Attorney-General's Opinion, in which it was advocated that the appeal should be dismissed, the fact that it was impossible for Mr Lobo Machado to obtain a copy of it and reply to it before judgment was given, infringed his right to adversarial proceedings. That right means in principle the opportunity for the parties to a criminal or civil trial to have knowledge of and comment on all evidence adduced or observations filed, even by an independent member of the national legal service, with a view to influencing the Court's decisions.

The important phrase is 'adversarial proceedings'. The usual understanding of those words is that the court will be independent, and will hear each side in the presence of the other, allowing each to challenge the other, and thereafter, applying the appropriate burden of proof, give a reasoned decision. This last sentence matches fairly well the constituent parts of Article 6. Thus, the European Court in *Lobo Machado* regarded Article 6 as applying to civil proceedings in most of its elements.

In England and Wales, the rules which govern civil procedure and the conduct of civil trials and proceedings were revised shortly before the Act came into effect, and drafted with some consideration of Article 6. In particular, for the first time, the new version of the rules, known as the Civil Procedure Rules, start with a general principle

---

[38] (1997) 23 EHRR 79.

which should inform all procedural decisions under the rules. This is referred to as the over-riding objective, which requires the court to deal with cases justly.[39] This includes ensuring that the parties are on an equal footing, which is a prime requirement of Article 6. Another requirement which echoes Article 6 is ensuring that cases are dealt with expeditiously and fairly. Other requirements are geared to the fact that the civil courts do not have unlimited time and resources, nor do litigants, and litigation which costs too much may deny some parties the ability to see their case through, especially if the costs are disproportionate to the amount in issue. It may be better to have a case dealt with inexpensively than not to have it dealt with at all. But interestingly, for our purpose, the obligation on the court is to deal with the case proportionately to the importance and complexity of the case, as well as bearing in mind the costs being incurred. The Court of Appeal has indicated that in general terms, the requirements of following the Civil Procedure Rules, are likely to involve similar considerations to the detail of Article 6 as it would apply to civil cases.[40]

QUESTIONS

1   Why is the impartiality of the court so important? Why should bias and interests in the case attract such attention and such a severe test be applied? Do you think the test goes far enough?

2   Why is the presumption of innocence so important? Do you consider that imposing a burden of proof on a defendant is ever justified? Does it matter how serious the burden is?

3   Consider evidence obtained in breach of someone's privacy: do you think it is fair or not that such evidence can be used in their trial for committing a crime?

4   Do you think that having juries hear serious criminal cases makes the trial more or less fair?

---

[39] Civil Procedure Rules 1998, rule 1.
[40] *Daniels v Walker* [2000] 1 WLR 1382.

Chapter 13

RETROSPECTIVE LEGISLATION

'If anything is said in this court to encourage a belief the Englishmen are entitled to jump off bridges for their own amusement the next thing to go will be the Constitution. It is not for me to say what offence the appellant has committed, but I am satisfied that he has committed *some* offence, for which he has been most properly punished.' (A.P. Herbert, *Uncommon Law*, 1935, per Lord Light LCJ in 'Is it a Free Country?')

> ARTICLE 7: NO PUNISHMENT WITHOUT LAW
> 1. No one shall be held guilty of any criminal offence on account of any act or omission which did not constitute a criminal offence under national or international law at the time when it was committed.
>   Nor shall a heavier penalty be imposed than the one that was applicable at the time the criminal offence was committed.
> 2. This Article shall not prejudice the trial and punishment of any person for any act or omission which, at the time when it was committed, was criminal according to the general principles of law recognised by civilised nations.

THE PRINCIPLE BEHIND ARTICLE 7

One of the principles of the rule of law is that criminal offences should be defined with certainty and precision.[1] In order to have a society regulated by law, one requirement is that people should be able to obey the law; they should be able to know, at any given time, what is legal and what is illegal. And it is not possible to obey the law if at a later time Parliament or the courts change the law, so as to make illegal what was done previously.

Article 7 deals with this. It prohibits retrospective application of the criminal law. Article 7 embodies three principles. First, the law must have been in place at the time when a person did a particular act, for a conviction to be based on that act. Second, a penalty imposed by the court must not be heavier than the penalty which was in force at the time when the crime was actually committed. Those two rules are contained in the first two sentences of Article 7(1).

The third rule is that the law – whether it be the definition of the offence or the penalty for a conviction for it – must be accessible and precise. That means it must be available and clear, albeit if necessary with legal advice. The ordinary person must be able

---

[1] Introduced in Chapter 2, pp. 13–14.

to foresee whether the court will say that any particular activity is legal or illegal. It may be that this requires some legal advice, for someone who is not a lawyer; but this is both understandable and fair. But it would be unfair if the law were elastic, so that the court could stretch the wording of the law, whether it be a statute or a previous court decision, simply to enable it to cover the particular circumstances. Of course, as we know, the courts develop the law; case law itself is a means of interpreting the law, and adapting it to changing situations. But provided that the development of the law is foreseeable, it will be regarded as fair.

An example of this is the case of *Kokkinakis*.[2]

Mr Kokkinakis was a retired businessman, of Greek nationality, and he had become a Jehovah's Witness. He had been arrested many times for the offence of proselytism, which was forbidden by Greek law. Mr Kokkinakis complained that this was not only a violation of Article 9, for infringing his freedom of belief, but also of Article 7: his complaint here was that because of the vague terms in which the offence was stated, its scope and meaning could be extended by the police. Thus he could be punished for something which was not obviously prohibited when he did it.

The European Court rejected his complaint under Article 7. The Court noted that the wording of many statutes, in all nations, is not absolutely precise. There is a need to avoid excessive rigidity, and to keep pace with changing circumstances. In this instance, in Greece, there existed a body of settled national case law on this topic of proselytism. This was published and accessible. Then the European Court said this:

> Article 7(1) of the Convention is not confined to prohibiting the retrospective application of the criminal law to an accused's disadvantage. It also embodies, more generally, the principle that only the law can define a crime and prescribe a penalty [and] the principle that the criminal law must not be extensively construed to an accused's detriment, for instance by analogy; it follows from this that an offence must be clearly defined in law. This condition is satisfied where the individual can know from the wording of the relevant provision and, if need be, with the assistance of the court's interpretation of it, what acts and omissions will make him liable.

In short, the law must be precise and must not be extended to any great extent without warning, that is, without legislation; but it is allowed to keep pace with developments, and especially, it is allowed to be developed by courts, particularly in the context of the interpretation of statutes, where it is part of a court's duty to resolve uncertainties. One of the reasons for this is precisely because it is a requirement of the rule of law that the law is clear: if it is not clear, one remedy is for a court to clarify it, even if that resolves an uncertainty against an accused.

RETROSPECTIVE LAW AND OUR CONSTITUTION

In our constitutional theory, in principle there are no limits to the legislative power of Parliament.[3] Thus, in principle, Parliament may pass Acts which are retrospective in their effect. And indeed Parliament has done so; the War Crimes Act and the Genocide Act are examples. But in the absence of clear provision, an Act will not be given retrospective application. Even before the incorporation of the European Convention, the

---

[2] (1994) 17 EHRR 397, discussed also in the context of Article 9, below, p. 211.
[3] Discussed above, Chapter 4, p. 39.

approach of English law was to construe an Act of Parliament as *not* having a retrospective effect.

In the case of *R v Miah*,[4] Mr Miah was charged with being an illegal immigrant, and being in possession of a false passport, contrary to the Immigration Act 1971; the Act came into force in 1973, but the events giving rise to the charge occurred before the Act came into force. His conviction was quashed: the House of Lords refused to interpret an Act of Parliament as having retrospective effect without clear words that said that that was the intention of Parliament.

Lord Reid said: 'there has for a very long time been a strong feeling against making legislation, and particularly criminal legislation, retrospective'. Lord Reid then referred to the Universal Declaration of Human Rights, and Article 7 of the European Convention, which are in virtually identical terms, and he said: 'So it is hardly credible that any government department would promote or that Parliament would pass retrospective criminal legislation.'

It may therefore be a natural question to ask, what has the incorporation of the Convention added to our law, since as long ago as 1974, Lord Reid was citing the European Convention, and declaring that the practice of our courts conformed to it? The answer is, as with the other articles, the Act enables the courts to apply the Convention directly, and so subject our law to greater scrutiny.

This scrutiny will follow the three principles of Article 7 we introduced above: what was the law in force at the time of the activity in question; what penalty followed on from that particular activity at that time; and was the law clear and precise on both of these questions. We have discussed already in other contexts the importance of this concept of precision and clarity in the law: it is the same idea reflected in requirements that something be 'in accordance with the law', which applies across all of the Convention rights.[5] The particular questions raised by this for Article 7 which we will consider are: is the law clear; what is meant by a penalty; and was a greater penalty imposed.

CLARITY IN THE LAW

We are talking here of both statute law and case law, and indeed about the orders of the courts. The law must be clear and foreseeable, and the defendant must know what he must do to remain within the law. We saw this in the statement of the law in *Kokkinakis*'s case; 'an offence must be clearly defined in law.' There is a good illustration of this in the case of *Hashman*,[6] in which hunt saboteurs were bound over to keep the peace and not to act *contra bonos mores* (against good behaviour). The European Court held that the order was not clear; the defendants could not know what it was they were forbidden to do. Thus the order of the court in imposing a penalty was unclear.

But the particular area where one might expect a defendant to claim that the law is unclear is the field of case law, where the law develops by judicial decisions. As was considered above in the *Kokkinakis* case, there is a real issue here, if a defendant claims that he acted in accordance with what he believed the law to be: if a court later decides the law is otherwise, that is unfair and retrospective, and a breach of Article 7.

---

[4] [1974] 1 WLR 683.
[5] Introduced above at p. 87.
[6] (2000) 30 EHRR 241; considered above in the context of Article 5, p. 135.

As we have seen, the European Court's answer is that it allows the law to be developed progressively, and if the judicial decision could reasonably be foreseen, then the judgment is not unfair, and not a violation of Article 7. That is so long as the law has not been, in the words of the European Court in the *Kokkinakis* case, 'extensively construed to an accused's detriment, for instance by analogy'; to use our earlier phrase, 'stretching the law'.

This principle, allowing for foreseeable development, is perfectly demonstrated in the case of *SW and CR v United Kingdom*,[7] two cases heard together with different facts but a similar conclusion; we shall consider the facts of *SW*. In both, the European Court considered that the removal by the English courts of a legal rule that a husband could not be guilty of the rape of his wife did not offend Article 7.

On 18 September 1990, SW attacked his wife, and she alleged that he raped her. On the following day he was charged with rape. On 19 April 1991 he was found guilty of rape, and sentenced to a term of imprisonment.

It had long been considered part of English law that as a rule a husband could not rape his wife. However, although this had been made subject to numerous exceptions, it was only removed altogether by the decision in a separate case called *R v R*. This was decided by Mr Justice Owen on 30 July 1990 and upheld by the Court of Appeal on 14 March 1991. The trial judge at SW's trial was bound by the Court of Appeal decision, which had been decided between the act which founded the case, and the trial. The House of Lords finally decided *R v R* on 23 October 1991.[8] In that case, the House of Lords confirmed that the general principle that a husband cannot rape his wife was no longer part of the law of England and Wales. The House stressed that the common law was capable of evolving in the light of changing social, economic and cultural developments. The old principle (dating from 1736) was out of date.

On the basis of this decision, SW withdrew his appeal against conviction, since, in short, he had no defence to the charge of rape. His complaint before the European Court was that the defence had been open to him when the rape took place and this had been taken away.

The European Court rejected that claim. Some quotations from the judgment show how the Court regarded the development of the criminal law. Thus:

> However clearly drafted a legal provision may be, in any system of law, including criminal law, there is an inevitable element of judicial interpretation. There will always be a need for elucidation of doubtful points and for adaptation to changing circumstances. Indeed, in the United Kingdom, as in the other Convention States, the progressive development of the criminal law through judicial law-making is a well entrenched and necessary part of legal tradition. [. . .] The decisions of the Court of Appeal and then the House of Lords [in this case] did no more than continue a perceptible line of case law development dismantling the immunity of a husband from prosecution for rape upon his wife. [. . .] This evolution had reached a stage where judicial recognition of the absence of immunity had become a reasonably foreseeable development of the law.

The European Court then stated the principle underlying the approach to Article 7:

> 'the object and purpose of Article 7 of the Convention [is] to ensure that no one should be subjected to arbitrary prosecution, conviction or punishment'.

That idea that the operation of the law should not be arbitrary is one we see often in the discussion – by the European Court or our courts – of any of the Convention

---

[7] (1996) 21 EHRR 363.
[8] *R v R* [1991] 4 All ER 481.

rights, and it is a key idea here. Behind the actual wording of Article 7 there is the requirement that the law should not be arbitrary in its application.

WHAT IS A PENALTY?

The question may arise also in some cases as to what is a 'penalty'. This is important, because the word 'penalty' is used expressly in Article 7(1). Parliament has provided in the case of some offences that there should be a further order imposing some liability upon the defendant in addition to imprisonment, or fine, or other penal orders. In two cases in our courts, Parliament had, after the criminal activity had been committed by the defendant, passed a law imposing new measures. The cases are *Welch* and *Ibbotson*.

In *Welch v UK*,[9] Mr Welch was arrested in 1986 for suspected drug offences. In that year the Drug Trafficking Offences Act 1986 was passed, but it came into force on 12 January 1987. Mr Welch was convicted in August 1988. The trial judge imposed a confiscation order upon him under the 1986 Act. Mr Welch complained that the confiscation order was a violation of Article 7(1), in that his drug activity had been committed before the coming into force of the Act. The question for the European Court was whether the confiscation order was a 'penalty'.

The Court found that it indeed was; it followed a conviction, it was directed to the proceeds involved in drug dealing, in default of its payment, imprisonment was a possibility, and in all these circumstances it had the appearance of a penalty. The Court said:

> Looking behind appearances at the realities of the situation, whatever the characterisation of the measure of confiscation, the applicant faced more far-reaching detriment as a result of the order than that to which he was exposed at the time of the commission of the offences for which he was convicted.

It will be a matter of judgement from case to case, but the European Court there found that the far-reaching nature of the confiscation order, added to the penalty of imprisonment, was itself a 'penalty'. Thus, there was a violation of Article 7, because it was something which came into effect after the commission of the drug activity which formed the crime. However, there was not held to be a penalty in the next case, *Ibbotson v UK*.[10]

In May 1996, Mr Ibbotson was convicted and sentenced to $3\frac{1}{2}$ years' imprisonment, regarding six charges of possession of obscene and indecent material; he was released on 20 August 1997. On 1 September 1997, the Sex Offenders Act 1997 came into force, requiring Mr Ibbotson to register with the police and to keep them informed of any change of name or home address. Thus, Parliament imposed upon him an order which had not existed at the time of his offending. He claimed that there was a violation of Article 7.

The European Court on this occasion held that this measure did *not* amount to a 'penalty'. The Court considered the case of *Welch*, but considered that the order to register was preventative rather than punitive, in the sense that inclusion on the register might help to dissuade an individual from re-offending. In short, the requirement for mere registration did not amount to a 'penalty'.

---

[9] (1995) 20 EHRR 247.
[10] [1999] Crim LR 153.

CHANGES IN SENTENCING

We are talking here about the second sentence in Article 7(1), where for some reason, a heavier penalty may be imposed by the court than was available at the time the offence was committed. In our courts, the level of sentencing does alter from time to time. One has only to read the newspapers to see calls for heavier sentences for particular crimes. Parliament may by statute increase the maximum sentence for a particular offence, or alternatively, the Court of Appeal deliver judgments in guideline cases, where the conclusion has been reached that the general level of sentencing for a particular offence has been too low. The question then arises as to whether there is a breach of the second sentence of Article 7(1).

Our courts have analysed this point, and they have concluded that increased sentencing guidelines do not violate Article 7. This was debated in the case of *R v Cathra*.[11]

Mr Cathra, at the age of 44, was convicted in 2001 of one count of rape, and several counts of indecent assault committed on several members of his family between 1970 and 1983, when he himself was aged between 14 and 26 years. In guideline cases the Court of Appeal had in 1986 increased the level of sentencing in such cases, so that had Mr Cathra been sentenced in, say, 1983 he would have faced lower guidelines. The maximum sentence for rape was always life imprisonment.

The Court of Appeal held that an enhanced level of sentencing which led to a higher level of sentence being imposed on Mr Cathra than was current at the time of his offence did not violate Article 7. The Court considered that Article 7 was not contravened as long as the court was entitled, at the time when the offence was committed, to impose the sentence actually passed, even though the then current guidelines might have indicated a lower sentence. What Article 7 prohibits is a court imposing a sentence which is greater than the *maximum penalty* prescribed at the time the offence was committed. The European Court does not, however, involve itself in considering the specific levels of sentencing by the national court, within the prescribed maximum.

The guideline cases had recommended to judges an increased level of sentencing because of concern, among the judiciary and the public, that sentences for rape were too low. The increase in the sentencing levels, suggested by the guideline cases, entirely fitted the approach which we have seen that the law should develop. What had *not* happened was an imposition of an increased maximum penalty since the date of Mr Cathra's offences.

There is a current tendency for Parliament to provide that a criminal should receive an increased sentence for offences which are repeated: 'two strikes and out' is an example. Section 2 of the Crime (Sentences) Act 1997 provides for the imposition of an automatic life sentence on a defendant who commits a serious offence, having previously been convicted of a similar serious offence.

In *R v Offen*[12] the defendant argued that this was a breach of Article 7. He had been convicted and sentenced for one serious offence, and after that, the 1997 Act came into force; he then committed the second offence, which the Court referred to as 'the trigger offence', and he then qualified

---

[11] [2001] (unreported) EWCA Crim. 2478.
[12] [2001] 1 WLR 253.

for the life sentence. He claimed that the penalty for the earlier offence was being increased. The Court of Appeal rejected this, holding that the life sentence was imposed only for the trigger offence. The sentence for the first and earlier offence remained the same.

It is noteworthy that the 1997 Act provides that the life sentence, which is automatic, should not be imposed if the court concludes that there are exceptional circumstances justifying it not being imposed. Undoubtedly that provision allows the court passing the sentence to consider whether or not it would be arbitrary to impose the life sentence, in accordance with the principles developed by the European Court.

CONDUCT WHICH IS ALWAYS CRIMINAL

Article 7(2) provides that there is no infringement of Article 7 if the conduct of the person being condemned was against international law or was 'criminal according to the general principles of law recognised by civilised nations'. This provision is justified because there are some acts which are wrong whether or not they are illegal under a given legal system, and punishing people for those is therefore allowed.

For example, if a law created a secret police who were allowed to shoot people for no good reason, that would be wrong and they should not act this way even if permitted to do so by law. It would therefore be morally permissible to punish them for this, and so not an infringement of the rights of any secret police who did go around shooting people. That act was 'criminal according to the general principles of law recognised by civilised nations'.

It is for this reason that it is considered morally acceptable to punish those who have committed war crimes, even if they acted within the law of their own country, because some acts are wrong whether or not they are permitted by law. Put another way, there are some things which cannot be made right just because they are made legal. So, the War Crimes Act 1991 provides retrospective criminal jurisdiction to courts in the United Kingdom regarding war crimes committed during the Second World War, in Germany, by persons who are British citizens or are now resident in the United Kingdom: this is not contrary to Article 7 because of Article 7(2).

This was another consideration in the case of *SW v UK*, the marital rape case. The European Court stated:

> The essentially debasing character of rape is so manifest that the result of these decisions [. . .] cannot be said to be at variance with the object and purpose of Article 7 of the Convention. [. . .] What is more, the abandonment of the unacceptable idea of a husband being immune against prosecution for rape of his wife was in conformity not only with a civilised concept of marriage but also, and above all, with the fundamental objectives of the Convention, the very essence of which is respect for human dignity and human freedom.

Thus the Court was affirming the principle that there is no breach of Article 7 where the law allows, or appears to allow, something which is inherently and seriously wrong. This is because it should be quite obvious to the person committing such an act that what they are doing is wrong, whether or not it is legal. It should not then be an excuse for them to hide behind a legal exception or technicality and the removal of such a legal protection does not infringe their rights, because the context is one in which they are only having to face the consequences of doing something they should not have done.

The Act itself allows for limited retrospective legislation in a comparable situation. We discussed earlier how, where a court makes a declaration of incompatibility, stating that a statute is incompatible with a Convention right, there is a procedure whereby a remedial order can be passed through Parliament to correct the infringement.[13] Schedule 2 of the Act specifically states that the remedial order can have retrospective effect. The retrospective effect allows the order, in principle, to reverse the decision of the court which was unable to grant someone a remedy for infringement of their rights because of the incompatible legislation. Thus the retrospectivity here is designed to correct an injustice and protect the Convention rights. It is then expressly stated that such an order shall not make any person retrospectively liable to a criminal penalty.[14] This ensures that Article 7 is complied with.

QUESTIONS

1   Why are clarity and accessibility so important for the law? What rights or interests of the individual do they protect? Do they justify being the subject of a separate article?

2   Do you agree that some conduct is so wrong that it can be punished even if it was not against the law when it was done? What about the situation where someone is ordered to do something they know is wrong, but it is not illegal and they have no choice in the matter?

---

[13] Above, pp. 58–9.
[14] Paragraph 4 of Schedule 2.

The actors Michael Douglas and Catherine Zeta-Jones, who are two of the celebrities who have sought to use Article 8 to protect their privacy from media intrusion, discussed in this chapter.

(*Source:* www.mirrorpix.com)

Chapter 14

THE RIGHT TO PRIVACY

'When the sanitary inspector of the Council arrived, the appellant obstructed him with all the rights of a free-born Englishman whose premises were being invaded and defied him with a clothes prop and a spade. He was entitled to do that unless the sanitary inspector had a right to enter . . . In the opinion of this court, the appellant now succeeds because the sanitary inspector had not done that which the statute required him to do before he had a right of entry.' (Lord Chief Justice Goddard, *Stroud v Bradbury*,[1] 1952)

ARTICLE 8: RIGHT TO RESPECT FOR PRIVATE AND FAMILY LIFE
1. Everyone has the right to respect for his private and family life, his home and his correspondence.
2. There shall be no interference by a public authority with the exercise of this right except such as is in accordance with the law and is necessary in a democratic society in the interests of national security, public safety or the economic well-being of the country, for the prevention of disorder or crime, for the protection of health or morals, or for the protection of the rights and freedoms of others.

THE AIMS OF ARTICLE 8

Powers of secret surveillance of citizens, characterising as they do the police state, are tolerable under the Convention only insofar as strictly necessary for safeguarding the democratic institutions . . .

This was the European Court's view of the importance of the rights protected by Article 8 in the case of *Klass v Federal Republic of Germany*,[2] a case about the German state authorities opening the mail and tapping the telephone of a private citizen. This emphasises that the key aim of this article is to protect the individual citizen against arbitrary interference in his or her private life.

In a civilised society, every person should have some freedom to be allowed to improve their life and lifestyle, to fulfil personal aims and ambitions, and to develop their individuality; we have previously referred to this as the idea of **moral autonomy**.[3] This is the core of what is protected by Article 8: it goes beyond the basic rights set out in the earlier parts of the Convention, which cover the physical integrity of the person from death, harm and detention without proper procedural protection. Article 8, and the

---

[1] [1952] 2 All ER 76.
[2] (1980) 2 EHRR 214.
[3] Considered above in Chapter 2.

articles which follow it, expand the conception of basic human entitlements to include privacy and autonomy, having a home which is free from interference, and space to do, think, learn, and express oneself.

However, in a modern society, we generally consider that some interference by the state even in one's private life is justified. So, for example, in our houses and gardens, we may not do things which cause harm or nuisance to our neighbours or to the area where we live; at home or at work or school, we may not create health hazards to other people; and in all these cases, interferences in our privacy, which lead to detection of harm being done or crimes being committed, are to some extent permissible. But at the same time, every person should have a bare minimum of freedom, and that bare minimum is what Article 8 protects.

Thus Article 8 sets out that the state must **respect** each person's **private** and **family life**, their **home** and their **correspondence**, albeit that this freedom can be limited as set out in Article 8(2) in certain circumstances. We have already seen in general terms how strictly the European Court interprets the limitations set out in articles such as Article 8:[4] the state's interference must be in accordance with the law, necessary in a democratic society, must follow one of the legitimate aims listed in Article 8(2), and the interference of the right must be proportionate to the interest which motivates the interference. Even where the interference is justified, this may still tell us something about the wide scope of interests which are potentially protected by Article 8.

Article 8 has been given a wide interpretation by the European Court, so that the words 'private life' have come to include living life with individuality and satisfaction, and with a capacity to develop a personality and an ability to follow individual pursuits; and this includes the individual's wish to express their sexual orientation. Looking at all the words of Article 8(1), they aim to provide protection of the home from invasion and intrusion, and allow the development of family life and relationships. This affects almost every aspect of one's personal life. And, of course, it is to a fair extent one's privacy that is being talked about, even though that word does not actually appear in the two paragraphs of Article 8. We shall consider whether there is in fact a 'right to privacy' under Article 8 shortly.

The wording of the right being protected by Article 8(1) bears close examination. There are four interests which paragraph (1) tells us are to be **respected**: private life, family life, home and correspondence. These are distinct ideas, although as we shall see, they do overlap in various situations. But before we look at those four elements of Article 8, it is worth pausing to consider the word **respect** here.

RESPECT

The acceptance of the idea of respect for private life means that the state has two duties: not only must the state refrain from interfering with one's private and family life, but also it must take positive steps to protect them. This connotation of the word 'respect' was considered by the European Court in the case of *Sheffield and Horsham v United Kingdom:*[5]

---

[4] For discussion of these general principles, see above, p. 86.
[5] (1999) 27 EHRR 163.

The applicants in this case had undergone gender reassignment surgery, in this case from male to female, and their complaint was that the state refused to give legal recognition to their new status as women, or to take positive steps to modify the system of state records which they claimed operated to their detriment, in violation of Article 8. In particular, the complaint was that they were obliged to keep their original name and sex in their birth certificates, social welfare documents and other official records. Although in this case the European Court held that there was no breach of the rights granted by Article 8, it did make it clear that the word 'respect' does indeed mean that the state has a positive duty to act to protect the private life of its citizens – as opposed to a duty merely to refrain from interference. The state must strike a fair balance between the community and the individual.

A RIGHT TO PRIVACY?

Strictly speaking, it is misleading to say that Article 8 protects a right to privacy, since, as we noted above, those words do not themselves appear in the article. Nonetheless, privacy is an important part of what this article does protect, and in this context the questions 'Is there a right to privacy?' or 'Should there be a right to privacy?' provoke a good deal of discussion.

For example, consider photographs being published of well-known people enjoying some private occasion. Is there, or should there be, a right to prevent one's photograph being printed in a newspaper? Does it matter in this context whether or not the person complaining about the pictures is a public figure, such as a member of the royal family or a politician, a television or film personality? We find here one of the best examples of the way the United Kingdom judges have used the Convention to develop our domestic law.

It used to be said that there was no right to privacy in English law, because there was no basis for suing someone who infringed the privacy of another just because they had invaded this privacy, but as we shall see, this has changed. This can be illustrated with four cases: in the first the judges deplore their inability to rely on a right of privacy; the second shows the courts developing a legal cause of action known as breach of confidence in this area; and then in two important cases decided since the Act, about Michael Douglas and Catherine Zeta-Jones and about the Bulger killers, and the cases which followed them, we shall see how the right of privacy really is being recognised.

In *Kaye v Robertson*,[6] the Court of Appeal had before it the case of an intrusion into a hospital ward. A newspaper reporter and photographer from the *Sunday Sport* had invaded the hospital room of the actor Gordon Kaye, actor in the television series *'Allo, 'Allo*, when he was recovering from serious head injuries. The Court of Appeal assumed there was no right of privacy in English law and decided that there was nothing it could do to restrain publication of the pictures taken, even though it considered that they were taken in circumstances which invaded Mr Kaye's privacy. Lord Justice Glidewell said:

> It is well known that in English law there is no right to privacy, and accordingly there is no right of action for breach of a person's privacy. The facts of the present case are a graphic illustration of the desirability of Parliament considering whether and in what circumstances statutory provision can be made to protect the privacy of individuals.

---

[6] [1991] FSR 62.

And Lord Justice Bingham agreed, saying:

> This case nonetheless highlights, yet again, the failure of both the common law of England and statute to protect in an effective way the personal privacy of individual citizens.

The words of the judges in that case speak for themselves: prior to the Act there was no right of privacy in English law. But in this next case we see a right developing out of the principles of an action for a breach of confidence. Breach of confidence is a well-established ground of complaint where a person wrongfully discloses information which has been given to them in confidence; for example, information about a new invention which is being kept secret, or security information about a place, or a business's lists of customers. As you can see from these examples, it has been traditionally used where the parties all appreciate, or ought to appreciate, that that information is actually confidential, or if it is the sort of information which is likely to be confidential. This was developed in the following case in particular:

In *Hellewell v Chief Constable of Derbyshire*,[7] the complaint was as follows. In May 1989, Mr Hellewell, who had 32 previous convictions, including 19 for theft, was arrested on suspicion of theft and taken to a police station where he was fingerprinted and photographed. He was charged with theft and attempted theft and later convicted of both offences. In 1992, an organisation of shopkeepers which was concerned about the level of local shoplifting asked the police to supply photographs of individuals known to be causing trouble in that area so that staff would recognise them. The police provided a number of photographs, including one of Mr Hellewell, which had clearly been taken when he was in custody. Traders were told not to display the photos publicly, but only to show them to their staff. Mr Hellewell learnt of the use being made of his photo and applied to the court for an injunction restraining the police from disclosing his photo to the public.

Mr Justice Laws (as he then was) decided that when the police took a photo of a suspect at a police station, they might well come under a duty of confidence towards him, but that, where the photo was used reasonably for preventing or investigating crime or for catching suspects, and where the photos were distributed only to people who had reasonable need to make use of them, the police would have a public interest defence to any action for breach of confidence.

So the court here in effect held that the police had done nothing unlawful. But the case is useful in showing how the duty to keep something confidential may give the other person a right of privacy. And the judge also gave the following example: if someone with a telephoto lens were to take a picture of someone else engaged in a private act without their permission, any subsequent disclosure of the photograph would as surely amount to a breach of confidence as if he had found or stolen and published a private – and therefore confidential – letter or diary in which the act was recounted. The same defence based on the public interest which was available to the police and the shopkeepers in this case might, however, also be available.

Thus, the court was saying that the law's recognition of confidentiality is a stepping stone to a right of privacy, and added that one answer to a claim for a breach of privacy would be that the invasion of privacy was in the public interest. Following the passing of the Act, this foundation was built on by the Court of Appeal in the important

---

[7] [1995] 1 WLR 804.

case of *Douglas v Hello! Ltd.*[8] In their judgment in this case, the Court of Appeal effectively recognised a right of privacy in English law by adapting the existing law of breach of confidence to allow them to protect aggrieved parties' rights under Article 8.

This case was brought by the film stars Michael Douglas and Catherine Zeta-Jones and the publishers of *OK!* magazine. That magazine and *Hello!*, the defendant, are rivals in the same tabloid magazine market. Michael Douglas and Catherine Zeta-Jones were married at the Plaza Hotel, New York, on 18 November 2000. They had contracted with *OK!* for the exclusive publicity rights regarding the wedding. There were strict security arrangements at the wedding designed to ensure that no one, including guests and staff, could take photographs. *Hello!* knew that exclusive rights were to be granted for coverage of the wedding, and indeed had bid for those rights but had failed to get them. However, *Hello!* did manage to obtain photographs of the wedding, and was about to publish them when the High Court granted an injunction restraining from doing so. The Court of Appeal noted the need for the courts ending the imagination, still to develop the law so that it gives appropriate recognition to Article 8(1) and in doing so recognised that there was a strong argument that Douglas and Zeta-Jones have a right to privacy.

The *Douglas* case was promptly followed in the case of *Thompson and Venables*.[9] We have already referred to this case in the context of Articles 2 and 3: the case concerned those convicted of the shocking murder of 2-year-old James Bulger. Their identities were protected from disclosure by the media, which is usual for those convicted of a crime when under 18. When Thompson and Venables turned 18, this issue was raised again by the press. The order to prevent disclosure of their whereabouts and identities was continued, because of the boys' rights to be protected from death or serious injury under Articles 2 and 3, which had been threatened, so there was more at stake than simply their privacy under Article 8. Indeed the judge, Lady Justice Butler-Sloss, President of the Family Division, was uncertain whether the threatened breach of Article 8 would, by itself, outweigh the newspapers' right to freedom of expression under Article 10, had it not been for the threats of death or serious injury. However, in the present context, the case was also important for the view taken by the judge as to the powers of the court to protect confidential information. The President said:

> Under the umbrella of confidentiality there will be information which may require a special quality of protection. In the present case the reason for advancing that special quality is that, if the information was published, the publication would be likely to lead to grave and possibly fatal consequences. In my judgement, the court does have the jurisdiction, in exceptional cases, to extend the protection of confidentiality of information, even to impose restrictions on the Press, where *not* to do so would be likely to lead to serious physical injury, or to death, of the person seeking that confidentiality, and there is no other way to protect the applicants other than by seeking relief from the court.

The development of the relatively limited law of breach of confidence to protect rights of privacy under Article 8 was expressly recognised in this case. This has since been consolidated in a number of further cases. The Court of Appeal, in the case of *A v B*,[10] set out some general principles which apply to considering this sort of case. The Court recognised that breach of confidence would be the appropriate cause of action where the protection of privacy was being sought, and considered that a duty of confidence

---

[8] [2001] 2 WLR 992, discussed further in the context of Article 10, below p. 230.
[9] *Thompson and Venables v News Group Newspapers* [2001] 2 WLR 1038.
[10] *A v B (a company)* [2002] 3 WLR 542; 'A' was in fact the footballer, Garry Flitcroft; see also, in the context of Article 10, below, p. 230.

would arise whenever the party subject to the duty was in a situation where he knew, or should have known, that the other person could reasonably expect his privacy to be protected. If there was an intrusion in a situation where a person could reasonably expect his privacy to be respected, that intrusion would be capable of giving rise to a liability for breach of confidence unless the intrusion could be justified. Where the person complaining of the intrusion is a public figure, their privacy should still be protected, but someone in a public position should expect a certain amount of media scrutiny, and if they courted public attention, there would be even less scope for objecting to any resulting intrusion.

Thus in *A v B* itself, which concerned an action to prevent the press reporting allegations of adultery by a premier league footballer, Garry Flitcroft, an injunction was refused, especially as it was the person with whom the extra-marital affair took place who chose to disclose the matter to a newspaper. In *Theakston*,[11] the complainant was a presenter of TV children's programmes. It was held that he was not entitled to an injunction restraining the printing of an account of his visit to a brothel, since he had put aspects of his life in the public domain; an injunction *was* granted to restrain the printing of photographs taken, since there was a reasonable expectation that such photographs would not be taken without consent, and this went beyond the sort of matters which the applicant had himself put into the public arena.

In *Campbell*,[12] the Court of Appeal confirmed that just because a person is a public figure, this does not mean that their private life can be laid bare by the media. However, where a public figure has said something which is untrue, the press are normally entitled to set the record straight. So in this case, the fashion model Naomi Campbell had not had her Article 8 rights infringed by newspaper reports which gave details of her treatment for narcotic addiction, since she had publicly denied that she had been addicted to drugs.

PRIVATE LIFE

We turn now to the first of the elements in Article 8(1). It should be noted at this point that many cases cover several of the divisions in this article: for example, 'private life' may well apply to the same circumstances as 'family' or 'correspondence'. But under the description of **private life** there are several cases which illustrate how the word 'life' has been construed, and, as we will see, private life has a much wider meaning than at first appears.

First of all, respect for a private life means ensuring, by positive measures, that a person's life is not made intolerable. In this next case the European Court made an interesting use of Article 8, when considering a woman's private or family life, and held that the state had a duty to make sure that her life was tolerable.

In *Airey v Ireland*,[13] Mrs Airey was a shop assistant, from a humble family background, in Cork. She sought a decree of judicial separation from her husband, but having no private means, she

---

[11] *Theakston v Mirror Group Newspapers* [2002] All ER (D) 182.
[12] *Naomi Campbell v Mirror Group Newspapers Ltd* [2003] 2 WLR 80.
[13] (1980) 2 EHRR 305.

could not pay for a lawyer, and no legal aid was available to her. The European Court held that this failure to provide legal aid, was a violation of Article 8. The European Court stated:[14]

> In Ireland, many aspects of private or family life are regulated by law. As regards marriage, husband and wife are in principle under a duty to cohabit but are entitled, in certain cases, to petition for a decree of judicial separation; this amounts to recognition of the fact that the protection of their private or family life may sometimes necessitate their being relieved from the duty to live together.

In other words, the Court was saying that respect for private life includes the right to be legally parted from one's spouse, if that is necessary for private happiness. And because the state had not provided the means for Mrs Airey to gain access to a court to seek a decree of separation – by providing free legal aid – the state had not taken proper steps to enable Mrs Airey to enforce her right.

The case is interesting for two points. First, the quality of a person's private life should be protected by the state, and the state should provide the means to ensure that protection; that will be important in decisions such as those taken by housing and education authorities. Second, the state may have the obligation of providing the assistance of free legal aid in cases where the quality of the person's life is jeopardised to ensure that that person can seek a remedy for the threat to their private life.

Students have private lives, yet the school or college may need to impose discipline. We considered in the context of Article 3 the case of *Costello-Roberts v UK*,[15] which was a case about corporal punishment in a school. Corporal punishment itself is no longer allowed by our law,[16] and raises issues as to whether it is inhuman or degrading treatment so as to infringe Article 3.[17] However, the relevance of the case here, is the principle that, in the field of education, a balance must be found when considering the rights of the individual and the interests of the community.

Costello-Roberts was a young boy at a boarding school, and he was given corporal punishment in accordance with the disciplinary rules in force at the school, by being slippered with a rubber-soled gym shoe by the headmaster, in private. Costello-Roberts claimed that his corporal punishment had given rise to a breach of Article 8, in that 'private life' covered a person's physical and moral integrity, and the punishment was a form of coercion through force and fear, and this constituted an interference with moral integrity as well as physical integrity. The Court held that in some circumstances there might be a breach of Article 8 in relation to disciplinary measures in a school. But the Court said:

> Having regard to the purpose and aim of the Convention taken as a whole, and bearing in mind that the sending of a child to school necessarily involves some degree of interference with his or her private life, the Court considers that the treatment complained of by the applicant did not entail adverse effects for his physical or moral integrity sufficient to bring it within the scope of the prohibition contained in Article 8.

Thus, on the particular facts there was no breach of the right to respect to a private life: any sort of communal life, such as school life, involves some sort of restriction on a participant's private life, although in principle this sort of situation might involve a breach of this right if the balance is not struck fairly.

---

[14] Paragraph 33.
[15] (1995) 19 EHRR 112.
[16] Discussed above, p. 115, and below, pp. 209–10.
[17] Discussed above, p. 115.

PERSONALITY AS AN ASPECT OF PRIVATE LIFE

The development of one's personality, or the widening of one's horizons, are part of the quality of a private life, and while the next case is perhaps unusual, it illustrates how the European Court takes a broad view of this aspect of private life.

In *Botta v Italy*,[18] Snr Botta complained that Article 8 had been violated in these circumstances: he was disabled and wanted to spend a holiday by the sea at Lido degli Estensi, but when he got there he found there were no facilities for the disabled which would enable him to bathe or use the facilities easily or readily; he simply could not get into the sea, or spend time on the beach. Snr Botta claimed that Article 8 gave him a right to a life in which he could enjoy relationships with other human beings, and so develop his personality. The European Court rejected his claim, on the ground that the spoiling of a seaside holiday was not such an event as would interfere with the development of his personality, even though the Court did accept that Article 8 may be applied to the kind of argument being advanced by Snr Botta. The Court stated:

> In the instant case, however, the right asserted by Snr Botta, namely the right to gain access to the beach and the sea at a place distant from his normal place of residence during his holidays, concerns interpersonal relations of such broad and indeterminate scope that there can be no conceivable direct link between the measures the state was urged to take in order to make good the omissions of the private bathing establishments and the applicant's private life.

This approach will be important in the fields which concern the provision of public facilities such as where local authorities take decisions about what facilities are to be provided in community centres or public places, especially for families or for the disabled. Public authorities will also have to consider what facilities must be provided in children's homes, hostels, or elderly people's homes to ensure that the people living there can develop their individual interests at least to some extent.

THE 'PRIVATE LIFE' OF PRISONERS

Respect must be given to every person, regardless of his or her status. This includes prisoners. Prison is a place where authority must be exercised; there is often a judgement to be made by prison staff regarding punishments and privileges and freedoms. In the relatively short time that the Act has been in force there have been already been a number of cases which concern the claims of prisoners under Article 8. An example from before the Act is the following:

In *X v UK*,[19] a prisoner serving a life sentence in Gartree Prison applied to the governor for a visitor's order for a visit from a member of the Citizens' Commission on human rights, which was sponsored by the Church of Scientology, in order to examine his medical records; the Governor refused, on the ground that the intended visitor had not been, before the sentence began, a relative or friend of the prisoner, and in addition there was concern about the potentially harmful effects of the Church of Scientology. The prisoner complained to the European Commission that, in violation of Article 8, he was being prevented from having contact with outside influences, which would assist his rehabilitation, and Article 8 gave him a right to a life which included relationships with

---

[18] (1998) 26 EHRR 241.
[19] (1983) 5 EHRR 260.

other human beings, in order to develop his emotional ties and so develop his own personality. The Commission accepted that the concept of a 'private life' could include the kind of features which the prisoner was seeking for himself, although it held that on the facts there was no violation of Article 8.

After the Act, the prison service, as a public authority, will need in the future to give thought to the kind of facilities in prisons to give a suitable effect to the rights of a prisoner to some form of private life. A prisoner also has family relationships, even if he or she is physically separated from their family; when the prisoner claims to exercise them, the prison authorities or the court must balance those rights against the state's right to impose custody.

In the case of *Lalley*,[20] Lalley had been convicted of murder and sentenced to life imprisonment. He was subsequently moved to a high-security hospital pursuant to the Mental Health Act 1983. Visits by Lalley's child nephews had been previously permitted in prison, but were not permitted in hospital until a risk assessment had been carried out, in accordance with a Ministry of Health circular. This circular restricted visits by children to high-security patients who had been convicted of murder, manslaughter or sexual offences unless a limited category of relationship existed and required the risk assessment in all cases. Lalley challenged the written Health Department direction by an application for judicial review. The categories of permitted relationship included those where the patient was the parent or relative of the child, including uncles. However, Lalley argued that the circular interfered with his right to family life within Article 8, because of the blanket nature of the ban on visits and the restrictions imposed by the circular.

The High Court decided that restrictions on child visits to patients at high-security hospitals who had committed murder, manslaughter or sexual offences were wholly justified and compatible with Article 8. So the prisoner's arguments were rejected. The Court said that it could not be argued that restricting visits to a limited category of relationship was irrational. No category of child was entirely excluded from visiting, as it was always possible to have recourse to the courts for a contact order. In any case, it was not obvious that the relationship between uncles and nephews necessarily fell within the meaning of family life under Article 8. Family life is a flexible concept and depends on the facts of each case.

In the case of *P*,[21] two prisoners challenged the prison service's policy to allow children to remain with their mothers in prison only until they were 18 months old, arguing that the separation of mother and child was a breach of Article 8. The Divisional Court held that Article 8 conferred not an absolute right to family life, but a right to respect for family life and that the policy was lawful because it gave sufficient respect in the circumstances. Prisoners are sent to prison as a punishment, to deter others and for rehabilitation. The impairment of the right of family life is a consequence of the deprivation of liberty which prison involves. Thus some form of policy is necessary to ensure that mothers with babies who are in prison are treated in the same manner and to balance the interests of the mother, the interests of the child and the interference resulting from the mother being in prison. Since the policy did not preclude reconsideration in individual cases and since it was kept under review, the mother and baby policy was lawful, and there was no breach of the Convention.

---

[20] R *(Lalley) v Secretary of State for Health* (2001) 1 FLR 406.
[21] R*(P) v Secretary of State for the Home Department* [2001] 1 WLR 2002.

In the case of *Mellor*,[22] M a prisoner serving a life sentence for murder challenged the refusal by the Secretary of State to grant him the opportunity to conceive a child with his wife via the aid of artificial insemination. The request had been refused on the basis that no exceptional circumstances existed to justify the grant of such facilities. M contended that the refusal infringed his right to respect for his private and family life and his right to found a family, contrary to Articles 8 and 12.

The High Court held that the Secretary of State had not acted in breach of M's right to respect for his family life or his right to marry and found a family. One aspect of the punishment meted out to him was the denial of precisely those rights which he now sought for himself. No interference with those rights would amount to a breach of his fundamental rights, provided that it was proportionate to the aim of operating a penal system designed for both punishment and deterrence. Nevertheless, the court said, in certain exceptional circumstances having regard to the principle of proportionality, it might *not* be appropriate to deny a prisoner the opportunity to conceive a child, whether by natural or artificial means. Thus, the court left open the possibility that a breach of Article 8 might occur in particular circumstances.

In the case of *Daly*[23] a prisoner complained that he was required to be absent when his cell was searched or his correspondence was opened. The House of Lords held that the policy of requiring a prisoner to be absent whenever prison officers examined his privileged legal correspondence, which he had in his cell, gave rise to the possibility that an officer might improperly read it, or the belief that he would read it, so that there was an inhibiting effect on the prisoner's willingness to communicate freely with his legal adviser; and this amounted to an interference with the prisoner's right to respect for his correspondence under Article 8. The House of Lords went on to consider whether the state was justified in interfering with the prisoner's right, and held that the routine or blanket policy of this kind of search, in the absence of the prisoner, was not proportionate. No account was being taken by the prison authorities of whether the particular prisoner was unruly, or likely to disrupt the search. In short, the prison authorities must take stock of each case and each situation before imposing this kind of condition.

In the case of *N*,[24] a patient in a secure hospital sought to challenge, as being in breach of Article 8, a provision in the safety and security written directions which applied to the Ashworth Special Hospital which entitled the hospital authority to record and listen to a random 10 per cent of patients' telephone calls. The High Court dismissed his challenge. The Court stated that while, on the one hand, it was clear that the written direction interfered with the Article 8 right to respect for private life, on the other, the hospital had a statutory duty to provide secure accommodation, and abuse of the telephone system could create a security risk, and in any event the 10 per cent system went no further than was strictly necessary, and so was proportionate.

SEXUAL ORIENTATION

Sexual fulfilment and orientation are bound up with the respect for a private life. This is not only relevant to discussions of people's privacy at home, but also in considering people's rights to privacy in the workplace, where rules which invade people's privacy as to their sexuality or practices which discriminate on the grounds of sexuality (which is an essentially private matter) may be a violation of Article 8.

---

[22] *R (Mellor) v Secretary of State for the Home Department* [2001] 3 WLR 533.
[23] *R (Daly) v Secretary of State for the Home Department* [2001] 2 WLR 1622.
[24] *R (N) v Ashworth Special Hospital Authority* (2001) HRLR 46.

In *Smith and Grady v UK*,[25] the applicants were members of the Royal Air Force, and they were homosexuals. When this fact was discovered by their superior officers, the applicants were subjected to very close and intrusive questioning, as indeed were their relatives and acquaintances. They were eventually discharged from the service because they were homosexuals. The Ministry of Defence had adopted a policy that homosexuals were not permitted to serve in the armed forces. There was undoubtedly an interference with their private lives, in breach of Article 8; the question was whether this interference was necessary in a democratic society. The European Court held that there was a violation of Article 8: the British government had not produced convincing or weighty reasons to justify the policy against homosexuals in the armed forces, or to justify the discharge of the applicants from the service.

APPEARANCE

Private life includes personal dignity, and pride in one's own appearance. The same applies to one's mode of dress. One can imagine that rules which unnecessarily restricted an individual's freedom as to how they dress might be considered an infringement of one's private life (as well as raising questions about freedom of expression).

In *McFeely v UK*,[26] the applicants were prisoners convicted of terrorist offences who were serving sentences in The Maze Prison in Northern Ireland. They were required to wear prison uniform, and the Commission considered that this constituted an interference with their right to respect for their private lives. However, the Commission observed that the purpose of a prison uniform is to facilitate identification of a prisoner with a view to preventing his escape or securing recapture in the event of an escape, and second, to enable the prison authorities to distinguish between the prison community and visitors dressed in ordinary clothes; therefore, the rule was justified under Article 8(2) as necessary in a democratic society in the interests of public safety and for the prevention of crime.

SEARCHES OF THE PERSON

We are often required, for example on entering many public buildings or approaching flight departures at an airport, to submit to a personal search of the body and belongings, whether directly or by passing through an X-ray machine. That is an obvious invasion of privacy: is it allowed? The answer is that it is, on the usual conditions set out in Article 8(2) – as long as it is in accordance with the law and necessary in a democratic society for one of the aims stated there. This may well be with the consent of the person being searched, which makes a search lawful; where a search is required before a person is allowed to enter a building or area, such as when going through an airport or entering a football stadium, unless the person consents to the search they will usually not be allowed in. However, not all searches are with consent. Consider the following Canadian case.

In *R v M*,[27] a case decided by the Supreme Court of Canada, a school vice-principal received information from several students that another student, M, would be selling drugs at a school dance.

---

[25] (2000) 29 EHRR 493 and (2001) 31 EHRR 24; also considered above p. 122.
[26] (1981) 3 EHRR 161.
[27] *R v M (MR)* [1998] 3 S.C.R. 393, 5 BHRC 474.

When M arrived at the dance, the police were called; and M was asked to go to the school office, where the police officer observed the schoolmaster search M, upon whom a packet of marijuana was found. M was arrested. The student complained of a violation of his rights of privacy. The court held that the student had a reasonable expectation of privacy, but this reasonable expectation was less than in other circumstances bearing in mind the responsibility of the school authorities for maintaining discipline and a safe environment, and students could not reasonably expect to be free from all searches.

The Canadian Supreme Court's conclusion applies also in the context of Article 8: the right of privacy is not an absolute right; it falls to be considered in a balancing exercise of the rights of the individual and the rights of the community.

PRIVATE LIFE: A WOMAN'S RIGHT TO AN ABORTION?

Although abortion as an issue is usually focused on rights to life – both the rights of the mother and of the child[28] – it is also an issue which is affected by considerations of private life as well as family life. One could argue that to have a life which is truly private means that the individual may do what he or she likes with their body. As we have seen, abortion is not prohibited by the Convention, although states may differ in their positions on this issue. Because of the width of views on the subject, this is one sphere where the European Court will especially defer to the social and moral attitudes of the individual state, in accordance with the margin of appreciation.[29] However, the topic has been considered in the context of Article 8.

In *Bruggemann and Scheuten v Germany*,[30] two women claimed that the state's laws restricting and defining the conditions in which an abortion could be carried out were in violation of the right to respect for a private life. The Commission found that many of the nations covered by the Convention had laws which set up regulations for the conduct of pregnancy and abortion. It concluded that the laws in the present case did not interfere with the private life of the two women: pregnancy and its termination are not matters solely for the private life of the mother. The Commission also said that it did not find it necessary to decide whether the unborn child was a 'life' for the purposes of Article 2.

FAMILY LIFE

This is the second protected interest in Article 8(1) – the right to respect for **family life**. This concept will obviously be important in cases and disputes involving spouses and partners and children, particularly relating to the custody of children, and divorce, and financial maintenance of members of a family. It will be necessary for the courts of the United Kingdom to consider whether the Convention increases the rights of individuals who may assert a right to be consulted about the life of the family or members of it. But the Convention has a much wider effect: it will impose an obligation on public authorities to take into account a family which may be affected by a decision.

---

[28] Discussed above in this context, p. 103.
[29] Introduced above, pp. 45–6.
[30] (1981) 3 EHRR 244.

The first thing to notice is that the 'family' in Convention terms is a broad concept. The object of family life is living together in order that family relationships can develop normally and family members can enjoy one another's company, but the family exists even when the members of it are not physically living together. So in the case of *Olsson v Sweden*,[31] a child had been taken into the care of the state authorities. The European Court was quite clear that:

> The mutual enjoyment by parent and child of each other's company constitutes a fundamental element of family life; furthermore, the natural family relationship is not terminated by reason of the fact that the child is taken into public care.

Nor is the word 'family' in Article 8 limited to relationships dependent on marriage.

In *Kroon v Netherlands*,[32] a child was born to a stable relationship between Mrs Kroon and Mr Zerrouk while Mrs Kroon was still married to Mr Kroon. Under Dutch law, it was impossible to obtain recognition of the biological father's paternity unless the husband denied paternity. The applicants complained that they were victims of a violation of Article 8. The Court said:

> The Court recalls that the notion of 'family life' in Article 8 is not solely confined to marriage-based relationships, and may encompass other *de facto* 'family ties' where partners are living together outside marriage. Although, as a rule, living together may be a requirement for such a relationship, exceptionally other factors may also serve to demonstrate that a relationship has sufficient constancy to create *de facto* 'family ties'; such is the case here, as since 1987 four children have been born to Mrs Kroon and Mr Zerrouk.

It has been clearly established by the European Court that Article 8 requires proper consideration to be given to preserving family relationships. So, for example, it is important that children are given proper access to their parents, and vice versa, even if the children are in the care of the state or in the process of being adopted; the child's interests are paramount, and interferences with rights of access can be justified if, but only if, they are in the child's best interests.

PUBLIC AUTHORITIES' DECISIONS ABOUT THE FAMILY

When local authorities and welfare agencies make decisions about families and individual members of families, those decisions may affect the rights of individuals under Article 8. The idea of respect for a family life in this context requires such agencies to consider fully the rights of the individual, and in particular the right of the individual to be consulted as to the future of their family.

In *TP v UK*,[33] T lived with her daughter K, a child, in a local authority area, and the authority owed duties to the child under the Child Care Act 1980. The authority suspected that the daughter had been sexually abused. K took part in a video interview, asserting that she had been sexually abused, by a man of the same name as T's boyfriend, but denying that he was the abuser. The authority obtained a place of safety order in respect of K, on the basis that T would be unable to protect K from abuse. One year later, T and her solicitors had sight of the video interview. The European

---

[31] (1989) 11 EHRR 259.
[32] (1995) 19 EHRR 263.
[33] (2002) 34 EHRR 2.

Court held that the delay in providing the video evidence amounted to a breach of Article 8, as T had not had the opportunity to participate in the decision-making procedures following K's removal from her home.

It is surprising in this case that no opportunity had been offered to her to see the video, as usually such evidence is made available. However, the principle is important and such considerations will be relevant to all cases concerning children, such as adoption decisions and child custody cases. Thus it is not just the outcome which is important: the individual must be allowed proper participation in the decision-making process, or that will itself be a breach of Article 8.

ANCESTORS OF THE FAMILY

The right to respect for family life applies equally to the cultural values of families, including values based on their ancestral histories. And there are several ways in which a family's interests in its ancestors may be affected by the activities of public authorities such as government, utilities such as railways or gas and electricity companies or building and construction authorities.

In *G & E v Norway*,[34] Lapp shepherds, fishermen, and hunters claimed that the proposed flooding of a 2.8-kilometre area of their ancestral hunting grounds by a hydroelectric project would be in breach of Article 8; the Commission held that their claim was capable of being covered by Article 8, but decided that the interference was justifiable under Article 8(2). Thus, the Commission was prepared to bring family livelihood and traditional occupation within this article.

In a decision by a comparable body, in *Hopu v France*,[35] the United Nations Human Rights Committee decided that the construction of hotel development over an ancestral burial site was capable of being an arbitrary interference with the family life of ethnic Polynesians.

Thus decisions on planning and land use and the undertaking of works by local authorities and public utilities are likely to be affected by such considerations. It has also been decided that to explore a shipwreck and enter it and remove artefacts is an interference with family privacy, when members of the family lie in the wreck.

TRADITIONAL FAMILY LIFESTYLES

Many people adhere to and cherish the faiths and traditions of their families. More than that, they may regard themselves as part of a culture, be proud of that and wish to live in a manner which is faithful to their tradition. However, sometimes this brings them into conflict with the laws of the land and a balance has to be struck. By way of example, we will consider two cases where gypsy families wished to pursue their traditional style of dwelling, and claimed that the law interfered with their traditions, so invading their right to respect for a private life.

---

[34] (1983) 35 DR 30.
[35] (1983) 3 BHRC 597.

In *Buckley v UK*,[36] Mrs Buckley and her three children were part of a family who had been gypsies for as long as they could trace back; they occupied caravans which stood on land owned by her. She applied for planning permission to have them on that land, and it was refused. The caravans were her home; yet it was apparently illegal to live in them. The local authority based their refusal on the contention that the caravans would spoil the amenity of the locality, yet there were buildings nearby, and the official gypsy site was very near. She complained to the European Court of a violation of Article 8.

The Court held that there was an interference with Mrs Buckley's family life, but (by a majority of 6 to 3) that it was justified under Article 8(2). There was a legitimate aim in limiting sites for caravans, on the grounds of public safety and economic wellbeing, and the health and rights of other persons; and it was necessary in a democratic society. The majority did not consider that Mrs Buckley was at any time penalised or subjected to any detrimental treatment for attempting to follow a traditional gypsy lifestyle. They did consider that the relevant national policy was aimed at enabling gypsies to cater for their own needs.

The judges in the minority were concerned about the fact that the gypsies are a minority people, who are vulnerable, and who had a special cultural heritage, and they were conscious that this was the first case before them dealing with gypsies; their judgment was that there was a violation of the right to family life, in breach of Article 8.

In *Chapman v UK*,[37] the European Court had to consider a case of gypsies who had been moved from various sites, whose applications for planning permissions had been refused, and who had been obliged to live in accommodation which they found unsuitable to their way of life. In this case, the Court found that the applicants' occupation of their caravans was an integral part of their ethnic identity as gypsies and that the enforcement measures and planning decisions interfered with their rights to respect for their private and family life.

However, the Court found that the measures were in accordance with the law and pursued the legitimate aim of protecting the rights of others through preservation of the environment. The planning inspectors, in the various cases, had identified strong environmental objections to the applicants' use of their land. The Court did not accept that there was a violation of Article 8 in a decision not to allow the applicants to occupy land where they wished to install their caravans, because, statistically, the number of gypsies was greater than the number of places available in authorised gypsy sites. Neither was the Court convinced that Article 8 could be interpreted to impose on the state an obligation to make available to the gypsy community an adequate number of suitably equipped sites. Article 8 did not give a right to be provided with a home, and whether the state provided funds to enable everyone to have a home was a matter for political not judicial decision.

IMMIGRANTS

Nowadays, movement of people from one state to another is a regular occurrence; they become immigrants or asylum seekers, and families are affected. The right to respect to a family life must be respected by host nations, or by deporting nations.

In the case of *R*,[38] the claimant, a Colombian national, had entered the United Kingdom in 1993 with his common-law wife and their two children; they had another child soon after arriving in the

---

[36] (1997) 23 EHRR 101.
[37] (2001) 33 EHRR 18.
[38] *R (R) v Secretary of State*, *The Times*, 29.11.00 [2000].

country. His asylum application was refused, and he was refused exceptional leave to remain. His wife's application for exceptional leave to remain was still outstanding. In 1999, the claimant was convicted of grievous bodily harm, possession of drugs, and drink driving, and he received a prison sentence of 18 months. On his release from prison the Secretary of State confirmed his decision to deport him to Colombia. The claimant argued that if he were returned it would breach his right to family life under Article 8. The High Court found that if indeed he were deported, there would be a serious risk of a breach of this article, and that to deport him because of his criminal conviction would be disproportionate.

HOME

This is the third element in Article 8(1), respect for the home; and what springs to mind now is the idea of protection of the home from invasion and intrusion. 'A man's house is his castle and each man's home is his safest refuge,' wrote Sir Edward Coke in 1628.[39] That is still the starting point of the modern law, and by and large the state or other public authorities may not enter private premises, unless the law permits it, as, for instance, on reasonable suspicion of crime, or under the power of a warrant. The application of Article 8 will not provide a lesser standard of protection for the individual than exists under the current law, since Article 8 itself requires that in order to be justified an invasion of privacy must be in accordance with the law. However, Article 8 may provide wider protection than previously, since it may limit the scope of a state authority to enter a home, even where it might otherwise be permitted by law.

Home has been given a broad interpretation by the European Court. So, for example, a home remains a home even though the owner may be away from the premises for a long period. In the case of *Gillow*,[40] the parties were absent from a house which they owned, but it was nonetheless held that they regarded it as their home.

Mr and Mrs Gillow owned a house in Guernsey, which they had built for themselves and furnished with the intention of eventually living there, although after building the house they lived away from Guernsey for about 18 years. They then returned to live in their house, but were then obliged to apply for a licence to occupy it, and this licence was refused. The purpose of the legislation was to ensure that houses were available for the population of Guernsey. They complained to the European Court of a violation of Article 8, as there had been an interference with their right to respect to their home. The European Court held that they should succeed: the national court had given insufficient weight to the circumstances of the particular case.

This approach will be relevant in a variety of situations where, for example, a local authority makes a decision about housing, or repossessing a property. It does not prevent such action, but suggests that due weight must be given to the facts of the case being considered.

---

[39] *Coke's Institutes of the Laws of England*, Third Part, p. 162; also *Semayne's Case*, 5 Co. Rep. 91b.
[40] (1986) 11 EHRR 335.

Likewise, respect for home and home life means more than just providing some form of a dwelling or shelter: it extends to maintaining the situation to which a person has become accustomed, and the very permanence of which gives comfort. Thus, in the case of *Coughlan*,[41] where a patient who was a paraplegic had become accustomed to a particular place of residence, and the promise had been given to her that she would not be moved, the health authority which indeed moved her was held to have breached her rights under Article 8.

QUALITY OF HOME LIFE

The enjoyment of a home may be spoilt by noise, and anyone who has experienced this might well refer to it as an invasion of their privacy. Aircraft noise pervades the lives of some people, and it may now be that they have a good cause of complaint under Article 8.

In *Powell and Rayner v UK*,[42] two families lived under the flight paths of aircraft taking off and landing at Heathrow Airport. One lived at Esher, several miles from the airport; the other lived about 1.5 miles from the runway. They had acquired their properties before the building of the runway extension, which had caused an increase in air traffic and noise. Their complaint was that the noise invaded their home life and so interfered with their private life. The European Court found, on balancing the rights of the householders and the general interest of the public in access to air travel, that there was *no* violation of Article 8.

However, in *Hatton v UK*,[43] the European Court held that the increase in the level of noise caused by aircraft using Heathrow Airport at night since 1993 *was* a breach of the applicants' right to respect for their private and family lives and homes, under Article 8.

A similar approach was taken in the following case about a chateau in France. In *S v France*,[44] a nuclear power station was situated less than 300 metres from an eighteenth-century chateau on the banks of the Loire. The power station caused noise, lights at night, and the creation of a micro-climate, so that the value of property was halved. All this was held by the Commission to be an interference under Article 8, but it was justified because of its benefit to the community.

This right of respect for a private home means that the state must either take a positive line, and rectify the cause of the interference, or justify the interference under Article 8(2).

In the case of *Guerra*,[45] the court applied this standard. The town of Manfredonia, in Foggia, Italy, was near to a factory which produced fertiliser compounds, and some of the emissions from the factory contained arsenic. There was a high risk from the gases and chemicals borne on the wind and in the air, but no information had been given to the nearby townsfolk about this risk.

---

[41] *R (Coughlan) v N. and E. Devon Health Authority* [2000] All ER 850.
[42] (1990) 12 EHRR 355; the Commission decision on the right to property is considered below, p. 253.
[43] (2002) 34 EHRR 1.
[44] (1990) 65 DR 250.
[45] (1998) 26 EHRR 357; considered above in the context of Article 2, p. 105.

The European Court held that in this case there was no interference with a right as such; but the state had been guilty of a failure to take *positive steps* to give essential information, despite their knowledge of the situation over quite some time. Thus the quality of the lives of nearby people had been diminished, and their home and private lives had been affected in breach of Article 8.

In *Lopez Ostra v Spain*,[46] the people of a village near an industrial plant, which treated waste water, complained of fumes and smells which made their lives intolerable, and this was a violation of Article 8, as damaging their private life; the state disputed that the situation was really as bad as it was described. The European Court held that severe environmental pollution may affect individuals' wellbeing and prevent them from enjoying their homes in such a way as to affect their private and family life adversely, even without seriously damaging their health.

Under our domestic law there are well-established remedies for people whose enjoyment of their home and property is affected by nuisances, such as noise or smells, or escaping or leaking industrial material, chemicals or waste. However, there are some limitations on these remedies under English law, in particular they are often not available to persons who are affected by such a nuisance where that person is not the occupier or owner of land or a house.

In *Hunter v Canary Wharf*,[47] it was claimed that the building of Canary Wharf in London's Docklands had significantly interfered with the television reception of neighbouring properties. The House of Lords decided that interference with television reception, whilst it might be inconvenient, was not something which could be restrained by the Court. The House of Lords also confirmed that in order to bring a claim of this sort (under the tort of nuisance) under English law it is necessary for the claimant to have property rights in the land where he lives and which are being interfered with.

This long-established restriction in English law in this sort of case may well have to be reconsidered if complaints such as this one infringe the right to respect for private and home life of people who live in a property but do not own it, such as family members of the owner. Such cases may therefore have to be reconsidered in light of the European jurisprudence on Article 8 – indeed, in *Hunter* itself, Lord Cooke, in a dissenting judgment, expressly referred to Article 8 as a possible basis for the householders' claim. As the interpretation of 'private life' in Article 8 covers this type of situation, a violation of the article will strengthen any claim and may require the domestic courts to expand the scope of those remedies which already exist.

Since the Act has been passed, the courts have recognised that the effect of Article 8 may well be to extend the existing law in this respect. In one case where there were complaints of emissions, noise pollution and invasion of privacy from a factory, the judge refused to summarily dismiss the claims, notwithstanding that the claimants were not home-owners, since there was an arguable case under Article 8, which might also require reconsideration of the law on nuisance.[48]

---

[46] (1995) 20 EHRR 277.
[47] [1997] 2 WLR 684.
[48] *Nora Mckenna v British Aluminium Ltd* (2002), *The Times*, 25 April 2002.

CORRESPONDENCE

The final category of protected interests under Article 8 is correspondence, the right to private mail. Although when this was originally drafted, only paper letters would have been in the minds of those setting out what rights Article 8 covers, this can now be applied very much more widely. With the growing number of forms of electronic communications, such as e-mails and text messages, it is a topical issue whether or not it is possible or appropriate for the state to monitor these forms of correspondence.

In a state which we like to consider a civilised democracy, it might be hard to imagine how the ordinary citizen might find the state interfering with his or her private correspondence. However, one should remember that the 'ordinary citizen' includes someone who is suspected of being involved in a crime, or who is a patient in a hospital or a prisoner in a prison. These are all situations where there might be a legitimate justification for monitoring correspondence or opening post.

In *Herczegfalvy v Austria*,[49] the applicant was resident in a psychiatric hospital, where the practice was adopted of passing all letters sent by him to the curator of the hospital, who would select those which could be sent on. This was done, argued the government, to protect his health, and was done in accordance with the relevant legal requirements. In other words, the government agreed that there was an interference with the patient's right of privacy of correspondence, but contended that it was justified under Article 8(2).

The European Court found that the terms of the statutes and the Civil Code were vaguely worded, and did not specify the scope of conditions of exercise of the discretionary power which was complained of: such specifications are all the more necessary in the case of detention in psychiatric institutions, because the person concerned is frequently at the mercy of the medical authorities, so that their correspondence is their only contact with the outside world. Thus, the government had failed to justify the interference and there was therefore a breach of Article 8.

In *Silver v UK*,[50] the applicants, all convicted prisoners, complained that controls over their mail constituted a breach of their rights under Article 8. There were restrictions on correspondence other than with a relative or friend, and on correspondence with journalists, or correspondence which held the authorities up to contempt, or letters to Members of Parliament containing complaints which had not been raised with the prison authorities, or letters calculated to stimulate public agitation. The Court held that such restrictions were not necessary in a democratic society, and that there had been breaches of Article 8.

In the case of *Hewitt v UK*,[51] officers of the National Council for Civil Liberties claimed that they had been the subject of telephone surveillance by the British Security Service, and that records had been kept about them, describing them as 'Communist sympathisers and subversives', based on sworn evidence from a former member of the Security Service. The European Court held that the recording and storing of information about the applicants' private lives, in a security and police register, interfered with the respect for private life. Since the rules governing this procedure were contained in non-binding and unpublished directives from the government and the Director General of the Secret Service, the framework for the surveillance was not sufficiently clear and so was not 'in accordance with the law'.

---

[49] (1993) 15 EHRR 437.
[50] (1983) 5 EHRR 347.
[51] (1992) 14 EHRR 657.

Thus it is clear that, in order to justify interference with correspondence, there must be not only a good reason for the interference, but the rules which govern such interference must themselves be clear and available to be seen. One can put this point as a matter of principle: broad discretionary powers such as those used in the above cases do not comply with the requirement that any interference should be in accordance with the law, since the powers are too vague and discretionary to qualify properly as 'law';[52] this is an important part of the Convention's protection against arbitrary powers.

INTRUSION BY SURVEILLANCE

The issues raised in the context of correspondence in fact apply more generally to all the interests being protected by Article 8: in respect of all of them there is the question of the extent to which it is permissible for the state to intrude on private activities for the purposes set out in Article 8(2). There is much modern technology which can be used to intrude on people's privacy and to check up on people: closed-circuit television cameras, binoculars, video recording, photography with long-range lenses, telephone tapping and bugging devices are all part of modern methods of watching and listening. These are all used by state officials in one context or another: police officers use these devices for the detection of crime; customs officers use them to intercept smuggling or drug running; television detectors use them to catch licence evaders; local authorities rely on CCTV to prevent crime, or even to spot traffic scheme evaders; and so on. It will be easily appreciated that the use of all these devices has the potential for infringing Article 8 and their use does get challenged. In particular in criminal prosecutions, the use of evidence obtained in breach of rights of privacy or without proper legal authority may be challenged by the defence, since without that evidence a criminal prosecution may fail; but such challenges are important because it is important that all criminal convictions are founded on properly obtained and reliable evidence. Where the use of such devices are challenged, the courts, following decisions of the European Court on this topic, will look at the particular circumstances of the intrusion, to see whether there is an interference with the right of respect to a private life, and then consider whether the interference can be justified on the basis that it is in accordance with the law and necessary in a democratic society for a specified purpose: the prevention of crime and so on.

In *Kopp v Austria*,[53] Herr Kopp was a lawyer who was suspected of criminal activity. The President of the Austrian court had authorised a phone tap, but he placed a limitation on it that conversations connected with Herr Kopp's work as a lawyer were not to be taken into account. However, the task of supervising and managing the tapping was entrusted not to a policeman but to an official in the legal department, who was a civil servant, and all the conversations on the telephone line were listened to. The European Court held that there was a breach of Article 8, and that the tapping had not been in accordance with the law (as required by Article 8(2)). The phone tap infringed Article 8 because no care had been taken with the carrying out of the tap and it had been done in an arbitrary way.

---

[52] This idea is discussed more generally above, pp. 87–8.
[53] (1999) 27 EHRR 91.

Thus it is a key requirement that surveillance be properly managed and supervised and be conducted in accordance with legal requirements and procedures. A similar type of case is *Khan v UK*,[54] to which we have already referred, since it raises the question of whether the reliance on evidence obtained in breach of Article 8 infringes the right to a fair trial under Article 6.

Mr Khan arrived in Britain, at Manchester Airport, from Pakistan. His cousin was on the same flight: his cousin was found to be in possession of £100,000 worth of heroin, and was charged and convicted of importing drugs. Mr Khan was not charged. However, some months later he visited a friend, who was himself under investigation for heroin dealing, at his home in Sheffield. A listening device had been fixed to the friend's house by police officers, unknown to the friend or to Mr Khan. During this visit the listening device was switched on, and Mr Khan was heard to admit that he was a party to the importing of the £100,000 heroin at Manchester Airport. He was arrested and charged, and at his trial the prosecution adduced the evidence of the conversation; the prosecution admitted that the fixing of the device was a trespass on the house, which is to say that it was obtained by unlawful means. Mr Khan argued at his trial that the evidence of the telephone conversation was based on an unlawful act and that it was unfair to admit it in the trial; the judge held that it was admissible and Mr Khan was convicted. The House of Lords held that although there was a breach of Article 8, the trial was not unfair.

The European Court held that there was indeed a violation of Article 8, although they considered that this did not mean that the trial was unfair in breach of Article 6. The Court did consider, however, that although the trial was not unfair, the United Kingdom had not provided any remedy for the breach of Article 8 (in breach of Article 13).

This suggests that after the Act, the United Kingdom courts will have to consider very carefully whether this subject should be revisited to provide a remedy for the breach of Article 8 in such situations, whether or not the result of using such evidence makes a trial unfair. Bear in mind that such evidence, although obtained improperly, may be perfectly reliable; but also that it is important that the police obey the law in all their actions and are not encouraged by the prospect of getting a conviction to obtain evidence of crime in ways which are themselves unlawful.

Since *Khan* was decided, one change to the law is that Parliament has passed the Regulation of Investigatory Powers Act 2000. This is important for our purposes because it is one of the requirements of Article 8 that, in order to be justified, conduct which would otherwise amount to a breach of Article 8 must be in accordance with the law. Where a state agency carries out surveillance which is not properly regulated or adequately covered by legislation or legal principles, it runs the risk of being found to be not in accordance with the law. If there is no relevant law, it is also harder for the state to say that it is necessary in a democratic society or proportionate. Until the Regulation of Investigatory Powers Act 2000, there were guidelines in place which applied to several forms of surveillance, but these were informal and not enshrined in statute. Thus the Regulation of Investigatory Powers Act provides a clear test for whether state surveillance is legal or illegal. This allows for a clearer assessment of whether surveillance infringes Article 8 because it is not in accordance with law, although this does not wholly answer the question of whether an infringement of privacy is justified. The

---

[54] (2001) 31 EHRR 45; also above, p. 164.

Regulation of Investigatory Powers Act provides regulation of, for example, the interception of communications, the use of covert surveillance and decryption of documents, including the disclosure of an encryption key in order to have access to protected material. Authority must be obtained for the carrying out of any of this; and the granting of any authorisation under the Act must take into account 'necessity' and 'proportionality'. Any surveillance which is performed other than under this Act, or without some other statutory authority, is unlawful.

QUESTIONS

1   How private do you think public records should be? You might like to think about examples such as the electoral roll and census forms, income tax returns, fingerprints, medical records or school records.

2   Do you think that prisoners deserve to have their rights to a private and family life respected?

3   Do you think that people should be able to prevent others interfering with the graves of their ancestors? Does your answer change if their ancestors' burial place is of archaeological or historical importance?

4   How private should correspondence such as e-mails and text messages be? Does your answer change where the messages are being used to plan a crime or to cause a nuisance to someone?

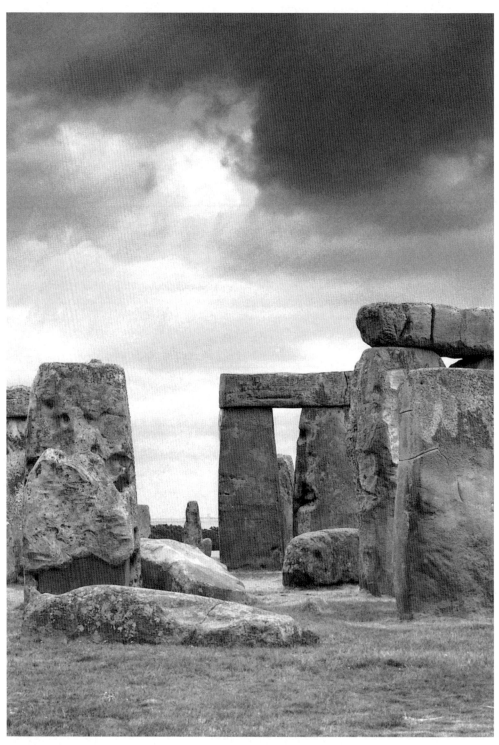

Stonehenge: access to this prehistoric religious site was the subject of *Pendragon v UK* (see p. 212).

Chapter 15

FREEDOM OF CONSCIENCE

'*Sapere aude*' – 'Dare to be wise' (The motto of Hugh Oldham, 1450–1519, Bishop of Exeter, and of The Manchester Grammar School, which he founded).

ARTICLE 9: FREEDOM OF THOUGHT, CONSCIENCE AND RELIGION
1. Everyone has the right to freedom of thought, conscience and religion; this right includes freedom to change his religion or belief and freedom, either alone or in community with others and in public or private, to manifest his religion or belief, in worship, teaching, practice and observance.
2. Freedom to manifest one's religion or beliefs shall be subject only to such limitations as are prescribed by law and are necessary in a democratic society in the interests of public safety, for the protection of public order, health or morals, or for the protection of the rights and freedoms of others.

FIRST PROTOCOL, ARTICLE 2: RIGHT TO EDUCATION
No person shall be denied the right to education. In the exercise of any functions which it assumes in relation to education and to teaching, the State shall respect the right of parents to ensure such education and teaching in conformity with their own religious and philosophical convictions.

FREEDOM OF THOUGHT

The European Court has said:

> Freedom of thought, conscience and religion is one of the foundations of a 'democratic society' within the meaning of the Convention. It is, in its religious dimension, one of the most vital elements that go to make up the identity of believers and their conception of life, but it is also a precious asset for atheists, agnostics, sceptics and the unconcerned. The pluralism indissociable from a democratic society, which has been dearly won over the centuries, depends on it.[1]

The word 'pluralism' is defined in the *Oxford English Dictionary* as the tolerance within society of a diversity of ethnic or multicultural groups and their beliefs and attitudes. And that word is echoed, by the phrase 'plural society', in a speech of an English judge, in 1979, some time before the Act, in the case of *R v Lemon*.[2] This case involved

---

[1] *Kokkinakis v Greece* (1994) 17 EHRR 397.
[2] [1979] AC 617.

a prosecution for blasphemous libel, brought against the editors and publishers of the magazine 'Gay News', in respect of a poem and a drawing, in that magazine, describing and depicting Christ in a scurrilous fashion. They had been convicted and the House of Lords dismissed their appeal. In his judgment, Lord Scarman said:

> In an increasingly plural society such as that of modern Britain it is necessary not only to respect the differing religious beliefs, feelings and practices of all but also to protect them from scurrility, vilification, ridicule and contempt. [. . .] People who know what they are doing will be criminally liable if the words they choose to publish are such as to cause grave offence to the religious feelings of some of their fellow citizens [, which] makes legal sense in a *plural society* which recognises the human rights and fundamental freedoms of the European Convention. Article 9 provides that every one has the right to freedom of religion, and the right to manifest his religion in worship, teaching, practice and observance. By necessary implication the Article imposes a duty on all of us to refrain from insulting or outraging the religious feelings of others. (emphasis added).

This emphasises that this freedom of conscience and religion is there to be exercised, but it should be expressed with due regard for others: there has to be a balance struck, and the rights of other persons to *their* freedom of religion imposes a duty not to insult gratuitously the religious views of others.

It is, however, extremely important to realise that such limitations on this right apply only to **manifesting** a belief and not to the right to **hold** a belief, which is not qualified in any way. This is because it would be wrong in principle for the state to attempt to legislate as to how people should **think**, as opposed to how they **act**. The attempt of any state to force people to think in a certain way is the hallmark of totalitarianism, and of some of the most evil regimes that have existed, such as Nazi Germany and Communist Russia. This is precisely because they attempted to stifle all freedom of thought, and not just freedom of action. This was also the enduring message of George Orwell's novel, *1984*, which painted a picture of a society where the state developed technology to try to control how its citizens thought. Although none of the states of modern Europe are anywhere near as oppressive as these, we will still see cases where, for example, the state has acted in a way which effectively attempts to impose on a citizen a religious attitude.

Thus, there are no qualifications at all on the distinct rights contained in Article 9(1) – the freedom *of* thought, conscience and religion, that is, a right to **hold** views or beliefs, and the freedom to **change** these beliefs. However, the right to **manifest** one's religion or beliefs, how one shows or exercises them, may be limited in accordance with Article 9(2), which sets out the legitimate aims that such limitations may pursue, and also includes the familiar phrases, that such limitations should be 'prescribed by law' and 'necessary in a democratic society'.[3] This brings into play the exercise of balancing rights, and as with most of the articles, there are a good number of cases which turn on whether or not an interference with an Article 9 right is justified under Article 9(2).

---

[3] Introduced above, p. 86.

THE RIGHT TO EDUCATION

We are considering Article 2 of the First Protocol[4] with Article 9, because both are aspects of the right to freedom of conscience. One of the hopes of many parents is that they will be able to bring up their children to share their fundamental beliefs about the world. This is recognised by the Convention as a legitimate aspiration in Article 2, the second sentence of which concerns just that, the right of parents to have their religious and philosophical convictions respected in the education of their children.

But at the same time, children must have their own freedom of conscience, a guarantee of their ability to form their own view of the world, including their own views of basic moral and religious issues. This fundamental aspect of personal growth and development can only be guaranteed by access to education. A denial of the right to education would be to deny a person the ability to explore the world in an informed manner, as well as to deny them the chance to improve themselves intellectually, and have the opportunity to pursue an occupation and lifestyle which will be fulfilling and worth while.

All these are important aspects of freedom of thought, but in a more concrete and specific context. And, as we will see, there are cases which reflect this, referring to both Articles 9 and 2. It should be noted also at the outset, that although Article 2 contains no second, qualifying paragraph, the requirement is to 'respect' the rights of parents, not to guarantee them. This is therefore not absolute, and the European Court has made clear that it can be interfered with by the state, so long as such interference is reasonably necessary and proportionate.

'BELIEF' OR 'RELIGION': IS THERE ONE?

The ordinary person may claim that his or her freedom of belief or religion has been violated, but the first question for the court is whether there is indeed a belief or religion which is clear enough to qualify for protection. Is it recognised by the court as coming within these articles? Obviously in many cases there will be no difficulty; the belief or religion is well known and established, and the case has reached court because of some other issue – whether there has been a violation, or whether the state's interference was justified.

But in some cases the claimant will not fall within these articles at all, because the conviction or belief, however sincerely or fervently held, is not one which falls within the scope of what is protected. In the next two cases we see how the questions can arise and the difficulty the courts have in answering it.

In *Campbell and Cosans v UK*,[5] Mrs Campbell and Mrs Cosans each had children of school age attending state schools in Scotland, where, at the time, corporal punishment was used as a disciplinary measure. Mrs Campbell objected to this form of punishment, although her son was never

---

[4] All references in this chapter to Article 2 should be taken to refer to this article, not Article 2 of the Convention itself.
[5] (1982) 4 EHRR 293.

punished in this way; Mrs Cosans' son refused to submit to the punishment and was suspended from school, and then denied readmission when his parents refused to accept the right of the school to administer corporal punishment. The European Court held that there had been a violation of 'religion and philosophical convictions' within the scope of Article 2. The Court said:

> Having regard to the Convention as a whole, including Article 17, the expression 'philosophical convictions' in the present context denotes, in the Court's opinion, such convictions as are worthy of respect in a 'democratic society' and are not incompatible with human dignity; in addition they must not conflict with the fundamental right of the child to education, the whole of Article 2 being dominated by its first sentence. The applicants' views relate to a weighty and substantial aspect of human life and behaviour, namely the integrity of the person, the propriety or otherwise of the infliction of corporal punishment and the exclusion of the distress which the risk of such punishment entails. They are views which satisfy each of the various criteria listed above; it is this that distinguishes them from opinions that might be held on other methods of discipline or on discipline in general.

In short, the beliefs of the parents, against corporal punishment, qualified as a philosophical conviction, and to ignore it amounted to a violation of their rights under Article 9. But suppose parents actually support the use of corporal punishment and claim it is part of their beliefs and convictions? This was the situation in the case of *Williamson*.[6]

Section 548 of the Education Act 1996 had removed the defence, previously available to teachers, that reasonable chastisement could be applied to pupils, and that if it was reasonable the teacher would not be guilty of assault. This meant that teachers naturally considered that they could no longer use corporal punishment, since they would be left open to a charge of assault. Some teachers and parents of children at certain Christian schools applied to the court for a ruling that the use of corporal punishment in independent schools had *not* been abolished by this section. These teachers and parents were in favour of corporal punishment; their argument was that physical discipline, admonished by teachers, was part of their Christian belief; but if that section had indeed abolished corporal punishment, that was a violation of their rights under Article 9 and Article 2.

The Court of Appeal acknowledged that the teachers and parents held Christian beliefs, and that they derived their view of corporal punishment from this belief, but the Court differed as to whether or not this qualified for protection. Lord Justice Buxton agreed with the High Court that this view was not a religious conviction in its own right, and therefore the Articles were not engaged. The majority of the Court, Lord Justice Rix and Lady Justice Arden, did consider that this was a religious conviction which was protected by these Articles; but they did not consider that the section interfered with a manifestation of that conviction, since it was not necessary for the parents' belief that the teachers should impose corporal punishment, as opposed to the parents themselves.

This shows that it will be a matter of evidence from case to case whether the view being put forward is sufficiently cogent to amount to a religious or philosophical belief, and that it is that belief which is being manifested – since in such cases, it is only the manifestation which is being considered, and not the right to believe what you like.

Article 9 also protects those who do not want any religious association at all, which echoes those words from *Kokkinakis*, which we quoted at the start of this chapter: the article is 'a precious asset for atheists, agnostics, sceptics and the unconcerned'. An example of this is the *Crawley Green Road Cemetery*[7] case.

---

[6] R (Williamson) v Secretary of State for Education [2003] 1 All ER 385.
[7] In re Crawley Green Road Cemetery, Luton [2001] 2 WLR 1175.

Mrs S was the widow of J, and during their life together they had lived in Luton. When he died, his funeral had been conducted in the humanist tradition, but his ashes had been interred in consecrated ground at a cemetery in Luton, although neither S nor J had had any affinity with the Christian faith. Then S had moved to London. S now sought to have the ashes exhumed, so that they could be re-interred nearer her home. S told the court that if she had been aware that J's ashes had been interred in ground 'with church associations', she would have regarded it as hypocritical, and she would not have permitted it. The Church Consistory Court held that Article 9 encompassed religious beliefs such as humanism, which S sincerely held, and to refuse her would be in violation of the article.

Of course, religious beliefs will vary from country to country, and the European Court has had to bear that in mind, when exercising its supervisory jurisdiction; the attitude of the particular country and its history will be relevant. Thus, in the *Kokkinakis*[8] case itself, where Mr Kokkinakis complained of interference by the state with his freedom of religion, the Court had to balance his rights with that of the state – and that balancing exercise required the Court to bear in mind the history of Greece.

Mr Kokkinakis was a Greek national and a Jehovah's Witness, and he was invited into an Orthodox Christian's home and entered into a discussion with her; he talked of the articles of faith of the Jehovah's Witnesses sect, and sought to persuade her to join the Jehovah's Witnesses; the police were informed, and he was arrested, and convicted of the offence of proselytism, contrary to Greek law, and fined. He claimed that to prosecute him and convict him was a violation of his rights under Article 9 of the Convention.

The European Court recognised that the Christian Eastern Orthodox Church, which during nearly four centuries of foreign occupation symbolised the maintenance of Greek culture and the Greek language, took an active part in the Greek people's struggle for emancipation, to such an extent that Hellenism is to some extent identified with the Orthodox faith. But the Court held that by prosecuting and convicting him the state had interfered with Mr Kokkinakis's right to freedom to manifest his religion or belief; the Greek government had failed to show that the conviction was justified by any pressing social need.

MANIFESTATION OF BELIEF

As we have noted above, only the freedom to *manifest* a belief is the subject of Article 9(2), and this is the only freedom guaranteed by Article 9 which may be limited: the right to hold or adhere to thought, conscience or religion may not be limited in any way. **Manifest** means to show and exercise something outwardly, and to demonstrate signs of it. It is therefore understandable that this is the aspect of Article 9 which may be limited, since what a person thinks is private, but how a person manifests that view may impinge on other people, and even harm them or society.

Quoting from the *Kokkinakis* case again, the European Court has referred to this distinction:

According to Article 9, freedom to manifest one's religion is not only exercisable in community with others, 'in public' and within the circle of those whose faith one shares, but

---

[8] (1994) 17 EHRR 397.

can also be asserted 'alone' and 'in private'; furthermore, it includes in principle the right to try to convince one's neighbour, for example through 'teaching', failing which, moreover, 'freedom to change one's religion or belief', enshrined in Article 9, would be likely to remain a dead letter. [. . .]

The fundamental nature of the rights guaranteed in Article 9(1) is also reflected in the wording of the paragraph providing for limitations on them. Unlike the second paragraphs of Article 8, 10 and 11, which cover all the rights mentioned in the first paragraphs of those Articles, that of Article 9 refers only to 'freedom to manifest one's religion or belief'. In so doing it recognises that in democratic societies, in which several religions co-exist within one and the same population, it may be necessary to place restrictions on this freedom in order to reconcile the interests of the various groups and ensure that everyone's beliefs are respected.

We shall look now at some cases where the Court considered various limitations on an Article 9 right. The Court applied the usual principles regarding such limitations in the Convention – the need to examine the aims of the limitation, and the principles implied in the words 'according to law', or 'necessary in a democratic society'. What emerges from the cases is the way in which the courts balance conflicting rights. And they must do so however sincerely and devoutly the relevant religion or belief is held and manifested. Our first case is *Pendragon v UK*.[9]

The applicant was the Honoured Pendragon of the Glastonbury Order of Druids. In 1995, he wished to hold a Druidic service for the Summer Solstice on 21 June at the Heel Stone, which is close to Stonehenge. Stonehenge is a monument predating the Iron Age, and it consists of a circle of stones which are aligned to the midsummer sunrise. The sun rises above the Heel Stone on the date of the midsummer sunrise. The modern Druid Orders have reconstructed their rituals, which have now taken place for about a century at Stonehenge.

In the mid-1980s, many non-Druids attended such events, and this resulted in disorder. The local authority and the Secretary of State therefore made orders under the Public Order Act 1986, forbidding assemblies at Stonehenge, because of the fear of mass invasion and disorder, and damage to the monument. But Pendragon attended anyway, in full ceremonial dress, and he was arrested. He complained that this was a violation of Article 9.

The European Commission accepted that his assembly had a legitimately religious nature, but the Commons considered that the state's interference – the banning orders and the arrest – was justified, as there was a real fear of a breakdown in public order if the assembly took place.

This case is a good example of the necessary balancing exercise: the freedom to manifest a belief or religion had to be balanced against the risk of disorder and the consequent damage to persons and property, especially in the context of an important national monument. In such cases, relevant factors will include the number of people involved, the importance of the religious ceremony, the likelihood of physical damage or injury, and so on.

Another case where we see this balancing act in a different context is the case of *Taylor*,[10] about religion and the use of narcotic drugs.

---

[9] (1999) 27 EHRR Co 179.
[10] *R v Taylor* (2002) 1 CAR 519.

Mr Paul Taylor was prosecuted and convicted of an offence of possession of cannabis, contrary to the Misuse of Drugs Act 1971. He was a Rastafarian, and it was agreed by the prosecution that this was a religion, in which drugs were used as an act of worship. Mr Taylor therefore argued that to prosecute him was a breach of Article 9.

The Court of Appeal held that there was no violation. The Court was entitled to consider that a ban on the possession of cannabis with intent to supply was in the interests of public safety to combat the danger of drugs from the point of view of health and safety. This was based on the policy of the Act itself and also on the fact that the United Kingdom had subscribed to various international treaties which prohibited certain drugs, such as the Single Convention on Narcotic Drugs 1961 and the United Nations Convention against Illicit Traffic in Narcotic Drugs and Psychotropic Substances 1988.

The Court said that a distinction should be drawn between legislation which prohibited conduct simply because it related to or was motivated by a religious belief, and legislation which was of general application and happened to prohibit conduct which was encouraged or required by a religious belief, where the prohibition was for reasons unconnected with that religious belief, as here. The Court took the view that the prohibition on the drugs in question was not aimed at religious conduct, but at general behaviour: the purpose of the legislation was not to prevent the manifestation of a belief, which would be more likely to infringe Article 9. Further, the ban on cannabis was justifiable under Article 9(2) as being necessary for public safety; when balancing the two interests, the religious rights of Mr Taylor were outweighed by the public interest in outlawing these drugs.

PRISONERS

Prisoners have human rights, including rights under Article 9, which they are entitled to exercise. But, as one might expect, prison rules may have priority. This was the situation in the case of *H v UK*.[11]

H was convicted by a court in the United Kingdom of common assault and sentenced to 3 years' imprisonment. In the prison where he was held, there was a policy that prisoners should spend time in the workshops, and H was told he should work in the print shop, but he refused, as he was a vegan, and he objected to working with products of animal origin, or products tested on animals – in this case the dyes in the print shop. He was disciplined for this refusal, and he complained to the European Court of a breach of Article 9.

His case came before the Commission, which agreed that veganism was a matter of conscience or belief, within Article 9. But the requirement that H should work in the print shop was a requirement which was justified under Article 9(2), as being 'prescribed by law', being provided for in the Prison Rules, which had the aim of good order in the prison. There had to be a system of allocation of work, which was fair and without favouritism, and so a prisoner could not enjoy a freedom of choice of employment. The system was a proportionate one, and there was no violation of Article 9.

Of course, one could not expect the prison authorities to act any differently in such a case, since the prison rules had to be observed, and did not allow for variations for individual prisoners. Nevertheless, even as against prisoners, it is important that such rules should still not interfere with rights except in a way which is proportionate, and should be enforced in a proportionate way, as the Commission found they were here.

---

[11] (1993) 16 EHRR CD 44.

CONSCIENTIOUS OBJECTORS

War, and the preparation for it, is in the eyes of many people, objectionable, and one part of that objection is that it is contrary to a philosophy of peace, which may or may not be founded on a religion or a faith; and 'conscientious objection' is a recognised belief or conviction. But the European Commission has said that conscientious objection is *not* recognised as a belief or conviction the manifestation of which is protected by Article 9. In the case of *Fadini v Switzerland*,[12] the Commission considered a claim that Article 9 had been violated in the case of Mr Fadini, who was required to carry out civil defence duty.

Mr Fadini, aged about 51, was required to report for compulsory civil defence duty, and in 1988, 1989 and 1991 he refused to report for duty, and was fined and imprisoned. His argument was that this civil defence duty was tantamount to the support of a war, and that his Christian conviction, which was against any form of violence, forbade him as a matter of conscience to participate in it. He therefore claimed that the punishment imposed on him by the state violated Article 9.

The Commission rejected his claim, holding that it was inadmissible; previous decisions of the Commission had held that conscientious objection to military service was not recognised as a right within Article 9, by the same token an objection to civil defence duty could not be recognised.

Part of the reason for the Commission's view about conscientious objectors is that Article 4, which refers to compulsory labour, specifically allows for compulsory military service or the equivalent service in the case of conscientious objectors 'in countries where they are recognised': thus the Convention itself allows countries the decision whether or not to recognise the rights of conscientious objectors to be exempt from service.

However, the actual belief that war is wrong is a genuine belief which qualifies in principle for the protection of Article 9, even if a particular manifestation may not be permitted, or may be justifiably interfered with. This is clear from the next case, that of *Arrowsmith v UK*,[13] where the European Court agreed that there existed a genuine belief, but held that the state's action – a prosecution – was not in fact an interference with *that* belief, since it held that the complainant was not manifesting that belief when she was arrested and prosecuted.

Miss Pat Arrowsmith, in September 1973, distributed leaflets at an Army centre in Warminster, where there were soldiers who were to be posted to Northern Ireland. The leaflets recounted views of ex-soldiers, and these leaflets advised the serving soldiers to go absent without leave, or to refuse to be posted to Northern Ireland. She was arrested near where the leaflets were being distributed. In May 1974, she was convicted of an offence under the Incitement to Disaffection Act 1934, and sentenced to a term of imprisonment. She was a convinced pacifist. She had campaigned in support of her views, and she was active in an organisation called the British Withdrawal from Northern Ireland Campaign.

The European Commission held that pacifism, as a philosophy, *is* a belief within the scope of Article 9, and *is* therefore protected. But the question arose, was the *distribution* protected, as being the manifestation of that belief of pacifism? The leaflets emphasised the Northern Ireland question;

---

[12] (1993) 16 EHRR CD 13.
[13] (1981) 3 EHRR 218.

the contents showed that the authors were opposed to the British policy in Northern Ireland. The leaflets did not express pacifist views. So, decided the Commission, her conviction and sentence did *not* interfere with the exercise of her pacifist views.

In one sense, this is an illustration of something obvious: to found a complaint of interference, the individual must show that the thing which suffered interference was the relevant belief or religion, and not something else, however nearly connected. Perhaps it is also a rather hard case: perhaps it would have made all the difference if Miss Arrowsmith had put at the top of the leaflets, 'In the name of pacifism'.

STATE CHURCHES

The Convention jurisprudence does not forbid or exclude the concept of a state church, that is, an official or established church, such as the Church of England. The fact that a state has established such a state church system does not violate Article 9. But a citizen must be free to join its membership, or to leave it. No-one can be obliged to join it. Those are the principles of the Convention, and they entirely reflect that attitude of pluralism which we mentioned earlier. And so we come to the case of *Darby v Sweden*,[14] which shows us how the European Commission regarded a state church and its tax laws.

Dr Peter Darby, a gentleman of British origin, and a Finnish citizen, was employed as a doctor by the Swedish State Railways, in Gavle, Sweden. He rented a flat in the town, but at weekends he lived with his family on the island of Lemland, in the Finnish archipelago of Aland. He was obliged to pay a special tax to the Lutheran Church of Sweden, which was the established church of Sweden. Membership of that church was reserved to Swedish citizens and to foreigners living in Sweden. Dr Darby was *not* a member of that church, and he complained that this tax violated his right to freedom of religion as guaranteed by Article 9.

The European Commission decided that there *was* a violation of Article 9. The Commission recognised that state church systems existed in several states who are parties to the Convention, and expressly stated that the fact that a state has established a state church system cannot in itself be considered to violate Article 9. But the Commission considered that, in order to satisfy the requirements of Article 9, a state church system must include specific safeguards for the individual's freedom of religion. It would be a breach of the article for people to be forced to enter or be prohibited from leaving the church in question. And the Commission found that the obligation to pay a tax to the church was in effect an obligation to be a member of it, in breach of Article 9.

(The European Court did not consider it necessary to decide the point under Article 9, since they found a violation of Article 14, the prohibition on discrimination, taken with Article 1 of the First Protocol: there was a discriminatory and unjustifiable difference of treatment between a resident and a non-resident in the application of a tax, which is a deprivation of property.)

This confirms a point that has been made in other cases as well, that freedom of religion includes freedom not to hold a religion, including freedom to abstain from membership of a church and to abstain from its ceremonies, and that includes a state church.

---

[14] (1991) 13 EHRR 774.

SECTION 13 OF THE ACT

Section 13 (1)   If a court's determination of any question arising under this Act might affect the exercise by a religious organisation (itself or its members collectively) of the Convention right to freedom of thought, conscience and religion, it must have particular regard to the importance of that right.

We have been discussing aspects of a state church and how Article 9 may be engaged. This is a convenient moment to mention section 13 of the Human Rights Act 1998 which refers to the rights of religious organisations generally. This section upholds and strengthens the Article 9 rights of a religious organisation and its members. It was inserted in the Act because concern was expressed, by a cross-section of society – religious leaders, the public and Members of Parliament – that the exercise of the Convention rights of others would damage the Article 9 rights of religious organisations and their members. And so the section was inserted. It requires the courts to 'have particular regard' to the importance of the Article 9 rights.

The Home Secretary gave assurances that the purpose of this section was to protect the religious organisations and their members: 'the new clause will send a clear signal to the courts that they must pay due regard to the rights guaranteed by Article 9, including, where relevant, the right of a Church to act in accordance with religious belief'.[15] And further, 'It is to reassure them against the [Act] being used to intrude upon genuinely religious beliefs or practices based on their beliefs. I emphasise the word "practices", as well as "beliefs".' The Home Secretary gave an example: 'The right of the Church, which we intend to strengthen, to refuse to marry divorced people remains protected by the Convention.' The Home Secretary's example shows how doctrinal beliefs and practices are preserved. He chose an example from the practice of the established Church, the Church of England; but it must be emphasised that section 13 extends to *any* religious organisation.

FREEDOM NOT TO HOLD A BELIEF

The principle of *Darby's* case is that there can be no obligation on a person to join a church or to pay deference to it. However, the protection provided by Article 9 goes further than this. Freedom to hold a belief means freedom *not* to hold a belief: there can be no obligation to hold a belief, or to swear by a belief, or to bow to it. That is the principle of the Convention, as shown in this next case of *Buscarini v San Marino*,[16] where members of a Parliament were obliged to swear on religious texts, contrary to their consciences.

Mr Buscarini, Mr Della Balda, and Mr Manzaroli were elected in 1993 to the General Grand Council (the Parliamentary body) of the Republic of San Marino. They asked permission to take the oath required by the Election Act, without making reference to any religious text. The Act prescribed

---

[15] House of Commons debates, 20 May 1998 (HC, Vol. 312, cols 1021–1024).
[16] (2000) 30 EHRR 208.

the words of the oath as being 'I . . . swear on the Holy Gospels ever to be faithful to and obey the Constitution of the Republic . . .'. At the General Grand Council session they took the oath, in writing, without reference to the Gospels, but the secretariat advised that this was invalid, and the General Grand Council resolved that they should retake the oath, on the Gospels, or else forfeit their parliamentary seats. They took the oath on the Gospels, albeit complaining that their right to freedom of religion and conscience had been infringed. The European Court agreed that this was in violation of their rights:

> That freedom entails, *inter alia*, freedom to hold or not to hold religious beliefs and to practise or not to practise a religion [. . .] In the instant case, requiring Mr. Buscarini and Mr. Della Balda to take an oath on the Gospels did indeed constitute a limitation within the meaning of the second paragraph of Article 9, since it required them to swear allegiance to a particular religion on pain of forfeiting their parliamentary seats. [. . .] Requiring the applicants to take the oath on the Gospels was tantamount to requiring two elected representatives of the people to swear allegiance to a particular religion, in a requirement which is not compatible with Article 9. [. . .] It would be contradictory to make the exercise of a mandate intended to represent different views of society within Parliament subject to a prior declaration of commitment to a particular set of beliefs.

That is an important case; there are institutions in the United Kingdom where the individual is obliged to attend an assembly, or to join in a ceremony which has some religious overtone – such as the pronouncement of a Grace – and which is objectionable to some persons attending it. And there may be occasions when one is obliged to take an oath which offends a conscientious belief.

CRITICISM

If the individual 'manifests' his belief or religion, he must expect the possibility of criticism; that is the approach of the European Court. There is no right to be exempt from criticism. This was clear in the case of *Otto-Preminger Institute v Austria*.[17]

The Institute announced a series of public showings of a satirical film, with a religious subject matter, 'The Council in Heaven'. It was a satirical tragedy, set in heaven, with trivial imagery and absurdities pointed at the Christian creed, and being a caricature of the Christian faith, and disparaging it. The Austrian Court found that it was an abusive attack on the Roman Catholic religion according to the conception of the Tyrolean public. The film was seized and forfeited, and the manager of the Institute complained that this was a violation of Article 10, the right of freedom of expression.

The European Court held that the Austrian authorities had been justified in seizing the film, and the case is principally concerned with Article 10. But the Court turned to consider the attack on the religion of the Austrian public, and how far the freedom of religion carried with it the obligation to put up with criticism. The Court said,

> Those who choose to exercise the freedom to manifest their religion, irrespective of whether they do so as members of a religious majority or minority, cannot reasonably expect to be exempt from all criticism. They must tolerate and accept the denial by others of their religious beliefs and even the propagation by others of doctrines hostile to their faith. However, the manner in which religious beliefs and doctrines are opposed or denied is a matter which may engage the responsibility of the State, notably its responsibility to ensure the peaceful enjoyment of the right guaranteed under Article 9 to the holders of those beliefs and doctrines.

---

[17] (1995) 19 EHRR 34.

This reflects the view of Lord Scarman, which we quoted earlier, from the case of *Lemon*: criticism is one thing, and must be tolerated, since that is a fundamental part of living in a plural society, but such criticism must not be gratuitously offensive. You need not share the beliefs or views of others, but you should not be needlessly insulting to them; and you should respect the rights of others to hold beliefs with which you disagree.

RESPECT FOR BELIEFS IN EDUCATION

As we have already mentioned, one aspect of the right to respect for the beliefs of others is the right to respect for religious and philosophical convictions in education protected by Article 2. Where the education of children is concerned, the religious and philosophical convictions of parents must be respected; we have seen how the European Court has applied this in the case of *Campbell and Cosans*.[18] But what does that word 'respect' mean in this context? The answer is that the use of the word respect has been understood to import a balancing exercise, and proportionality in any interference with religious convictions, such as is implicit in Article 9(2). But there is still a positive requirement to respect the religious convictions of parents – as opposed to merely taking them into account.

In the case of *Kjeldsen, Busk Madsen and Pedersen v Denmark*,[19] the three sets of applications were six parents who had children of school age, and who objected to compulsory sex education in state schools; they could not educate the children at private schools, nor at home themselves. They argued that this compulsory sex education was contrary to the beliefs they held as Christian parents, and that the state had failed to accord respect to their religious or philosophical convictions in this regard.

The European Court held that the parents had religious and philosophical convictions, which came within Article 9; but the policy of this sex education did *not* offend them to the extent forbidden by the second sentence of Article 2, so there was no violation. First, the Court made it clear that under Convention law the state is forbidden to indoctrinate its citizens – in the sense of imposing a particular religious or moral lesson, or making it paramount; that was *not* suggested in this case. On the other hand, Article 2 does not prevent the state from importing, through teaching or education, information or knowledge of a directly or indirectly religious or philosophical kind – provided it does so in an objective critical and pluralistic way. In the present case, the Court took account of the fact that although the education involved considerations of a moral order, these were very general in character. So the education did not fail to respect the convictions of the parents who brought the complaint.

The Court added that the respect which is due from the state under Article 9, applies to the whole field of the state's functions in relation to education and training; it is not limited to religious instruction, but is required throughout the entire educational curriculum.

---

[18] (1982) 4 EHRR 293, above p. 209.
[19] (1976) 1 EHRR 711.

In a country such as the United Kingdom, where society is multi-ethnic, this duty on the state – of respect in education – is becoming more important. This appears in the next case of *K v Newham London Borough Council*.[20]

K was a parent of a girl of secondary school age. The local authority's policy was that parents were entitled to express a preference, and that a preference for a single-sex school was one of several considerations, which would be taken into account when deciding where a child would be placed. K had stated a preference for a single-sex school on the basis of being a devout Muslim. The local authority had decided that the girl would *not* be given a place at a single-sex school, and an appeal from this decision was refused. These decisions did not mention religious grounds, but stated that the decision was on the basis of efficient use of resources. K sought judicial review of the decisions in the High Court.

The High Court quashed the decisions, as being in violation of Article 2. The Court held that K's religious convictions were genuine; and they came within the meaning of Article 2. There is an obligation under the Article to recognise and take into account the religion of the parent, and the application book, provided to the parent, should have had space for this, but did not do so; the decisions had therefore been taken without the respect required by Article 2. The local authority should have taken positive steps to ensure that the religious beliefs and reasons of the parents were sought and recorded so that they could at least be considered when the decision as to placement was made.

However, this does not mean that a parent has the right to insist on a particular form of education, or education at a particular school.

In the case of *O*,[21] it was argued that where a religious school refused to admit a pupil on the grounds that their classes were full, this was a breach of Article 2, and also of Article 8, the right to family life, since the pupil already had a sister at the school.

The Administrative Court held that there was no breach of these rights: Article 2 did not confer any absolute right to admission to a particular school, and other considerations could also affect whether or not a pupil was allowed entry; and Article 8 did not require admission to the same school as a sibling. The requirements of the articles were met because the school's admissions policy did have a sibling criterion, so the point would be considered when the decision was made.

THE SCOPE OF ARTICLE 2

It is important to note that Article 2 does not provide a positive right to education. This was not necessary because when the Convention was drawn up, all parties to it had education systems. What it does is require that no-one shall be denied access to such education systems as exist, not that there is a positive right to any particular type of education.[22] It is in that context that respect is required for the parents' religious

---

[20] *R (on the application of K) v Newham London Borough Council* (2002) *Times*, 28.2.02.
[21] *R (O) v J Roman Catholic Primary School Appeal Panel* (2001) LTL 22.10.01.
[22] *Belgian Linguistics* case (1979–80) 1 EHRR 241 & 252, considered above in the context of Article 14, p. 92.

and philosophical convictions; that is another reason why Article 2 cannot be used to ensure education in accordance with any particular preference.

However, although the second sentence of Article 2 is phrased in terms of parents, it would be misleading to assume that the right of access to education applies only to children, or at any rate, young students. The first sentence refers to the right to education of *every* person; mature students may claim to have a right under this article.

RESERVATION TO ARTICLE 2

UK RESERVATION:
At the time of signing the present (First) Protocol, I declare that, in view of certain provisions of the Education Acts in the United Kingdom, the principle affirmed in the second sentence of Article 2 is accepted by the United Kingdom only so far as it is compatible with the provision of efficient instruction and training, and the avoidance of unreasonable public expenditure. Dated 20 March 1952 Made by the United Kingdom Permanent Representative to the Council of Europe.

The above is the Reservation entered by the United Kingdom with regard to Article 2.[23] The key provision is that the principle affirmed in the second sentence of Article 2 is accepted only so far as it is compatible with the provision of efficient instruction and training, and the avoidance of unreasonable public expenditure.

The reason for this Reservation was that at the time the Convention was signed by the United Kingdom, there was a concern that this right might not be complied with by the Education Act then in force, which governed the rights to education. The Reservation still applies, although the European Commission has expressed the view that this Reservation may be questioned.[24]

However, since Article 2 does not specify what sort of education the state should provide, the Reservation does not undermine the effect of the main right, since it does not inhibit access to *an* education, it is simply a further factor in considering whether the views of the parents as to the *type* of education have been respected: the United Kingdom does not accept that this requirement for respect of parents' convictions can entail unreasonable public expenditure or an inefficient use of resources. If these factors alone mean that a certain sort of education is not available, then the fact that the result may be a lack of respect for a parent's convictions should not amount to a breach of the Convention right. This is likely to be part of the proportionality calculation in any event; but, of course, when the Reservation was entered, the Court had not come into being, so none of the cases which developed the way the Court approaches such questions had been decided.

---

[23] The effect of a reservation is discussed above, p. 85.
[24] *SP v UK* (1997) 23 EHRR CD 139.

QUESTIONS

1   Freedom of conscience: are there any views which you would not consider should be protected as 'beliefs'? Do you agree that not all manifestations of beliefs should qualify for protection?

2   The right to education: should there be a positive right? You may like to compare Article 2 with Article 26 of the Universal Declaration of Human Rights (in Appendix 4), which does include a positive right to education, and goes into rather more detail, including requiring compulsory and free elementary education.

Speaker's Corner in Hyde Park, London, where anyone has been allowed to express freely any view about anything since 1872.

(*Source:* Aaron Robson/PA Photos.)

Chapter 16

FREEDOM OF EXPRESSION

'Nothing is more apt to surprise a foreigner, than the extreme liberty, which we enjoy in this country, of communicating whatever we please to the public, and of openly censuring every measure, entered into by the king or his ministers.' (David Hume, *Essays Moral, Political, and Literary*, 1875)

FREE SPEECH

'The freedom of expression constitutes one of the essential foundations of a democratic society, one of the basic conditions for its progress and for the development of every man.'[1] Those are words of high principle, spoken by the European Court. They reflect the attitude of judges and statesmen, in many societies and nations, who emphasise the right of freedom of speech.

'Free speech', the words of the heading above, is a phrase used regularly: 'It's a free country', 'I can say what I like'. Article 10 certainly protects the right of free speech: but it also provides a good deal more. 'Expression' covers human activity beyond mere speech, and we shall see in this chapter what means of expression have come within the article. Furthermore, the words of Article 10(1) are not limited to expression; they provide also a right to *receive* information.

The judges of our courts, even before the incorporation of the Convention, recognised the right to freedom of expression. In one case, Mr Justice Laws in the High Court said:

---

[1] *Handyside v UK* (1979–80) 1 EHRR 737.

There is a general principle in our law that the expression of opinion and the conveyance of information will not be restrained by the courts, save on pressing grounds. Freedom of expression is as much a sinew of the common law as it is of the European Convention.[2]

In that case the Advertising Standards Authority had compiled a report criticising Vernons Pools, and Vernons applied to the court for an order preventing publication; the judge refused the order. These words were spoken long before the incorporation of the Convention. Note the description of the freedom of expression as a 'sinew' of the law, meaning an essential part of the common law, and a working part.

A more recent case, but one which also predated the coming into force of the Act, in which the House of Lords have upheld the status of freedom of expression as a fundamental principle of our law, even without the Convention, is the case of *Simms*.[3]

This case concerned restrictions on the rights of prisoners to speak to journalists. The House of Lords held that the prison rules which imposed restrictions on the rights of prisoners were in principle justified, but that they had to be applied in a way which gave effect to the fundamental right to freedom of expression. Thus the policy of the Home Secretary in imposing an indiscriminate ban on interviews with journalists aimed at publicising an alleged wrongful conviction could not stand. Although it was an inevitable consequence of imprisonment that a prisoner's rights are limited, such interference has to be the minimum necessary to achieve the objectives of the sentence of deprivation of liberty, and discipline and order in prisons. A refusal to allow consultation with a journalist for the investigation of new evidence which could lead to a reference back of a case to the Court of Appeal was an unjustified limitation on freedom of expression since it endangered the prisoner's access to justice.

But undoubtedly the Convention has added something to the previous law: there are cases in our courts which have been decided with the Convention principles in mind, especially in the exercise of dealing with situations where there is a conflict of rights. We shall see that particularly in the field of privacy – where newspapers have sought to exercise their freedom of expression, by publishing confidential material.

THE SCOPE OF THE FREEDOM

The question is this: how far may one go; how outrageous or how offensive may the content of your 'expression' be? What kind of material is actually protected by Article 10? The answer has been given by the European Court, again in *Handyside*,[4] which we quoted earlier.

Mr Handyside had published and distributed to schools and colleges a booklet entitled '*The Little Red Schoolbook*' which contained offensive and obscene material. It was intended to be read by schoolchildren and adolescents. He was prosecuted and convicted of distributing an obscene publication. The European Court found that the prosecution and conviction of Mr Handyside were indeed interferences with his right to impart information and ideas, within the meaning of Article 10(1). The Court in fact held that the interference was justified under Article 10(2) for the protection of morals;

[2] *R. v Advertising Standards Authority, ex parte Vernons Organisation* [1992] 1 WLR 1289 at 1293.
[3] *R (Simms) v Secretary of State for the Home Department* [2000] 2 AC 115.
[4] (1979–80) 1 EHRR 737, see also above, p. 60.

but the key statement of principle for our purposes is that although the material was offensive, he had a right to publish it. The Court said:

> Subject to Article 10(2), [Article 10] is applicable not only to single 'information' or 'ideas' that are favourably received or regarded as inoffensive or a matter of indifference, but also to those that offend, shock or disturb the State or any section of the population. Such are the demands of that pluralism, tolerance and broadmindedness without which there is no 'democratic society'.

This includes the key idea of pluralism, which echoes what the European Court has said about the right to freedom of conscience and belief in Article 9. This is perfectly appropriate: freedom of expression and freedom to manifest one's belief will overlap, because the value of freedom of expression is to express what one believes. However, the focus with Article 10 is on the expression, how far one is allowed to express oneself, as opposed to the underlying belief. This will raise questions such as how far expression should be limited, if ever, if what is being said is offensive or objectionable, for example if it is threatening, sexist, racist or pornographic. An overlapping question is how far one may be allowed to disseminate information, and this will involve considering questions such as whether this should be restricted if the information is false, or if it is confidential.

Some of these questions will be considered in our discussion of Article 10(2), which imposes certain limitations on the right set out in Article 10(1). However, there is one further limitation, which is worth referring to at the outset, and that is the limitation contained in Article 17.[5] This removes the protection of the Convention from those seeking to use rights, such as the right to freedom of expression, to engage in any activity or perform any act aimed at the destruction of the Convention rights. What it is important to realise is that this does not simply refer to arguments or statements which are objectionable.

So, for example, in the case of *Lehideux v France*,[6] a statement which was sympathetic to an individual who had been convicted of collaboration with the Nazis, the French Vichy leader, Marshal Petain, did not fall outside the protection of Article 10, since it was not expressing a pro-Nazi policy but was part of a historical debate. But the European Court was quite clear that statements seeking to justify a pro-Nazi policy or denying the holocaust, would not enjoy the protection of Article 10, because of Article 17. Such positions and statements take themselves outside Article 10, not because they are not genuinely held, but because the Convention rights are not there to protect those who wish to attack fundamentally the values on which it is based; and the Nazi regime is an example of one which clearly did not conform to even the basic standards of morality.

TYPES OF EXPRESSION

Expression clearly includes speech and the written word. It would also extend to painting, drawing and sculpture, the making of a television or radio programme or film: these are all forms of expression. But someone who wishes to express themselves may do it by their actions. Sometimes this will be something we might think of as artistic, such as acting in a play, cultivating a garden, using craft skills to make something. Or

---

[5] Discussed in more detail above, p. 94.
[6] (2000) 30 EHRR 665; see above, p. 95.

it may be a pastime, indulging in a hobby such as a sport or collecting something may be a means of self-expression.

But self-expression may be more political. Taking part in a protest, and simply being at a particular place, may be a means of expression, and a means of exercising the right under Article 10. This is a more contentious area, because it is in such situations that the expression of a view, or a position, or a loyalty, may reach the point where it threatens to, or does, interfere with the rights of others. This is what happened in the case of *Steel v UK*.[7] This case concerned several protesters, at different places, who were arrested as they carried out their protests.

One of them, as part of a protest against a grouse shoot, walked in front of an armed member of the shoot, thus physically preventing him from firing. Another, taking part in a protest against the building of a motorway extension, placed herself in front of machinery in order to impede the engineering works. Others, at the Queen Elizabeth Conference Centre in Westminster, where a 'Fighter Helicopter II' Conference was being held, protested against the sale of fighter helicopters, and handed out leaflets and held up banners. Each of them was arrested for a breach of the peace, and was convicted. They each complained to the European Court that their conviction was a violation of Article 10.

The European Court found that indeed they had been exercising their right of expression, and that it had been violated by being stopped, and by the prosecution. Although the Court considered that the convictions were, in the circumstances, not a disproportionate interference with the right, the important point is that their freedom of expression by way of protest was recognised as coming within Article 10.

The same applies to the case of *Hashman and Harrup v UK*.[8] The applicants, acted to try to disrupt the activities of the Portman Hunt; they blew a hunting horn and engaged in hallooing, so that hounds were drawn towards them, and the hunt staff had to be deployed to recover the hounds. They also were convicted of breaches of the peace, and complained to the European Court. Here too, the Court held that they also were exercising their right of freedom of expression. The Court did not consider whether the interference was justified, because it was held not to be 'prescribed by law', given the uncertainty relating to the order made against the applicants.

THE RIGHT TO RECEIVE INFORMATION

It is not really surprising that part of Article 10(1) is the right to **receive** and **impart** information: a right to impart information is of no use unless there is a right for others to receive that information. The wish to express something is accompanied by the right to hear it: without both sides of this coin, there can be no debate, and without debate, the article would fail to protect the pluralism that is at the heart of this freedom.

A newspaper's claim that it has a right to publish information is also a claim that its readers have a right to receive it. But there may be countervailing considerations: governments or other public authorities may wish to keep something secret; yet the public, on the other hand, may wish to know about it. The principle of Article 10(1) is that access should not be denied to information that is being freely provided, and which is intended to be read. But the right to receive information does not provide a

---

[7] (1999) 28 EHRR 603; for discussion in the context of Article 5, see above, p. 134.
[8] (2000) 30 EHRR 241; also above, p. 135.

right to freedom of information as such: it does not provide a positive right to be given information or to access to information. The following case is one where the European Court held that the individual had no right to receive information, in the particular circumstances of the case.

The case was *Leander v Sweden*.[9] Mr Leander was a carpenter by occupation, and applied for employment as a museum technician with the National Naval Museum. This involved access to certain sensitive areas. He was refused employment, after the authorities had considered secret information about him. He contended that he had a right to receive the information, and complained to the European Court.

The European Court held that Article 10 did not, in the circumstances of the case, confer on Mr Leander a right of access to the register which contained information on his personal position; the Court found that there was no violation of either Article 10 or Article 8 (respect for privacy). The Court carried out a balance of the circumstances in the case, especially bearing in mind what particular protections the state had put in place for supervising and monitoring the recording of information about employees; the Court came to the view that the citizen was sufficiently protected.

However, that is not to say that in an appropriate case there may not be a justification for access to personal files, or other information. A good example where there may be a clear public interest in access to information is where there has been a public emergency of some sort, or serious crime, and there is a clear public interest in what has happened, which may fall within the right to receive information. The following are examples of cases where what has been sought is that an inquiry into such a matter should be conducted in public.

The first case, *Wagstaff*,[10] concerned a decision to set up an inquiry following the conviction of Dr Harold Shipman for the murder of 15 of his patients. The inquiry was announced, to be chaired by Lord Laming, and the decision was that it should be held in private.

The Divisional Court held that this decision, to hold the inquiry in private, was in breach of Article 10. The reasons for holding the inquiry in private, reasons of efficiency and speed, and that witnesses might feel more free to speak in private, did not outweigh the public interest in the conduct of a medical practice, and in the question whether there had been appropriate controls and supervision. There was a breach of Article 10 because there was an interference with the reception of information which others were willing to impart.

Another case raising the same point was *Persey*.[11] In August 2001, the Secretary of State set up inquiries into the outbreak of foot and mouth disease, with the evidence to be received in private. The applicants, who were farmers, veterinary surgeons, hoteliers, and media organisations, applied for a court order that the Lessons Learned Inquiry should be conducted in public, because to hold it in private violated Article 10 of the Convention. They contended that an open public inquiry would restore public confidence in the government's handling of the crisis.

The Divisional Court rejected this argument. The central point of the judgment is this: Article 10 guarantees freedom of expression, and not access to information. It imposes no positive duty on a government to provide an open forum to achieve wider dissemination of views than exists already. For this reason, the Court considered that it was different from *Wagstaff*.

---

[9] (1987) 9 EHRR 433.

[10] *R (Wagstaff) v Secretary of State for Health* [2001] 1 WLR 292.

[11] *R (Persey) v Secretary of State for Environment, Food and Rural Affairs* [2002] 3 WLR 704.

RESTRICTIONS ON FREEDOM OF EXPRESSION

Article 10(2) is the only one of the sets of express qualifications to one of the Convention rights which expressly refers to the freedoms carrying with them **duties and responsibilities**, as well as setting out the interests which can justify an interference with the right. This is important: the duties and responsibilities upon the person or body who wishes to exercise their right to freedom of expression must be brought into the balance. The European Court has considered these words, for example in the case of *Handyside* again:

> Whoever exercises his freedom of expression undertakes 'duties and responsibilities' the scope of which depends on his situation and the technical means he uses. The Court cannot overlook such a person's 'duties' and 'responsibilities' when it enquires, as in this case, whether 'restrictions' or 'penalties' were conductive to the protection of morals which made them 'necessary' in a 'democratic society'.

In other words, Mr Handyside had duties and responsibilities as a publisher, since he had the power to reach a wide audience by his ability to print and publish and distribute. Those duties and responsibilities were relevant when it came to judging whether the interference with his Article 10 rights was proportionate.

Article 10(2) also includes the familiar phrase 'prescribed by law', with its meaning that the law should be clear, foreseeable and precise:[12] this was where the state's case failed in the case of *Hashman*, discussed above. Then there is the list of grounds which may justify an interference with the right, so long as they are necessary in a democratic society and proportionate in extent. These include grounds found in comparable paragraphs of other articles, such as national security, the prevention of disorder or crime, and the protection of health or morals. It also includes some purposes which are specific to freedom of expression: preventing the disclosure of information received in confidence, which as we will see gives rise to a significant conflict of rights for the press; the protection of the reputation or rights of others; and maintaining the authority and impartiality of the judiciary.

All these grounds are already reflected in our law, which contains a variety of limitations on the right of freedom of speech, but which in principle fall within the grounds for interference in Article 10(2), depending on how they are applied in practice. Thus, there is the law of defamation, which protects reputation from libel and slander. There are laws forbidding obscenity and blasphemy, which are grounded in protecting the rights of others, especially children. The authority and impartiality of the judiciary is protected by the law of contempt of court, which, for example, prohibits the publication of information which is designed to influence improperly the outcome of a trial. It is an offence to incite another person to commit a crime or to incite racial hatred, or to use speech to foment disorder or racial divisions; all of this again is aimed at protecting the rights of others. Each of those laws will in proper circumstances fall within the 'conditions, restrictions or penalties' allowed by Article 10(2).

One example of a situation where freedom of expression threatens the rights of others, is in the situation we discussed earlier, where the expression is in the form of a protest or disturbance, which can threaten harm or damage. There are laws which

---

[12] This idea is discussed above, p. 87.

prohibit harassment, violence and criminal damage, and these do not, of themselves, infringe the right to free speech.

In the case of *Silverton v Gravett*,[13] the claimants were a company, including its directors and their families, that sold furs. Their complaint was that they were being harassed by animal rights activists opposed to the selling of furs, mainly at the company's premises, but also at one of the director's homes. There had been damage to windows, offensive letters and material, obstruction of customers, and the directors' home addresses had been published. The High Court considered that, in such a situation, the claimants were entitled to the protection of the law from harassment. The rights set out in Article 10, and also Article 11, which protects political gatherings, could be restricted to prevent disorder or crime or to protect the reputation or rights of others, and that justified the restrictions here.

PRESS FREEDOM

'Any interference with press freedom must be justified': this was the headline in *The Times* newspaper for the report of *A v B*, a case about press coverage of the private life of a footballer. And the reference to duties and responsibilities, and some of the restrictions in Article 10(2), will be especially relevant when considering a claim for the exercise of freedom of expression by a newspaper or media organisation, since some of these can have real power and influence.

   Because of concerns expressed about press freedom, there is a particular section of the Act which is relevant here, section 12:

> **Section 12 (4)** The court must have particular regard to the importance of the Convention right to freedom of expression and, where the proceedings relate to material which the respondent claims, or which appears to the court, to be journalistic, literary or artistic material (or to conduct connected with such material), to –
> (a) the extent to which –
> > (i)   the material has, or is about to, become available to the public; or
> > (ii) it is, or would be, in the public interest for the material to be published;
> (b) any relevant privacy code.

The words of section 12 make a special point of preserving freedom of expression. The section applies only to the freedom of expression, and to no other right or freedom under the Convention. It applies if a court is considering whether to grant any relief which might affect the exercise of the right to freedom of expression; that means relief which might stifle the right, or prevent expression. The court must have particular regard to the importance of the freedom of expression; and where the court is asked to prevent publication, notice must be given to the person who has the right of expression, and an order restraining publication should be made only if the court is satisfied that publication is likely to be prevented; it is in considering such an order that the court

---

[13] (2001) LTL 31.10.01.

must have 'particular regard to the importance of the Convention right to freedom of expression'.[14]

The courts have now had the opportunity to consider the effect of section 12, in the context of the desire of newspapers to publish material, when faced with a claim that such publication would infringe a right to privacy or confidentiality. We have already looked at these cases in the context of Article 8, which protects privacy.[15] We saw there how the courts have expanded the law to protect confidential or private information. All of the cases discussed there are situations where there is a conflict between Article 8 and Article 10. We shall consider a couple of them again here, from the point of view of Article 10 and section 12.

Douglas v Hello!,[16] concerned the celebrity couple, Michael Douglas and Catherine Zeta-Jones, who had given *OK!* magazine exclusive rights to publish photographs of their wedding. Their claim was against *Hello!*, which was proposing to publish photographs of the couple's wedding, which had been taken without permission.

The Court of Appeal recognised that Article 8 justifies a restriction on Article 10 to protect privacy. They also paid especial regard to section 12. However, on the facts of the case they declined to make an injunction restraining publication, especially because they considered that there were no exceptional circumstances to justify restraining the right of freedom of expression. In particular, this was not in fact a private wedding, since the couple were proposing in any event that some photographs would be published.

Then there is the case of *A v B*.[17] A was a married professional footballer who had sexual relationships with a woman, referred to as C, and another woman, D, neither of whom was his wife (as a result of this decision, A was revealed to be Garry Flitcroft, captain of Blackburn Rovers). A newspaper intended to publish an article which would identify the parties, and therefore his wife would learn the facts; he applied for an injunction to prevent that publication. The women C and D did not ask that the relationship be kept confidential; indeed it was they who had disclosed the relationship to the press.

The Court of Appeal refused to make the injunction forbidding publication. The Court refused to accord the same protection to transient sexual relationships, such as these, as to sexual relationships within marriage, as the Court was not in a position to decide whether or not it is in the wife's interest to be kept in ignorance of the affairs. The fact that A was a professional footballer meant he was a role model and so there was a corresponding public and press interest in him.

The Court also specifically referred to section 12(4): any interference with the press has to be justified because it inevitably has some effect on the ability of the press to perform its role in society, and because the existence of a free press is in itself desirable. Such interference can be justified by the right of privacy under Article 8, but the weaker the claim for privacy the more likely that it would be outweighed by the claim based on freedom of expression.

JOURNALISTS' SOURCES

A 'scoop' is an exclusive piece of news for a newspaper; it means the paper is first, and ahead of its competitors. A scoop is sometimes headline-grabbing, and the newspaper's circulation figures go up. Presumably, editors and reporters dream of scoops. A reporter

---

[14] Section 12 is also considered above, p. 77.
[15] Above, pp. 185–8.
[16] [2001] 2 WLR 992; see also above, p. 187.
[17] *A v B (a company)* [2002] 2 WLR 542; also discussed above, pp. 78 and 187.

keeps his ear to the ground, so that he gets the information early. Some information may come to him from an informant who will extract a promise that his identity will be kept secret.

But if the newspaper publishes the information, an interested party may ask for the identity of the source. The information may be an official secret, or it may have come from company documents which are confidential, and which must remain so, and the company may consider that it is important to retrieve the documents, or to prevent any further breach of confidence. The information may reveal that there is an employee who bears a grudge, and it is important to identify him. The newspaper's answer to this is that its sources are secret, and that it must be free to publish information after giving an assurance of secrecy. It will rely upon its freedom of expression, under Article 10. The interested party, on the other hand, will rely upon Article 8 – the right to respect for a private life – and contend that its privacy has been invaded. We have seen examples of the tension between the two articles in the discussion of the celebrities' cases. In the next case, *Goodwin v UK*,[18] we see how the European Court upheld a claim of freedom of expression when the newspaper is ordered to reveal the identity of its informant.

William Goodwin was a British journalist on the staff of *The Engineer*. In 1989, he was telephoned by a person, 'X', who had previously supplied information to him on various companies, and X gave him information about a company, Tetra, to the effect that it had financial problems. It was sensitive information. The information was unsolicited by Mr Goodwin, and was not given in exchange for any money; it had come from a confidential memo, which had been taken from Tetra. Mr Goodwin telephoned Tetra to get assistance for an article which he planned to write for *The Engineer*. Tetra obtained an injunction restraining the publication of the article; the High Court ordered Mr G to divulge the identity of X, and he refused, and he was fined £5,000 for contempt of court. Mr G complained to the European Court that this was a violation of Article 10, contending that the public interest in disclosure outweighed the public interest in confidentiality. The Contempt of Court Act 1981 provided that a court shall not require a person to disclose their source of information unless it is satisfied that disclosure is necessary in the interests of justice, or national security or the prevention of disorder or crime.

The European Court held that a feature to be borne in mind was that publication had been prevented; while Tetra had an interest in learning who was X and whether it was a disloyal employee, and preventing further publication, the need for a free press outweighed that. The Court said:

> Protection of journalistic sources is one of the basic conditions for press freedom, as is reflected in the laws and the professional codes of conduct in a number of Contracting States and is affirmed in several international instruments on journalistic freedoms. Without such protection, sources may be deterred from assisting the press in informing the public on matters of public interest. [. . .] Having regard to the importance of the protection of journalistic sources for press freedom in democratic society and the potentially chilling effect an order of source disclosure has on the exercise of that freedom, such a measure cannot be compatible with Article 10 of the Convention unless it is justified by an overriding requirement in the public interest.

QUESTIONS

1 Freedom of speech is the only right which is expressed to carry with it duties and responsibilities. Why do you think this is? Do you agree? How does this relate to the list of limitations?

2 How important is the freedom of the press, and why? Do you agree with the protection given to journalists' sources?

---

[18] (1996) 22 EHRR 123.

One of the more militant trade union strikes of recent years was the Miners' strike in 1984–5, which saw clashes between police and the miners' picket lines: the picture shows a confrontation outside the Orgreave Coking Plant near Rotherham in May 1984, later the site of something approaching a pitched battle.

(*Source*: Reproduced courtesy of People's History Museum)

Chapter 17

FREEDOM OF ASSEMBLY

'[In 1819] public meetings were generally prohibited. It would have been better if none had been allowed at all, for when a vast but orderly concourse of working men and women assembled on St. Peter's Fields, Manchester, to demand Parliamentary Reform, the magistrates, seized by sudden panic, let loose a charge of yeomanry which killed a dozen and seriously injured hundreds of both sexes . . . It was called "Peterloo," because it seemed to cancel the debt of the nation's gratitude for Waterloo.' (G.M. Trevelyan, *Illustrated History of England*, on Peterloo (16 August 1819))

> *ARTICLE 11: FREEDOM OF ASSEMBLY AND ASSOCIATION*
> 1. Everyone has the right to freedom of peaceful assembly and to freedom of association with others, including the right to form and to join trade unions for the protection of his interests.
>   No restrictions shall be placed on the exercise of these rights other than such as are prescribed by law and are necessary in a democratic society in the interests of national security or public safety, for the prevention of disorder or crime, for the protection of health or morals or for the protection of the rights and freedoms of others. This Article shall not prevent the imposition of lawful restrictions on the exercise of these rights by members of the armed forces, of the police or of the administration of the State.

THE FREEDOM DEFINED

A demonstration may annoy or give offence to persons opposed to the ideas or claims that it is seeking to promote. The participants must however be able to hold the demonstration without having to fear that they will be subjected to physical violence by their opponents; such a fear would be liable to deter associations or other groups supporting common ideas or interests from openly expressing their opinions on highly controversial issues affecting the community. In a democracy the right to counter-demonstrate cannot extend to inhibiting the exercise of the right to demonstrate.[1]

Those are the words of the European Court, and they come to this: there is a right to hold a demonstration, even though it is in favour of something unpopular or objectionable. This is part of the same group of rights as Articles 9 and 10, freedom to manifest a belief, and freedom of expression, and there may be an overlap between them. In a

---

[1] *Plattform Arzte fur das Leben v Austria* (1991) 13 EHRR 204.

tolerant and open democracy, it is important not just that people are free to hold whatever belief they choose, but also that they are free to manifest that belief, share it with others, and collectively meet to discuss, debate and demonstrate. Of course, the more that the right of freedom of association involves a physical demonstration, the more likely it is to raise questions about whether an interference with it is justified, using the principles we have seen in other articles, for a legitimate aim, such as public order or safety, and in a way which is proportionate to that aim.

So what does Article 11 protect? Obviously, Article 11 is about demonstrations and meetings; but it goes far beyond that. Article 11 covers a wide variety of people who assemble and associate together. It is about trade unions, and political assemblies, and societies. And in a political climate, where across Europe national or ethnic minorities are making claims to recognition, it is about associations of people who claim a national identity in a larger community. For instance, protection has been given to an organisation to promote the interests of the Macedonian minority in Bulgaria, which the Bulgarian court held was divisive of national unity and was dangerous for the territorial unity of Bulgaria,[2] or the Union of People of Silesian Nationality, to promote Silesian consciousness, culture and rights in Poland.[3]

WHAT IS AN ASSEMBLY?

An assembly or meeting might take place in all sorts of situations and places; but **assembly** does not just mean something static, but includes marches and processions, as we shall see in the next case, *Plattform Arzte fur das Leben v Austria*.[4]

The Plattform was an association of doctors campaigning against legalised abortion, and in 1980, it organised a march of supporters along public roads, ending in a religious service at an altar on a hillside; counter-demonstrators were expected, and indeed they came and did disrupt the march, by shouting down the Plattform members' recitation of the rosary. At the service, the counter-demonstrators used loudspeakers and threw eggs and clumps of grass at the congregation. In 1982, Plattform held a second demonstration in Salzburg Cathedral Square, and counter-demonstrators shouted opposition; police formed a protective cordon, but eventually the police cleared the square.

Plattform claimed that there had been a violation of Article 11 in respect of both demonstrations, in that the police had failed to provide protection to Plattform, and had failed to ensure their freedom of assembly.

The European Court accepted that Article 11 was applicable, to the meeting and to the march along public roads, and the Court regarded those places as legitimate places for processions and meetings which came within Article 11. But the Court rejected the claim on the facts of the situation; it dismissed the claim of Plattform that the police had remained passive; it found that the police had deployed themselves in sufficient numbers and with suitable tactics, and that no serious clashes occurred.

---

[2] *Stankov and United Macedonia Organisation Ilenden v Bulgaria* (2001) 2 October, 29221/95.
[3] *Gorzelik v Poland* (2001), *unreported* 20 December 44158/98.
[4] (1991) 13 EHRR 204.

THE STATE'S DUTY

On a literal reading of Articles 11(1) and 11(2), one might conclude that the state's duty is simply to permit the freedom to exist; there seems to be nothing more than a negative duty – to refrain from interference, except in accordance with 11(2). But we have already seen what the European Court said in the *Plattform* case in our quotation at the start of this chapter; there is a positive duty as well as a negative one.

In the *Plattform* case the Court was dealing with facts which brought up this point directly: had the state fulfilled its duty, by ensuring enough police and proper tactics? The Court said:

> Genuine, effective freedom of peaceful assembly cannot, therefore, be reduced to a mere duty on the part of the State not to interfere: a purely negative conception would not be compatible with the object and purpose of Article 11. Like Article 8, Article 11 sometimes requires positive measures to be taken, even in the sphere of relations between individuals, if need be.

It is not a guarantee; and the Court made that clear:

> While it is the duty of Contracting States to take reasonable and appropriate measures to enable lawful demonstrations to proceed peacefully, they cannot guarantee this absolutely and they have a wide discretion in the choice of the means to be used.

ARTICLE 10 AND ARTICLE 11

The relationship of these two articles is close; and one finds cases where both are in issue, and where both are part of the same claim made by the claimant. This is because, as we noted earlier, a person who joins an association is in effect expressing a view – that is, a view in favour of that association. Whether the particular 'assembly' is a meeting, or a procession, or a trade union association, the very fact of joining it is an expression of a view or an opinion; the person is allying himself or herself with its ideas or opinions. That is how the European Court put it in the case of *Ahmed v UK*.[5]

Messrs Ahmed, Perrin, Bentley and Brough lived in various parts of England. They were each permanently employed in different capacities by local authorities – as (respectively) solicitor, principal valuer, planning manager, and adviser to committees. Each of them wished to take part in political activities, as a candidate or assisting a constituency party. In 1990, Regulations were made so that persons holding certain posts in local authority could not participate in political activities, although they were allowed to join a political party; the posts were in a 'politically restricted' category. If they wished to continue their political activities, they were obliged to resign from their employment. The applicants were in that category. They sought exemption from the English courts, and failed, and so claimed before the European Court that there had been violations of Articles 10 and 11.

The European Court found that the creation of the restricted category was indeed a violation of both Articles 10 and 11, but that it was necessary in a democratic society to have such a restriction in order to maintain political neutrality in the local authority permanent staff.

---

[5] (2000) 29 EHRR 1.

The interesting point for us is the statement made by the Court about the relationship of the two articles. The Court considered that:

> Notwithstanding its autonomous role and particular sphere of application, Article 11 must in the present case also be considered in the light of Article 10 having regard to the fact that the freedom to hold opinions and to receive and impart information and ideas is one of the objectives of freedom of assembly and association as enshrined in Article 11.

In short, one of the purposes of entering an association, and exercising *that* right, is to receive and impart information, which is at the heart of Article 10. In the *Ahmed* case, the embargo was on both expressing a political view and on taking a meaningful part in politics.

POLITICAL ACTIVITIES

It is especially in the political field that one would expect the right of expression and assembly to dovetail with each other; debate, after all, is usually carried on in an assembly. Debate, however, may be forceful, and when it offers criticism, especially of the state or state agents, the state may be tempted to suppress it. We shall see in this section examples where the state has not merely forbidden participation in the particular politics, but has gone to the length of dissolving the political association or party, or outlawing it. In the United Kingdom, that is unusual; the attitude here is usually one of tolerance. That tolerance is the mark of a democratic society, which is not afraid of debate; that is the reasoning of the European Court in this next case, of *The People's Party v Turkey*,[6] where the facts were as follows.

The HEP, the People's Labour Party, was founded in 1990, and the case was brought by its Chairman, Vice Chairman, and Secretary General, all of whom were Turkish nationals. HEP stood for principles of self-determination and the recognition of language rights. The Party had severely criticised Turkey's armed forces, which had carried out an anti-terrorist campaign. The Turkish Constitutional Court dissolved the Party on the grounds that it had undermined the integrity of the State by these criticisms, on the grounds that it had lent assistance to illegal acts. Thus, these officers of HEP complained to the European Court of violations of Article 11.

The European Court held that there had been a violation of Article 11. Merely to criticise the armed forces did not mean that the Party was equivalent to the armed groups pursuing violence; and the advocating of ideas advanced by these armed groups did not mean that the Party was supporting terrorism. The state, by forbidding the propounding of those ideas, diminished the possibility of airing those questions in democratic debate.

This is a strong case: there had been violence caused by terrorists in Turkey, and the Turkish courts had doubtless been concerned to see that terrorism did not flourish, and the HEP's views were unpalatable. But the European Court considered that the order dissolving the Party was disproportionate; it was in breach of Article 11.

There is a provision in our law for the proscription of an organisation. This is in the Terrorism Act 2000, which allows the banning of an organisation which the Secretary

---

[6] *Yazar, Karatas, Aksoy and the People's Party (HEP) v Turkey* (2003) 36 EHRR 59.

of State believes is concerned in terrorism, so that membership or support of it is unlawful. Political activity on the part of an organisation will not be enough to justify proscription; it will have to be involved in terrorism in some way, which includes elements of the planning or execution of violence and attempts to intimidate or threaten the government or the public. We will consider this in more detail in our discussion of terrorism;[7] but it is worth noting in the present context, that this power will raise an issue in each case as to whether such an order will be proportionate under Article 11.

TRADE UNIONS

Trade unions are expressly mentioned in the words of Article 11(1): the individual has the right to form and join one, for the protection of his interests. This wording is fairly wide, and might support an argument that *any* activity, which protects the member's interests, will fall within Article 11. However, whilst this may be the starting point, it is subject to the limitations in Article 11(2), restrictions which are prescribed by law, and necessary in a democratic society. And the next case, *UNISON v UK*,[8] is a good example of this.

UNISON was a union for public service employees, and it had members employed by University College Hospital ('UCLH'). A substantial proportion of them were on terms of employment negotiated by UNISON at a national level. In 1998 UCLH was negotiating to transfer parts of its business, under a Private Finance Initiative, to private companies, who would erect and run a new hospital for UCLH, and would make further transfers of staff with subcontracting to specialist companies. Some, but not all, of the UNISON members would be transferred in this way.

UNISON sought protection for its members, so there would be terms of employment on all the private companies lasting 30 years. When UCLH refused, UNISON held a pre-strike ballot, which favoured striking. UCLH then obtained a High Court injunction to prevent the strike, on the grounds that it was not in contemplation of a trade dispute, and so did not fall within the statutory protection for strikes in furtherance of a trade dispute.[9] UNISON complained to the European Court that the injunction was a breach of Article 11.

The European Court considered that the prohibition of the strike was a restriction on UNISON's power to protect its members' interests, and therefore was a restriction on freedom of association. However, the Court rejected UNISON's claim, on the grounds that the injunction was prescribed by law, and was proportionate in protecting the rights of UCLH. The principle of having private finance initiatives was an acceptable one, and UNISON remained able to take strike action if UCLH dismissed an employee, or changed their contracts; and against any private company taking over employees who threatened to dismiss an employee or threatened to 'de-recognise' UNISON. In all these circumstances, the European Court found that the injunction preventing UNISON from striking *was* a proportionate measure.

However, the Court also made some interesting observations about the scope of Article 11. The Court noted that Article 11(1) did not set out any particular treatment of trade union members by the state or any particular set of powers or freedoms which

---

[7] Below, Chapter 21.
[8] 10 January 2002, 53574/99.
[9] Section 219 of the Trade Union and Labour Relations (Consolidation) Act 1992.

a trade union should have, and left states with a choice as to how the freedom of trade unions should be safeguarded. They said:

> There is no express inclusion of a right to strike or an obligation on employers to engage in collective bargaining. At most, Article 11 may be regarded as safeguarding the freedom of trade unions to protect the occupational interests of their members. While the ability to strike represents one of the most important of the means by which trade unions can fulfil this function, there are others.

The right under Article 11 is not just to join a trade union, and for a trade union to protect its members. It is also to *leave* a trade union, or *to refrain* from membership.

In the case of *Young, James and Webster v UK*,[10] the three applicants were employed by British Rail, which had negotiated a closed-shop agreement between the company and trade unions, so that membership of a union was a condition of employment. The three men failed to join a union, and were dismissed from their employment. They claimed breaches of Article 11, and the European Court agreed. The Court said:

> One of the purposes of freedom of association guaranteed by Article 11 is, like Articles 9 and 10, the protection of personal opinion; and the kind of pressure exerted on the applicants to compel them to join particular unions, contrary to their convictions, strikes at the very substance of Article 11 and constitutes an interference with the rights guaranteed by it.

Since the events of this case, the law has been changed; it is now illegal to impose a condition of this kind on an employee.[11]

PRIVATE ASSOCIATIONS

The terms of Article 11 are quite unlimited in their scope; an 'assembly' or an 'association' may be of any kind, public or private, so long as it is peaceful, to qualify for protection under Article 11(1). And it nonetheless may suffer interference as strictly defined by Article 11(2). We have so far been mainly considering associations or organisations which one would term 'public' – political parties, and trade unions, although the association in the *Plattform* case could be regarded as a private one. The following is a case from Italy, which demonstrates that a purely private association will attract the protection of Article 11. The case is *Grande Oriente D'Italia Di Palazzo Guistini v Italy*,[12] concerning the public scrutiny of freemasonry.

Grande Oriente D'Italia Di Palazzo Guistini was an Italian Masonic association with the legal status of an unrecognised private law association. An Italian law required candidates for certain public offices, *not* part of the public administration, to declare that they were not freemasons. The Masonic Association complained to the European Court that this law breached its right to freedom of association under Article 11.

The European Court agreed, and held that the interference was not justified under Article 11(2). The Court said that an association of this kind was entitled to claim the protection of Article 11. The Italian law might well cause the Masonic Association to lose members, if candidates for office

---

[10] (1982) 4 EHRR 39.
[11] Trade Union and Labour Relations (Consolidation) Act 1992.
[12] (2002) 34 EHRR 22.

preferred to leave rather than make the declaration. The state had a legitimate concern to reassure public opinion at a time when activities of freemasons in public life was under scrutiny. But a balance had to be struck, and, especially as the offices specified in the law were not part of public administration, the Italian law went too far in creating this blanket requirement to make a declaration in each and every case.

AN ASSOCIATION AND ITS MEMBERS

All clubs and societies wish to limit their membership in some way or other; usually, membership of the society will be based on those with a particular interest, or outlook; or a club or society may wish to have members of a certain background. Likewise, clubs and societies will usually have some form of rules, or even a legal framework, to govern their relationship with their members or would-be members. However, Article 11 may have an effect here, especially if the organisation performs a public function, for example if it is a charity. Apart from any other considerations, if it performs a public function, it may qualify as a public authority, in which case it will be obliged to act in a way which is compatible with the Convention rights.[13] So, in making decisions, such as those about membership, associations may find that they have to apply the principles of Article 11, which means making decisions in a way which is fair, not arbitrary and where the decision is proportionate to its purpose. An example is the decision in the case of *RSPCA v Attorney General*.[14]

The Royal Society for the Prevention of Cruelty to Animals (RSPCA) wished to adopt and administer a selective membership policy, so that it could freely exclude or remove from membership any individual whom the RSPCA suspected would not promote its aims and objectives – in effect, it believed certain people would damage its interests, and it wished to exclude them. The RSPCA went to the High Court and sought a declaration that its rules permitted this.

The High Court first stated that Article 11 provides freedom of association, and also of non-association. This permits the RSPCA to exclude persons who might damage its interests. However, it must do so in a non-arbitrary way; and this was so especially considering that it is a charitable organisation. Fairness here would require an opportunity for the person excluded to make representations in their defence; and any policy of exclusion should be announced on an application form for membership; if someone was excluded they had to be invited to make representations why their admission was appropriate.

Thus, Article 11 limits the freedom of action of the association here, because it requires certain standards to be applied to dealings with their membership, or prospective membership. It is worth noting here that clubs, associations and societies may also find that other Convention rights are engaged in such dealings. So, in making decisions regulating membership, officers, committees, subscriptions, penalties, and awards, Article 6 may be relevant if there is a question about a committee making a fair decision; or Article 8 may apply to a decision to exclude someone from an association, where the effect is to prevent them from pursuing a sport or pastime, if this is a genuine part of their private or family life.

---

[13] Section 6 of the Act, above, p. 61.
[14] [2002] 1 WLR 448.

BANNING DEMONSTRATIONS

There are often very good reasons for seeking to prevent a demonstration from taking place. It may be that the demonstration is likely to lead to violence of some sort, or at least disruption; it may be that a police presence will be required; it may be that if an unpopular organisation is allowed to hold a meeting, there will be a counter-demonstration, and a fear that the two will clash. Sometimes, it is the unpopular organisation which is allowed to hold a meeting, and a more moderate counter-demonstration which is banned, precisely for fear of disorder. It will be a matter of balancing rights, and ensuring that the relevant decision is not an arbitrary one. That was the picture in *Rai, Allmond and 'Negotiate Now' v UK*.[15]

Milan Rai and Gill Almond were members of 'Negotiate Now', which was a non-governmental organisation seeking to promote peace in Northern Ireland, and advocating a policy that the government should support peace negotiations without a prior ceasefire. In May 1994, they wished to hold a rally, in Trafalgar Square in London, to promote their views. This is a well-known venue for public demonstrations, and has been described as traditionally available to any individual or organisation who wishes to use it.

The police view was that there was no danger to public order. But the Secretary of State refused permission to hold the rally, on the grounds that the subject was controversial, being of great sensitivity, and the applicants' attempt to have the decision judicially reviewed failed. They complained of a violation of Article 11.

The Commission acknowledged that the intentions of the applicants was peaceful, and found that the ban was a violation of the applicants' right to freedom of assembly. However, the ban did not amount to a blanket prohibition of the holding of the rally, but only prevented the use of this high-profile location, other venues being available in central London. There were sensitive and complex issues connected with the affairs of Northern Ireland, and public order was a legitimate consideration. In these circumstances, the decision was not arbitrary, and was proportionate.

This will be the test in cases concerning such banning orders; the public authority, whether it be the police, a local authority, or whoever, will be obliged to show that the ban is proportionate.

STATE OFFICIALS

The final sentence of Article 11(2) refers expressly to members of the armed forces, the police, and members of the administration of the state. All of these might be described as agents of the state, and may, by Article 11(2), have restrictions placed upon them limiting their Article 11 rights. The reason for this special treatment is that because of the nature of their jobs, it may be justifiable to prevent them from joining certain associations. They may be privy to secret information, or it may be desirable that people doing certain jobs do not fall under political pressure, or are not encouraged to strike or take industrial action of certain sorts. This was the sort of situation in the *Ahmed* case, where local government officers were barred from engaging in political activity. It is likely to arise from time to time in any state, if there is a conflict between an

---

[15] (1995) 19 EHRR 93.

individual's job and political interests. Once again, it will be a matter of a balance. An example is the case of *Rekvenyi v Hungary*.[16]

Mr Rekvenyi was a police officer and Secretary General of the Police Independent Trade Union, in Hungary. In 1993, a law was passed so that from 1 January 1994 members of the police service were prohibited from joining any political activity, and a letter was sent to all police officers demanding that they refrain from political activity or leave the force. The trade union complained to the Hungarian Constitutional Court that the new law infringed the constitutional rights of career members of the police force, but the Court rejected the claim, and the trade union then complained to the European Court that the new law was a violation of both Articles 10 and 11.

The Court took particular account of the history of Hungary, which had, between 1949 and 1989, been ruled by one political party. Membership of that party was expected as a manifestation of the individual's commitment to the regime, an expectation even more pronounced in the military and the police, as the ruling party's decisions were directly implemented by the police. This was what the rules on political neutrality were designed to prevent, the police being the instruments of just one political party. On this ground, the new law was not disproportionate, and the restriction imposed on Mr Rekvenyi was not arbitrary.

QUESTIONS

1 Why do you think that trade unions are especially mentioned as a form of association in this article? Do you think this special reference is necessary?
2 Consider the limitations allowed on the political activities of state officials. Do you think these are justified?

---

[16] (1999) 30 EHRR 519.

Chapter 18

THE RIGHT TO MARRY

'It is a truth universally acknowledged, that a single man in possession of a good fortune, must be in want of a wife.' (Jane Austen, *Pride and Prejudice*, 1813)

> **ARTICLE 12: RIGHT TO MARRY**
> Men and women of marriageable age have the right to marry and to found a family, according to the national laws governing the exercise of this right.

THE RIGHTS PROTECTED

The right to marry and found a family is not one that has given rise to much case law. This is perhaps understandable, since it is recognised in most countries: it is not a right with which it is common for a state to interfere. On the other hand, as with so many of the other Convention rights, this does not mean that there was no point in including it in the Convention as a basic right, since the very fact of its inclusion *has* allowed challenges to previously accepted positions. At the very least, it ensures that consideration can be given to whether this right is being properly respected.

The title of the Article 12 refers to the right to marry. But in fact this article provides two quite separate rights, namely the right to marry, and the right to found a family. Both of them are expressed in fairly simple terms; there are no restrictions similar to those found in some of the other articles, where there are express limits on the rights. The European Commission have referred to this as an 'absolute' right. But the rights do indeed have the qualification 'according to the national laws governing the exercise of the right'.

In the case of *Hamer*,[1] the Commission said:

[the rights being absolute] does not mean that the scope afforded to the national law is unlimited. If it did, Article 12 would be redundant. The role of the national law, as the wording of Article 12 indicates, is to *govern the exercise of the right*. (original emphasis)

The Commission went on to give examples of those words in italics. National law may provide rules for such things as the notices, publicity, and formalities required for solemnising marriage; and such rules may govern capacity, consent, prohibited degrees or the prevention of bigamy. These are the kind of national rules which the European Court will recognise; and they will obviously differ from one nation to another.

---

[1] *Hamer v UK* (1979) 24 DR 5.

However, what the national law will not be allowed to do is to 'interfere substantially with the exercise of the right'. In other words, the national law should not prevent the marriage of someone who ought to be allowed to marry. The case of *Hamer* is a good example.

Mr Hamer was a prisoner in a UK prison, and he wished to marry his fiancée, even though the ceremony would take place in prison; but the law would not permit a marriage ceremony in a prison, and the Secretary of State refused to allow him a temporary release to enable him to be married elsewhere.

The Commission found this obstacle to Mr Hamer was a violation of Article 12, and it interfered with his right. The right under the article was essentially a right to form a legal relationship, to acquire a status, and simply to allow prisoners to marry would involve no general threat to prison security, since the ceremony would take place under the supervision of prison authorities.

The strict factual result of the case of *Hamer* has been superseded by a change in the law which allows marriages to take place in prison. But the case remains a valuable analysis of the rights guaranteed by Article 12, and gives guidance about the reference to 'national laws'.

The other right given by Article 12 – the right to found a family – has been raised in another case concerning a prisoner, and the Court of Appeal looked at this right rather differently. This is the case of *Mellor*,[2] which we have already considered in the context of Article 8, since there is an overlap between the right to found a family and the right to a private and family life.

Mr Mellor was serving a life sentence for murder, and was not likely even to be released on licence – that is, on strict conditions, if he behaved in prison – until he was 35 and his wife was 31. He applied for permission for access to artificial insemination facilities to start a family. This was refused on the basis that no exceptional circumstances existed to justify the grant of such facilities. Mr Mellor challenged this refusal as a breach of his right to found a family, contrary to Article 12, as well a failure to respect his private life, in breach of Article 8.

The Court of Appeal rejected his claim. The Court agreed that imprisonment is *not* compatible with the exercise of the full rights and liberties which a husband and wife can enjoy, in particular, the ability and freedom to start a family, so it does involve an interference with the right to found a family under Article 12. However, the interference is justifiable under Article 12, which should be read consistently with the express criteria in Article 8(2), since this also applied to this situation. One aspect of being punished by the state was the denial of precisely those rights which were now sought, which were therefore not unjustifiably infringed, so long as the interference was proportionate to the aim of operating a penal system designed for both punishment and deterrence.

Thus the Court recognised the importance of the Article 12 right to found a family, even though it considered that it was not infringed. The analysis of Article 12 as consistent with Article 8(2) is also noteworthy, and we will see that it is based on a similar analysis by the European Court.

---

[2] *R (Mellor) v Secretary of State for the Home Department* [2001] 3 WLR 533; above, p. 192.

WHO CAN MARRY?

In modern times, sexual orientation and gender reassignment have become matters of public debate. All courts have been obliged to consider these matters. A particularly difficult area is the question of treatment of transsexuals, those who have undergone a sex change operation. There are a number of cases which consider the rights of transsexuals and whether they can enter into valid marriages and found families, under Articles 12 and 8.

The first case is *Rees v UK*.[3] Mark Rees, as the applicant came to be known, was born in 1942 with female characteristics, and was registered as a female. But after exhibiting male behaviour, and receiving treatment, in 1977 he changed his name to Mark Rees, and since then he had been socially accepted as a male. He was a female to male transsexual. However, his birth certificate remained with the female registration. In the United Kingdom, a birth certificate is required to be produced from time to time, for the purposes of pensions and employment; and he would be regarded as female for the purposes of marriage. He sought to have his birth certificate altered to show his sex as male, but the Registrar General refused this request. He then complained of violations of Articles 8 and 12.

The European Court noted that different states in Europe had varying practices regarding transsexuals, so that some, unlike the United Kingdom, gave transsexuals the option of changing status to fit their new-found identity. The European Court considered there was no overall consensus, so the matter fell within the margin of appreciation, and there was therefore no violation of Articles 8 and 12. In particular, the European Court regarded Article 12 as referring to a marriage between persons of the opposite biological sex, that being the prevalent tradition.

But it is clear that the European Court was ready to consider evidence of social changes in the states of Europe, and scientific and biological evidence and the European Court advised nations to keep measures under review, especially having regard to scientific and societal developments.

Rees was simply a case of seeking to alter the birth certificate. But the next case sought to argue the right for a transsexual to take the further step to marry and have children.

In the case of *Cossey*,[4] Caroline Cossey, as she later became, was born in 1954, and was registered at birth as a male; she realised that psychologically she was female, and from the age of 18 dressed as a woman. At 20, she underwent gender reassignment surgery. As a transsexual, she was able to have sexual intercourse with a man. She was about to marry a man, but the Registrar General informed her that the marriage would be void. She complained that the refusal to issue a birth certificate recognising her female gender, and her inability to contract a marriage, were violations of Articles 8 and 12.

The European Court decided that there were *no* violations. But it noted that some states would now regard as valid a marriage between a man and a person such as Caroline Cossey but still regarded the diversity of treatment, among European states, as important. Thus, it could not take a new approach to the interpretation of Article 12.

---

[3] (1985) 7 EHRR 429.
[4] *Cossey v UK* (1991) 13 EHRR 622.

That was 1990; in a case in 1997, the factual situation was even more pronounced, as the parties entered into a marriage, and had a child. The case is *X, Y and Z v United Kingdom*.[5]

X was a female to male transsexual, and he had lived in a permanent relationship with Y since 1979. In 1992 after AID treatment, Y gave birth to Z, but X was not allowed to register as Z's father. They made their complaint under Article 8.

The European Court held that there was no violation of the article, as there was no common European standard regarding transsexuals, and in this particular case the legal consequences would not cause undue hardship to Z.

But we now reach the stage where the English court is required to consider a marriage of transsexuals. The case is *Bellinger v Bellinger*.[6]

Mrs Bellinger went to the English court to get a declaration that the marriage celebrated between herself and Mr Bellinger was valid. She made this application because, having been classified at birth as a male, she regarded herself as female, and she underwent gender reassignment surgery. Then followed the marriage ceremony.

The Court of Appeal, by a majority, held that the ceremony was *not* valid, as Mrs Bellinger's status for the purpose of marriage was male; she had been a biological male at birth, and that fact determined her gender for the purposes of the legal definition of marriage, and she could not marry a man. However, one member of the Court dissented, and this was Lord Justice Thorpe; he stated that the law should be flexible enough to accommodate social change, and to recognise human dignity, and so recognise this marriage. He noted that in 1972, Sweden led the way by legislation enabling transsexuals to change their legal sex, and to marry a person of their former sex; and he referred to other jurisdictions.

We have seen a most interesting progression of cases. The European Court pays attention to the phrase in Article 12, 'according to the national laws governing the exercise of the right'; and in addition pays deference to the margin of appreciation. But at the same time, it takes into account the attitudes of the states of Europe, and their practices, and in certain circumstances the European Court would say that a particular nation's practices were so lacking in progress, when compared with the practices of other states, that they should be held to be disproportionate. The European Court has now reached the stage where it is prepared to recognise the international trend towards increased social acceptance of transsexuals and increased legal recognition of their new sexual identity, as no longer being a matter of controversy, in *Goodwin v UK*.[7]

Christine Goodwin was a post-operative male-to-female transsexual. Her particular claim related to problems with sexual harassment at work. She also faced having to pay National Insurance contributions until she was aged 65, since she was legally a man, instead of being able to stop paying in 1997 at age 60, as she would have been able to do if she was recognised as a woman. But she also complained about her inability to marry, and her legal status in general.

---

[5] (1997) 24 EHRR 143.
[6] [2002] 2 WLR 411.
[7] *The Times*, 12 July 2002; also considered above, p. 47, as an example of the margin of appreciation, now followed in an employment context: *A v C.C. W Yorkshire* (2003) 1 FLR 233.

The European Court considered that it was artificial to assert that Ms Goodwin's right to marry had not been denied to her: legally she was a man, so could only marry a woman. Since the applicant now lived as a woman, and was denied the right to marry a man, the European Court considered that the very essence of her right to marry had been infringed. The Court considered that there was no justification for preventing the applicant from marrying under any circumstances, and so found a breach of Article 12.

THE RIGHT TO DIVORCE?

The 'right to marry' presumably includes the right to be in a position to marry. At any rate, that is an attractive way of putting the argument, and it would be a convenient argument when there is some obstacle which prevents one getting married. But however good that argument is in some circumstances, it is not valid when it is presented as a right to a divorce. In the case we are about to consider, one party could not exercise his right to marry, because he was already married, and could not obtain a dissolution of that marriage. The case is *Johnston v Ireland*.[8]

Roy Johnston was married to a woman in 1952, but by 1965 it was clear that the marriage had broken down and they decided to live separately. Mr Johnston started to live in 1971 with his partner, who then gave birth to a child. They wished to be married, but under the Irish Constitution, divorce was not permitted. They complained that the absence of any provision for divorce was a violation of Articles 8 and 12.

The European Court rejected their claims. In short, the right to marry did not include a right to a divorce. The Court paid attention to the phrase 'according to the national laws'; and the Court found that the prohibition, in the Irish Constitution, on divorce was not such an interference with the substance of the right guaranteed by Article 12. Once again, as we have seen in other cases, the Court had regard to the practices of varying nations. It referred in this case to a 'society adhering to the principle of monogamy'. In essence, a decision characterising the failure to provide a system of divorce as a violation of Article 12 would be tantamount to finding that the state must provide a system of divorce. The Court declined to do this.

But it is worth noting that if there is a system of divorce or separation of some sort in place, there may be a breach of a Convention right if there is no access to it: we considered in the context of Article 8, the case of *Airey v Ireland*,[9] where the European Court held that a lack of legal aid was a breach of Article 8, since it prevented Mrs Airey from having access to a court to seek a decree of separation.

QUESTIONS

1 Why should the right to marry be a legal right? Why do people have a legitimate interest in having marriage legally recognised?
2 Do you agree that transsexuals should be allowed to marry? What about homosexual couples – is there any good reason for treating such couples differently from heterosexual couples?

---

[8] (1987) 9 EHRR 203.
[9] (1980) 2 EHRR 305; above, p. 188.

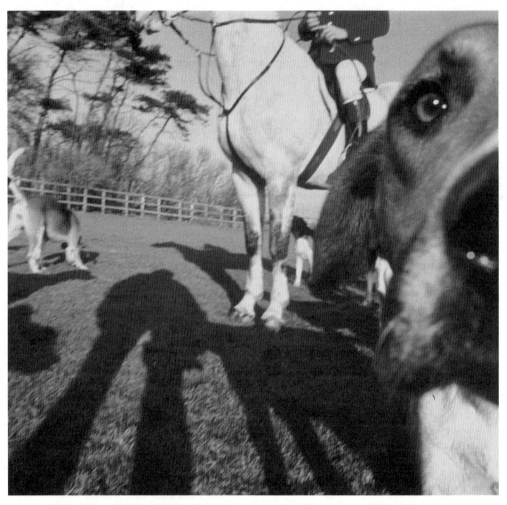

A fox-hunt: an activity which impinges on the use of property, foxhunting has been the subject of more than one human rights case (see p. 256).

(*Source:* www.gettyimages.com)

Chapter 19

THE RIGHT TO PROPERTY

'Wemmick's house was a little wooden cottage in the midst of plots of garden, and the top of it was cut out and painted like a battery mounted with guns. [. . . .] "At the back, there's a pig, and there are fowls and rabbits; then I knock together my own little frame, you see, and grow cucumbers; and you'll judge at supper what sort of salad I can raise. [So,] if you can suppose the little place besieged, it would hold out a devil of a time in point of provisions."' (Charles Dickens, *Great Expectations*, 1861)

FIRST PROTOCOL, ARTICLE 1: PROTECTION OF PROPERTY[1]
Every natural or legal person is entitled to the peaceful enjoyment of his possessions. No one shall be deprived of his possessions except in the public interest and subject to the conditions provided for by law and by the general principles of international law.

The preceding provisions shall not, however, in any way impair the right of a State to enforce such laws as it deems necessary to control the use of property in accordance with the general interest or to secure the payment of taxes or other contributions or penalties.

All democratic societies recognise that while there are certain basic rights which attach to the ownership of property, they are heavily qualified by considerations of the public interest. This is reflected in the terms of Article 1 of Protocol 1 to the Convention . . . Thus, under the first paragraph, property may be taken by the state, on payment of compensation, if the public interest so requires. And, under the second paragraph, the use of property may be restricted without compensation on similar grounds.

These are the words of Lord Hoffmann, in the House of Lords in the *Alconbury* case,[2] and they absolutely set the tone for this chapter. Article 1 provides the right to property, which may be interfered with – this right is 'heavily qualified' in Lord Hoffmann's phrase – but that interference must, following the Convention jurisprudence, be lawful, non-arbitrary, and proportionate.

This chapter will look at how a claim to the right of property may arise, and how the right may be limited. We shall consider a variety of situations, which are common enough, where the possession or use of property is limited by the state. They may occur, for example, in town and country planning, or in decisions by national or local government about the environment, or road building, or in some other way which has an

---

[1] All references in this chapter to Article 1 should be taken to refer to this article, not Article 1 of the Convention itself.
[2] [2001] 2 WLR 1389 at 1411; the case is considered at p. 41 above.

adverse effect upon the property of an individual, as to its value, or its use, or the enjoyment they derive from it. And this will apply equally whether the person complaining is an individual or a company, which may be a large business, since a company also enjoys the right to property.

ENGLISH LAW AND THE RIGHT TO PROPERTY

In order to gauge the effect of the Convention, one must have some idea as to what is provided by the national law. First of all, what is meant by **property**? Property includes what is known in legal terminology as 'real' property, land and buildings. Then there is 'personal' property, goods such as cars and other vehicles, furniture, clothes – the whole range of things that one can buy or possess. Animals will also count as property, since they can belong to someone who is entitled to protect them and protect their rights to them. Property does not have to be tangible, that is, it need not physically exist: so, for example, there is what is referred to as 'intellectual' property, rights such as trademarks, copyright in written material or confidential information. Money is also property, perhaps the most common example of property in court cases, whether we are talking about physical coins, or far more often, a *right* to money, such as money in a bank account, or money which is claimed from someone else as being a debt or payable for some other reason.

There are a number of ways in which our law provides substantial protection for people's property. In cases of damage to land, the owner or occupier has a number of remedies for damage to or interference with their property: trespass, nuisance and negligence. Where there is interference with or damage to goods, there are actions available of trespass, negligence, or conversion. Further, a person may enter into a contract which gives him property rights, such as a sale, a hiring, or a lease, and he will have an action for the breach of it. And the law of landlord and tenant provides rules which create rights of possession and property, for both the landlord and the tenant, where there is the relevant legal relationship of the lease of a property. Then there is the criminal law. It protects rights of property, by creating the offence of theft, and other offences of dishonesty, and the offences of robbery and burglary, and criminal damage. Criminals may be ordered to forfeit money or other property, and to pay compensation.

However, there are also established ways in which property *can* be interfered with. There is the right of the state to impose taxes, as is recognised in the words of the second paragraph of Article 1. There are also situations such as planning controls, which limit the use that can be made of land to protect the rights of other people. Then there are situations where the state seeks to deprive a person of property because it has been used to commit a crime or because it is the proceeds of crime, or where a particular use of property is prevented: here this article is particularly relevant, since the interference is directly by the state.

Indeed, most of the cases in our discussion of this article will involve some form of state interference, mainly because of the existing variety of protections against, and remedies for, interferences with private property, which we have mentioned above. Where the parties to a case are both individuals, arguing, for example, over who an item belongs to, the Convention right will have little if any application. But where the state is proposing to interfere with property, by a legislative provision, or the application of such legislation, then the general principles of Article 1 will apply. Just as we have seen in our discussion of many of the other articles, the courts will now have to consider the substantive justification for any such interference, and especially whether it is proportionate, whereas previously the courts usually only had to consider whether the interference was lawful, that is, whether it complied with the relevant formal and statutory requirements.

'POSSESSIONS' AND 'PROPERTY'

Both these words are used in Article 1; what is the difference? In fact there is no real difference, and when we look at the cases we shall not be troubled by any distinction. The next case demonstrates that the phrases can be used interchangeably. More importantly, the case defines Article 1, and announces how the Convention principles – lawfulness, absence of any arbitrary decision, and proportionality – govern the whole of the article. The case is *Marckx v Belgium*,[3] where a claim was made under this article.

Paula Marckx had a daughter who, according to Belgian law, was 'illegitimate', and therefore could not inherit from her mother; so Paula could not leave property to her. Paula claimed that this was a violation of Article 1, since the right to property included the right to dispose of one's property. The European Court agreed that the right to dispose of one's property was part of the right to property, and said:

> By recognising that everyone has the right to the peaceful enjoyment of his possessions, Article 1 is in substance guaranteeing the right of property. This is the clear impression left by the words 'possessions' and 'use of property' . . . the right to dispose of one's property constitutes a traditional and fundamental aspect of the right of property.

Thus, the court drew no distinction between 'possessions' and 'property': the right to dispose of one's possessions is a right of property. The European Court's decision, on the facts of the case, was that the Belgian laws of succession regulating the right to dispose of property were not arbitrary and were permitted under the second paragraph of Article 1, which allows the control of the use of property in accordance with the 'general interest', although the European Court did find that this law was discriminatory against children, in breach of Article 14.

ANALYSIS OF THE ARTICLE

The European Court in the *Marckx* case also analysed the wording of Article 1 as being composed of three rules, each based on a sentence of the article. The first, found in the first sentence of Article 1, is of a general nature, and sets out the principle of the **peaceful enjoyment** of property. The second, in the second sentence, covers **deprivation** of property, subject to certain conditions. The third, in the third sentence, recognises that states are entitled to **control the use** of property for the general interest and the payment of taxes and the like. The European Court added this, and it is of the utmost importance:

> The second and third rules are concerned with particular instances of interference with the right to peaceful enjoyment of property, and should therefore be construed in the light of the general principle enunciated in the first rule.

---

[3] (1980) 2 EHRR 330.

But what is the general principle of the first rule? There is no expression of principle beyond the actual words establishing the right to peaceful enjoyment. The answer is that the European Court has read into those words the requirement that there must be a fair balance achieved between the interests of the community and the rights of the individual. We shall see the Court's expression of it in the *Air Canada*[4] case. Thus, each part of Article 1, each 'rule', is subject to the principle that any interference with the right must be **lawful, not arbitrary** and **proportionate**. We shall repeatedly see this as we travel through examples.

THE GENERAL APPROACH

We shall make some reference to this division into 'peaceful enjoyment', 'depriving of possessions' and 'control of use'. This is not always easy; sometimes it is not clear under which head the case falls, or the court does not specifically announce under which head it falls, as in the next case. But this does not greatly matter. What is more important are the general principles, which apply whichever classification applies. One example of this general approach being applied in our courts is *Wilson v First County*.[5]

First County were pawnbrokers, and they made an agreement with Mr Wilson which was a credit agreement for a loan; Mr Wilson provided security for the loan, and this was a BMW car. The Consumer Credit Act 1974 applied to this agreement, which required the agreement to be in a precise form; if it was not, neither the pawnbrokers nor the court could enforce it. The agreement was not in the correct form, and the Court of Appeal held that the Consumer Credit Act prevented enforcement. The pawnbrokers argued that this interfered with their right to property, in breach of Article 1, so that the section was incompatible with the Convention.

The Court of Appeal agreed and made a declaration of incompatibility. It considered that the pawnbrokers did indeed have property rights under their contract with Mr Wilson, and the Consumer Credit Act did not prevent those existing, but it did prevent them being enforced, and this amounted to an interference with their rights. The principle of consumer protection, protecting consumers from credit which they could not afford, and from creditors who might put pressure on them, is a valid one, but the interference still has to be proportionate. Since this prohibition was inflexible, and the court had no discretion to enforce the property rights however unjust that might be, this was a disproportionate interference.

The salient point is that Article 1 requires a fair balance, whichever part of the article applies. Indeed the general approach is more important than the precise classification, the insistence on the principles that the interference is lawful, not arbitrary, and proportionate.

PEACEFUL ENJOYMENT

The first sentence of the article, referring to the basic principle of peaceful enjoyment, is short, but the European Court finds in it the implication of the balancing exercise.

---

[4] (1995) 20 EHRR 150, below, p. 252.
[5] *Wilson v First County Trust Limited (No. 2)* [2001] 3 WLR 42.

So, in *Iatridis v Greece*,[6] a case about a local authority taking over a man's property, and damaging his livelihood.

This case concerned an open-air cinema, the Ilioupolis, built in 1950 with the appropriate permit. An open-air cinema played an important role in local cultural life in Greece, and the clientele of such cinemas was made up mainly of local residents. A dispute arose between the state and the cinema owners as to the ownership of the land. In 1978, Mr Iatridis took a lease of the cinema from the owners, and completely restored the cinema. He then operated it for 11 years, and built up the clientele, which was an asset. The town council then evicted Mr Iatridis, and assigned the cinema to themselves. A judge quashed the eviction order, and that meant that the town council was in possession of the cinema, but unlawfully. The appropriate government minister refused to revoke the assignment, so the town council remained in possession. Mr Iatridis complained of a violation of his right to property in the cinema.

   The European Court held in his favour. The Court expressly said that he had a right to peaceful enjoyment of his possession or property, and it was being denied him; this amounted to an interference with it; this was not an outright appropriation, only because he held a lease, which is a limited right and was properly terminated. The European Court considered whether the interference was justified by any of the grounds in the article, and found that the interference was unlawful even by Greek law, so there was no point in looking any further; once found to be outside the national law, it could not be 'lawful' within any of the meanings of the European Convention.

So this is a case within the first sentence of Article 1. And although the 13 words of that sentence do not make any reference to 'lawful', or to any other concept of the Convention jurisprudence, that concept is to be understood as being part of the rights protected by the article.

DEPRIVATION OF PROPERTY

'Deprivation' is the word coming from the phrasing of the second sentence of Article 1; and it is the word used in the next case by the European Commission. It is also certainly a case of enjoyment which was not peaceful. The interest for us is the readiness of the Commission to accept that damage to the environment may be a part of a claim under this article. The case is *Rayner v UK*.[7]

Michael Anthony Rayner was a partner with members of his family in the management of agricultural land. In 1961, he took up residence at Colnbrook, at a place which was about 1.3 miles west of Heathrow Airport North runway, and in a direct line with it. Aircraft regularly flew over the house, taking off and landing, and this produced very high noise levels. As well as a violation of Article 8, Mr Rayner claimed a violation of Protocol 1, Article 1. The Commission said:

> This provision is mainly concerned with the arbitrary confiscation of property and does not, in principle, guarantee a right to the peaceful enjoyment of possessions in a pleasant environment. It is true that aircraft noise nuisance of considerable importance both as to level and frequency may seriously affect the value of real property or even render it unsaleable and thus amount to a *partial taking of property*, necessitating payment of compensation. (emphasis added)

---

[6] (2000) 30 EHRR 97.
[7] (1987) 9 EHRR 375, see also above, p. 199, in the context of Article 8.

In short, you may get a violation of Article 1 in a situation like this. However, unfortunately for Mr Rayner, he had not produced any evidence that his house had suffered any loss of value, and so on that basis the Article 1 claim failed. But the words of the Commission above are interesting, especially the words in italics. They mean that where there is proof of financial damage, because the value of the house – or other premises – is reduced, some environmental feature will be enough to come within Article 1, even though there is no 'depriving of possession' – the phrase of the second sentence – nor any 'control of use' by the state – the phrase in the last sentence. It would be loss of 'peaceful enjoyment'.

COMPENSATION

There is one more point in *Rayner*, and it relates to compensation, referred to at the end of the quotation from the Commission. The point is that in cases where there is some taking of property – as opposed to simply a control of it – the European Court has regarded the payment of compensation, or the lack of it, as an important feature in deciding whether the act of the state was proportionate or not. The lack of compensation will lead more easily to a conclusion that there was a lack of proportionality. This will be especially relevant in cases of deprivation of property.

The next case is an example where lack of compensation was an important factor in the argument put forward. One incidental point about the case is that some of the claimants were companies, expressly provided for here by the opening words of Article 1, which mention 'every natural or legal person' – a company is a 'legal person'. The case is *James v UK*.[8]

The four claimants in this case were the trustees of the will of the Second Duke of Westminster, including the Sixth Duke. In the area of Belgravia in Central London, on a site which was once farmland on the outskirts of the City of London, the Westminster family and its trustees had developed a large estate comprising about 2,000 houses which became one of the most desirable residential areas in London. By the Leasehold Reform Act 1967, occupiers of these houses who were tenants were given the right to purchase compulsorily the freehold of the house. This was called 'leasehold enfranchisement'; British governments had for nearly one hundred years sought to implement this policy, which enabled tenants to purchase the house in which they had invested money. The claimants, on the other hand, pointed out that the purchase price was often below the market value, and the tenant, having made the purchase, was able to sell again at a profit. They claimed that they were, by the compulsory sale, 'deprived of their possessions' in breach of Article 1.

The European Court dealt with the phrases 'in the public interest' and 'subject to the conditions provided for by law', and said:

The Court has consistently held that the terms 'law' or 'lawful' in the Convention do not merely refer back to domestic law but also relate to the quality of the law, requiring it to be compatible with the rule of law. However, on the facts [. . .] there are *no grounds* for finding that the enfranchisement of the applicants' properties was *arbitrary* because of the terms of compensation provided for under the leasehold reform legislation. (emphasis added)

---

[8] (1986) 8 EHRR 123.

There is the reference to compensation; it was a central part of the case, and despite the claims of the applicants, the European Court found that there was nothing arbitrary about the scheme. This case is a perfect illustration of the balancing exercise the court will carry out. And it is a foretaste of what the Convention will bring to our law in this area – a close examination of state interference. Another case about compensation, which also underlines the principle that the taking of property under Article 1 requires proportionality, is *Lithgow v UK*.[9]

The applicants were shipbuilders, ship repairers, marine engineers, and aerospace manufacturers. Their interests were nationalised by the Aircraft and Shipbuilding Industries Act 1977, which provided compensation to businesses which were nationalised. The applicants claimed that the compensation they received was grossly inadequate, and so was in violation of Article 1.

The European Court held that there had been a taking of property – a 'depriving of possessions' – within Article 1, but that on the facts the compensation was *not* so inadequate as to be a breach. The Court stated the principle that the payment of compensation is a necessary condition for the taking of property, and to take property without it would be justifiable only in exceptional circumstances. Then the Court said:

> In this connection, the Court recalls that not only must a measure depriving a person of his property pursue, on the facts as well as in principle, a legitimate aim 'in the public interest', but there must also be a reasonable relationship of proportionality between the means employed and the aim sought to be realised.

This is the 'fair balance' point; and the amount of compensation is relevant to it. On this point of the importance of compensation, we shall consider one more case, where a company brought an action arising out of the deprivation of its property without compensation: the case is *Booker Aquaculture*.[10]

McConnell Salmon Ltd occupied a farm site on the island of Gigha, Scotland, and they reared turbot. In 1994, they suspected that some of the turbot were infected with a disease. They informed the Secretary of State, who then served a notice under the Disease of Fish (Control) Regulations 1994, requiring McConnell to destroy all their fish, but some fish could be slaughtered for commercial purposes on particular conditions. The Regulations were made by government to implement a European Union (EU) Directive, and so were part of the system of EU regulation. McConnell claimed compensation of over £600,000, which the Secretary of State refused. McConnell assigned their rights to Booker, who claimed a violation of Article 1.

The Inner House of the Court of Session found that McConnell's Article 1 rights had been violated – they were deprived of their property when they had to destroy their fish, and they were restricted in the use of the fish which could be used commercially on conditions; further, the Court regarded the availability of compensation as relevant to the question whether there had been a violation, and this was also the appropriate approach under EU law.

(There was also an uncertain point of EU law involved, so the question of the determination of compensation was in fact referred to the EU's court, the European Court of Justice.)

The case is important. Government departments from time to time, and increasingly so, introduce legislation preventing the use of various types of property, on the ground

---

[9] (1986) 8 EHRR 329.
[10] *Booker Aquaculture Limited v The Secretary of State for Scotland* [2000] UKHRR 1.

of health or safety. Fur farming, for example, is to be controlled, and businesses will be affected by the regulation of it. The judgment in the *Booker* case shows that there may well be a violation of Article 1 if no proper provision is made for compensation.

CONTROL OF USE

Control of use may cover a variety of rights to use land, and this will also involve the right *not* to use property. One example of a case which involved the control of the use of land was the case of *Chassagnou v France*.[11]

In this case, a French law compelled certain landowners to allow hunting across their land and to join a hunting association. The applicants all had ethical objections to hunting and so objected to the law. The European Court considered that, although the applicants had not been deprived of their right to use their property, the compulsory transfer of the hunting rights to a statutory hunting association prevented them from making use of one of the rights over their land. The fact that the applicants' intention was to make *no* use of that right – that is, the applicants wished to use their rights as landowners to *prohibit* hunting over their land – did not prevent this being a control of the use of land, and therefore an interference with their rights as owners of the property. The Court went on to consider that the law was a disproportionate interference with these rights and therefore an unjustified interference with Article 1; the Court also found violations of Article 14, because the law applied differently to small and large landowners; and of Article 11, because the law compelled membership of the hunting association.

The same right has been invoked, but on the other side of the argument, in a challenge to an Act of the Scottish Parliament banning foxhunting:[12] it was argued that the ban on foxhunting was an interference with the right to use of property under Article 1. The Court of Session held that the ban was a control of the use of property, namely the land and hounds previously used for hunting, and so Article 1 applied, but the Court found no violation of Article 1. The Court considered that the activity of hunting was not central to the economic exploitation of the property, that there was no identifiable loss, and that in any event, the interference was justified in accordance with the general interest in the prevention of cruelty to animals.

TAXATION

It has been said: 'Tax legislation lacks charm.'[13] Tax law can be very technical, and raises many issues of detail, rather than issues of principle. But behind it is a very important political and legal reality: the state has the power, and the right, to impose taxes; and these will interfere with the property of an individual or a business. The second paragraph of Article 1 refers expressly to taxation, in connection with the need to 'control the use' of property. But whether it is a situation of 'depriving of possessions' or 'control of use', or simply 'peaceful enjoyment', as with other interferences, it must be lawful, not arbitrary, and proportionate.

---

[11] (2000) 29 EHRR 615; see also above, p. 89.
[12] *Adams v Lord Advocate* [2002] UKHRR 1189.
[13] H.H. Monroe QC, *Intolerable Inquisition? Reflections on the Law of Tax*, 1981 Hamlyn Lecture.

An example of the requirement that the tax should not be arbitrary is the case of *Wallbank*.[14]

Mr and Mrs Wallbank were owners of a field. Over 250 years ago, an obligation had been attached to the field which made it rectorial property. This meant that ownership of the field made whoever owned it lay rectors of the parish where the field was located, which meant that they had an obligation to repair the chancel of the parish church, if called upon to do so. A notice requiring the Wallbanks to pay for the cost of repairing the church was served on them by the Parish Council, the cost being over £95,000. The Wallbanks argued that this infringed their Article 1 rights.

The Court of Appeal agreed. They considered that the liability of someone who was not otherwise connected to the church to pay for the cost of repairs was contrary to Article 1. It could no longer be characterised as a voluntary, private obligation, as it would have been considered in past centuries; in the modern day, it was clearly a form of taxation. As such it was arbitrary, since it no longer had any connection with the church property itself, and because it might arise at any time and for any amount. It was also discriminatory (in breach of Article 14), because it fell upon some landowners and not others.

The question of proportionality in taxation will be more difficult, since the amount and principles of any particular tax are the sort of question which all courts prefer to leave to legislation. This is because there is a very wide range of taxes that *could* be imposed within the range of what will be proportionate: this is a very real example of a situation where the court is being asked to consider what we have described as a policy decision which is most appropriate for a democratically elected Parliament, since what taxes are imposed is precisely the question at stake when people choose which political party to vote for in a general election. Indeed, a policy on the imposition of higher or lower taxation is often one of the key distinctions between political parties. Therefore, the courts will be slow to interfere just because a person happens to disagree with the amount of a particular tax, so long as it is generally applied and does not offend general principles, such as only taxing people on money upon which they are expecting to be taxed, so that they can plan their tax payments accordingly.

The next case is an example of an unsuccessful challenge to a rather unusual tax provision as being disproportionate. It was unusual because what was being challenged was a retrospective provision to cover a period for which no tax had been payable because of a drafting oversight in the relevant legislation. Here, the argument was whether in fact the result was that the building societies challenging the law had had to pay tax twice as a result.

One other point of introduction to the case is to consider the nature of the property. Just as debts owed to a business are part of its assets, so a claim to money or property may be part of the possessions or property of an individual or a business. In this case, the claim in question was a claim to repayment of tax previously paid. This was the property which was alleged to have been interfered with; the case is that of the *National and Provincial Building Society*.[15]

---

[14] *Aston Cantlow Parochial Church Council v Wallbank* [2001] 3 WLR 1323.
[15] (1998) 25 EHRR 127.

Three building societies had all paid tax on the interest they paid to their investors. There was a change in the tax laws governing taxation of interest, which accidentally left a period of time for which *no* tax was payable. So regulations were passed which dealt with this gap, but which had the effect of making some tax payable twice on the same income. These regulations were successfully challenged by the Woolwich Building Society, which then recovered the money it had paid in tax under the regulations.

The National and Provincial, the Leeds, and the Yorkshire Building Societies then issued proceedings to make the same claim, but before these came to trial, the government passed legislation retrospectively legalising the regulations, so the building societies' actions were barred; only the Woolwich, whose court case was over, was allowed to keep the money recovered by it. The other three societies claimed that this retrospective legislation deprived them of their 'possessions', namely their claim to the tax money which they had paid over twice, in breach of Article 1.

The European Court was prepared for the purposes of the case to proceed on the basis that these legal claims were 'possessions'. As such, it considered that they had been interfered with and went on to examine the matter as a control of the use of property in the general interest to secure the payment of tax. The Court concluded that the legislation had not acted improperly or disproportionately: if the building societies were right, they would effectively receive a windfall from the changeover in the tax regime, which would not be in the public interest; nor was the burden resulting from the regulations excessive. The balance between the protection of the building societies' claims and the public interest in the payment of taxes was not upset.

The European Court was able to regard the buildings societies' claims as 'possessions' for the purposes of this case, although we are really talking about an intangible asset, a claim to money, which is relevant to other situations where what is being interfered with is not a tangible possession. But the essential point is the balancing exercise: although the retrospective application of the Act of Parliament seemed unfair to the building societies, the state is entitled to take measures to ensure that a tax is applied fairly and without the exploitation of loopholes.

The 'fair balance' will sometimes involve difficult questions – and, as we have seen, can also involve claims involving very large sums of money, such as the millions of pounds at stake in the Building Societies' case. Likewise, there were millions of pounds in gaming licence duty claimed by Customs and Excise in the next case, *Lydiashourne Ltd.*[16]

Lydiashourne operated Maxim's Casino, where a Mr Al Shamlan was accustomed to gamble; on one occasion he obtained gaming chips or tokens to the value of £6,700,000 from the Casino, by means of a banker's draft; he staked the chips and lost. The draft turned out to be forged and valueless. The Casino were therefore not paid for the chips. Nonetheless Customs and Excise demanded the payment of the relevant gaming tax of £2,240,000 on the draft. The Casino contended that the banker's draft was accepted by them in total and unconditional payment, which was now a bad debt, so that they were entitled to bad debt relief. The Value Added Tax and Duties Tribunal disagreed, holding that the draft was received conditionally on the bank paying it. The Casino appealed to the Court of Appeal, contending that they were entitled to bad debt relief, and that if the statutory provisions did not allow such relief, that was a violation of Article 1, in that it was an excessive and unjustifiable interference with the Casino's enjoyment of its property. They had not received payment: they should not have to pay tax on it.

---

[16] *Lydiashourne Ltd v The Commissioners of Customs and Excise* (2000) LTL 2.10.00.

The Court of Appeal considered the final sentence of Article 1, which permits the state to enforce laws to control the use of property to secure the payment of taxes; and the central question was proportionality. Lord Justice Robert Walker said:

> With that must be read the references [to] the need to achieve a fair balance and to the need for proportionality. Nevertheless it is plain that a challenge to tax laws as infringing Article 1 is a very steep hill to climb. It seems to me that the language of [the tax statute] is clear. I can see nothing disproportionate or exorbitant in laws which insist on the principle that gaming of this sort, conducted at casinos for very high stakes, should be carried out on a cash basis or what is tantamount to a cash basis, and that [the Casino] should bear the risk of being taxed on the amount of any gaming tokens which it issues if, despite the rigours of the system, bad debts arise. Such tax laws cannot in my judgment be called devoid of reasonable foundation.

CUSTOMS AND THE PORTS

The duty imposed on goods imported into the country is a form of taxation. Like any other power which adversely affects the citizen's right of property, it must be applied with balance and proportion. Further, large organisations, such as government departments, have policies to cover particular situations; they oil the wheels, by making decisions faster and easier. But a policy, or a policy document, may give the appearance of an inflexible, or arbitrary, approach. We see that in the case of *Lindsay*.[17]

Customs and Excise officers on duty at ports check persons and vehicles for cigarettes and alcohol, on which duty is payable. In this case, they were operating a policy that in cases where a motor vehicle was seized, because duty was being evaded, Customs would return the vehicle to the owner only in exceptional circumstances; no distinction was made between large-scale, so-called 'commercial' smuggling and those bringing in goods on a non-commercial basis, for private use. Mr Lindsay, about to board a cross-Channel ferry at Calais, was stopped with substantial quantities of alcohol and cigarettes in his car. His vehicle was confiscated; the Customs officer applied the policy, and his car was not returned to him.

The Court of Appeal held there was a violation of Article 1. The question was whether there was sufficient justification for the interference with property. The deprivation of property would be justified where it was necessary and proportionate and in the public interest specifically 'to secure the payment of taxes or other contributions'. However, where, as here, no distinction was drawn between commercial and non-commercial smuggling, proportionality required that each case be considered on its facts; this included the scale of the importation, whether or not it was a first offence, whether there was any attempt to conceal the goods, the value of the vehicle, and any hardship which would be caused to the individual. Mr Lindsay was clearly importing goods for his family and friends and therefore should not have been subject to an automatic forfeiture.

CONFISCATION OF PROCEEDS OF CRIME

Article 1 has also been relied on in the criminal courts, in the context of the confiscation of the proceeds of crime, and again the important principle of proportionality has been applied. Two cases, considered together, raised this issue where convicted criminals faced confiscation of their assets and claimed that this was an interference with their property. The cases are *Rezvi* and *Benjafield*.[18]

---

[17] *Lindsay v Commissioners of Customs and Excise* [2002] 1 WLR 1766.
[18] *R v Rezvi, R v Benjafield* [2002] 2 WLR 235.

Karl Robert Benjafield was convicted of charges connected with drug supplying, and the judge made an order of confiscation of his assets to the extent of £327,971; and Syed Rezvi was convicted of offences of theft, and a confiscation order was made in his case of £214,389. The confiscation orders were made under Acts of Parliament, which empowered the court to confiscate assets following conviction of offences; the statutes permitted the court to make assumptions against the defendant that his property and expenditure originated from criminal activity, unless the defendant showed them to be incorrect.

The House of Lords considered Article 1 and agreed that these were instances of interference with property, but held that confiscation was a reasonable and proportionate reaction to the danger of drug trafficking and serious crime, so long as the court making the order did not consider that there was a risk of real or serious injustice. On the principle which justified the institution of confiscation, Lord Steyn said:

> It is a notorious fact that professional and habitual criminals frequently take steps to conceal their profits from crime. Effective but fair powers of confiscating the proceeds of crime are therefore essential. The provisions of the 1988 Act are aimed at depriving such offenders of the proceeds of their criminal conduct. Its purposes are to punish convicted offenders, to deter the commission of further offences and to reduce the profits available to fund further criminal enterprises. These objectives reflect not only national but also international policy. The United Kingdom has undertaken, by signing and ratifying treaties agreed under the auspices of the United Nations and the Council of Europe, to take measures necessary to ensure that the profits of those engaged in drug trafficking or other crimes are confiscated.

FORFEITURE OF GOODS

We have seen good examples of the balancing exercise in the taxation cases; and the court will require to be satisfied that the imposition of the tax is fair. These powers are far-reaching, and large sums of money are at stake. In this next case we see how a large asset was involved, and the European Court had to make a judgment on the proportionality of the exercise of the power of forfeiture. The case is *Air Canada v UK*.[19]

Between 1983 and 1986, at Heathrow Airport, a number of incidents gave rise to concern regarding the adequacy of Air Canada's security procedures; drugs disappeared from freight or premises, or drugs were secreted in freight, and two Air Canada employees were convicted of offences connected with the importation of cannabis resin. Customs and Excise wrote letters warning that deductions could be made from the security bonds deposited by the airline. On 26 April 1987, a Tristar aircraft, worth over £60,000,000, owned and operated by Air Canada, and on a regular scheduled passenger flight, landed at Heathrow, where it discharged cargo including a container holding 331 kg of cannabis resin valued at about £800,000. The airway bill was false, and Air Canada's cargo computer did not hold any detail of the consignment. Customs officers seized the aircraft as liable to forfeiture, but the officers delivered it back on payment by Air Canada of a banker's draft of £50,000. Air Canada complained that there had been a violation of Article 1 by the seizing of the aircraft as liable to forfeiture.

The European Court regarded this as a control of use case, and so considered the case under the second paragraph of Article 1. The Court said:

> According to the Court's well-established case law, the second paragraph of Article 1 must be construed in the light of the principle laid down in the Article's first sentence. Consequently, any interference must achieve a 'fair balance' between the demands of the general interest of the community and the requirements of the protection of the individual's fundamental rights. The concern to achieve this balance is reflected

---

[19] (1995) 20 EHRR 150.

in the structure of Article 1 as a whole, including the second paragraph: there must therefore be a reasonable relationship of proportionality between the means employed and the aim pursued.

The Court found that bearing in mind the history of incidents, and the warnings, a fair balance had been achieved when the aircraft had been seized, and so the interference with the right of property was justified.

BUSINESS AND LIVELIHOOD

We have looked at a number of cases which have concerned the business of the people claiming the protection of the right of property. However, where the alleged interference with property would have the effect of removing a person's ability to run their business, it will be particularly important to strike the right balance between the needs of that individual and the needs of the wider community. This is shown by the next case, which concerned an application for a licence of a public house. Such applications are heard daily, and the court will now have to consider whether to renew or refuse an application will be a proportionate interference with a right to property. The case is *Catscratch Ltd.*[20]

Catscratch Limited operated premises as a night club, under a public house licence, and had in the past enjoyed regular extensions of permitted hours until 2 a.m. from Monday to Sunday and 2.30 to 6.30 p.m. on Sundays. In June 2000, at the statutory meeting of the licensing board, Catscratch's annual application for a regular extension in relation to an entertainment licence was refused. And the same thing happened again in 2001. Although a number of objections had been lodged, none were from the police or the local authority. The company claimed it suffered loss of business as a result of the withdrawing of the licences and sought judicial review of the decision of the licensing board, complaining of a breach of Article 1.

The Court of Session accepted that the failure to obtain a permitted licensing extension, so leading to the closure of the business amounted to a 'control of the use of the property' of the premises within Article 1, and so was an interference with Catscratch's rights. But applying the fair balance test, there was sufficient evidence to lead the licensing board to conclude that there was a need to protect the environment, and the refusal of the licence was necessary for this purpose and not disproportionate.

PROTECTION OF THE HOME

This is something which is also protected under Article 8, as we have discussed earlier. But where the alleged intrusion into the home also affects the use or enjoyment of property, then Article 1 will also be engaged. One example where there were breaches of both articles, is the next case, *Marcic v Thames Water.*[21]

Mr Marcic's complaint was about flooding of his house and garden by sewers and drains operated by Thames Water. This was caused by heavy rain. Although the sewers had been properly constructed and maintained, they did not have the capacity to cope with large rainfall. Thames Water

---

[20] *Catscratch Limited v Glasgow City Licensing Board* [2001] UKHRR 1309.
[21] *Marcic v Thames Water Utilities Limited* [2002] 2 WLR 932 (CA).

had not carried out the substantial works needed to reduce the risk of flooding because of the cost: Thames Water operated a system for prioritising such works, and the works required to solve Mr Marcic's problem were not therefore likely to be done for some considerable time.

It was held by the High Court that this was a breach of Article 8 and Article 1 of the Protocol. The judge took the view that there was no remedy outside of the Act, in particular, since the statutory provisions which apply to the provision of sewers have a very limited scope for allowing compensation for complaints of this sort. However, the judge did consider that there was an interference with property and with the home, which had not been properly justified by Thames Water, under Article 1 or Article 8(2).

In principle Thames Water has a measure of discretion as to how to perform its statutory duties of provision of drainage, and it clearly has to strike some sort of balance in dealing with flooding problems, depending on their urgency. However, the judge did not consider that they had dealt with Mr Marcic in a fair or proportionate way: in particular, because there was no provision for cases of external flooding, as here, where there was no flooding to the inside of a house; Mr Marcic had been waiting nine years for something to be done and had spent a considerable amount of money himself to try to limit the damage; and there was no prospect of anything being done about it under the present system. Thames Water had therefore failed to strike a fair balance between Mr Marcic and the needs of its other customers. The Court of Appeal agreed with this analysis, although they also considered that Mr Marcic had a remedy under the law of nuisance in any event.

This case also makes a point which we have come across previously in the context of other articles: it will not be enough to defend a claim for breach of a Convention right just to rely on the cost of remedying the situation, unless in all the circumstances, the cost would be wholly disproportionate.

QUESTIONS

1 The wording of Article 1 contains a number of limitations set out in broad and general terms. What are the general interests which these limitations protect? Are they too broad, too narrow, or about right, and why?

2 Is taxation justified? Does it matter what the purpose of the taxation is?

3 Do you consider that the law is correct to confiscate the proceeds of crime? Why?

Voting by secret ballot: the right to participate in democratic elections is enshrined in Article 3 of the First Protocol, discussed in this chapter.

Chapter 20

FREE ELECTIONS

'The courts owe a special responsibility to the public as the constitutional guardian of the freedom of political debate.' (Lord Justice Laws, in *R (Pro-Life Alliance) v BBC*,[1] 2002)

FIRST PROTOCOL, ARTICLE 3: RIGHT TO FREE ELECTIONS[2]
The High Contracting parties undertake to hold free elections at reasonable intervals by secret ballot, under conditions which will ensure free expression of the opinion of the people in the choice of the legislature.

THE IMPORTANCE OF DEMOCRACY

Democracy is without doubt a fundamental feature of the European public order. That is apparent, from the Preamble to the Convention,[3] which establishes a very clear connection between the Convention and democracy by stating that the maintenance and further realisation of human rights and fundamental freedoms are best ensured on the one hand by an effective political democracy and on the other by a common understanding and observance of human rights. [It notes] the prime importance of Article 3 of Protocol No. 1 which enshrines a characteristic principle of an effective political democracy.

This was the statement of the European Court in the case of *United Communist Party of Turkey v Turkey*,[4] where the Turkish Constitutional Court had made an order dissolving the Turkish Communist Party on the grounds that its programme contained statements to undermine the integrity of the state and the unity of the nation, since its programme referred to the Kurdish nation as well as the Turkish nation, and the Turkish Constitution prohibited self-determination and regional autonomy. The European Court did not in fact determine the complaint under Article 3, since it found a clear breach of the Article 11 right to freedom of association.

Nonetheless, the statement of principle above is important, and it sets the scene for our examination of this article. Democracy is something we usually consider to be one of the key features of a free society. This is partly because the right to vote has been hard-won, as has the right to be governed by elected representatives. After all,

---

[1] [2002] 3 WLR 1080.
[2] All references in this chapter to Article 3 should be taken to refer to this Article, not Article 3 of the Convention itself.
[3] This can be found in the text of the Convention in Appendix 2.
[4] (1998) 26 EHRR 121.

the English Civil War (1642–49) was fought over who should govern the country, and Parliament won. Likewise, the Bill of Rights 1688 was based on a forced change of sovereign, the 'Glorious Revolution', which is why it set out a number of important Parliamentary privileges and protections for democracy, including the right to free elections.[5] This right in some form has therefore been a part of our law for centuries, although as with many other basic rights, its content and scope has developed with time. After all, in 1688, the number of people who could actually vote was severely limited; full universal suffrage, the right of all adults to vote, cannot really be said to have been in place until 1950.[6]

It is also worth bearing in mind that what we mean by democracy, and what is protected by Article 3, is representative democracy. That is, the rights protected are the rights to vote for representatives – in the United Kingdom, these are Members of Parliament – to make up a legislature. This is not the only possible meaning of democracy – it is a far cry from the system for which the term was invented, that of ancient Athens, where the state was effectively the city, and government, at least in part, was by an assembly of all adult males, which was considered at the time to be government by the people (the 'demos'). But it is the only form of democracy which is practicable in a modern country, given the number of citizens. It is therefore necessary to concentrate on how to ensure that elections are free, properly express the views of the electorate, and occur at sufficiently regular intervals so that the government never gets to the stage where it does not have to consider that it will be accountable to the electorate.

THE STATE'S OBLIGATION

'The High Contracting parties . . .' – these are the opening words of this article, and no other article of the Convention guaranteeing a right or freedom opens in this manner. It emphasises that the article expressly imposes an obligation on the state to ensure the right. In the case of *Mathieu-Mohin and Clerfayt v Belgium*[7] the European Court referred to these opening words of this article.

Mrs Mathieu-Mohin, a French-speaking Belgian citizen, had been elected to the Senate, one of the two Houses of the Belgian Parliament. She had taken the parliamentary oath in French, and therefore could not be a member of the Flemish Council; that was the relevant regional body for representatives elected from her area. She complained that French-speaking electors, who had elected herself, were disadvantaged in that their candidates suffered these limitations. In this sense, she complained, the 'free expression of the opinion of the people' was impaired. The European Court rejected the claim, on the facts of the case. But it did refer to these first words of Article 3:

> The inter-State colouring of the wording of Article 3 does not reflect any difference of substance from the other substantive clauses in the Convention and Protocols. The reason for it would seem to lie rather in the desire to give greater solemnity to the commitment undertaken and in the fact that the primary obligation in the field concerned is not one of abstention or non-interference, as with the majority of the civil and political rights, but one of adoption by the State of positive measures to 'hold' democratic elections.

[5] Discussed above, p. 18.
[6] In 1928, women were given the vote on the same terms as men; in 1950, the residence qualification was removed.
[7] (1988) 10 EHRR 1.

THE SCOPE OF ARTICLE 3

Article 3 does not contain any express limitation or restriction, such as are contained, for example, in Articles 8, 9, 10 and 11. There is no reference in the wording of Article 3 to proportionality, and no reference to any reservation.

But Article 3 is not absolute; that was the express statement of the European Court in the case of *Ahmed v United Kingdom*.[8] We have examined this case in our discussion of Article 10, the right to freedom of expression. The case concerned local government officers who were interested in taking part in the activities of political parties, but were forbidden to do so by Regulations which restricted such activities of officers in 'politically restricted posts'. They claimed that their rights under Article 10 had been violated. The European Court rejected their claims, holding that there was a pressing social need for restrictions of this kind, and that these restrictions could not be said to be disproportionate. But the Court also considered Article 3:

> The Court recalls that Article 3 of Protocol No. 1 implies subjective rights to vote and to stand for election. As important as those rights are, they are not, however, absolute. Since Article 3 recognises them without setting them forth in express terms, let alone defining them, there is room for implied limitations.

This approach is consistent with the Court's treatment of other articles: we have seen examples in other articles of the Convention, where there are no express limitations or reservations, but where the Court has implied limitations, sometimes even where the wording appears to be absolute. As with other such implied limitations, the underlying feature of the Court's approach is the question of proportionality.

We see this perfectly illustrated in another election case. It is the case of *Robertson*.[9]

Mr Robertson was an elector, and wished to have his name removed from an electoral register before that register was sold to a commercial concern for marketing purposes. Electoral registration officers were by statute charged with the duty of preparing and publishing each year a register of parliamentary and local government electors for their area, and were required to supply a copy to any person upon payment of a fee. Mr Robertson, although knowing it was a criminal offence to fail to return an application form duly completed, wrote to the officer in Wakefield stating that he did not intend to complete the form for inclusion on the register because he opposed the practice of selling copies of the register to commercial interests. The officer replied that the compilation of the register was separate from the uses made of it, and that he intended to include the name and address of Mr Robertson.

Mr Robertson applied for judicial review on the ground that he was unlawfully being required to tolerate the dissemination of the register to commercial interests, and that his enfranchisement could not lawfully be made conditional upon acceptance of that practice. He complained of a breach of Article 8 (the right to respect for his private life) and Article 3.

The Judge held that the practice of selling the register to commercial concerns without affording individual electors a right of objection was a *disproportionate* way in which to give effect to the legitimate objective of retaining a commercially available register, so that there was a violation of Article 8. Further, to the extent that the relevant Regulations made the right to vote conditional upon the acquiescence in that practice, with no individual right of objection, they operated in a

---

[8] (2000) 29 EHRR 1, above, p. 235.
[9] *R (Robertson) v Wakefield Metropolitan District Council* [2002] 2 WLR 889.

manner which contravened Article 3 on the same reasoning of justification and proportionality that was applied in the case of Article 8.

Thus we see the principle of proportionality applied to this article, here by reference also to the express limitations in Article 8; and we should bear this in mind as we turn to other aspects of elections. We shall consider first the position of the voter – systems of voting, and the franchise – and then the position of the candidate.

VOTING SYSTEMS

Possibly the two most important rights for a voter are the **system of voting**, and his **franchise**. The wording of Article 3 does not specify any particular method of voting. The election process must be 'free', and must ensure 'a secret ballot', and a 'free expression of the opinion of the people'. But that is all. There is no mention of how these should be achieved. Of course, the underlying principle is that of democracy, that there should be a true expression of the preference of the people. How that is achieved is a matter on which the European Court will allow a margin of appreciation, since the article does not specify any particular electoral system, and since different systems are used in different countries, so long as the degree of accuracy is comparable with the systems of other European democracies.

We see this illustrated in the case of *The Liberal Party v United Kingdom*.[10]

Here, the Liberal Party (as it then was) was questioning the British electoral system. Our elections are run on the basis of a simple majority, known as the first past the post system. The Liberal Party was rather smaller than the two main parties, the Conservative and Labour Parties.

The Liberal Party claimed that the number of candidates elected to Parliament did not properly reflect the number of electors who voted Liberal, because it was a smaller party, and so it was disproportionately disadvantaged by the electoral system. Thus the system did not ensure the 'free expression of the opinion of the people'. The Liberal Party claimed that if one of the generally recognised systems for proportional representation had been used – such as voting for candidates on a national list, using an additional number system, or using a single transferable vote, which allows second-preference votes to count – more Liberal candidates would have been elected, which would have been a more accurate reflection of the views of the electorate. The Liberal Party therefore claimed that there were violations of Article 3, as well as Article 14 (which prohibits discrimination). The Conservative and Labour Parties opposed this, unsurprisingly, on the basis that they would lose seats.

The Commission rejected the claim. It considered that Article 3 was careful not to bind the states as to the electoral system they should use. It does not add any requirement of 'equality' to the 'secret ballot'. Furthermore, even countries with a formal requirement for equality of voting still accept that the simple majority system complies with that requirement: for example, the Federal Republic of Germany, and the United States of America.

It is of interest to note that this was notwithstanding the opinion, relied upon by the Liberal Party and cited by the Commission, of Professor Wade, who has described the

---

[10] (1982) 4 EHRR 106.

British electoral system of parliamentary representation as 'probably the worst that could be devised'.[11]

THE FRANCHISE

Another key aspect of elections is the **right to vote**, the franchise. In a democracy it is a valuable thing – even if some people stay away from the polling booth and so do not use it. Indeed, over the course of history, there have been long and bitter struggles by various groups to obtain the right to vote, and was only relatively recently that it could be said that all adults have the right to vote. Article 14 would be relevant here if there was ever an attempt to limit the franchise on arbitrary grounds, since although that might not breach Article 3 by itself, it would be likely to breach Article 3 taken together with Article 14, which prevents discrimination in the application of the other articles.

However, having the franchise is no use if a person is not allowed to vote. In two cases which we will now examine, electors wished to use their franchise, and could not. Bearing in mind that the European Court accepts that the Article 3 right is not absolute, the question in both cases was whether the interference was justified and proportionate. In the first case, *Moore v UK*,[12] when Mr Moore's claim showed that the interference was not justified, Parliament changed the law.

Mr Moore had been detained since 1993 in Colchester under the Mental Health Acts; in 1996, he wrote to the Electoral Registration Officer asking to be entered on the electoral roll; the Officer's reply was that the Representation of the People Act 1983 prevented detained patients from being resident at the place of their detention, so Mr Moore should approach the Officer of his parents' area. Mr Moore did so, but that Officer refused to register him, as he had not lived there for 6 months. Thus Mr Moore had no way of registering to vote.

He complained to the European Court of a breach of his electoral rights, claiming that he had been disenfranchised, denied his right to vote. Before the case was decided by the European Court, Parliament amended the 1983 Act to include a provision that patients could be registered for the area of the hospital where they resided. This complaint therefore brought about a change in the law, because it was realised that there was a breach of Article 3.

But in the next case, concerning a prisoner, the Divisional Court was clear that although the applicants were disenfranchised, this was *not* a disproportionate result. The case is *Pearson and Martinez*.[13]

Mr Pearson was a prisoner serving a 10-year sentence for drug offences, and Mr Martinez was a discretionary life-sentence prisoner convicted of arson. They had applied to the Electoral Registration Officer for the relevant districts, to be registered on the electoral roll, and the Officers had refused. They complained of violations of Article 3 of the First Protocol and Article 14 of the Convention. Section 3(1) of the Representation of the People Act 1983 provided that a convicted person detained in a penal institution was legally incapable of voting at parliamentary or local government elections.

---

[11] *Constitutional Fundamentals*, 1980 Hamlyn Lectures.
[12] (2000) 30 EHRR CD 90.
[13] *R (on the application of Pearson) v Secretary of State for the Home Department* [2001] HRLR 39.

The Divisional Court noted that the implied right to vote enshrined in Article 3 was not absolute. It considered a number of decisions by the European Commission which have established that in principle it is not an infringement of Article 3 for convicted prisoners to be restricted in their rights: this does not thwart the free expression of the opinion of the people in the choice of the legislature. Convicted prisoners are by definition being treated differently from other citizens: the key question is what extent of differential treatment is acceptable and proportionate. Parliament is entitled to consider that disenfranchisement should follow as part of the punishment of imprisonment following conviction.

THE LEGISLATURE

This word is not limited to the national Parliament of the state. The word must be interpreted in the light of the constitutional structure of the nation in question. This was the attitude of the European Court in the case of *Matthews v UK*.[14]

Ms Matthews was a British citizen, residing in Gibraltar; she applied to the Electoral Registration Officer to be registered as a voter at the elections to the European Parliament, but received the reply that Gibraltar was not included in the franchise for the European parliamentary elections, so she therefore could not vote. She complained to the European Court of a violation of Article 3. The European Commission had previously found that non-national institutions, such as the European Parliament, were not to be regarded as 'the legislature' within Article 3.

The Court noted that Gibraltar is part of the European Union, and that according to the case law of the European Court of Justice, it is an inherent aspect of EU law that such law sits alongside, and indeed has precedence over, domestic law. The European Parliament was a legislature within the fullest sense of the word, and was indeed the European legislature for Gibraltar. The fact that a body was not envisaged by the drafters of the Convention cannot prevent that body from falling within the scope of the Convention. And the Court added:

> The Court thus considers that to accept the Government's contention that the sphere of activities of the European Parliament falls outside the scope of Article 3 of Protocol No. 1 would risk undermining one of the fundamental tools by which 'effective political democracy' can be maintained.

THE POSITION OF CANDIDATES

The 'free expression of the opinion of the people in the choice of the legislature' is the object of this article. But that free expression, and choice, might be impaired if some obstacle is put in the way of a candidate: the people may have voted for the candidate, but he is prevented from taking his seat. In the case of *Buscarini v San Marino*[15] this happened with members of the General Grand Council, which is the legislature of the Republic of San Marino. They were obliged to swear an oath on the Gospels. They did so under protest, complaining that their right to freedom of religion and conscience had been infringed. The European Court agreed that this was in violation of their rights under Article 9. Whilst this case is primarily about freedom of conscience, it is also relevant as an example of the Convention's impact on the democratic process, which is very much what is protected by Article 3.

---

[14] (1999) 28 EHRR 361.
[15] (2000) 30 EHRR 208, discussed in the context of Article 9, above, p. 216.

Of a similar kind is the case of *Bowman v UK*,[16] and again this is not a case under Article 3, because the complaint was of a violation of Article 10, freedom of expression; but it is instructive of the attitude of the European Court on a matter which is part of the election process, in this case, limitations on the amount that can be spent on election publicity.

Mrs Bowman was a director of the SPUC, the Society for the Protection of the Unborn Child, which was opposed to abortion and human embryo experimentation and which sought to change the law which permits abortion up to 22 weeks. In the Parliamentary election of 1992, Mrs Bowman was not an election candidate; but she distributed leaflets, which assisted one of the candidates in the election. Mrs Bowman brought to the attention of electors the views and opinions of the candidates regarding abortion and related issues, by distributing leaflets in Halifax. The Representation of the People Act 1983 prohibited expenditure exceeding £5 on the conveying of information to electors with a view to promoting or procuring the election of a candidate. She was prosecuted for exceeding this figure, although she was acquitted when it was shown that the prosecution had been brought out of time. She complained to the European Court of a violation of Article 10.

The Court agreed that the prosecution was a violation of Article 10; the limitation on expenditure, to so low a figure as £5, and the subsequent prosecution, were disproportionate to the legitimate aim of pursuing and securing equality between candidates.

The picture is clear: in the context of elections Articles 9 and 10 can be as relevant as Article 3 in ensuring that overall the electoral process is fair.

PARTY POLITICAL BROADCASTS

One of the best-known modern features of general elections is the party political broadcast. It is almost an institution in itself. A broadcast of this kind is obviously 'an expression of opinion'. Again, even if Article 3 is not directly engaged, Articles 9 and 10 may well be, in a context in which they are supportive of free elections. In 2002 the Court of Appeal gave judgment in a case where the BBC had refused to allow a party political broadcast. The judgment does not refer to Article 3, but it does describe the right to free elections, and the right to freedom of political speech, in full and trenchant terms, which clearly fits in with the Convention jurisprudence. It is the case of *Pro-Life Alliance v BBC*.[17]

The Pro-Life Alliance, a political party registered under the Political Parties, Election and Referendums Act 2000, campaigned for absolute respect for human life, and opposed abortion, euthanasia, destructive embryo research and human cloning. The party sought to make a party election broadcast in May 2001, but the BBC and other broadcasters declined to transmit it, on the grounds that the content did not comply with the BBC's and Independent TV's Guidelines and Code in respect of matters of taste and decency. The Court viewed the video, and described it as 'graphic and disturbing'.

The Court of Appeal, on an application for judicial review, held that the BBC's decision was unlawful as interfering with the freedom of speech of an accredited party at a public election. This

---

[16] (1998) 26 EHRR 1.
[17] *R (Pro-Life Alliance) v British Broadcasting Corporation* [2002] 2 WLR 1080.

freedom, said the Court, must not be interfered with save on the most pressing grounds, and such grounds would very rarely be shown by appeal to considerations of taste and decency alone. Lord Justice Laws referred to the courts, in the quote at the start of this chapter, as the 'constitutional guardian of the freedom of political debate' and said:

> We are concerned with the protection of free expression in the context of political debate. In the rancour and asperity of a general election this duty, owed to the people, is surely at its highest. [This duty] has its origin in a deeper truth, which is that the courts are ultimately the trustees of our democracy's framework. [. . .]
>
>   Freedom of expression is plainly a constitutional right, and its enjoyment by an accredited political party in an election contest must call, if anything, for especially heightened protection. [Where] the context is day-to-day news reporting the broadcasters' margin of discretion may be somewhat more constrained but will remain very considerable. But the *milieu*, the cockpit of a general election, is inside the veins and arteries of the democratic process.

Lord Justice Laws referred to the fact that the BBC had declined to make the broadcast on the grounds of taste, but he said:

> There might be instances, even in the context of a general election, in which political speech may justifiably be censored on the ground of taste or offensiveness. But in my judgment it would take a very extreme case, most likely involving factors [. . .] such as gratuitous sensationalism and dishonesty. [On] the facts of this case the broadcasters have in my judgment failed altogether to give sufficient weight to the pressing imperative of free political expression.

QUESTIONS

1   Why is democracy important? Why should it matter that people are given the right to elect their government?

2   Does Article 3 provide sufficient safeguards for the democratic process?

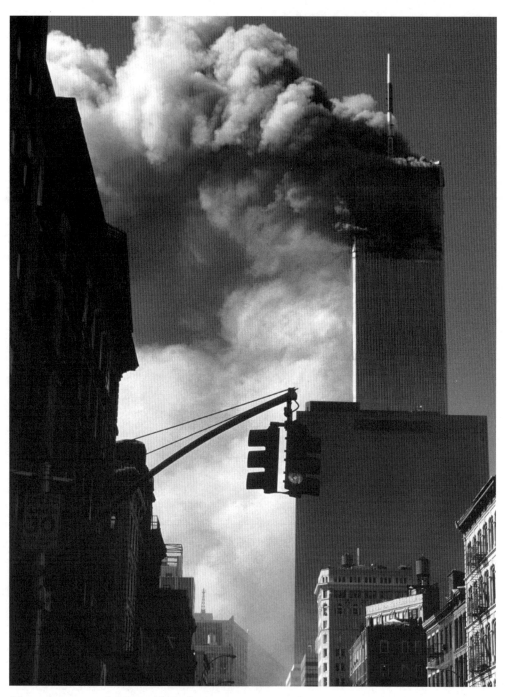

The twin towers of the World Trade Centre in New York were destroyed on 11th September 2001 by a terrorist attack which killed some 2,800 people. This prompted a legislative reaction: the Anti-terrorism Crime and Security Act 2001, discussed in this chapter.

(*Source:* Susan Meiselas/Magnum Photos)

Chapter 21

THE PROBLEM OF TERRORISM

'*Silent enim leges inter arma*' (In the midst of arms, the laws are dumb). Marcus Tullius Cicero, *Pro Milone*, 52 BCE

TERRORISM AND THE RULE OF LAW

Arms were literally surrounding the place when the Roman orator Cicero spoke those words to the court in Rome, in the midst of political crisis. The renowned general Pompey had stationed his army in the nearby Forum, and in all the temples round about. Cicero was acting as the advocate for Milo, who was charged with murdering a populist political leader and rabble-rouser, Clodius. Cicero was drawing attention to the fact that the threatening presence of Pompey's soldiers was intended to make the court forget the law and act only in accordance with the political pressure which was being put on them. He himself was reputed to be so afraid that he was shaking; and Milo was convicted.

Nowadays we would not expect courts to be deciding questions under siege, at least not in Britain, although there are recent examples from around the world, where state pressure has been brought to bear on courts to deal with real or perceived enemies of the state as the government wishes. But certainly, in time of war, when the state is under attack, the rule of law may come under strain. Exceptional measures may be thought necessary, to preserve the community from those using force against it, and the usual procedures of the law may have to be suspended.

In the United Kingdom there have, over the centuries, been a large number of instances where **emergency powers** have been passed to respond to a situation where the normal safeguards provided by the law were perceived as inhibiting the action which was needed to combat the threat. Indeed, as one looks at the history of particular legal safeguards, the development of exceptions to a particular safeguard in times of emergency often goes back as far as the development of the safeguard itself. So, for many centuries, one device used in a civil emergency was the suspension of habeas corpus, which meant that there could be no judicial scrutiny of detention of suspects; this was last used in Ireland in 1866–69. A similar measure was **martial law**, which refers to rule by military authority during a state of war. It was last used in Britain in 1780, but was invoked in Ireland in 1916 and 1920, and then in a number of colonial situations later in the twentieth century, although its use declined after the Amritsar Massacre in India in 1919, which occurred whilst martial law was in force. During both the First World

War (1914–18) and the Second World War (1939–45), there were emergency powers in force in the United Kingdom.[1]

Although a terrorism campaign does not pose as grave a threat to national security and public safety as does a full-scale war, the threat of terrorism may still be a serious one. Over the last few decades, there have been a number of terrorist bombings on mainland Britain with serious consequences, especially those committed by the Irish Republican Army (IRA) and its offshoots, and even more so in Northern Ireland. Then, of course, the events of 11 September 2001, when the twin towers of the World Trade Center in New York were destroyed by terrorists using hijacked aircraft as flying bombs, demonstrated that terrorism can be carried out on a massive scale, and that a terrorist may attack any corner of the world. Terror organisations can have the resources to do real damage, even without the backing of a state or government.

This raises the question as to whether special laws are required to deal with terrorists, and whether it is justified for these laws to interfere with human rights if necessary to tackle this threat. Because of the particular issues and problems of having to balance the need to combat a serious threat against the potential for infringements of human rights, the terrorism legislation is worth considering as a separate topic, rather than within the previous discussions of the separate articles of the Convention.

WHAT IS TERRORISM?

The first thing we should do is to define what we mean by **terrorism**. The definition adopted by section 1 of the Terrorism Act can be distilled into: the threat or use of any action which involves **serious violence** against persons or property, **endangers life**, creates a serious **risk to public health or safety** or is designed seriously to interfere with or **disrupt an electronic system**, where this action has the **purpose of intimidating or coercing** a government or the public, in order to advance a **political, religious or ideological cause**.

Thus, the emphasis is on serious violence or damage, or the threat of it, carried out for a particular cause, and aimed at the government or the public and the government or public in question need not be those of the country where the attack is carried out. The reference to electronic systems has in mind what is termed cyber-terrorism, the threat of taking advantage of our reliance nowadays on technological systems for controlling safety, such as air-traffic control, or national arms control systems.

During the passage of the Terrorism Bill, the Home Secretary said:

> Terrorism is premeditated, and aimed to create a climate of extreme fear. While the direct victims may be specific or symbolic targets, they may also be selected at random. In any event, terrorism is aimed at influencing a wider target than its immediate victims. Although all crime to some degree plainly threatens the stability of the social and political order, terrorism differs from crime motivated solely by greed, in that it is directed at undermining the foundations of Government.[2]

---

[1] We highly recommend Chapter 2 of Professor Simpson's *Human Rights and the End of Empire*, for a rather more detailed discussion of the history of emergency and martial laws in the UK and its colonies.

[2] Rt. Hon. Jack Straw M.P., *Hansard*, HC, Vol. 341, col. 152.

There are some particular situations which fall outside the statutory definition. In particular, industrial or trade disputes are not intended to be caught by the definition in the Terrorism Act. Although that is action for a political cause, aimed at influencing the government, it does not have the aim of causing harm. Indeed reference was made in Parliament to the fact that unions which represent those who provide essential services usually go to considerable lengths to seek to avoid serious risk to life, health and safety as a result of the way in which they pursue industrial disputes.[3]

Likewise ordinary political protest, of the sort we have discussed in the context of Articles 10 and 11,[4] will fall outside the definition, unless it involves serious violence. Much civil disobedience is without any violence, or it may involve only the risk of harm to the protesters themselves. In order that this latter situation does not qualify as terrorism, the reference to endangering a person's life, in the definition of terrorism in section 1, specifically excludes endangering the life of the person committing the action.

This tells us what we are talking about when we are considering measures to deal with terrorists. One could say that in such cases, we are dealing with people who are willing to cause great damage to others to make a political point, and try to intimidate a government through fear and violence, rather than through the mechanisms of debate and political expression which are the acceptable ways of influencing government. Such violence is not justifiable in a democratic society where free expression is available and so there is ample opportunity to demonstrate how one feels about an issue or situation without harming others.

DEALING WITH THE THREAT

Most acts of terrorism involve breaches of the ordinary criminal law: for example, a terrorist who uses a firearm to kill a member of the public can be charged with the usual offence of murder. But there are two particular aspects of terrorism which make it a particular threat. The first is the scale of the threat: when terrorism strikes, it is often part of a campaign, with repeated incidents committed by an organisation. The second is the nature of the threat: terrorists may be especially dangerous because they are in the category of people who clearly do not respect the rights of others to life and physical integrity.

When a campaign of violence is being pursued by terrorists, there may be a real perception that it is necessary to subordinate human rights to extraordinary laws intended to prevent or detect terrorism. This in particular is what drives governments to pass special laws to deal with it, going beyond the ordinary law of the land, and suspending the established safeguards of the law. This is what can lead to violations of human rights; either because the law itself, by its very terms, contravenes a human right, or because the way in which the law is put into effect infringes a human right.

But the fact that human rights are infringed does not *necessarily* mean that these laws are unnecessary. Perhaps breaches of human rights are justified. The threat of terrorism may be so great, at a particular time, that extraordinary measures may be

---

[3] Lord Bassam of Brighton, *Hansard*, HL, Vol. 614, col. 1449.
[4] Above, Chapters 16 and 17.

genuinely necessary to prevent them from committing outrages, or to detect the perpetrators of an attack as a matter of urgency. Measures may be considered necessary, such as powers of arrest without an offence being committed or suspected; detention without trial; an obligation to give incriminating answers to questioning; abolition of the right to remain silent in the face of an accusation; and the placing of a burden of proof on an accused person.

These sorts of far-reaching powers are examples of those which have been put in place in the United Kingdom. Parliament has passed two Acts to deal with terrorism, within a little over a year of each other. They are the Terrorism Act 2000, and the Anti-Terrorism, Crime and Security Act 2001 (which we shall refer to here as 'the Terrorism Act', 'the ATCS Act' and collectively as 'the Terrorism Acts'). Each of them contains powers which may give rise to breaches of human rights, raising the problem of balancing the threat against the potential or actual interference with a Convention right: even where the threat is serious, one must still consider whether the means chosen to deal with it are proportionate.

The courts have also recognised that terrorism may have to be treated as a special case. This comes across in the House of Lords' case of *Kebilene*, which we will consider later. And in the case of *Fox, Campbell and Hartley v UK*,[5] the European Court, considering the question of reasonable suspicion founding an arrest, said:

> What may be 'reasonable' will depend upon all the circumstances. In this respect, terrorist crime falls into a special category. Because of the attendant risk of loss of life and human suffering, the police are obliged to act with utmost urgency in following up all information, including information from secret sources. Further, the police may frequently have to arrest a suspected terrorist on the basis of information which is reliable but which cannot, without putting in jeopardy the source of the information, be revealed to the suspect or produced in court to support a charge [. . .] in view of the difficulties inherent in the investigation and prosecution of terrorist-type offences in Northern Ireland, the 'reasonableness' of the suspicion justifying such arrests cannot always be judged according to the same standards as are applied in dealing with conventional crime.

The Court in that case decided that even allowing for this being a terrorist case, insufficient facts had been shown to reach a conclusion that the arresting officer's belief was reasonable. But the important point is that terrorism may be taken into account when considering whether a measure is arbitrary or proportionate.

Both of the Terrorism Acts raise questions about how the Convention rights might be engaged by the operation of the powers they provide. We shall consider some of the ways in which the various Convention rights may be engaged by the exercise of the various powers which have been thought necessary to combat terrorism, after a short introduction to the two Acts.

THE TERRORISM ACT 2000

The Terrorism Act 2000 completely reformed the law relating to terrorist activity. It applies, with a few exceptions, to the whole of the United Kingdom, including terrorism

---

[5] (1991) 13 EHRR 157.

connected with the affairs of Northern Ireland. It also extends to terrorism abroad: it creates a wide range of offences connected with the commission of acts of terrorism outside the United Kingdom.

One of its main features is the procedure for proscribing and deproscribing an organisation. Proscription is a way of denouncing a person or organisation, by making them illegal, and is used nowadays to outlaw organisations involved in terrorism. The Terrorism Act provides for the proscription of an organisation by the Secretary of State if he believes that it is concerned in terrorism; his decision may be based upon sensitive intelligence which cannot be published or shown to the suspect. A person or organisation may appeal against the Secretary of State's decision to a Proscribed Organisations Appeal Commission. Once an organisation is proscribed, it is an offence to undertake most activity connected with it, such as being a member, or joining, supporting or funding it.

There are also specific offences relating to fundraising for terrorist organisations, using money or property for terrorism, money laundering, and failing to disclose information about such offences. Then there are also wide powers of investigation, and search procedures, including a provision requiring financial institutions to reveal details of customers and their accounts. In addition, there are specific counter-terrorist powers of stop, search, questioning and arrest.

THE ANTI-TERRORISM, CRIME AND SECURITY ACT 2001

The Terrorism Act came into force on 19 February 2001. Then on 11 September 2001 there occurred the terrorist attacks in the United States of America; these had been well planned and managed and organised, with the application of much effort and money; the terrorists who carried them out were skilled and trained, and they were supported by organisations which clearly had access to great financial resources. And they operated on an international basis. After 11 September, the general perception was that further attacks could well occur, and that they might happen anywhere in the world, and that nuclear, chemical or biological weapons might be used. Thus on 12 November 2001, the Anti-Terrorism, Crime and Security Bill was presented and read in Parliament for the first time. It was carried through Parliament with expedition: it received the Royal Assent on 14 December 2001.

One of the main provisions is the power to confiscate funds used for terrorism. There are further provisions ordering financial institutions to provide information about their customers' accounts. The assets of overseas governments and persons may be frozen, where there is a threat to the economic interests of the United Kingdom. There are provisions for the disclosure of information by public authorities and government departments to the security services.

One of the most contentious sections was a power to detain persons suspected of being international terrorists. This provision involved a derogation from Article 5 of the Convention, which we will consider below. There are also provisions which relate to the security of various industries and activities, including the security of the nuclear and aviation industries, and the regulation of transactions with nuclear, chemical and biological weapons or hazardous material.

THE RIGHT TO LIFE

Terrorism raises particular issues in the context of the right to life, because it leads to situations which are on the frontier between normal policing, and responding to an armed attack on society. There are therefore particular risks that decisions or actions will be taken which do not adequately protect the right to life, which in a civilised society should be extended in principle even to those who are acting to try to harm that society, subject to the right to defend against their attacks. Thus police officers and members of the armed forces are deployed from time to time in places and situations where terrorism is suspected, or expected, or where it has actually occurred; and in these situations, the use of force may bring about a death, or cause the risk of it.

Article 2 covers such situations, by imposing a twofold duty on the state: the positive obligation to take steps to protect life, as well as the duty to refrain from taking life. Article 2(2) provides that deprivation of life shall not be regarded as being in breach of 2(1) when it results from the use of force which is no more than absolutely necessary and strictly proportionate to protect people from violence (but *not* property), to effect an arrest, or to quell a riot or insurrection. Additionally, where death results from the acts or omissions of an agent of the state, there must be an effective official investigation into the death. It will be a matter of judging, from case to case, whether there has been effective control and management of the situation, to limit as far as possible the risk to life, in the guidance and instructions issued to the security forces, and whether there has been a proper investigation into any death which might have occurred.

These principles were illustrated in the case of *McCann*.[6] SAS soldiers shot and killed three IRA suspects in Gibraltar. The European Court held that in order to judge whether only such force was used as was absolutely necessary, there must be proper planning, control and organisation of the operation. In this case, the Court found that the planning and control of the operation failed properly to protect the right to life of the suspects, although the Court did find that there was a sufficient investigation into the deaths.

The Terrorism Acts themselves do not regulate the use of firearms or explosives by the police or armed forces. Section 114 of the Terrorism Act provides that a police officer may use reasonable force for the purpose of exercising a power given by that Act, which means that consideration of reasonable force may additionally apply to the various powers we will be considering below. Section 95 is an equivalent provision for the armed forces in Northern Ireland.

FREEDOM FROM TORTURE

Article 3 provides the right to be free of torture, inhuman or degrading treatment or punishment. We have already considered the case of *Ireland v United Kingdom*,[7] where methods used by the security forces in Northern Ireland to try to obtain information about IRA activities were held to amount to inhuman and degrading treatment. The Terrorism Acts do not contain provisions which directly threaten to infringe Article 3.

---

[6] *McCann v UK* (1996) 21 EHRR 97, considered above p. 107.

[7] (1980) 2 EHRR 25, discussed in detail above, pp. 112–13.

But there is a real temptation on the part of those investigating, or trying to prevent, serious terrorist crimes to take such steps; again, it is the mark of a civilised society not to stoop to the level of those who do *not* respect the rights of individuals to be free from physical violence.

ARREST WITHOUT WARRANT

Section 41 of the Terrorism Act provides for particular powers of detention by the police of someone suspected of being a terrorist: a constable may arrest without a warrant a person who is reasonably suspected to be a terrorist. The definition of a terrorist here includes a person who is or has been concerned in the commission, preparation, or instigation of terrorism; but these are not of themselves criminal offences. Thus a police officer making an arrest under section 41 need have no suspicion that any particular offence has been committed.

This may give rise to a violation of Article 5, the right to freedom from arbitrary detention. Article 5 contains an exhaustive list of circumstances in which a person may be justifiably deprived of their liberty.[8] The relevant ground here is (c), which permits the deprivation of liberty on 'the lawful arrest or detention of a person effected for the purpose of bringing him before the competent legal authority *on reasonable suspicion of having committed an offence . . .*' (emphasis added). Since terrorism as such is not an offence, it follows that an arrest under section 41 of a person suspected of being a terrorist may be a violation of his rights under Article 5.

This was raised in the case of *Brogan*.[9] Mr Brogan was arrested in Northern Ireland under the Prevention of Terrorism Act then in force. He was detained for 5 days and 11 hours, and then released without having been charged with any offence, or taken before a magistrate or judge. In custody, he was questioned about an offence of murder of a police officer, and about suspected membership of the Provisional IRA. He argued that he had been deprived of his liberty, but this had been in breach of Article 5(3)(c) in that he had not been arrested 'for having committed an offence'.

The European Court held that the definition of 'terrorism' (for which he *was* arrested) – namely 'the use of violence for the purpose of putting the public in fear' – was well in keeping with the idea of an offence; and in addition he was questioned about a specific offence. Thus there was no violation of Article 5.

Section 41 has not been the subject of any cases yet. However, support for the suggestion that an arrest under section 41 may well violate Article 5, comes from the following, said by Lord Lloyd, one of the Law Lords, during the debate on the Terrorism Act in Parliament:

The whole point of [*Brogan*] was that the applicants there were suspected of being members of a proscribed organisation which is a specific offence, and suspected of various other specific offences. They were not suspected of being involved generally in acts of terrorism, as the Government were at great pains to point out. It was not on that ground that the European court decided that point in favour of the United Kingdom. Therefore if the

---

[8] These are discussed in detail above, in Chapter 11.
[9] *Brogan v UK* (1989) 11 EHRR 117.

Government still rely on *Brogan* in support of that defence of [section 41] I suggest they are on very weak ground.[10]

Under section 41 and Schedule 8, there are extended periods for detention for suspected terrorists. With such measures, it will be important to ensure that the Article 5 safeguards are still applied, especially review of the detention by a proper authority. Thus, under the Terrorism Act, a detainee may be held for 48 hours before being taken before a magistrate, which may be extended to 7 days; the usual periods are 36 hours and 96 hours.[11] Likewise, a person so detained may be delayed in consulting a solicitor, or having a named person informed of his arrest, for up to 48 hours; the usual period is 30 hours.[12] There is a similar power of detention under section 53 of the Terrorism Act, for detention for questioning at a port or border: the person may be detained for up to 9 hours, and again may suffer a delay in consulting a solicitor or having a person informed of the detention. In any of these cases, there must be at least a risk that the conditions of the detention will be such that they could amount to a violation of Article 3.

PORT AND BORDER CONTROLS

The same considerations apply to section 53 and Schedule 7 of the Terrorism Act. These provide a comprehensive code for the exercise of port and border control powers and empower a police or customs officer at a port or border to stop and question a person in order to determine *whether* that person is involved in the commission, preparation, or instigation of acts of terrorism. The officer need entertain no suspicion about the person – whether of terrorism or any offence. The officer may require information, proof of identity, and disclosure of documents, and he may detain the person.

Again, therefore, there is a real possibility that detention can fall outside the list of permitted forms of detention listed in Article 5(1), and in particular that it will not fall within 5(1)(c), arrest on suspicion of having committed an offence, since no such suspicion is required. There is one case where the European Commission considered that a similar provision did fall within (b), arrest or detention in order to secure the fulfilment of an obligation prescribed by law, but the case is not easy to follow;[13] it is not clear why there is a legal obligation here. The conclusion must be that there is a real risk of a violation of Article 5 in the operation of these provisions.

DETENTION OF SUSPECTED TERRORISTS
AND THE DEROGATION

Section 21 of the ATCS Act enables the Secretary of State to certify that a person is a 'suspected international terrorist', and under section 23 the certified suspect may be detained. The reason why section 21 may conflict with Article 5 is as follows. There

---

[10] *Hansard* HL, Vol. 613, col. 677.
[11] Police and Criminal Evidence Act 1984, sections 43(5) and 44(3).
[12] Police and Criminal Evidence Act 1984, section 58(5).
[13] *McVeigh v UK* (1982) 25 DR 15.

are, says the government, foreign nationals present in this country who are suspected of being concerned in terrorism, or of having links with international terrorist groups. There are three possible ways of dealing with them. The first is to allow them to leave the country voluntarily and to return to their own country; but not many of them wish to do so, because they would return to a regime which is oppressive. The second is to prosecute them, which means that any detention would be in accordance with Article 5(1)(c); but that may not be possible, because the evidence against them is based on sensitive intelligence which cannot be presented to a court. It may also be that there has been a prosecution, which has not resulted in a conviction for some reason, but there is still a concern that the person is a terrorist; or it may even be that they have been prosecuted and convicted and served their sentence, but there is a continuing concern about the risk they pose. The third is to deport them; detention for the purpose of deportation is permitted by Article 5(1)(f); and there is power under the Immigration Act 1971 to remove or deport them, because their presence here is not conducive to the public good, on national security grounds. However, there may be reasons why deportation is not possible, because their removal or deportation would be a violation of Article 3, if they were liable to suffer torture or inhuman or degrading treatment or punishment in the destination country, or because there are practical reasons why they cannot be sent to a particular country, or reasons of international law.[14] In addition, there is European Court authority that Article 5(1)(f) requires deportation proceedings to be taken with due diligence,[15] and that cannot be guaranteed under section 21.

Thus, to detain such a person may well be a violation of Article 5, if they are not being brought before a court on suspicion of having committed an offence, or deported within a reasonable time, within Articles 5(1)(c) and (f) respectively.[16]

Nonetheless, Parliament, by section 21 of the ATCS Act, gave the Secretary of State power to certify a person to be a 'suspected international terrorist', if he reasonably believes that the person's presence in the United Kingdom is a risk to national security, and he reasonably suspects he is a terrorist. There is no requirement, before the Secretary of State issues the certificate, that any offence should have been committed. Here too, 'terrorist' is defined without reference to a specific offence, as a person who is or has been concerned in international terrorism, or is a member of or belongs to an international terrorist group, or has links with it. This power applies to foreign nationals only, not to British subjects. Once certified, the suspect may be detained under section 23 and has a right of appeal to the Special Immigration Appeals Commission (SIAC). It is in order to avoid the possibility that these powers might violate Article 5.

It is in order to avoid the possibility that these powers might violate Article 5 that the United Kingdom government has entered a **derogation** with regard to the Article in respect of these provisions, on the ground of an emergency threatening the life of the nation. The derogation[17] expressly refers to Article 5(1)(f), and indicates the view that a public emergency exists in the United Kingdom (within the meaning of Article 15)

---

[14] This is specifically covered by section 22 of the ATCS Act.

[15] *Chahal v UK* (1997) 23 EHRR 413.

[16] The purpose of a derogation is discussed above, p. 85.

[17] *The Human Rights Act 1998 (Designated Derogation) Order 2001* (SI 2001 No. 3644); the text can be found in Appendix 1.

which justifies a possible interference with Article 5 for the reasons we have discussed. This derogation took effect on 13 November 2001.

It is open to a person who complains of a violation of Article 5 to challenge the derogation, on the ground that there was *not* such a state of emergency as to justify the derogation, or that the particular circumstances were not warranted by the emergency. An example of this under a Turkish derogation is in the case of *Demir v Turkey*.[18]

Mr Demir was detained by Turkish security forces in the course of anti-terrorism operations, and he complained that his detention was unduly long. The European Court considered the point in two stages. First, it found that the local terrorism amounted to circumstances which could be described as an emergency threatening the life of the nation; but second, the detention in this particular case exceeded the extent strictly required by the nature of the crisis. Thus, they applied a test of proportionality, even to a derogation.

And indeed the relevance of proportionality was acknowledged in the case of *A v Home Secretary*,[19] where detainees appealed to the SIAC against their detention under section 23 of the ATCS Act.

A number of foreign nationals had been detained under the provisions of sections 21 and 23 of the ATCS Act, and they raised several points, in particular that their detention violated Article 3 of the Convention, because no term had been fixed for their detention; and also that it violated Article 14, since the fact that British nationals were not liable to be detained meant that there was discriminatory treatment of the applicants.

SIAC considered that a belief that the risk of a terrorist attack in the United Kingdom was greater than in other states that were also signatories to the Convention was reasonable, so the derogation was permissible under Article 15 of the Convention. SIAC rejected the detainees' claims under Article 3, stating that the mere fact that the terms were not fixed did not render their detention a breach of that article. SIAC did find, however, that there was indeed a difference of treatment that amounted to discrimination for the purposes of Article 14, and there was no reasonable relationship of proportionality between the state's objective of obviating danger from terrorism and the means employed, namely the detention of foreign nationals only.

However, the Court of Appeal disagreed with the finding on discrimination. It considered that there is an objective difference between nationals and non-nationals for the purpose of Article 14, where a non-national has no right to remain in the country but cannot be deported for their own safety. Further, there is an objectively justifiable ground for interfering only with the rights of non-nationals, based on the nature of the threat of terrorism. This is also in accordance with the established principle of international law, that states can treat non-nationals differently from nationals in times of national emergency.[20]

THE PRESUMPTION OF INNOCENCE

This is the first of two aspects of Article 6 which are particularly engaged by terrorism legislation. In our discussion of Article 6, we introduced the idea of the presumption of innocence, that it is for the prosecution to prove a criminal charge and not for the

---

[18] (2001) 33 EHRR 43.
[19] (2002) UKHRR 1141.
[20] This is the basis of Article 16, discussed above, p. 93.

defence to disprove it. We also introduced the idea of a reverse burden, where a defendant has to prove some facts which would amount to a defence to the charge, which may be evidential – a burden simply to produce some evidence raising an issue which the prosecution have to disprove – or persuasive – a burden to actually prove, as being more likely than not, that the defence is made out.[21] Such a burden is not necessarily a breach of Article 6; it depends on the particular offence.

There are a number of offences in the Terrorism Act which put reverse burdens on defendants. One example is section 57, which creates an offence where a person possesses an article in circumstances which give rise to a reasonable suspicion that it is for terrorist purposes; note that what is required here is reasonable suspicion and not proof that the item is possessed for a terrorist purpose. It is then a defence for the accused to prove that possession of the article was not for that purpose: the burden is on the defendant. Further if the article was simply on the same premises as the defendant, or on premises occupied or used by him, the court may *assume* that he was in possession of the article, unless the defendant *proves* that he did not know or have control of the article. This is a further reverse burden: before we even get to the question of purpose, the defendant may have to prove that they were *not* in possession of the article.

This provision reproduced a previous offence, which was considered in the case of *Kebilene*,[22] a case we considered in some detail in our discussion of Article 6.

The defendants were suspected Algerian terrorists, and they were found with maps and other documents on them, which could be useful in the planning of an attack. They argued that the burdens placed on them by the statute amounted to a breach of the presumption of innocence set out in Article 6(2). The House of Lords considered that an evidential burden would not infringe Article 6(2); a persuasive burden might do; although they did not find it necessary to decide which this section imposed. However, the House of Lords did specifically refer to the purpose of the statute, dealing with terrorism. Lord Hope referred to the principle that, in balancing the rights of the individual and the community, the court has to consider the nature of the threat faced by society which the provision is designed to combat.

Those who drafted the Terrorism Act took into account the House of Lords' judgment in *Kebilene*, and section 118 expressly requires the court to read certain sections of the Terrorism Act, which create offences and have a reverse burden relating to a defence, in such a way as to place upon the defendant only an evidential burden – that is, the less onerous burden. Section 57 is one such section, so the burdens imposed on a defendant by that section are burdens to adduce evidence only, not to persuade the court that the defence is made out.

For those offences to which section 118 does not apply, the court have to consider this Article 6 point, in considering what sort of burden is imposed, and in any event to ensure that the defendant has a fair trial. This is especially so where the charge is as emotive a crime as anything related to terrorism. So, for example, in one case decided in the Newcastle-upon-Tyne Crown Court, for an offence under section 11, which makes it an offence to be a member of a proscribed organisation. The judge there held that

---

[21] Discussed above, pp. 56–7, 100–2.
[22] *R v DPP, ex parte Kebilene* [2000] 2 AC 321, see above, pp. 160–1.

the burden on the defendant was only an evidential one, even though this was not a section specifically mentioned in section 118.[23]

UNKNOWN EVIDENCE

The second point under Article 6 is the right to know the case against you and be able to challenge it, which is enshrined in Article 6(3)(d). There are situations brought about by the Terrorism Acts where the defendant will not be allowed to know who is giving evidence against them, or what that evidence is. In the process of proscription and deproscription under the Terrorism Act, the Secretary of State may act on sensitive and secret intelligence, which cannot be revealed to the individual or organisation being proscribed. The same applies in the process of certifying a suspected international terrorist under section 21 of the ATCS Act. In both instances an advocate can be appointed to represent the interests of the person or organisation. The advocate may see or hear the sensitive intelligence, but may not communicate it to the person represented.

The European Court has considered this kind of situation, where the defendant or person affected may not hear all the evidence, and the decisions of the Court have shown that it is not necessarily a violation of Article 6. Provided that there is an adequate framework, or system, for monitoring the decision, it will not necessarily be unfair, even though the evidence is given against a person in their absence. Thus, the procedure is likely to be more fair if it is a court rather than an administrative or executive officer making the decision, provided the court sees or hears the whole of the evidence, and can make a fair decision about whether the subject should be informed of the sensitive information. The court will, of course, bear in mind the subject's own rights, especially the right to a fair trial and the right to respect for their private life.

PRECISION IN THE LAW

Article 7 is defined in terms of freedom from punishment without law, which is primarily concerned with freedom from being held guilty under retrospective legislation. But Article 7 also underlines the principle of Convention law that the law should be clear and precise and its effect foreseeable.[24] It is upon this latter aspect that we now concentrate, because the term 'terrorist', used in both the Terrorism Acts, is vague and imprecise, and therefore, at least arguably, its meaning is not foreseeable.

The essence of this point is that the definition of 'terrorism' does not refer to any specific offence, and terrorism is not itself an offence. The definition of 'terrorism' relies upon ingredients of violence or the threat of it, in order to influence the government or the public for a political or similar cause. There is no requirement of the commission of a particular offence, which makes the meaning of the term uncertain.

The Terrorism Act then uses the term 'terrorist investigation', meaning an investigation into acts of terrorism, the resources of a proscribed organisation, and so on. If an investigation is a terrorist investigation, a number of specific powers for the investigation and detection of terrorism and terrorist activity apply. Again, there is

---

[23] *R v Abdellah*, unreported, 22 May 2002; HH Judge Hodson.
[24] See above, Chapter 13.

no requirement that a specific criminal offence should be investigated or even suspected, which means that this term too is imprecise.

So, for example, to support a terrorist investigation, the police may obtain a warrant to enter premises, or a court order for the production of documents, or the explanation of documents; this is provided by section 37 and Schedule 5 of the Terrorism Act; and there are offences connected with these powers. Likewise, for the purposes of a terrorist investigation, the police may obtain a court order under section 38 and Schedules 6 and 6A of the Terrorism Act requiring financial institutions to give details of their customers and accounts. Section 19 of the Terrorism Act makes it an offence for a person to fail to disclose their knowledge, belief or suspicion that an offence has been committed relating to fundraising or money laundering for terrorist purposes. Under section 1 of the ATCS Act, money may be forfeited where it is intended for terrorist purposes, or was obtained by terrorism. All these powers and offences are rooted in the definition of terrorism, which requires no specific offence to be proved to substantiate the allegation that terrorism is involved.

Finally, under section 4 of the ATCS Act, the Treasury has the power to make an order to freeze the assets of persons or governments overseas, whom the Treasury reasonably believes are acting to the detriment of the economy of the United Kingdom, or constituting a threat to the life or property of nationals of the United Kingdom. It will be realised at once that the conditions allowing the making of such an order are vague, and again there is no requirement that there should be any suspicion of criminal activity, let alone that actual criminal activity be proven.

DISCLOSURE OF INFORMATION

Here we are considering the rights protected by Article 8, respect for private life. Article 8 will be engaged by some of the procedures and orders to which we have just referred, the entry, search and seizure and financial information provisions in Schedules 5, 6, and 6A of the Terrorism Act, because all of these relate to private information. The provisions on forfeiture of money and freezing orders under sections 1 and 4 of the ATCS Act will engage Article 8, and also Article 1 of the First Protocol, since they are also an interference with the enjoyment of property. In all these situations, there may be an infringement of these articles if an order is made which is not reasonably necessary and proportionate, albeit taking into account the nature of the threat of terrorism, following the principles set out in *Fox, Campbell and Hartley* and *Kebilene*. They may also fall foul of these articles for the same reason they may fall foul of Article 7, if they are too vague to be 'in accordance with the law', that is, if they offend the principle of legality. There is, however, some guidance for some of the provisions which involve questioning suspects, taking audio and video recordings of interviews and the forfeiture of terrorist money, because in these areas the Terrorism Act requires the issuing of codes of conduct. These will provide some standards on whether particular conduct is proper or not, whether or not it should be considered arbitrary or disproportionate.

However, there are also further provisions which engage Article 8. One is covered by those parts of the ATCS Act which deals with the retention of communications data, intrusions by the state into information on telephone, postal, or electronic communications.

Communications providers – the postal or telephone authorities, or Internet service providers in the case of e-mail – commonly maintain records relating to the use of their services. This is 'communications data' – the information on a customer's telephone bill, the address of a website visited by a customer, the date, time, and title of an e-mail, and the identities of the sender and recipient. It does *not* include the contents of the telephone call or e-mail message. The providers may retain it for commercial purposes, but if it is retained for any other purpose, it must be made anonymous. Under the Regulation of Investigatory Powers Act 2000, law-enforcement agencies may gain access to such data, for the purpose of protecting national security, economic wellbeing, public safety or health, preventing crime or preventing death or damage, or collecting taxes. There is no statutory requirement that this data should be retained for any particular period.

Sections 102 to 107 of the ATCS Act enable the Secretary of State to issue codes of practice for the retention of data on grounds of national security, or for the prevention or detection of crime or for the prosecution of offenders, when the crime or the offender affects national security. The Act provides, in the first instance, for a voluntary agreement as to the codes of practice, but if this does not operate satisfactorily, the Secretary of State may impose a regime. No violation of Article 8 arises from these sections themselves. However, this is another situation where any disclosure by a communications provider may well violate their customer's right under Article 8, and therefore must be strictly justified, and must be proportionate. In order to assist in the assessment of what is proper conduct in this area, section 102 provides for a code of practice for the retention of communications data.

There is a further power in the ATCS Act which relates to the disclosure of information, and that is section 17, which extends the power of security services to obtain access to private information; it enlarges the number of sources which they may use in order to obtain intelligence.

This section inserts a new provision into the statutes which create a number of public authorities, set out in Schedule 4. For example, the Harbours Act 1964 makes provision for a National Ports Council, and the Airports Act 1986 for the Civil Aviation Authority. Each of these is authorised by the statute creating it to make enquiries and to obtain information, in order to assist its usual functions. In each case the statute provides that this information shall not be disclosed, by the public authority, to a third person, except for particular reasons, such as for the proper functioning of the authority, or for legal proceedings, or with the consent of the person originally providing the information.

Section 17 of the ATCS Act provides that each of the statutes listed in the schedule should be amended so as to permit disclosure for the purposes of assisting *any* criminal investigation or criminal proceedings in the United Kingdom, or abroad, or to assist in the task of deciding whether *any* investigation or proceedings should begin or end. It may be that no criminal offence has been committed, or that there is no suspicion of any offence; and disclosure is permitted even before an investigation has started. The wording of section 17(2) will cover an investigation into conduct falling within section 41 of the Terrorism Act, 'a person suspected to be a terrorist', which may be conduct not even amounting to an offence.

The provisions of this section are available in terrorism cases, but they are not limited to such cases; the disclosure of information may be made for the purpose of *any* criminal proceedings. No order of the court is necessary. And there is no provision for any subsequent check by any supervisory authority.

Clearly, proportionality is essential to the exercise of the powers under this section. There will be a violation of Article 8 on any disclosure of information under section 17, and that disclosure must be justified under Article 8(2). Also, a disclosure may produce material which is later used in evidence in a trial; if the disclosure is in violation of Article 8, the use of the evidence may make the trial unfair, in breach of Article 6. All this is indeed reflected in the section itself; section 17(5) of the ATCS Act provides that no disclosure shall be made under this section unless the public authority doing so is satisfied that the making of the disclosure is *proportionate* to what is sought to be achieved by it. The policing of this power is vital to ensuring that its use is properly restrained, since in principle, it could be a very serious invasion of privacy.

FREEDOM OF ASSOCIATION

An order under section 3 of the Terrorism Act, proscribing an organisation, makes the organisation illegal, and it is unlawful to be a member of it. In effect, a person is prohibited from joining. That will engage Article 11; there will be an interference with the freedom of association.

The next question is whether the interference is justified under Article 11(2). The Secretary of State has power to proscribe an organisation if he 'believes that it is concerned in terrorism' (section 3(4)). The test is a subjective one; there is no condition that he must 'reasonably believe'. But an organisation or person affected by his decision may appeal to the Proscribed Organisations Appeal Commission, and the appeal will be decided in the light of the principles of judicial review (section 5(3)); therefore, the principles of the European Convention will apply. Here too, at all stages, the use of the power must be proportionate and must not be arbitrary.

QUESTIONS

1   Should terrorism be a special case? Do you agree with the principles which are used to justify special provisions to deal with terrorists?
2   Considering the particular measures which have been adopted, do they meet the standards of being necessary and proportionate interferences with the various Convention rights we have discussed, and why/why not? What is your overall assessment?

Chapter 22

CONCLUSION

'There are two things which I am confident I can do very well: one is an introduction to any literary work, stating what it is to contain, and how it should be executed in the most perfect manner; the other is a conclusion, shewing from various causes why the execution has not been equal to what the author promised to himself and to the public.' (Samuel Johnson, 1755)

So there it is: the Human Rights Act 1998, and the rights set out in the European Convention on Human Rights. We hope that you now have an understanding of the basic principles of the Act, and of the way in which the Convention rights are to be analysed, as well as some understanding of the different areas in which the Act will affect United Kingdom law.

The passing of this Act should not make us complacent. The fact that there is statutory recognition of a number of basic rights – including, it should be said, the most fundamental, the rights to life and personal security and liberty – should not prevent us from considering whether other rights should be accepted in the same way. Should our law recognise a right to social security? A positive right to a free education? Should there be a general right to freedom of information? These are not easy questions, so we will not try to give quick answers. But the incorporation of the Convention is a welcome step, and a fine starting point for ensuring the greater protection of individual rights. The United Kingdom helped to draft the Convention and was the first to ratify it. The delay in allowing it to be used in our courts has led to a rather greater number of decisions against the United Kingdom in the European Court than there should have been. Our courts now have the opportunity to make their own contribution to the wider debate on rights, and to allow the Convention to permeate our law.

We should not expect the effects of the Act to be felt overnight, or even within only a few years: anyone who expected the Act to work immediate and radical alterations to our law was, predictably, incorrect. If our law so badly failed to protect the basic rights of its citizens that the Act was required to create basic rights, then there would have been a political outcry for its implementation long ago. The view of the British civil servants involved in the drafting of the Convention in 1950 was broadly correct, that it embodied, in the main, basic principles and underlying rights, which are to be found in our law – although their view that English law adequately protected all those rights was seriously deficient, as the European Court has shown.

However, neither has the Act been a 'damp squib'. We have seen, in our discussion of the individual Convention rights, a whole host of areas where the Convention jurisprudence has forced a reassessment of the previous law, the standards applied to everyday decisions and situations, the way in which the courts scrutinise governmental decisions and actions. Whilst the effects have been mostly incremental, that is what one would expect from the way our common law develops. There have been significant departures from the previous law in some areas – perhaps the most notable is the courts' newfound ability to protect the right to privacy, something which they had quite obviously felt unable to do before the Act was passed.

It has also provided an important new ground for the scrutiny of executive action. This is perhaps the main effect of the Act: to oblige the courts to consider cases concerning basic rights in a more substantive way than they did before, applying the principles developed by the European Court, of balance, legality and proportionality. The government is now required to justify its actions and decisions more closely. Before the Act, if a decision was lawful and within the bounds of a 'reasonable' decision, it could not be challenged. Now, the courts expect a more substantive justification if a Convention right is at stake. This has been expressly recognised:

> The intensity of review is somewhat greater under the proportionality approach. [The] doctrine of proportionality may require the reviewing Court to assess the balance which the decision maker has struck [. . . and] attention to be directed to the relative weight accorded to interests and considerations.[1]

Although there was a growing tendency, even before the Act, to give more recognition to basic rights,[2] this has been accelerated and brought into focus by the express provisions of the Act.

In all cases, there is also a greater identification of issues of rights, a focus in the argument before the courts, in cases in which basic rights are at stake. This is one of the benefits we identified at the outset of this book: rights are not the end of the matter, since one must also consider duties and the rights of others, but discussion in terms of rights ensures that no-one's rights are ridden over roughshod.

But none of this means that there has been, or is likely to be, a wholesale shift in power from Parliament and the executive to the courts. Our judges are acutely aware of the potential political difficulties the Act could get them into. The Act's preservation of Parliamentary sovereignty means that Parliament – the elected representatives of the people – ultimately has the last word. And then there is the important idea of judicial deference, allowing that where there is a range of acceptable solutions to a problem, it may be appropriate to accept the view of Parliament or the person or body who is best placed to consider the matter. So long as deference does not stifle judicial protection of rights, this plays an important part in keeping judges from areas which are not appropriate to their form of decision-making. And it does not appear to have stifled such protection so far, although there have been some decisions which may suggest a tendency towards an over-deferential attitude.

This again is another benefit of the Act, which is in its own way profoundly democratic. The process of getting legislation through Parliament is so slow, especially for

---

[1] Lord Steyn in *R (Daly) v Secretary of State for the Home Department* [2001] 2 AC 532 at 547.
[2] Some examples can be found above, pp. 44 and 54.

matters which may be important in principle, but are not high in political priority, that the incorporation of the Convention means that the courts at least provide a forum for questions of rights affecting individuals to be aired. The benefit to democracy in society is that at least questions concerning basic rights can now be argued by litigation in the public forum of the courts – and if Parliament doesn't like the result, it will have to do something about it.

In many ways, the Act has been a breath of fresh air for the law. It has forced a rethink in a whole variety of areas. It provides an opportunity for the courts, the lawyers, journalists, academics, and the public as a whole to consider whether the law *really does* protect the rights that we tend to assume we have. It would be stating the position too strongly to say that the courts have in fact immediately begun the 'fundamental process of review and, where necessary, reform by the judiciary' which Lord Hope referred to in *Kebilene*.[3] But the potential is there. We hope that this process will continue, and that our judges will continue gradually to review and develop our law against the benchmark of the Convention rights.

---

[3] [2000] 2 AC 326 at 375.

THE HUMAN RIGHTS ACT 1998

An Act to give further effect to rights and freedoms guaranteed under the European Convention on Human Rights; to make provision with respect to holders of certain judicial offices who become judges of the European Court of Human Rights; and for connected purposes.

[9th November 1998]

BE IT ENACTED by the Queen's most Excellent Majesty, by and with the advice and consent of the Lords Spiritual and Temporal, and Commons, in this present Parliament assembled, and by the authority of the same, as follows: –

INTRODUCTION

The Convention rights

1. – (1) In this Act 'the Convention rights' means the rights and fundamental freedoms set out in –
  (a)   Articles 2 to 12 and 14 of the Convention,
  (b)   Articles 1 to 3 of the First Protocol, and
  (c)   Articles 1 and 2 of the Sixth Protocol,
  as read with Articles 16 to 18 of the Convention.
(2)   Those Articles are to have effect for the purposes of this Act subject to any designated derogation or reservation (as to which see sections 14 and 15).
(3)   The Articles are set out in Schedule 1.
(4)   The Lord Chancellor[1] may by order make such amendments to this Act as he considers appropriate to reflect the effect, in relation to the United Kingdom, of a protocol.
(5)   In subsection (4) 'protocol' means a protocol to the Convention –
  (a)   which the United Kingdom has ratified; or
  (b)   which the United Kingdom has signed with a view to ratification.
(6)   No amendment may be made by an order under subsection (4) so as to come into force before the protocol concerned is in force in relation to the United Kingdom.

---

[1] Substituted for 'Secretary of State' by the Transfer of Functions (Miscellaneous) Order 2001 (SI 2001 No. 3500).

Interpretation of Convention rights

2. – (1)   A court or tribunal determining a question which has arisen in connection with a Convention right must take into account any –

(a)   judgment, decision, declaration or advisory opinion of the European Court of Human Rights,

(b)   opinion of the Commission given in a report adopted under Article 31 of the Convention,

(c)   decision of the Commission in connection with Article 26 or 27(2) of the Convention, or

(d)   decision of the Committee of Ministers taken under Article 46 of the Convention,

whenever made or given, so far as, in the opinion of the court or tribunal, it is relevant to the proceedings in which that question has arisen.

(2)   Evidence of any judgment, decision, declaration or opinion of which account may have to be taken under this section is to be given in proceedings before any court or tribunal in such manner as may be provided by rules.

(3)   In this section 'rules' means rules of court or, in the case of proceedings before a tribunal, rules made for the purposes of this section –

(a)   by the Lord Chancellor or the Secretary of State, in relation to any proceedings outside Scotland;

(b)   by the Secretary of State, in relation to proceedings in Scotland; or

(c)   by a Northern Ireland department, in relation to proceedings before a tribunal in Northern Ireland –

(i)   which deals with transferred matters; and

(ii)   for which no rules made under paragraph (a) are in force.

LEGISLATION

Interpretation of legislation

3. – (1)   So far as it is possible to do so, primary legislation and subordinate legislation must be read and given effect in a way which is compatible with the Convention rights.

(2)   This section –

(a)   applies to primary legislation and subordinate legislation whenever enacted;

(b)   does not affect the validity, continuing operation or enforcement of any incompatible primary legislation; and

(c)   does not affect the validity, continuing operation or enforcement of any incompatible subordinate legislation if (disregarding any possibility of revocation) primary legislation prevents removal of the incompatibility.

Declaration of incompatibility

4. – (1)   Subsection (2) applies in any proceedings in which a court determines whether a provision of primary legislation is compatible with a Convention right.

(2)   If the court is satisfied that the provision is incompatible with a Convention right, it may make a declaration of that incompatibility.

(3) Subsection (4) applies in any proceedings in which a court determines whether a provision of subordinate legislation, made in the exercise of a power conferred by primary legislation, is compatible with a Convention right.

(4) If the court is satisfied –
(a) that the provision is incompatible with a Convention right, and
(b) that (disregarding any possibility of revocation) the primary legislation concerned prevents removal of the incompatibility,
it may make a declaration of that incompatibility.

(5) In this section 'court' means –
(a) the House of Lords;
(b) the Judicial Committee of the Privy Council;
(c) the Courts-Martial Appeal Court;
(d) in Scotland, the High Court of Justiciary sitting otherwise than as a trial court or the Court of Session;
(e) in England and Wales or Northern Ireland, the High Court or the Court of Appeal.

(6) A declaration under this section ('a declaration of incompatibility') –
(a) does not affect the validity, continuing operation or enforcement of the provision in respect of which it is given; and
(b) is not binding on the parties to the proceedings in which it is made.

Right of Crown to intervene

5. – (1) Where a court is considering whether to make a declaration of incompatibility, the Crown is entitled to notice in accordance with rules of court.

(2) In any case to which subsection (1) applies –
(a) a Minister of the Crown (or a person nominated by him),
(b) a member of the Scottish Executive,
(c) a Northern Ireland Minister,
(d) a Northern Ireland department,
is entitled, on giving notice in accordance with rules of court, to be joined as a party to the proceedings.

(3) Notice under subsection (2) may be given at any time during the proceedings.

(4) A person who has been made a party to criminal proceedings (other than in Scotland) as the result of a notice under subsection (2) may, with leave, appeal to the House of Lords against any declaration of incompatibility made in the proceedings.

(5) In subsection (4) –
'criminal proceedings' includes all proceedings before the Courts-Martial Appeal Court; and 'leave' means leave granted by the court making the declaration of incompatibility or by the House of Lords.

PUBLIC AUTHORITIES

Acts of public authorities

6. – (1) It is unlawful for a public authority to act in a way which is incompatible with a Convention right.

(2) Subsection (1) does not apply to an act if –
    (a) as the result of one or more provisions of primary legislation, the authority could not have acted differently; or
    (b) in the case of one or more provisions of, or made under, primary legislation which cannot be read or given effect in a way which is compatible with the Convention rights, the authority was acting so as to give effect to or enforce those provisions.
(3) In this section 'public authority' includes –
    (a) a court or tribunal, and
    (b) any person certain of whose functions are functions of a public nature, but does not include either House of Parliament or a person exercising functions in connection with proceedings in Parliament.
(4) In subsection (3) 'Parliament' does not include the House of Lords in its judicial capacity.
(5) In relation to a particular act, a person is not a public authority by virtue only of subsection (3)(b) if the nature of the act is private.
(6) 'An act' includes a failure to act but does not include a failure to –
    (a) introduce in, or lay before, Parliament a proposal for legislation; or
    (b) make any primary legislation or remedial order.

Proceedings

7. – (1) A person who claims that a public authority has acted (or proposes to act) in a way which is made unlawful by section 6(1) may –
    (a) bring proceedings against the authority under this Act in the appropriate court or tribunal, or
    (b) rely on the Convention right or rights concerned in any legal proceedings, but only if he is (or would be) a victim of the unlawful act.
(2) In subsection (1)(a) 'appropriate court or tribunal' means such court or tribunal as may be determined in accordance with rules; and proceedings against an authority include a counterclaim or similar proceeding.
(3) If the proceedings are brought on an application for judicial review, the applicant is to be taken to have a sufficient interest in relation to the unlawful act only if he is, or would be, a victim of that act.
(4) If the proceedings are made by way of a petition for judicial review in Scotland, the applicant shall be taken to have title and interest to sue in relation to the unlawful act only if he is, or would be, a victim of that act.
(5) Proceedings under subsection (1)(a) must be brought before the end of –
    (a) the period of one year beginning with the date on which the act complained of took place; or
    (b) such longer period as the court or tribunal considers equitable having regard to all the circumstances, but that is subject to any rule imposing a stricter time limit in relation to the procedure in question.
(6) In subsection (1)(b) 'legal proceedings' includes –
    (a) proceedings brought by or at the instigation of a public authority; and
    (b) an appeal against the decision of a court or tribunal.

(7) For the purposes of this section, a person is a victim of an unlawful act only if he would be a victim for the purposes of Article 34 of the Convention if proceedings were brought in the European Court of Human Rights in respect of that act.

(8) Nothing in this Act creates a criminal offence.

(9) In this section 'rules' means –
   (a) in relation to proceedings before a court or tribunal outside Scotland, rules made by the Lord Chancellor or the Secretary of State for the purposes of this section or rules of court,
   (b) in relation to proceedings before a court or tribunal in Scotland, rules made by the Secretary of State for those purposes,
   (c) in relation to proceedings before a tribunal in Northern Ireland –
      (i)   which deals with transferred matters; and
      (ii) for which no rules made under paragraph (a) are in force,
   rules made by a Northern Ireland department for those purposes,
   and includes provision made by order under section 1 of the Courts and Legal Services Act 1990.

(10) In making rules, regard must be had to section 9.

(11) The Minister who has power to make rules in relation to a particular tribunal may, to the extent he considers it necessary to ensure that the tribunal can provide an appropriate remedy in relation to an act (or proposed act) of a public authority which is (or would be) unlawful as a result of section 6(1), by order add to –
   (a) the relief or remedies which the tribunal may grant; or
   (b) the grounds on which it may grant any of them.

(12) An order made under subsection (11) may contain such incidental, supplemental, consequential or transitional provision as the Minister making it considers appropriate.

(13) 'The Minister' includes the Northern Ireland department concerned.

Judicial remedies

8. – (1) In relation to any act (or proposed act) of a public authority which the court finds is (or would be) unlawful, it may grant such relief or remedy, or make such order, within its powers as it considers just and appropriate.

(2) But damages may be awarded only by a court which has power to award damages, or to order the payment of compensation, in civil proceedings.

(3) No award of damages is to be made unless, taking account of all the circumstances of the case, including –
   (a) any other relief or remedy granted, or order made, in relation to the act in question (by that or any other court), and
   (b) the consequences of any decision (of that or any other court) in respect of that act,
   the court is satisfied that the award is necessary to afford just satisfaction to the person in whose favour it is made.

(4) In determining –
   (a) whether to award damages, or
   (b) the amount of an award,

the court must take into account the principles applied by the European Court of Human Rights in relation to the award of compensation under Article 41 of the Convention.

(5) A public authority against which damages are awarded is to be treated –

(a) in Scotland, for the purposes of section 3 of the Law Reform (Miscellaneous Provisions) (Scotland) Act 1940 as if the award were made in an action of damages in which the authority has been found liable in respect of loss or damage to the person to whom the award is made;

(b) for the purposes of the Civil Liability (Contribution) Act 1978 as liable in respect of damage suffered by the person to whom the award is made.

(6) In this section –

'court' includes a tribunal;

'damages' means damages for an unlawful act of a public authority; and

'unlawful' means unlawful under section 6(1).

9. – (1) Proceedings under section 7(1)(a) in respect of a judicial act may be brought only –

(a) by exercising a right of appeal;

(b) on an application (in Scotland a petition) for judicial review; or

(c) in such other forum as may be prescribed by rules.

(2) That does not affect any rule of law which prevents a court from being the subject of judicial review.

(3) In proceedings under this Act in respect of a judicial act done in good faith, damages may not be awarded otherwise than to compensate a person to the extent required by Article 5(5) of the Convention.

(4) An award of damages permitted by subsection (3) is to be made against the Crown; but no award may be made unless the appropriate person, if not a party to the proceedings, is joined.

(5) In this section –

'appropriate person' means the Minister responsible for the court concerned, or a person or government department nominated by him;

'court' includes a tribunal;

'judge' includes a member of a tribunal, a justice of the peace and a clerk or other officer entitled to exercise the jurisdiction of a court;

'judicial act' means a judicial act of a court and includes an act done on the instructions, or on behalf, of a judge; and

'rules' has the same meaning as in section 7(9).

REMEDIAL ACTION

Power to take remedial action

10. – (1) This section applies if –

(a) a provision of legislation has been declared under section 4 to be incompatible with a Convention right and, if an appeal lies –

(i) all persons who may appeal have stated in writing that they do not intend to do so;

(ii) the time for bringing an appeal has expired and no appeal has been brought within that time; or

(iii) an appeal brought within that time has been determined or abandoned; or

(b) it appears to a Minister of the Crown or Her Majesty in Council that, having regard to a finding of the European Court of Human Rights made after the coming into force of this section in proceedings against the United Kingdom, a provision of legislation is incompatible with an obligation of the United Kingdom arising from the Convention.

(2) If a Minister of the Crown considers that there are compelling reasons for proceeding under this section, he may by order make such amendments to the legislation as he considers necessary to remove the incompatibility.

(3) If, in the case of subordinate legislation, a Minister of the Crown considers –

(a) that it is necessary to amend the primary legislation under which the subordinate legislation in question was made, in order to enable the incompatibility to be removed, and

(b) that there are compelling reasons for proceeding under this section,

he may by order make such amendments to the primary legislation as he considers necessary.

(4) This section also applies where the provision in question is in subordinate legislation and has been quashed, or declared invalid, by reason of incompatibility with a Convention right and the Minister proposes to proceed under paragraph 2(b) of Schedule 2.

(5) If the legislation is an Order in Council, the power conferred by subsection (2) or (3) is exercisable by Her Majesty in Council.

(6) In this section 'legislation' does not include a Measure of the Church Assembly or of the General Synod of the Church of England.

(7) Schedule 2 makes further provision about remedial orders.

OTHER RIGHTS AND PROCEEDINGS

Safeguard for existing human rights

11. A person's reliance on a Convention right does not restrict –

(a) any other right or freedom conferred on him by or under any law having effect in any part of the United Kingdom; or

(b) his right to make any claim or bring any proceedings which he could make or bring apart from sections 7 to 9.

Freedom of expression

12. – (1) This section applies if a court is considering whether to grant any relief which, if granted, might affect the exercise of the Convention right to freedom of expression.

(2) If the person against whom the application for relief is made ('the respondent') is neither present nor represented, no such relief is to be granted unless the court is satisfied –

(a) that the applicant has taken all practicable steps to notify the respondent; or

(b) that there are compelling reasons why the respondent should not be notified.

(3) No such relief is to be granted so as to restrain publication before trial unless the court is satisfied that the applicant is likely to establish that publication should not be allowed.

(4) The court must have particular regard to the importance of the Convention right to freedom of expression and, where the proceedings relate to material which the respondent claims, or which appears to the court, to be journalistic, literary or artistic material (or to conduct connected with such material), to –

(a) the extent to which –

(i)   the material has, or is about to, become available to the public; or

(ii) it is, or would be, in the public interest for the material to be published;

(b) any relevant privacy code.

(5) In this section –

'court' includes a tribunal; and

'relief' includes any remedy or order (other than in criminal proceedings).

Freedom of thought, conscience and religion

13. – (1) If a court's determination of any question arising under this Act might affect the exercise by a religious organisation (itself or its members collectively) of the Convention right to freedom of thought, conscience and religion, it must have particular regard to the importance of that right.

(2) In this section 'court' includes a tribunal.

DEROGATIONS AND RESERVATIONS

Derogations

14.[2] – (1) In this Act 'designated derogation' means any derogation by the United Kingdom from an Article of the Convention, or of any protocol to the Convention, which is designated for the purposes of this Act in an order made by the Lord Chancellor.[3]

(2) [. . .][2]

(3) If a designated derogation is amended or replaced it ceases to be a designated derogation.

(4) But subsection (3) does not prevent the Lord Chancellor from exercising his power under subsection (1) to make a fresh designation order in respect of the Article concerned.

---

[2] The Human Rights Act (Amendment) Order 2001 (SI 2001 No. 1216) amended this section to remove the reference to the previous derogation to Article 5(3), including the removal of subsection (2).

[3] Substituted for 'Secretary of State' in this section by the Transfer of Functions (Miscellaneous) Order 2001 (SI 2001 No. 3500).

(5) The Lord Chancellor must by order make such amendments to Schedule 3 as he considers appropriate to reflect –
(a) any designation order; or
(b) the effect of subsection (3).

(6) A designation order may be made in anticipation of the making by the United Kingdom of a proposed derogation.

Reservations

15. – (1) In this Act 'designated reservation' means –
(a) the United Kingdom's reservation to Article 2 of the First Protocol to the Convention; and
(b) any other reservation by the United Kingdom to an Article of the Convention, or of any protocol to the Convention, which is designated for the purposes of this Act in an order made by the Lord Chancellor.[4]

(2) The text of the reservation referred to in subsection (1)(a) is set out in Part II of Schedule 3.

(3) If a designated reservation is withdrawn wholly or in part it ceases to be a designated reservation.

(4) But subsection (3) does not prevent the Lord Chancellor from exercising his power under subsection (1)(b) to make a fresh designation order in respect of the Article concerned.

(5) The Lord Chancellor must by order make such amendments to this Act as he considers appropriate to reflect –
(a) any designation order; or
(b) the effect of subsection (3).

Period for which designated derogations have effect

16.[5] – (1) If it has not already been withdrawn by the United Kingdom, a designated derogation ceases to have effect for the purposes of this Act at the end of the period of five years beginning with the date on which the order designating it was made.

(2) At any time before the period –
(a) fixed by subsection (1), or
(b) extended by an order under this subsection,
comes to an end, the Lord Chancellor[6] may by order extend it by a further period of five years.

(3) An order under section 14(1) ceases to have effect at the end of the period for consideration, unless a resolution has been passed by each House approving the order.

---

[4] Substituted for 'Secretary of State' in this section by the Transfer of Functions (Miscellaneous) Order 2001 (SI 2001 No. 3500).
[5] As amended by the Human Rights Act (Amendment) Order 2001 (SI 2001 No. 1216).
[6] Substituted for 'Secretary of State' in this section by the Transfer of Functions (Miscellaneous) Order 2001 (SI 2001 No. 3500).

(4) Subsection (3) does not affect –
    (a) anything done in reliance on the order; or
    (b) the power to make a fresh order under section 14(1).

(5) In subsection (3) 'period for consideration' means the period of forty days beginning with the day on which the order was made.

(6) In calculating the period for consideration, no account is to be taken of any time during which –
    (a) Parliament is dissolved or prorogued; or
    (b) both Houses are adjourned for more than four days.

(7) If a designated derogation is withdrawn by the United Kingdom, the Lord Chancellor must by order make such amendments to this Act as he considers are required to reflect that withdrawal.

Periodic review of designated reservations

17. – (1) The appropriate Minister must review the designated reservation referred to in section 15(1)(a) –
    (a) before the end of the period of five years beginning with the date on which section 1(2) came into force; and
    (b) if that designation is still in force, before the end of the period of five years beginning with the date on which the last report relating to it was laid under subsection (3).

(2) The appropriate Minister must review each of the other designated reservations (if any) –
    (a) before the end of the period of five years beginning with the date on which the order designating the reservation first came into force; and
    (b) if the designation is still in force, before the end of the period of five years beginning with the date on which the last report relating to it was laid under subsection (3).

(3) The Minister conducting a review under this section must prepare a report on the result of the review and lay a copy of it before each House of Parliament.

JUDGES OF THE EUROPEAN COURT OF HUMAN RIGHTS

Appointment to European Court of Human Rights

18. – (1) In this section 'judicial office' means the office of –
    (a) Lord Justice of Appeal, Justice of the High Court or Circuit judge, in England and Wales;
    (b) judge of the Court of Session or sheriff, in Scotland;
    (c) Lord Justice of Appeal, judge of the High Court or county court judge, in Northern Ireland.

(2) The holder of a judicial office may become a judge of the European Court of Human Rights ('the Court') without being required to relinquish his office.

(3) But he is not required to perform the duties of his judicial office while he is a judge of the Court.

(4) In respect of any period during which he is a judge of the Court –
    (a) a Lord Justice of Appeal or Justice of the High Court is not to count as a judge of the relevant court for the purposes of section 2(1) or 4(1) of the Supreme Court Act 1981 (maximum number of judges) nor as a judge of the Supreme Court for the purposes of section 12(1) to (6) of that Act (salaries etc.);
    (b) a judge of the Court of Session is not to count as a judge of that court for the purposes of section 1(1) of the Court of Session Act 1988 (maximum number of judges) or of section 9(1)(c) of the Administration of Justice Act 1973 ('the 1973 Act') (salaries etc.);
    (c) a Lord Justice of Appeal or judge of the High Court in Northern Ireland is not to count as a judge of the relevant court for the purposes of section 2(1) or 3(1) of the Judicature (Northern Ireland) Act 1978 (maximum number of judges) nor as a judge of the Supreme Court of Northern Ireland for the purposes of section 9(1)(d) of the 1973 Act (salaries etc.);
    (d) a Circuit judge is not to count as such for the purposes of section 18 of the Courts Act 1971 (salaries etc.);
    (e) a sheriff is not to count as such for the purposes of section 14 of the Sheriff Courts (Scotland) Act 1907 (salaries etc.);
    (f) a county court judge of Northern Ireland is not to count as such for the purposes of section 106 of the County Courts Act (Northern Ireland) 1959 (salaries etc.).

(5) If a sheriff principal is appointed a judge of the Court, section 11(1) of the Sheriff Courts (Scotland) Act 1971 (temporary appointment of sheriff principal) applies, while he holds that appointment, as if his office is vacant.

(6) Schedule 4 makes provision about judicial pensions in relation to the holder of a judicial office who serves as a judge of the Court.

(7) The Lord Chancellor or the Secretary of State may by order make such transitional provision (including, in particular, provision for a temporary increase in the maximum number of judges) as he considers appropriate in relation to any holder of a judicial office who has completed his service as a judge of the Court.

PARLIAMENTARY PROCEDURE

Statements of compatibility

19. – (1) A Minister of the Crown in charge of a Bill in either House of Parliament must, before Second Reading of the Bill –
    (a) make a statement to the effect that in his view the provisions of the Bill are compatible with the Convention rights ('a statement of compatibility'); or
    (b) make a statement to the effect that although he is unable to make a statement of compatibility the government nevertheless wishes the House to proceed with the Bill.

(2) The statement must be in writing and be published in such manner as the Minister making it considers appropriate.

SUPPLEMENTAL

Orders etc. under this Act

20. – (1) Any power of a Minister of the Crown to make an order under this Act is exercisable by statutory instrument.

(2) The power of the Lord Chancellor or the Secretary of State to make rules (other than rules of court) under section 2(3) or 7(9) is exercisable by statutory instrument.

(3) Any statutory instrument made under section 14, 15 or 16(7) must be laid before Parliament.

(4) No order may be made by the Lord Chancellor or the Secretary of State under section 1(4), 7(11) or 16(2) unless a draft of the order has been laid before, and approved by, each House of Parliament.

(5) Any statutory instrument made under section 18(7) or Schedule 4, or to which subsection (2) applies, shall be subject to annulment in pursuance of a resolution of either House of Parliament.

(6) The power of a Northern Ireland department to make –
   (a)   rules under section 2(3)(c) or 7(9)(c), or
   (b)   an order under section 7(11),
is exercisable by statutory rule for the purposes of the Statutory Rules (Northern Ireland) Order 1979.

(7) Any rules made under section 2(3)(c) or 7(9)(c) shall be subject to negative resolution; and section 41(6) of the Interpretation Act (Northern Ireland) 1954 (meaning of 'subject to negative resolution') shall apply as if the power to make the rules were conferred by an Act of the Northern Ireland Assembly.

(8) No order may be made by a Northern Ireland department under section 7(11) unless a draft of the order has been laid before, and approved by, the Northern Ireland Assembly.

Interpretation, etc.

21. – (1) In this Act –
   'amend' includes repeal and apply (with or without modifications);
   'the appropriate Minister' means the Minister of the Crown having charge of the appropriate authorised government department (within the meaning of the Crown Proceedings Act 1947);
   'the Commission' means the European Commission of Human Rights;
   'the Convention' means the Convention for the Protection of Human Rights and Fundamental Freedoms, agreed by the Council of Europe at Rome on 4th November 1950 as it has effect for the time being in relation to the United Kingdom;
   'declaration of incompatibility' means a declaration under section 4;
   'Minister of the Crown' has the same meaning as in the Ministers of the Crown Act 1975;
   'Northern Ireland Minister' includes the First Minister and the deputy First Minister in Northern Ireland;
   'primary legislation' means any –

(a)   public general Act;
(b)   local and personal Act;
(c)   private Act;
(d)   Measure of the Church Assembly;
(e)   Measure of the General Synod of the Church of England;
(f)   Order in Council –
       (i)   made in exercise of Her Majesty's Royal Prerogative;
       (ii)   made under section 38(1)(a) of the Northern Ireland Constitution Act 1973
               or the corresponding provision of the Northern Ireland Act 1998; or
       (iii)   amending an Act of a kind mentioned in paragraph (a), (b) or (c);
and includes an order or other instrument made under primary legislation (otherwise than by the National Assembly for Wales, a member of the Scottish Executive, a Northern Ireland Minister or a Northern Ireland department) to the extent
to which it operates to bring one or more provisions of that legislation into force
or amends any primary legislation;
'the First Protocol' means the protocol to the Convention agreed at Paris on 20th
March 1952;
'the Sixth Protocol' means the protocol to the Convention agreed at Strasbourg
on 28th April 1983;
'the Eleventh Protocol' means the protocol to the Convention (restructuring the
control machinery established by the Convention) agreed at Strasbourg on 11th
May 1994;
'remedial order' means an order under section 10;
'subordinate legislation' means any –
(a)   Order in Council other than one –
       (i)   made in exercise of Her Majesty's Royal Prerogative;
       (ii)   made under section 38(1)(a) of the Northern Ireland Constitution
               Act 1973 or the corresponding provision of the Northern Ireland Act
               1998; or
       (iii)   amending an Act of a kind mentioned in the definition of primary leg-
               islation;
(b)   Act of the Scottish Parliament;
(c)   Act of the Parliament of Northern Ireland;
(d)   Measure of the Assembly established under section 1 of the Northern
       Ireland Assembly Act 1973;
(e)   Act of the Northern Ireland Assembly;
(f)   order, rules, regulations, scheme, warrant, byelaw or other instrument made
       under primary legislation (except to the extent to which it operates to bring
       one or more provisions of that legislation into force or amends any primary
       legislation);
(g)   order, rules, regulations, scheme, warrant, byelaw or other instrument made
       under legislation mentioned in paragraph (b), (c), (d) or (e) or made under
       an Order in Council applying only to Northern Ireland;
(h)   order, rules, regulations, scheme, warrant, byelaw or other instrument made
       by a member of the Scottish Executive, a Northern Ireland Minister or a
       Northern Ireland department in exercise of prerogative or other executive

functions of Her Majesty which are exercisable by such a person on behalf of Her Majesty;

'transferred matters' has the same meaning as in the Northern Ireland Act 1998; and

'tribunal' means any tribunal in which legal proceedings may be brought.

(2) The references in paragraphs (b) and (c) of section 2(1) to Articles are to Articles of the Convention as they had effect immediately before the coming into force of the Eleventh Protocol.

(3) The reference in paragraph (d) of section 2(1) to Article 46 includes a reference to Articles 32 and 54 of the Convention as they had effect immediately before the coming into force of the Eleventh Protocol.

(4) The references in section 2(1) to a report or decision of the Commission or a decision of the Committee of Ministers include references to a report or decision made as provided by paragraphs 3, 4 and 6 of Article 5 of the Eleventh Protocol (transitional provisions).

(5) Any liability under the Army Act 1955, the Air Force Act 1955 or the Naval Discipline Act 1957 to suffer death for an offence is replaced by a liability to imprisonment for life or any less punishment authorised by those Acts; and those Acts shall accordingly have effect with the necessary modifications.

Short title, commencement, application and extent

22. – (1) This Act may be cited as the Human Rights Act 1998.

(2) Sections 18, 20 and 21(5) and this section come into force on the passing of this Act.

(3) The other provisions of this Act come into force on such day as the Secretary of State may by order appoint; and different days may be appointed for different purposes.

(4) Paragraph (b) of subsection (1) of section 7 applies to proceedings brought by or at the instigation of a public authority whenever the act in question took place; but otherwise that subsection does not apply to an act taking place before the coming into force of that section.

(5) This Act binds the Crown.

(6) This Act extends to Northern Ireland.

(7) Section 21(5), so far as it relates to any provision contained in the Army Act 1955, the Air Force Act 1955 or the Naval Discipline Act 1957, extends to any place to which that provision extends.

SCHEDULE 1 – THE ARTICLES

PART I   THE CONVENTION RIGHTS AND FREEDOMS

ARTICLE 2   RIGHT TO LIFE

1. Everyone's right to life shall be protected by law. No one shall be deprived of his life intentionally save in the execution of a sentence of a court following his conviction of a crime for which this penalty is provided by law.

2. Deprivation of life shall not be regarded as inflicted in contravention of this Article when it results from the use of force which is no more than absolutely necessary:

    (a)   in defence of any person from unlawful violence;

    (b)   in order to effect a lawful arrest or to prevent the escape of a person lawfully detained;

    (c)   in action lawfully taken for the purpose of quelling a riot or insurrection.

ARTICLE 3   PROHIBITION OF TORTURE

No one shall be subjected to torture or to inhuman or degrading treatment or punishment.

ARTICLE 4   PROHIBITION OF SLAVERY AND FORCED LABOUR

1. No one shall be held in slavery or servitude.

2. No one shall be required to perform forced or compulsory labour.

3. For the purpose of this Article the term 'forced or compulsory labour' shall not include:

    (a)   any work required to be done in the ordinary course of detention imposed according to the provisions of Article 5 of this Convention or during conditional release from such detention;

    (b)   any service of a military character or, in case of conscientious objectors in countries where they are recognised, service exacted instead of compulsory military service;

    (c)   any service exacted in case of an emergency or calamity threatening the life or well-being of the community;

    (d)   any work or service which forms part of normal civic obligations.

ARTICLE 5   RIGHT TO LIBERTY AND SECURITY

1. Everyone has the right to liberty and security of person. No one shall be deprived of his liberty save in the following cases and in accordance with a procedure prescribed by law:

    (a)   the lawful detention of a person after conviction by a competent court;

    (b)   the lawful arrest or detention of a person for non-compliance with the lawful order of a court or in order to secure the fulfilment of any obligation prescribed by law;

    (c)   the lawful arrest or detention of a person effected for the purpose of bringing him before the competent legal authority on reasonable suspicion of having committed an offence or when it is reasonably considered necessary to prevent his committing an offence or fleeing after having done so;

    (d)   the detention of a minor by lawful order for the purpose of educational supervision or his lawful detention for the purpose of bringing him before the competent legal authority;

    (e)   the lawful detention of persons for the prevention of the spreading of infectious diseases, of persons of unsound mind, alcoholics or drug addicts or vagrants;

(f)   the lawful arrest or detention of a person to prevent his effecting an unau-
      thorised entry into the country or of a person against whom action is being
      taken with a view to deportation or extradition.

2. Everyone who is arrested shall be informed promptly, in a language which he understands, of the reasons for his arrest and of any charge against him.

3. Everyone arrested or detained in accordance with the provisions of paragraph 1(c)
of this Article shall be brought promptly before a judge or other officer authorised by
law to exercise judicial power and shall be entitled to trial within a reasonable time or
to release pending trial. Release may be conditioned by guarantees to appear for trial.

4. Everyone who is deprived of his liberty by arrest or detention shall be entitled to
take proceedings by which the lawfulness of his detention shall be decided speedily by
a court and his release ordered if the detention is not lawful.

5. Everyone who has been the victim of arrest or detention in contravention of the
provisions of this Article shall have an enforceable right to compensation.

ARTICLE 6   RIGHT TO A FAIR TRIAL

1. In the determination of his civil rights and obligations or of any criminal charge
against him, everyone is entitled to a fair and public hearing within a reasonable time
by an independent and impartial tribunal established by law. Judgment shall be pronounced publicly but the press and public may be excluded from all or part of the trial
in the interest of morals, public order or national security in a democratic society, where
the interests of juveniles or the protection of the private life of the parties so require,
or to the extent strictly necessary in the opinion of the court in special circumstances
where publicity would prejudice the interests of justice.

2. Everyone charged with a criminal offence shall be presumed innocent until proved
guilty according to law.

3. Everyone charged with a criminal offence has the following minimum rights:
    (a)   to be informed promptly, in a language which he understands and in detail,
          of the nature and cause of the accusation against him;
    (b)   to have adequate time and facilities for the preparation of his defence;
    (c)   to defend himself in person or through legal assistance of his own choosing
          or, if he has not sufficient means to pay for legal assistance, to be given it
          free when the interests of justice so require;
    (d)   to examine or have examined witnesses against him and to obtain the attend-
          ance and examination of witnesses on his behalf under the same conditions
          as witnesses against him;
    (e)   to have the free assistance of an interpreter if he cannot understand or speak
          the language used in court.

ARTICLE 7   NO PUNISHMENT WITHOUT LAW

1. No one shall be held guilty of any criminal offence on account of any act or omission which did not constitute a criminal offence under national or international law at
the time when it was committed. Nor shall a heavier penalty be imposed than the one
that was applicable at the time the criminal offence was committed.

2. This Article shall not prejudice the trial and punishment of any person for any act or omission which, at the time when it was committed, was criminal according to the general principles of law recognised by civilised nations.

ARTICLE 8   RIGHT TO RESPECT FOR PRIVATE AND FAMILY LIFE

1. Everyone has the right to respect for his private and family life, his home and his correspondence.
2. There shall be no interference by a public authority with the exercise of this right except such as is in accordance with the law and is necessary in a democratic society in the interests of national security, public safety or the economic well-being of the country, for the prevention of disorder or crime, for the protection of health or morals, or for the protection of the rights and freedoms of others.

ARTICLE 9   FREEDOM OF THOUGHT, CONSCIENCE AND RELIGION

1. Everyone has the right to freedom of thought, conscience and religion; this right includes freedom to change his religion or belief and freedom, either alone or in community with others and in public or private, to manifest his religion or belief, in worship, teaching, practice and observance.
2. Freedom to manifest one's religion or beliefs shall be subject only to such limitations as are prescribed by law and are necessary in a democratic society in the interests of public safety, for the protection of public order, health or morals, or for the protection of the rights and freedoms of others.

ARTICLE 10   FREEDOM OF EXPRESSION

1. Everyone has the right to freedom of expression. This right shall include freedom to hold opinions and to receive and impart information and ideas without interference by public authority and regardless of frontiers. This Article shall not prevent States from requiring the licensing of broadcasting, television or cinema enterprises.
2. The exercise of these freedoms, since it carries with it duties and responsibilities, may be subject to such formalities, conditions, restrictions or penalties as are prescribed by law and are necessary in a democratic society, in the interests of national security, territorial integrity or public safety, for the prevention of disorder or crime, for the protection of health or morals, for the protection of the reputation or rights of others, for preventing the disclosure of information received in confidence, or for maintaining the authority and impartiality of the judiciary.

ARTICLE 11   FREEDOM OF ASSEMBLY AND ASSOCIATION

1. Everyone has the right to freedom of peaceful assembly and to freedom of association with others, including the right to form and to join trade unions for the protection of his interests.

2. No restrictions shall be placed on the exercise of these rights other than such as are prescribed by law and are necessary in a democratic society in the interests of national security or public safety, for the prevention of disorder or crime, for the protection of health or morals or for the protection of the rights and freedoms of others. This Article shall not prevent the imposition of lawful restrictions on the exercise of these rights by members of the armed forces, of the police or of the administration of the State.

ARTICLE 12   RIGHT TO MARRY

Men and women of marriageable age have the right to marry and to found a family, according to the national laws governing the exercise of this right.

ARTICLE 14   PROHIBITION OF DISCRIMINATION

The enjoyment of the rights and freedoms set forth in this Convention shall be secured without discrimination on any ground such as sex, race, colour, language, religion, political or other opinion, national or social origin, association with a national minority, property, birth or other status.

ARTICLE 16   RESTRICTIONS ON POLITICAL ACTIVITY OF ALIENS

Nothing in Articles 10, 11 and 14 shall be regarded as preventing the High Contracting Parties from imposing restrictions on the political activity of aliens.

ARTICLE 17   PROHIBITION OF ABUSE OF RIGHTS

Nothing in this Convention may be interpreted as implying for any State, group or person any right to engage in any activity or perform any act aimed at the destruction of any of the rights and freedoms set forth herein or at their limitation to a greater extent than is provided for in the Convention.

ARTICLE 18   LIMITATION ON USE OF RESTRICTIONS ON RIGHTS

The restrictions permitted under this Convention to the said rights and freedoms shall not be applied for any purpose other than those for which they have been prescribed.

PART II   THE FIRST PROTOCOL

ARTICLE 1   PROTECTION OF PROPERTY

Every natural or legal person is entitled to the peaceful enjoyment of his possessions. No one shall be deprived of his possessions except in the public interest and subject to the conditions provided for by law and by the general principles of international law. The preceding provisions shall not, however, in any way impair the right of a State to enforce such laws as it deems necessary to control the use of property in accordance with the general interest or to secure the payment of taxes or other contributions or penalties.

ARTICLE 2   RIGHT TO EDUCATION

No person shall be denied the right to education. In the exercise of any functions which it assumes in relation to education and to teaching, the State shall respect the right of parents to ensure such education and teaching in conformity with their own religious and philosophical convictions.

ARTICLE 3   RIGHT TO FREE ELECTIONS

The High Contracting Parties undertake to hold free elections at reasonable intervals by secret ballot, under conditions which will ensure the free expression of the opinion of the people in the choice of the legislature.

PART III   THE SIXTH PROTOCOL

ARTICLE 1   ABOLITION OF THE DEATH PENALTY

The death penalty shall be abolished. No one shall be condemned to such penalty or executed.

ARTICLE 2   DEATH PENALTY IN TIME OF WAR

A State may make provision in its law for the death penalty in respect of acts committed in time of war or of imminent threat of war; such penalty shall be applied only in the instances laid down in the law and in accordance with its provisions. The State shall communicate to the Secretary General of the Council of Europe the relevant provisions of that law.

SCHEDULE 2 – REMEDIAL ORDERS

Orders

1. – (1) A remedial order may –
   - (a)   contain such incidental, supplemental, consequential or transitional provision as the person making it considers appropriate;
   - (b)   be made so as to have effect from a date earlier than that on which it is made;
   - (c)   make provision for the delegation of specific functions;
   - (d)   make different provision for different cases.
   (2)   The power conferred by sub-paragraph (1)(a) includes –
   - (a)   power to amend primary legislation (including primary legislation other than that which contains the incompatible provision); and

    (b)   power to amend or revoke subordinate legislation (including subordinate legislation other than that which contains the incompatible provision).

(3)   A remedial order may be made so as to have the same extent as the legislation which it affects.

(4)   No person is to be guilty of an offence solely as a result of the retrospective effect of a remedial order.

Procedure

2. No remedial order may be made unless –
    (a)   a draft of the order has been approved by a resolution of each House of Parliament made after the end of the period of 60 days beginning with the day on which the draft was laid; or
    (b)   it is declared in the order that it appears to the person making it that, because of the urgency of the matter, it is necessary to make the order without a draft being so approved.

Orders laid in draft

3. – (1) No draft may be laid under paragraph 2(a) unless –
    (a)   the person proposing to make the order has laid before Parliament a document which contains a draft of the proposed order and the required information; and
    (b)   the period of 60 days, beginning with the day on which the document required by this sub-paragraph was laid, has ended.

(2)   If representations have been made during that period, the draft laid under paragraph 2(a) must be accompanied by a statement containing –
    (a)   a summary of the representations; and
    (b)   if, as a result of the representations, the proposed order has been changed, details of the changes.

Urgent cases

4. – (1) If a remedial order ('the original order') is made without being approved in draft, the person making it must lay it before Parliament, accompanied by the required information, after it is made.

(2)   If representations have been made during the period of 60 days beginning with the day on which the original order was made, the person making it must (after the end of that period) lay before Parliament a statement containing –
    (a)   a summary of the representations; and
    (b)   if, as a result of the representations, he considers it appropriate to make changes to the original order, details of the changes.

(3)   If sub-paragraph (2)(b) applies, the person making the statement must –
    (a)   make a further remedial order replacing the original order; and
    (b)   lay the replacement order before Parliament.

(4)   If, at the end of the period of 120 days beginning with the day on which the original order was made, a resolution has not been passed by each House approving the original or replacement order, the order ceases to have effect (but without that affecting anything previously done under either order or the power to make a fresh remedial order).

Definitions

5.   In this Schedule –

'representations' means representations about a remedial order (or proposed remedial order) made to the person making (or proposing to make) it and includes any relevant Parliamentary report or resolution; and

'required information' means –

(a)   an explanation of the incompatibility which the order (or proposed order) seeks to remove, including particulars of the relevant declaration, finding or order; and

(b)   a statement of the reasons for proceeding under section 10 and for making an order in those terms.

Calculating periods

6.   In calculating any period for the purposes of this Schedule, no account is to be taken of any time during which –

(a)   Parliament is dissolved or prorogued; or

(b)   both Houses are adjourned for more than four days.

7.[7] (1) This paragraph applies in relation to –

(a)   any remedial order made, and any draft of such an order proposed to be made, –

(i)   by the Scottish Ministers; or

(ii)   within devolved competence (within the meaning of the Scotland Act 1998) by Her Majesty in Council; and

(b)   any document or statement to be laid in connection with such an order (or proposed order).

(2)   This Schedule has effect in relation to any such order (or proposed order), document or statement subject to the following modifications.

(3)   Any reference to Parliament, each House of Parliament or both Houses of Parliament shall be construed as a reference to the Scottish Parliament.

(4)   Paragraph 6 does not apply and instead, in calculating any period for the purposes of this Schedule, no account is to be taken of any time during which the Scottish Parliament is dissolved or is in recess for more than four days.

---

[7] Inserted by the Scotland Act 1998 (Consequential Modifications) Order 2000 (SI 2000 No. 2040).

SCHEDULE 3 – DEROGATION AND RESERVATION

PART I   DEROGATION[8]

United Kingdom's derogation from Article 5(1)

The United Kingdom Permanent Representative to the Council of Europe presents his compliments to the Secretary General of the Council, and has the honour to convey the following information in order to ensure compliance with the obligations of Her Majesty's Government in the United Kingdom under Article 15(3) of the Convention for the Protection of Human Rights and Fundamental Freedoms signed at Rome on 4 November 1950.

Public emergency in the United Kingdom

The terrorist attacks in New York, Washington, D.C. and Pennsylvania on 11th September 2001 resulted in several thousand deaths, including many British victims and others from 70 different countries. In its resolutions 1368 (2001) and 1373 (2001), the United Nations Security Council recognised the attacks as a threat to international peace and security.

The threat from international terrorism is a continuing one. In its resolution 1373 (2001), the Security Council, acting under Chapter VII of the United Nations Charter, required all States to take measures to prevent the commission of terrorist attacks, including by denying safe haven to those who finance, plan, support or commit terrorist attacks.

There exists a terrorist threat to the United Kingdom from persons suspected of involvement in international terrorism. In particular, there are foreign nationals present in the United Kingdom who are suspected of being concerned in the commission, preparation or instigation of acts of international terrorism, of being members of organisations or groups which are so concerned or of having links with members of such organisations or groups, and who are a threat to the national security of the United Kingdom.

As a result, a public emergency, within the meaning of Article 15(1) of the Convention, exists in the United Kingdom.

The Anti-terrorism, Crime and Security Act 2001

As a result of the public emergency, provision is made in the Anti-terrorism, Crime and Security Act 2001, *inter alia*, for an extended power to arrest and detain a foreign national which will apply where it is intended to remove or deport the person from the United Kingdom but where removal or deportation is not for the time being possible, with the consequence that the detention would be unlawful under existing domestic law powers. The extended power to arrest and detain will apply where the

---

[8] The derogation which was included in the Act when it was passed was repealed by the Human Rights Act (Amendment) Order 2001 SI 2001 No. 1216; the new derogation was inserted by the Human Rights Act (Amendment No. 2) Order 2001 SI 2001 No. 4032.

Secretary of State issues a certificate indicating his belief that the person's presence in the United Kingdom is a risk to national security and that he suspects the person of being an international terrorist. That certificate will be subject to an appeal to the Special Immigration Appeals Commission ('SIAC'), established under the Special Immigration Appeals Commission Act 1997, which will have power to cancel it if it considers that the certificate should not have been issued. There will be an appeal on a point of law from a ruling by SIAC. In addition, the certificate will be reviewed by SIAC at regular intervals. SIAC will also be able to grant bail, where appropriate, subject to conditions. It will be open to a detainee to end his detention at any time by agreeing to leave the United Kingdom.

The extended power of arrest and detention in the Anti-terrorism, Crime and Security Act 2001 is a measure which is strictly required by the exigencies of the situation. It is a temporary provision which comes into force for an initial period of 15 months and then expires unless renewed by Parliament. Thereafter, it is subject to annual renewal by Parliament. If, at any time, in the Government's assessment, the public emergency no longer exists or the extended power is no longer strictly required by the exigencies of the situation, then the Secretary of State will, by Order, repeal the provision.

Domestic law powers of detention (other than under the Anti-terrorism, Crime and Security Act 2001)

The Government has powers under the Immigration Act 1971 ('the 1971 Act') to remove or deport persons on the ground that their presence in the United Kingdom is not conducive to the public good on national security grounds. Persons can also be arrested and detained under Schedules 2 and 3 to the 1971 Act pending their removal or deportation. The courts in the United Kingdom have ruled that this power of detention can only be exercised during the period necessary, in all the circumstances of the particular case, to effect removal and that, if it becomes clear that removal is not going to be possible within a reasonable time, detention will be unlawful (*R v Governor of Durham Prison, ex parte Singh* [1984] 1 All ER 983).

Article 5(1)(f) of the Convention

It is well established that Article 5(1)(f) permits the detention of a person with a view to deportation only in circumstance where 'action is being taken with a view to deportation' (*Chahal v United Kingdom* (1997) 23 EHRR 413 at paragraph 112). In that case the European Court of Human Rights indicated that detention will cease to be permissible under Article 5(1)(f) if deportation proceedings are not prosecuted with due diligence and that it was necessary in such cases to determine whether the duration of the deportation proceedings was excessive (paragraph 113).

In some cases, where the intention remains to remove or deport a person on national security grounds, continued detention may not be consistent with Article 5(1)(f) as interpreted by the Court in the *Chahal* case. This may be the case, for example, if the person has established that removal to their own country might result in treatment contrary to Article 3 of the Convention. In such circumstances, irrespective of the gravity of the threat to national security posed by the person concerned, it is well established that Article 3 prevents removal or deportation to a place where there is a real risk that the person will suffer treatment contrary to that article. If no alternative destination is immediately available then removal or deportation may not, for the time being, be possible even though the ultimate intention remains to remove or deport the person once satisfactory arrangements can be made. In addition, it may not be possible to prosecute the person for a criminal offence given the strict rules on the admissibility of evidence in the criminal justice system of the United Kingdom and the high standard of proof required.

Derogation under Article 15 of the Convention

The Government has considered whether the exercise of the extended power to detain contained in the Anti-terrorism, Crime and Security Act 2001 may be inconsistent with the obligations under Article 5(1) of the Convention. As indicated above, there may be cases where, notwithstanding a continuing intention to remove or deport a person who is being detained, it is not possible to say that 'action is being taken with a view to deportation' within the meaning of Article 5(1)(f) as interpreted by the Court in the *Chahal* case. To the extent, therefore, that the exercise of the extended power may be inconsistent with the United Kingdom's obligations under Article 5(1), the Government has decided to avail itself of the right of derogation conferred by Article 15(1) of the Convention and will continue to do so until further notice.

Strasbourg, 18 December 2001

PART II RESERVATION

At the time of signing the present (First) Protocol, I declare that, in view of certain provisions of the Education Acts in the United Kingdom, the principle affirmed in the second sentence of Article 2 is accepted by the United Kingdom only so far as it is compatible with the provision of efficient instruction and training, and the avoidance of unreasonable public expenditure. Dated 20 March 1952 Made by the United Kingdom Permanent Representative to the Council of Europe.

SCHEDULE 4 – JUDICIAL PENSIONS

Duty to make orders about pensions

1. – (1) The appropriate Minister must by order make provision with respect to pensions payable to or in respect of any holder of a judicial office who serves as an ECHR judge.
(2) A pensions order must include such provision as the Minister making it considers is necessary to secure that –
    (a) an ECHR judge who was, immediately before his appointment as an ECHR judge, a member of a judicial pension scheme is entitled to remain as a member of that scheme;

(b)   the terms on which he remains a member of the scheme are those which would
      have been applicable had he not been appointed as an ECHR judge; and

(c)   entitlement to benefits payable in accordance with the scheme continues to
      be determined as if, while serving as an ECHR judge, his salary was that
      which would (but for section 18(4)) have been payable to him in respect of
      his continuing service as the holder of his judicial office.

Contributions

2. A pensions order may, in particular, make provision –

(a)   for any contributions which are payable by a person who remains a mem-
      ber of a scheme as a result of the order, and which would otherwise be payable
      by deduction from his salary, to be made otherwise than by deduction from
      his salary as an ECHR judge; and

(b)   for such contributions to be collected in such manner as may be determined
      by the administrators of the scheme.

Amendments of other enactments

3. A pensions order may amend any provision of, or made under, a pensions Act in
such manner and to such extent as the Minister making the order considers necessary
or expedient to ensure the proper administration of any scheme to which it relates.

Definitions

4. In this Schedule –

   'appropriate Minister' means –

(a)   in relation to any judicial office whose jurisdiction is exercisable exclusively
      in relation to Scotland, the Secretary of State; and

(b)   otherwise, the Lord Chancellor;

   'ECHR judge' means the holder of a judicial office who is serving as a judge of
   the Court;

   'judicial pension scheme' means a scheme established by and in accordance with
   a pensions Act;

   'pensions Act' means –

(a)   the County Courts Act (Northern Ireland) 1959;

(b)   the Sheriffs' Pensions (Scotland) Act 1961;

(c)   the Judicial Pensions Act 1981; or

(d)   the Judicial Pensions and Retirement Act 1993; and

   'pensions order' means an order made under paragraph 1.

Appendix 2

THE EUROPEAN CONVENTION FOR THE PROTECTION OF HUMAN RIGHTS AND FUNDAMENTAL FREEDOMS[1]

The governments signatory hereto, being members of the Council of Europe,
Considering the Universal Declaration of Human Rights proclaimed by the General Assembly of the United Nations on 10th December 1948;
Considering that this Declaration aims at securing the universal and effective recognition and observance of the Rights therein declared;
Considering that the aim of the Council of Europe is the achievement of greater unity between its members and that one of the methods by which that aim is to be pursued is the maintenance and further realisation of human rights and fundamental freedoms;
Reaffirming their profound belief in those fundamental freedoms which are the foundation of justice and peace in the world and are best maintained on the one hand by an effective political democracy and on the other by a common understanding and observance of the human rights upon which they depend;
Being resolved, as the governments of European countries which are like-minded and have a common heritage of political traditions, ideals, freedom and the rule of law, to take the first steps for the collective enforcement of certain of the rights stated in the Universal Declaration,
Have agreed as follows:

Article 1 – Obligation to respect human rights
The High Contracting Parties shall secure to everyone within their jurisdiction the rights and freedoms defined in Section I of this Convention.

SECTION I – RIGHTS AND FREEDOMS
Article 2 – Right to life
1   Everyone's right to life shall be protected by law. No one shall be deprived of his life intentionally save in the execution of a sentence of a court following his conviction of a crime for which this penalty is provided by law.

---

[1] The text is as amended by Protocol 11.

2 Deprivation of life shall not be regarded as inflicted in contravention of this article when it results from the use of force which is no more than absolutely necessary:
   a in defence of any person from unlawful violence;
   b in order to effect a lawful arrest or to prevent the escape of a person lawfully detained;
   c in action lawfully taken for the purpose of quelling a riot or insurrection.

Article 3 – Prohibition of torture
No one shall be subjected to torture or to inhuman or degrading treatment or punishment.

Article 4 – Prohibition of slavery and forced labour
1 No one shall be held in slavery or servitude.
2 No one shall be required to perform forced or compulsory labour.
3 For the purpose of this article the term 'forced or compulsory labour' shall not include:
   a any work required to be done in the ordinary course of detention imposed according to the provisions of Article 5 of this Convention or during conditional release from such detention;
   b any service of a military character or, in case of conscientious objectors in countries where they are recognised, service exacted instead of compulsory military service;
   c any service exacted in case of an emergency or calamity threatening the life or well-being of the community;
   d any work or service which forms part of normal civic obligations.

Article 5 – Right to liberty and security
1 Everyone has the right to liberty and security of person. No one shall be deprived of his liberty save in the following cases and in accordance with a procedure prescribed by law:
   a the lawful detention of a person after conviction by a competent court;
   b the lawful arrest or detention of a person for non-compliance with the lawful order of a court or in order to secure the fulfilment of any obligation prescribed by law;
   c the lawful arrest or detention of a person effected for the purpose of bringing him before the competent legal authority on reasonable suspicion of having committed an offence or when it is reasonably considered necessary to prevent his committing an offence or fleeing after having done so;
   d the detention of a minor by lawful order for the purpose of educational supervision or his lawful detention for the purpose of bringing him before the competent legal authority;
   e the lawful detention of persons for the prevention of the spreading of infectious diseases, of persons of unsound mind, alcoholics or drug addicts or vagrants;
   f the lawful arrest or detention of a person to prevent his effecting an unauthorised entry into the country or of a person against whom action is being taken with a view to deportation or extradition.

2   Everyone who is arrested shall be informed promptly, in a language which he under-
    stands, of the reasons for his arrest and of any charge against him.
3   Everyone arrested or detained in accordance with the provisions of paragraph 1.c
    of this article shall be brought promptly before a judge or other officer authorised
    by law to exercise judicial power and shall be entitled to trial within a reasonable
    time or to release pending trial. Release may be conditioned by guarantees to appear
    for trial.
4   Everyone who is deprived of his liberty by arrest or detention shall be entitled to
    take proceedings by which the lawfulness of his detention shall be decided speed-
    ily by a court and his release ordered if the detention is not lawful.
5   Everyone who has been the victim of arrest or detention in contravention of the
    provisions of this article shall have an enforceable right to compensation.

Article 6 – Right to a fair trial

1   In the determination of his civil rights and obligations or of any criminal charge
    against him, everyone is entitled to a fair and public hearing within a reasonable
    time by an independent and impartial tribunal established by law. Judgment shall
    be pronounced publicly but the press and public may be excluded from all or
    part of the trial in the interests of morals, public order or national security in a
    democratic society, where the interests of juveniles or the protection of the private
    life of the parties so require, or to the extent strictly necessary in the opinion of
    the court in special circumstances where publicity would prejudice the interests of
    justice.
2   Everyone charged with a criminal offence shall be presumed innocent until proved
    guilty according to law.
3   Everyone charged with a criminal offence has the following minimum rights:
    a   to be informed promptly, in a language which he understands and in detail, of
        the nature and cause of the accusation against him;
    b   to have adequate time and facilities for the preparation of his defence;
    c   to defend himself in person or through legal assistance of his own choosing or,
        if he has not sufficient means to pay for legal assistance, to be given it free when
        the interests of justice so require;
    d   to examine or have examined witnesses against him and to obtain the atten-
        dance and examination of witnesses on his behalf under the same conditions as
        witnesses against him;
    e   to have the free assistance of an interpreter if he cannot understand or speak
        the language used in court.

Article 7 – No punishment without law

1   No one shall be held guilty of any criminal offence on account of any act or omis-
    sion which did not constitute a criminal offence under national or international law
    at the time when it was committed. Nor shall a heavier penalty be imposed than
    the one that was applicable at the time the criminal offence was committed.
2   This article shall not prejudice the trial and punishment of any person for any act
    or omission which, at the time when it was committed, was criminal according to
    the general principles of law recognised by civilised nations.

Article 8 – Right to respect for private and family life

1 Everyone has the right to respect for his private and family life, his home and his correspondence.

2 There shall be no interference by a public authority with the exercise of this right except such as is in accordance with the law and is necessary in a democratic society in the interests of national security, public safety or the economic well-being of the country, for the prevention of disorder or crime, for the protection of health or morals, or for the protection of the rights and freedoms of others.

Article 9 – Freedom of thought, conscience and religion

1 Everyone has the right to freedom of thought, conscience and religion; this right includes freedom to change his religion or belief and freedom, either alone or in community with others and in public or private, to manifest his religion or belief, in worship, teaching, practice and observance.

2 Freedom to manifest one's religion or beliefs shall be subject only to such limitations as are prescribed by law and are necessary in a democratic society in the interests of public safety, for the protection of public order, health or morals, or for the protection of the rights and freedoms of others.

Article 10 – Freedom of expression

1 Everyone has the right to freedom of expression. This right shall include freedom to hold opinions and to receive and impart information and ideas without interference by public authority and regardless of frontiers. This article shall not prevent States from requiring the licensing of broadcasting, television or cinema enterprises.

2 The exercise of these freedoms, since it carries with it duties and responsibilities, may be subject to such formalities, conditions, restrictions or penalties as are prescribed by law and are necessary in a democratic society, in the interests of national security, territorial integrity or public safety, for the prevention of disorder or crime, for the protection of health or morals, for the protection of the reputation or rights of others, for preventing the disclosure of information received in confidence, or for maintaining the authority and impartiality of the judiciary.

Article 11 – Freedom of assembly and association

1 Everyone has the right to freedom of peaceful assembly and to freedom of association with others, including the right to form and to join trade unions for the protection of his interests.

2 No restrictions shall be placed on the exercise of these rights other than such as are prescribed by law and are necessary in a democratic society in the interests of national security or public safety, for the prevention of disorder or crime, for the protection of health or morals or for the protection of the rights and freedoms of others. This article shall not prevent the imposition of lawful restrictions on the exercise of these rights by members of the armed forces, of the police or of the administration of the State.

Article 12 – Right to marry

Men and women of marriageable age have the right to marry and to found a family, according to the national laws governing the exercise of this right.

Article 13 – Right to an effective remedy
Everyone whose rights and freedoms as set forth in this Convention are violated shall have an effective remedy before a national authority notwithstanding that the violation has been committed by persons acting in an official capacity.

Article 14 – Prohibition of discrimination
The enjoyment of the rights and freedoms set forth in this Convention shall be secured without discrimination on any ground such as sex, race, colour, language, religion, political or other opinion, national or social origin, association with a national minority, property, birth or other status.

Article 15 – Derogation in time of emergency
1   In time of war or other public emergency threatening the life of the nation any High Contracting Party may take measures derogating from its obligations under this Convention to the extent strictly required by the exigencies of the situation, provided that such measures are not inconsistent with its other obligations under international law.
2   No derogation from Article 2, except in respect of deaths resulting from lawful acts of war, or from Articles 3, 4 (paragraph 1) and 7 shall be made under this provision.
3   Any High Contracting Party availing itself of this right of derogation shall keep the Secretary General of the Council of Europe fully informed of the measures which it has taken and the reasons therefor. It shall also inform the Secretary General of the Council of Europe when such measures have ceased to operate and the provisions of the Convention are again being fully executed.

Article 16 – Restrictions on political activity of aliens
Nothing in Articles 10, 11 and 14 shall be regarded as preventing the High Contracting Parties from imposing restrictions on the political activity of aliens.

Article 17 – Prohibition of abuse of rights
Nothing in this Convention may be interpreted as implying for any State, group or person any right to engage in any activity or perform any act aimed at the destruction of any of the rights and freedoms set forth herein or at their limitation to a greater extent than is provided for in the Convention.

Article 18 – Limitation on use of restrictions on rights
The restrictions permitted under this Convention to the said rights and freedoms shall not be applied for any purpose other than those for which they have been prescribed.

SECTION II – EUROPEAN COURT OF HUMAN RIGHTS
Article 19 – Establishment of the Court
To ensure the observance of the engagements undertaken by the High Contracting Parties in the Convention and the Protocols thereto, there shall be set up a European Court of Human Rights, hereinafter referred to as 'the Court'. It shall function on a permanent basis.

Article 20 – Number of judges
The Court shall consist of a number of judges equal to that of the High Contracting Parties.

Article 21 – Criteria for office
1 The judges shall be of high moral character and must either possess the qualifications required for appointment to high judicial office or be jurisconsults of recognised competence.
2 The judges shall sit on the Court in their individual capacity.
3 During their term of office the judges shall not engage in any activity which is incompatible with their independence, impartiality or with the demands of a full-time office; all questions arising from the application of this paragraph shall be decided by the Court.

Article 22 – Election of judges
1 The judges shall be elected by the Parliamentary Assembly with respect to each High Contracting Party by a majority of votes cast from a list of three candidates nominated by the High Contracting Party.
2 The same procedure shall be followed to complete the Court in the event of the accession of new High Contracting Parties and in filling casual vacancies.

Article 23 – Terms of office
1 The judges shall be elected for a period of six years. They may be re-elected. However, the terms of office of one-half of the judges elected at the first election shall expire at the end of three years.
2 The judges whose terms of office are to expire at the end of the initial period of three years shall be chosen by lot by the Secretary General of the Council of Europe immediately after their election.
3 In order to ensure that, as far as possible, the terms of office of one-half of the judges are renewed every three years, the Parliamentary Assembly may decide, before proceeding to any subsequent election, that the term or terms of office of one or more judges to be elected shall be for a period other than six years but not more than nine and not less than three years.
4 In cases where more than one term of office is involved and where the Parliamentary Assembly applies the preceding paragraph, the allocation of the terms of office shall be effected by a drawing of lots by the Secretary General of the Council of Europe immediately after the election.
5 A judge elected to replace a judge whose term of office has not expired shall hold office for the remainder of his predecessor's term.
6 The terms of office of judges shall expire when they reach the age of 70.
7 The judges shall hold office until replaced. They shall, however, continue to deal with such cases as they already have under consideration.

Article 24 – Dismissal
No judge may be dismissed from his office unless the other judges decide by a majority of two-thirds that he has ceased to fulfil the required conditions.

Article 25 – Registry and legal secretaries
The Court shall have a registry, the functions and organisation of which shall be laid down in the rules of the Court. The Court shall be assisted by legal secretaries.

Article 26 – Plenary Court
The plenary Court shall

a   elect its President and one or two Vice-Presidents for a period of three years; they may be re-elected;
b   set up Chambers, constituted for a fixed period of time;
c   elect the Presidents of the Chambers of the Court; they may be re-elected;
d   adopt the rules of the Court, and
e   elect the Registrar and one or more Deputy Registrars.

Article 27 – Committees, Chambers and Grand Chamber
1   To consider cases brought before it, the Court shall sit in committees of three judges, in Chambers of seven judges and in a Grand Chamber of seventeen judges. The Court's Chambers shall set up committees for a fixed period of time.
2   There shall sit as an *ex officio* member of the Chamber and the Grand Chamber the judge elected in respect of the State Party concerned or, if there is none or if he is unable to sit, a person of its choice who shall sit in the capacity of judge.
3   The Grand Chamber shall also include the President of the Court, the Vice-Presidents, the Presidents of the Chambers and other judges chosen in accordance with the rules of the Court. When a case is referred to the Grand Chamber under Article 43, no judge from the Chamber which rendered the judgment shall sit in the Grand Chamber, with the exception of the President of the Chamber and the judge who sat in respect of the State Party concerned.

Article 28 – Declarations of inadmissibility by committees
A committee may, by a unanimous vote, declare inadmissible or strike out of its list of cases an application submitted under Article 34 where such a decision can be taken without further examination. The decision shall be final.

Article 29 – Decisions by Chambers on admissibility and merits
1   If no decision is taken under Article 28, a Chamber shall decide on the admissibility and merits of individual applications submitted under Article 34.
2   A Chamber shall decide on the admissibility and merits of inter-State applications submitted under Article 33.
3   The decision on admissibility shall be taken separately unless the Court, in exceptional cases, decides otherwise.

Article 30 – Relinquishment of jurisdiction to the Grand Chamber
Where a case pending before a Chamber raises a serious question affecting the interpretation of the Convention or the protocols thereto, or where the resolution of a question before the Chamber might have a result inconsistent with a judgment previously delivered by the Court, the Chamber may, at any time before it has rendered

its judgment, relinquish jurisdiction in favour of the Grand Chamber, unless one of the parties to the case objects.

Article 31 – Powers of the Grand Chamber

The Grand Chamber shall

1. a determine applications submitted either under Article 33 or Article 34 when a Chamber has relinquished jurisdiction under Article 30 or when the case has been referred to it under Article 43; and

   b consider requests for advisory opinions submitted under Article 47.

Article 32 – Jurisdiction of the Court

1 The jurisdiction of the Court shall extend to all matters concerning the interpretation and application of the Convention and the protocols thereto which are referred to it as provided in Articles 33, 34 and 47.

2 In the event of dispute as to whether the Court has jurisdiction, the Court shall decide.

Article 33 – Inter-State cases

Any High Contracting Party may refer to the Court any alleged breach of the provisions of the Convention and the protocols thereto by another High Contracting Party.

Article 34 – Individual applications

The Court may receive applications from any person, non-governmental organisation or group of individuals claiming to be the victim of a violation by one of the High Contracting Parties of the rights set forth in the Convention or the protocols thereto. The High Contracting Parties undertake not to hinder in any way the effective exercise of this right.

Article 35 – Admissibility criteria

1 The Court may only deal with the matter after all domestic remedies have been exhausted, according to the generally recognised rules of international law, and within a period of six months from the date on which the final decision was taken.

2 The Court shall not deal with any application submitted under Article 34 that

   a is anonymous; or

   b is substantially the same as a matter that has already been examined by the Court or has already been submitted to another procedure of international investigation or settlement and contains no relevant new information.

3 The Court shall declare inadmissible any individual application submitted under Article 34 which it considers incompatible with the provisions of the Convention or the protocols thereto, manifestly ill-founded, or an abuse of the right of application.

4 The Court shall reject any application which it considers inadmissible under this Article. It may do so at any stage of the proceedings.

Article 36 – Third party intervention

1 In all cases before a Chamber or the Grand Chamber, a High Contracting Party one of whose nationals is an applicant shall have the right to submit written comments and to take part in hearings.

2 The President of the Court may, in the interest of the proper administration of justice, invite any High Contracting Party which is not a party to the proceedings or any person concerned who is not the applicant to submit written comments or take part in hearings.

Article 37 – Striking out applications

1 The Court may at any stage of the proceedings decide to strike an application out of its list of cases where the circumstances lead to the conclusion that

a   the applicant does not intend to pursue his application; or

b   the matter has been resolved; or

c   for any other reason established by the Court, it is no longer justified to continue the examination of the application.

However, the Court shall continue the examination of the application if respect for human rights as defined in the Convention and the protocols thereto so requires.

2 The Court may decide to restore an application to its list of cases if it considers that the circumstances justify such a course.

Article 38 – Examination of the case and friendly settlement proceedings

1 If the Court declares the application admissible, it shall

a   pursue the examination of the case, together with the representatives of the parties, and if need be, undertake an investigation, for the effective conduct of which the States concerned shall furnish all necessary facilities;

b   place itself at the disposal of the parties concerned with a view to securing a friendly settlement of the matter on the basis of respect for human rights as defined in the Convention and the protocols thereto.

2 Proceedings conducted under paragraph 1.b shall be confidential.

Article 39 – Finding of a friendly settlement

If a friendly settlement is effected, the Court shall strike the case out of its list by means of a decision which shall be confined to a brief statement of the facts and of the solution reached.

Article 40 – Public hearings and access to documents

1 Hearings shall be in public unless the Court in exceptional circumstances decides otherwise.

2 Documents deposited with the Registrar shall be accessible to the public unless the President of the Court decides otherwise.

Article 41 – Just satisfaction

If the Court finds that there has been a violation of the Convention or the protocols thereto, and if the internal law of the High Contracting Party concerned allows only partial reparation to be made, the Court shall, if necessary, afford just satisfaction to the injured party.

Article 42 – Judgments of Chambers

Judgments of Chambers shall become final in accordance with the provisions of Article 44, paragraph 2.

Article 43 – Referral to the Grand Chamber

1 Within a period of three months from the date of the judgment of the Chamber, any party to the case may, in exceptional cases, request that the case be referred to the Grand Chamber.
2 A panel of five judges of the Grand Chamber shall accept the request if the case raises a serious question affecting the interpretation or application of the Convention or the protocols thereto, or a serious issue of general importance.
3 If the panel accepts the request, the Grand Chamber shall decide the case by means of a judgment.

Article 44 – Final judgments

1 The judgment of the Grand Chamber shall be final.
2 The judgment of a Chamber shall become final
   a when the parties declare that they will not request that the case be referred to the Grand Chamber; or
   b three months after the date of the judgment, if reference of the case to the Grand Chamber has not been requested; or
   c when the panel of the Grand Chamber rejects the request to refer under Article 43.
3 The final judgment shall be published.

Article 45 – Reasons for judgments and decisions

1 Reasons shall be given for judgments as well as for decisions declaring applications admissible or inadmissible.
2 If a judgment does not represent, in whole or in part, the unanimous opinion of the judges, any judge shall be entitled to deliver a separate opinion.

Article 46 – Binding force and execution of judgments

1 The High Contracting Parties undertake to abide by the final judgment of the Court in any case to which they are parties.
2 The final judgment of the Court shall be transmitted to the Committee of Ministers, which shall supervise its execution.

Article 47 – Advisory opinions

1 The Court may, at the request of the Committee of Ministers, give advisory opinions on legal questions concerning the interpretation of the Convention and the protocols thereto.
2 Such opinions shall not deal with any question relating to the content or scope of the rights or freedoms defined in Section I of the Convention and the protocols thereto, or with any other question which the Court or the Committee of Ministers might have to consider in consequence of any such proceedings as could be instituted in accordance with the Convention.
3 Decisions of the Committee of Ministers to request an advisory opinion of the Court shall require a majority vote of the representatives entitled to sit on the Committee.

Article 48 – Advisory jurisdiction of the Court

The Court shall decide whether a request for an advisory opinion submitted by the Committee of Ministers is within its competence as defined in Article 47.

Article 49 – Reasons for advisory opinions

1   Reasons shall be given for advisory opinions of the Court.

2   If the advisory opinion does not represent, in whole or in part, the unanimous opinion of the judges, any judge shall be entitled to deliver a separate opinion.

3   Advisory opinions of the Court shall be communicated to the Committee of Ministers.

Article 50 – Expenditure on the Court

The expenditure on the Court shall be borne by the Council of Europe.

Article 51 – Privileges and immunities of judges

The judges shall be entitled, during the exercise of their functions, to the privileges and immunities provided for in Article 40 of the Statute of the Council of Europe and in the agreements made thereunder.

SECTION III – MISCELLANEOUS PROVISIONS

Article 52 – Inquiries by the Secretary General

On receipt of a request from the Secretary General of the Council of Europe any High Contracting Party shall furnish an explanation of the manner in which its internal law ensures the effective implementation of any of the provisions of the Convention.

Article 53 – Safeguard for existing human rights

Nothing in this Convention shall be construed as limiting or derogating from any of the human rights and fundamental freedoms which may be ensured under the laws of any High Contracting Party or under any other agreement to which it is a Party.

Article 54 – Powers of the Committee of Ministers

Nothing in this Convention shall prejudice the powers conferred on the Committee of Ministers by the Statute of the Council of Europe.

Article 55 – Exclusion of other means of dispute settlement

The High Contracting Parties agree that, except by special agreement, they will not avail themselves of treaties, conventions or declarations in force between them for the purpose of submitting, by way of petition, a dispute arising out of the interpretation or application of this Convention to a means of settlement other than those provided for in this Convention.

Article 56 – Territorial application

1   Any State may at the time of its ratification or at any time thereafter declare by notification addressed to the Secretary General of the Council of Europe that the present Convention shall, subject to paragraph 4 of this Article, extend to all or any of the territories for whose international relations it is responsible.

2   The Convention shall extend to the territory or territories named in the notification as from the thirtieth day after the receipt of this notification by the Secretary General of the Council of Europe.

3   The provisions of this Convention shall be applied in such territories with due regard, however, to local requirements.

4   Any State which has made a declaration in accordance with paragraph 1 of this
    article may at any time thereafter declare on behalf of one or more of the territor-
    ies to which the declaration relates that it accepts the competence of the Court to
    receive applications from individuals, non-governmental organisations or groups of
    individuals as provided by Article 34 of the Convention.

Article 57 – Reservations

1   Any State may, when signing this Convention or when depositing its instrument
    of ratification, make a reservation in respect of any particular provision of the
    Convention to the extent that any law then in force in its territory is not in con-
    formity with the provision. Reservations of a general character shall not be per-
    mitted under this article.
2   Any reservation made under this article shall contain a brief statement of the law
    concerned.

Article 58 – Denunciation

1   A High Contracting Party may denounce the present Convention only after the expiry
    of five years from the date on which it became a party to it and after six months'
    notice contained in a notification addressed to the Secretary General of the Council
    of Europe, who shall inform the other High Contracting Parties.
2   Such a denunciation shall not have the effect of releasing the High Contracting Party
    concerned from its obligations under this Convention in respect of any act which,
    being capable of constituting a violation of such obligations, may have been per-
    formed by it before the date at which the denunciation became effective.
3   Any High Contracting Party which shall cease to be a member of the Council of
    Europe shall cease to be a Party to this Convention under the same conditions.
4   The Convention may be denounced in accordance with the provisions of the pre-
    ceding paragraphs in respect of any territory to which it has been declared to extend
    under the terms of Article 56.

Article 59 – Signature and ratification

1   This Convention shall be open to the signature of the members of the Council of
    Europe. It shall be ratified. Ratifications shall be deposited with the Secretary General
    of the Council of Europe.
2   The present Convention shall come into force after the deposit of ten instruments
    of ratification.
3   As regards any signatory ratifying subsequently, the Convention shall come into
    force at the date of the deposit of its instrument of ratification.
4   The Secretary General of the Council of Europe shall notify all the members of the
    Council of Europe of the entry into force of the Convention, the names of the High
    Contracting Parties who have ratified it, and the deposit of all instruments of
    ratification which may be effected subsequently.

Done at Rome this 4th day of November 1950, in English and French, both texts being
equally authentic, in a single copy which shall remain deposited in the archives of the
Council of Europe. The Secretary General shall transmit certified copies to each of the
signatories.

Protocol to the Convention for the Protection of Human Rights and Fundamental Freedoms (as amended by Protocol No. 11)
Paris, 20.III.1952

The governments signatory hereto, being members of the Council of Europe, Being resolved to take steps to ensure the collective enforcement of certain rights and freedoms other than those already included in Section I of the Convention for the Protection of Human Rights and Fundamental Freedoms signed at Rome on 4 November 1950 (hereinafter referred to as 'the Convention'),

Have agreed as follows:

Article 1 – Protection of property
Every natural or legal person is entitled to the peaceful enjoyment of his possessions. No one shall be deprived of his possessions except in the public interest and subject to the conditions provided for by law and by the general principles of international law. The preceding provisions shall not, however, in any way impair the right of a State to enforce such laws as it deems necessary to control the use of property in accordance with the general interest or to secure the payment of taxes or other contributions or penalties.

Article 2 – Right to education
No person shall be denied the right to education. In the exercise of any functions which it assumes in relation to education and to teaching, the State shall respect the right of parents to ensure such education and teaching in conformity with their own religious and philosophical convictions.

Article 3 – Right to free elections
The High Contracting Parties undertake to hold free elections at reasonable intervals by secret ballot, under conditions which will ensure the free expression of the opinion of the people in the choice of the legislature.

Article 4 – Territorial application
Any High Contracting Party may at the time of signature or ratification or at any time thereafter communicate to the Secretary General of the Council of Europe a declaration stating the extent to which it undertakes that the provisions of the present Protocol shall apply to such of the territories for the international relations of which it is responsible as are named therein. Any High Contracting Party which has communicated a declaration in virtue of the preceding paragraph may from time to time communicate a further declaration modifying the terms of any former declaration or terminating the application of the provisions of this Protocol in respect of any territory. A declaration made in accordance with this article shall be deemed to have been made in accordance with paragraph 1 of Article 56 of the Convention.

Article 5 – Relationship to the Convention
As between the High Contracting Parties the provisions of Articles 1, 2, 3 and 4 of this Protocol shall be regarded as additional articles to the Convention and all the provisions of the Convention shall apply accordingly.

Article 6 – Signature and ratification

This Protocol shall be open for signature by the members of the Council of Europe, who are the signatories of the Convention; it shall be ratified at the same time as or after the ratification of the Convention. It shall enter into force after the deposit of ten instruments of ratification. As regards any signatory ratifying subsequently, the Protocol shall enter into force at the date of the deposit of its instrument of ratification.

The instruments of ratification shall be deposited with the Secretary General of the Council of Europe, who will notify all members of the names of those who have ratified.

Done at Paris on the 20th day of March 1952, in English and French, both texts being equally authentic, in a single copy which shall remain deposited in the archives of the Council of Europe. The Secretary General shall transmit certified copies to each of the signatory governments.

Protocol No. 4 to the Convention for the Protection of Human Rights and Fundamental Freedoms, securing certain rights and freedoms other than those already included in the Convention and in the first Protocol thereto, as amended by Protocol No. 11
Strasbourg, 16.IX.1963

The governments signatory hereto, being members of the Council of Europe,

Being resolved to take steps to ensure the collective enforcement of certain rights and freedoms other than those already included in Section 1 of the Convention for the Protection of Human Rights and Fundamental Freedoms signed at Rome on 4th November 1950 (hereinafter referred to as the 'Convention') and in Articles 1 to 3 of the First Protocol to the Convention, signed at Paris on 20th March 1952,

Have agreed as follows:

Article 1 – Prohibition of imprisonment for debt

No one shall be deprived of his liberty merely on the ground of inability to fulfil a contractual obligation.

Article 2 – Freedom of movement

1 Everyone lawfully within the territory of a State shall, within that territory, have the right to liberty of movement and freedom to choose his residence.
2 Everyone shall be free to leave any country, including his own.
3 No restrictions shall be placed on the exercise of these rights other than such as are in accordance with law and are necessary in a democratic society in the interests of national security or public safety, for the maintenance of *ordre public*, for the prevention of crime, for the protection of health or morals, or for the protection of the rights and freedoms of others.
4 The rights set forth in paragraph 1 may also be subject, in particular areas, to restrictions imposed in accordance with law and justified by the public interest in a democratic society.

Article 3 – Prohibition of expulsion of nationals

1   No one shall be expelled, by means either of an individual or of a collective measure, from the territory of the State of which he is a national.
2   No one shall be deprived of the right to enter the territory of the state of which he is a national.

Article 4 – Prohibition of collective expulsion of aliens

Collective expulsion of aliens is prohibited.

Article 5 – Territorial application

1   Any High Contracting Party may, at the time of signature or ratification of this Protocol, or at any time thereafter, communicate to the Secretary General of the Council of Europe a declaration stating the extent to which it undertakes that the provisions of this Protocol shall apply to such of the territories for the international relations of which it is responsible as are named therein.
2   Any High Contracting Party which has communicated a declaration in virtue of the preceding paragraph may, from time to time, communicate a further declaration modifying the terms of any former declaration or terminating the application of the provisions of this Protocol in respect of any territory.
3   A declaration made in accordance with this article shall be deemed to have been made in accordance with paragraph 1 of Article 56 of the Convention.
4   The territory of any State to which this Protocol applies by virtue of ratification or acceptance by that State, and each territory to which this Protocol is applied by virtue of a declaration by that State under this article, shall be treated as separate territories for the purpose of the references in Articles 2 and 3 to the territory of a State.
5   Any State which has made a declaration in accordance with paragraph 1 or 2 of this Article may at any time thereafter declare on behalf of one or more of the territories to which the declaration relates that it accepts the competence of the Court to receive applications from individuals, non-governmental organisations or groups of individuals as provided in Article 34 of the Convention in respect of all or any of Articles 1 to 4 of this Protocol.

Article 6 – Relationship to the Convention

As between the High Contracting Parties the provisions of Articles 1 to 5 of this Protocol shall be regarded as additional articles to the Convention, and all the provisions of the Convention shall apply accordingly.

Article 7 – Signature and ratification

1   This Protocol shall be open for signature by the members of the Council of Europe who are the signatories of the Convention; it shall be ratified at the same time as or after the ratification of the Convention. It shall enter into force after the deposit of five instruments of ratification. As regards any signatory ratifying subsequently, the Protocol shall enter into force at the date of the deposit of its instrument of ratification.
2   The instruments of ratification shall be deposited with the Secretary General of the Council of Europe, who will notify all Members of the names of those who have ratified.

In witness whereof the undersigned, being duly authorised thereto, have signed this Protocol.

Done at Strasbourg, this 16th day of September 1963, in English and in French, both texts being equally authoritative, in a single copy which shall remain deposited in the archives of the Council of Europe. The Secretary General shall transmit certified copies to each of the signatory states.

Protocol No. 6 to the Convention for the Protection of Human Rights and Fundamental Freedoms concerning the abolition of the death penalty, as amended by Protocol No. 11
Strasbourg, 28.IV.1983

The member States of the Council of Europe, signatory to this Protocol to the Convention for the Protection of Human Rights and Fundamental Freedoms, signed at Rome on 4 November 1950 (hereinafter referred to as 'the Convention'),

Considering that the evolution that has occurred in several member States of the Council of Europe expresses a general tendency in favour of abolition of the death penalty,

Have agreed as follows:

Article 1 – Abolition of the death penalty
The death penalty shall be abolished. No-one shall be condemned to such penalty or executed.

Article 2 – Death penalty in time of war
A State may make provision in its law for the death penalty in respect of acts committed in time of war or of imminent threat of war; such penalty shall be applied only in the instances laid down in the law and in accordance with its provisions. The State shall communicate to the Secretary General of the Council of Europe the relevant provisions of that law.

Article 3 – Prohibition of derogations
No derogation from the provisions of this Protocol shall be made under Article 15 of the Convention.

Article 4 – Prohibition of reservations
No reservation may be made under Article 57 of the Convention in respect of the provisions of this Protocol.

Article 5 – Territorial application
1 Any State may at the time of signature or when depositing its instrument of ratification, acceptance or approval, specify the territory or territories to which this Protocol shall apply.
2 Any State may at any later date, by a declaration addressed to the Secretary General of the Council of Europe, extend the application of this Protocol to any

other territory specified in the declaration. In respect of such territory the Protocol shall enter into force on the first day of the month following the date of receipt of such declaration by the Secretary General.

3   Any declaration made under the two preceding paragraphs may, in respect of any territory specified in such declaration, be withdrawn by a notification addressed to the Secretary General. The withdrawal shall become effective on the first day of the month following the date of receipt of such notification by the Secretary General.

Article 6 – Relationship to the Convention

As between the States Parties the provisions of Articles 1 to 5 of this Protocol shall be regarded as additional articles to the Convention and all the provisions of the Convention shall apply accordingly.

Article 7 – Signature and ratification

The Protocol shall be open for signature by the member States of the Council of Europe, signatories to the Convention. It shall be subject to ratification, acceptance or approval. A member State of the Council of Europe may not ratify, accept or approve this Protocol unless it has, simultaneously or previously, ratified the Convention. Instruments of ratification, acceptance or approval shall be deposited with the Secretary General of the Council of Europe.

Article 8 – Entry into force

1   This Protocol shall enter into force on the first day of the month following the date on which five member States of the Council of Europe have expressed their consent to be bound by the Protocol in accordance with the provisions of Article 7.

2   In respect of any member State which subsequently expresses its consent to be bound by it, the Protocol shall enter into force on the first day of the month following the date of the deposit of the instrument of ratification, acceptance or approval.

Article 9 – Depositary functions

The Secretary General of the Council of Europe shall notify the member States of the Council of:

a   any signature;

b   the deposit of any instrument of ratification, acceptance or approval;

c   any date of entry into force of this Protocol in accordance with Articles 5 and 8;

d   any other act, notification or communication relating to this Protocol.

In witness whereof the undersigned, being duly authorised thereto, have signed this Protocol. Done at Strasbourg, this 28th day of April 1983, in English and in French, both texts being equally authentic, in a single copy which shall be deposited in the archives of the Council of Europe. The Secretary General of the Council of Europe shall transmit certified copies to each member State of the Council of Europe.

Protocol No. 7 to the Convention for the Protection of Human Rights and Fundamental Freedoms, as amended by Protocol No. 11 Strasbourg, 22.XI.1984

The member States of the Council of Europe signatory hereto, Being resolved to take further steps to ensure the collective enforcement of certain rights and freedoms by means of the Convention for the Protection of Human Rights and Fundamental Freedoms signed at Rome on 4 November 1950 (hereinafter referred to as 'the Convention'), Have agreed as follows:

Article 1 – Procedural safeguards relating to expulsion of aliens

1   An alien lawfully resident in the territory of a State shall not be expelled therefrom except in pursuance of a decision reached in accordance with law and shall be allowed:
   a   to submit reasons against his expulsion,
   b   to have his case reviewed, and
   c   to be represented for these purposes before the competent authority or a person or persons designated by that authority.
2   An alien may be expelled before the exercise of his rights under paragraph 1.a, b and c of this Article, when such expulsion is necessary in the interests of public order or is grounded on reasons of national security.

Article 2 – Right of appeal in criminal matters

1   Everyone convicted of a criminal offence by a tribunal shall have the right to have his conviction or sentence reviewed by a higher tribunal. The exercise of this right, including the grounds on which it may be exercised, shall be governed by law.
2   This right may be subject to exceptions in regard to offences of a minor character, as prescribed by law, or in cases in which the person concerned was tried in the first instance by the highest tribunal or was convicted following an appeal against acquittal.

Article 3 – Compensation for wrongful conviction

When a person has by a final decision been convicted of a criminal offence and when subsequently his conviction has been reversed, or he has been pardoned, on the ground that a new or newly discovered fact shows conclusively that there has been a miscarriage of justice, the person who has suffered punishment as a result of such conviction shall be compensated according to the law or the practice of the State concerned, unless it is proved that the non-disclosure of the unknown fact in time is wholly or partly attributable to him.

Article 4 – Right not to be tried or punished twice

1   No one shall be liable to be tried or punished again in criminal proceedings under the jurisdiction of the same State for an offence for which he has already been finally acquitted or convicted in accordance with the law and penal procedure of that State.
2   The provisions of the preceding paragraph shall not prevent the reopening of the case in accordance with the law and penal procedure of the State concerned, if there

is evidence of new or newly discovered facts, or if there has been a fundamental defect in the previous proceedings, which could affect the outcome of the case.

3 No derogation from this Article shall be made under Article 15 of the Convention.

Article 5 – Equality between spouses

Spouses shall enjoy equality of rights and responsibilities of a private law character between them, and in their relations with their children, as to marriage, during marriage and in the event of its dissolution. This Article shall not prevent States from taking such measures as are necessary in the interests of the children.

Article 6 – Territorial application

1 Any State may at the time of signature or when depositing its instrument of ratification, acceptance or approval, specify the territory or territories to which the Protocol shall apply and state the extent to which it undertakes that the provisions of this Protocol shall apply to such territory or territories.

2 Any State may at any later date, by a declaration addressed to the Secretary General of the Council of Europe, extend the application of this Protocol to any other territory specified in the declaration. In respect of such territory the Protocol shall enter into force on the first day of the month following the expiration of a period of two months after the date of receipt by the Secretary General of such declaration.

3 Any declaration made under the two preceding paragraphs may, in respect of any territory specified in such declaration, be withdrawn or modified by a notification addressed to the Secretary General. The withdrawal or modification shall become effective on the first day of the month following the expiration of a period of two months after the date of receipt of such notification by the Secretary General.

4 A declaration made in accordance with this Article shall be deemed to have been made in accordance with paragraph 1 of Article 56 of the Convention.

5 The territory of any State to which this Protocol applies by virtue of ratification, acceptance or approval by that State, and each territory to which this Protocol is applied by virtue of a declaration by that State under this Article, may be treated as separate territories for the purpose of the reference in Article 1 to the territory of a State.

6 Any State which has made a declaration in accordance with paragraph 1 or 2 of this Article may at any time thereafter declare on behalf of one or more of the territories to which the declaration relates that it accepts the competence of the Court to receive applications from individuals, non-governmental organisations or groups of individuals as provided in Article 34 of the Convention in respect of Articles 1 to 5 of this Protocol.

Article 7 – Relationship to the Convention

As between the States Parties, the provisions of Articles 1 to 6 of this Protocol shall be regarded as additional Articles to the Convention, and all the provisions of the Convention shall apply accordingly.

Article 8 – Signature and ratification

This Protocol shall be open for signature by member States of the Council of Europe which have signed the Convention. It is subject to ratification, acceptance or approval.

A member State of the Council of Europe may not ratify, accept or approve this Protocol without previously or simultaneously ratifying the Convention. Instruments of ratification, acceptance or approval shall be deposited with the Secretary General of the Council of Europe.

Article 9 – Entry into force

1 This Protocol shall enter into force on the first day of the month following the expiration of a period of two months after the date on which seven member States of the Council of Europe have expressed their consent to be bound by the Protocol in accordance with the provisions of Article 8.
2 In respect of any member State which subsequently expresses its consent to be bound by it, the Protocol shall enter into force on the first day of the month following the expiration of a period of two months after the date of the deposit of the instrument of ratification, acceptance or approval.

Article 10 – Depositary functions

The Secretary General of the Council of Europe shall notify all the member States of the Council of Europe of:

a any signature;
b the deposit of any instrument of ratification, acceptance or approval;
c any date of entry into force of this Protocol in accordance with Articles 6 and 9;
d any other act, notification or declaration relating to this Protocol.

In witness whereof the undersigned, being duly authorised thereto, have signed this Protocol. Done at Strasbourg, this 22nd day of November 1984, in English and French, both texts being equally authentic, in a single copy which shall be deposited in the archives of the Council of Europe. The Secretary General of the Council of Europe shall transmit certified copies to each member State of the Council of Europe.

Protocol No. 12 to the Convention for the Protection of Human Rights and Fundamental Freedoms [*not in force yet*]
Rome, 4.XI.2000

The member States of the Council of Europe signatory hereto,

Having regard to the fundamental principle according to which all persons are equal before the law and are entitled to the equal protection of the law;

Being resolved to take further steps to promote the equality of all persons through the collective enforcement of a general prohibition of discrimination by means of the Convention for the Protection of Human Rights and Fundamental Freedoms signed at Rome on 4 November 1950 (hereinafter referred to as 'the Convention');

Reaffirming that the principle of non-discrimination does not prevent States Parties from taking measures in order to promote full and effective equality, provided that there is an objective and reasonable justification for those measures,

Have agreed as follows:

Article 1 – General prohibition of discrimination

1   The enjoyment of any right set forth by law shall be secured without discrimination on any ground such as sex, race, colour, language, religion, political or other opinion, national or social origin, association with a national minority, property, birth or other status.

2   No one shall be discriminated against by any public authority on any ground such as those mentioned in paragraph 1.

Article 2 – Territorial application

1   Any State may, at the time of signature or when depositing its instrument of ratification, acceptance or approval, specify the territory or territories to which this Protocol shall apply.

2   Any State may at any later date, by a declaration addressed to the Secretary General of the Council of Europe, extend the application of this Protocol to any other territory specified in the declaration. In respect of such territory the Protocol shall enter into force on the first day of the month following the expiration of a period of three months after the date of receipt by the Secretary General of such declaration.

3   Any declaration made under the two preceding paragraphs may, in respect of any territory specified in such declaration, be withdrawn or modified by a notification addressed to the Secretary General of the Council of Europe. The withdrawal or modification shall become effective on the first day of the month following the expiration of a period of three months after the date of receipt of such notification by the Secretary General.

4   A declaration made in accordance with this article shall be deemed to have been made in accordance with paragraph 1 of Article 56 of the Convention.

5   Any State which has made a declaration in accordance with paragraph 1 or 2 of this article may at any time thereafter declare on behalf of one or more of the territories to which the declaration relates that it accepts the competence of the Court to receive applications from individuals, non-governmental organisations or groups of individuals as provided by Article 34 of the Convention in respect of Article 1 of this Protocol.

Article 3 – Relationship to the Convention

As between the States Parties, the provisions of Articles 1 and 2 of this Protocol shall be regarded as additional articles to the Convention, and all the provisions of the Convention shall apply accordingly.

Article 4 – Signature and ratification

This Protocol shall be open for signature by member States of the Council of Europe which have signed the Convention. It is subject to ratification, acceptance or approval. A member State of the Council of Europe may not ratify, accept or approve this Protocol without previously or simultaneously ratifying the Convention. Instruments of ratification, acceptance or approval shall be deposited with the Secretary General of the Council of Europe.

Article 5 – Entry into force

1   This Protocol shall enter into force on the first day of the month following the expiration of a period of three months after the date on which ten member States of the Council of Europe have expressed their consent to be bound by the Protocol in accordance with the provisions of Article 4.

2   In respect of any member State which subsequently expresses its consent to be bound by it, the Protocol shall enter into force on the first day of the month following the expiration of a period of three months after the date of the deposit of the instrument of ratification, acceptance or approval.

Article 6 – Depositary functions

The Secretary General of the Council of Europe shall notify all the member States of the Council of Europe of:

a   any signature;

b   the deposit of any instrument of ratification, acceptance or approval;

c   any date of entry into force of this Protocol in accordance with Articles 2 and 5;

d   any other act, notification or communication relating to this Protocol.

In witness whereof the undersigned, being duly authorised thereto, have signed this Protocol.

Done at Rome, this 4th day of November 2000, in English and in French, both texts being equally authentic, in a single copy which shall be deposited in the archives of the Council of Europe. The Secretary General of the Council of Europe shall transmit certified copies to each member State of the Council of Europe.

Protocol No. 13 to the Convention for the Protection of Human Rights and Fundamental Freedoms, concerning the abolition of the death penalty in all circumstances
[Vilnius, 3.V.2002]

The member States of the Council of Europe signatory hereto,

Convinced that everyone's right to life is a basic value in a democratic society and that the abolition of the death penalty is essential for the protection of this right and for the full recognition of the inherent dignity of all human beings;

Wishing to strengthen the protection of the right to life guaranteed by the Convention for the Protection of Human Rights and Fundamental Freedoms signed at Rome on 4 November 1950 (hereinafter referred to as 'the Convention');

Noting that Protocol No. 6 to the Convention, concerning the Abolition of the Death Penalty, signed at Strasbourg on 28 April 1983, does not exclude the death penalty in respect of acts committed in time of war or of imminent threat of war;

Being resolved to take the final step in order to abolish the death penalty in all circumstances, Have agreed as follows:

Article 1 – Abolition of the death penalty
The death penalty shall be abolished. No one shall be condemned to such penalty or executed.

Article 2 – Prohibition of derogations
No derogation from the provisions of this Protocol shall be made under Article 15 of the Convention.

Article 3 – Prohibition of reservations
No reservation may be made under Article 57 of the Convention in respect of the provisions of this Protocol.

Article 4 – Territorial application
1   Any State may, at the time of signature or when depositing its instrument of ratification, acceptance or approval, specify the territory or territories to which this Protocol shall apply.
2   Any State may at any later date, by a declaration addressed to the Secretary General of the Council of Europe, extend the application of this Protocol to any other territory specified in the declaration. In respect of such territory the Protocol shall enter into force on the first day of the month following the expiration of a period of three months after the date of receipt of such declaration by the Secretary General.
3   Any declaration made under the two preceding paragraphs may, in respect of any territory specified in such declaration, be withdrawn or modified by a notification addressed to the Secretary General. The withdrawal or modification shall become effective on the first day of the month following the expiration of a period of three months after the date of receipt of such notification by the Secretary General.

Article 5 – Relationship to the Convention
As between the States Parties the provisions of Articles 1 to 4 of this Protocol shall be regarded as additional articles to the Convention, and all the provisions of the Convention shall apply accordingly.

Article 6 – Signature and ratification
This Protocol shall be open for signature by member States of the Council of Europe which have signed the Convention. It is subject to ratification, acceptance or approval. A member State of the Council of Europe may not ratify, accept or approve this Protocol without previously or simultaneously ratifying the Convention. Instruments of ratification, acceptance or approval shall be deposited with the Secretary General of the Council of Europe.

Article 7 – Entry into force
1   This Protocol shall enter into force on the first day of the month following the expiration of a period of three months after the date on which ten member States of the Council of Europe have expressed their consent to be bound by the Protocol in accordance with the provisions of Article 6.

2 In respect of any member State which subsequently expresses its consent to be bound by it, the Protocol shall enter into force on the first day of the month following the expiration of a period of three months after the date of the deposit of the instrument of ratification, acceptance or approval.

Article 8 – Depositary functions

The Secretary General of the Council of Europe shall notify all the member States of the Council of Europe of:

a   any signature;
b   the deposit of any instrument of ratification, acceptance or approval;
c   any date of entry into force of this Protocol in accordance with Articles 4 and 7;
d   any other act, notification or communication relating to this Protocol.

In witness whereof the undersigned, being duly authorised thereto, have signed this Protocol. Done at Vilnius, this 3rd day of May 2002, in English and in French, both texts being equally authentic, in a single copy which shall be deposited in the archives of the Council of Europe. The Secretary General of the Council of Europe shall transmit certified copies to each member State of the Council of Europe.

Appendix 3

MEMBERS OF THE COUNCIL OF EUROPE AND CONVENTION RATIFICATIONS

I: MEMBERS OF THE COUNCIL OF EUROPE, as at February 2003
(with date of joining)

Albania (13.07.1995)
Andorra (10.10.1994)
Armenia (25.1.2001)
Austria (16.04.1956)
Azerbaijan (25.1.2001)
Belgium (5.5.1949)
Bosnia & Herzegovina (24.04.2002)
Bulgaria (7.5.1992)
Croatia (6.11.1996)
Cyprus (24.5.1961)
Czech Republic (30.6.1993)
Denmark (5.5.1949)
Estonia (14.5.1993)
Finland (5.5.1989)
France (5.5.1949)
Georgia (27.4.1999)
Germany (13.7.1950)
Greece (9.8.1949)
Hungary (6.11.1990)
Iceland (9.3.1950)
Ireland (5.5.1949)
Italy (5.5.1949)
Latvia (10.2.1995)

Liechtenstein (23.11.1978)
Lithuania (14.5.1993)
Luxembourg (5.5.1949)
(the former Yugoslav Republic of)
Macedonia (9.11.1995)
Malta (29.4.1965)
Moldova (13.7.1995)
Netherlands (5.5.1949)
Norway (5.5.1949)
Poland (29.11.1991)
Portugal (22.9.1976)
Romania (7.10.1993)
Russian Federation (28.2.1996)
San Marino (16.11.1988)
Slovakia (30.6.1993)
Slovenia (14.5.1993)
Spain (24.11.1977)
Sweden (5.5.1949)
Switzerland (6.5.1963)
Turkey (9.8.1949)
Ukraine (9.11.1995)
United Kingdom (5.5.1949)

Special Guests to the Parliamentary Assembly
Federal Republic of Yugoslavia (22.1.2001)

Observers to the Committee of Ministers
Canada (29.05.1996)
Holy See (7.03.1970)

Japan (20.11.1996)
Mexico (1.12.1999)
United States of America (10.01.1996)

Observers to the Parliamentary Assembly
Canada (28.05.1997)
Israel (2.12.1957)
Mexico (4.11.1999)

Map showing Members of the Council of Europe
Member States Special Guest to the Parliamentary Assembly

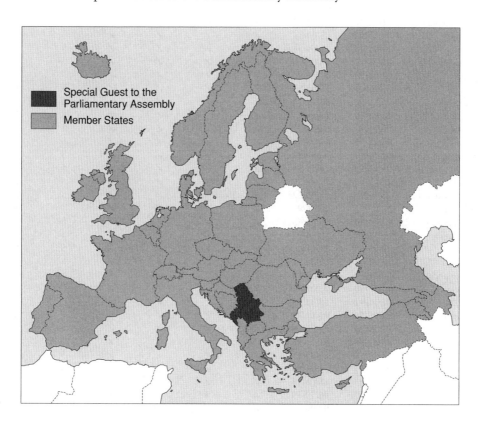

II: RATIFICATIONS OF CONVENTION PROTOCOLS, **as at February 2003**
This table lists which states have signed up to which of the Protocols which add substantive rights to the Convention; none of the other Protocols are still in effect, except
the 11th, which has amended the procedure and has been ratified by all parties to the
Convention.

(Key: 3 – ratified and in force; S – signed but not ratified; R – ratified, for a protocol
not in force; 10R indicates number of Ratifications required for the Protocol to come
into force)

Member State	Signature of Convention	Entry into force of Convention	1st Protocol	4th Protocol	6th Protocol	7th Protocol	12th Protocol	13th Protocol
Albania	13/07/95	02/10/96	✓	✓	✓	✓		
Andorra	10/11/94	22/01/96	–	–	✓	–		S
Armenia	25/01/01	26/04/02	✓	✓	S	✓		
Austria	13/12/57	03/09/58	✓	✓	✓	✓	S	S
Azerbaijan	25/01/01	15/04/02	✓	✓	✓	✓		
Belgium	04/11/50	14/06/55	✓	✓	✓	–	S	S
Bosnia and Herzegovina	24/04/02	12/07/02	✓	✓	✓	✓	S	S
Bulgaria	07/05/92	07/09/92	✓	✓	✓	✓		R
Croatia	06/11/96	05/11/97	✓	✓	✓	✓	R	R
Cyprus	16/12/61	06/10/62	✓	✓	✓	✓	R	S
Czech Republic	21/02/91	01/01/93	✓	✓	✓	✓	S	S
Denmark	04/11/50	03/09/53	✓	✓	✓	✓		R
Estonia	14/05/93	16/04/96	✓	✓	✓	✓	S	S
Finland	05/05/89	10/05/90	✓	✓	✓	✓	S	S
France	04/11/50	03/05/74	✓	✓	✓	✓		S
Georgia	27/04/99	20/05/99	✓	✓	✓	✓	R	S
Germany	04/11/50	03/09/53	✓	✓	✓	S	S	S
Greece	28/11/50	28/11/74	✓	–	✓	✓	S	S
Hungary	06/11/90	05/11/92	✓	✓	✓	✓	S	S
Iceland	04/11/50	03/09/53	✓	✓	✓	✓	S	S
Ireland	04/11/50	03/09/53	✓	✓	✓	✓	S	R
Italy	04/11/50	26/10/55	✓	✓	✓	✓	S	S
Latvia	10/02/95	27/06/97	✓	✓	✓	✓	S	S
Liechtenstein	23/11/78	08/09/82	✓	–	✓	✓	S	R
Lithuania	14/05/93	20/06/95	✓	✓	✓	✓		S
Luxembourg	04/11/50	03/09/53	✓	✓	✓	✓	S	S
Macedonia	09/11/95	10/04/97	✓	✓	✓	✓	S	S
Malta	12/12/66	23/01/67	✓	✓	✓	–	S	R
Moldova	13/07/95	12/09/97	✓	✓	✓	✓	S	S
Netherlands	04/11/50	31/08/54	✓	✓	✓	S	S	S
Norway	04/11/50	03/09/53	✓	✓	✓	✓		S
Poland	26/11/91	19/01/93	✓	✓	✓	✓		S
Portugal	22/09/76	09/11/78	✓	✓	✓	S	S	S
Romania	07/10/93	20/06/94	✓	✓	✓	✓	S	S
Russia	28/02/96	05/05/98	✓	✓	S	✓	S	
San Marino	16/11/88	22/03/89	✓	✓	✓	✓	S	S
Slovakia	21/02/91	01/01/93	✓	✓	✓	✓	S	S
Slovenia	14/05/93	28/06/94	✓	✓	✓	✓	S	S
Spain	24/11/77	04/10/79	✓	S	✓	S		S
Sweden	28/11/50	03/09/53	✓	✓	✓	✓		S
Switzerland	21/12/72	28/11/74	S	–	✓	✓		R
Turkey	04/11/50	18/05/54	✓	S	–	S	S	
Ukraine	09/11/95	11/09/97	✓	✓	✓	✓	S	S
United Kingdom	04/11/50	03/09/53	✓	S	✓	–		S
Total parties (signed but not ratified)		44(0)	42(1)	37(3)	41(3)	35(5)	3(27)	7(32)
Entered into force		03/09/53	18/05/54	02/05/68	01/03/85	01/11/88	10R	10R

THE UNIVERSAL DECLARATION OF HUMAN RIGHTS

Preamble

Whereas recognition of the inherent dignity and of the equal and inalienable rights of all members of the human family is the foundation of freedom, justice and peace in the world,

Whereas disregard and contempt for human rights have resulted in barbarous acts which have outraged the conscience of mankind, and the advent of a world in which human beings shall enjoy freedom of speech and belief and freedom from fear and want has been proclaimed as the highest aspiration of the common people,

Whereas it is essential, if man is not to be compelled to have recourse, as a last resort, to rebellion against tyranny and oppression, that human rights should be protected by the rule of law,

Whereas it is essential to promote the development of friendly relations between nations,

Whereas the peoples of the United Nations have in the Charter reaffirmed their faith in fundamental human rights, in the dignity and worth of the human person and in the equal rights of men and women and have determined to promote social progress and better standards of life in larger freedom,

Whereas Member States have pledged themselves to achieve, in cooperation with the United Nations, the promotion of universal respect for and observance of human rights and fundamental freedoms,

Whereas a common understanding of these rights and freedoms is of the greatest importance for the full realization of this pledge,

Now, therefore, the General Assembly proclaims this Universal Declaration of Human Rights as a common standard of achievement for all peoples and all nations, to the end that every individual and every organ of society, keeping this Declaration constantly in mind, shall strive by teaching and education to promote respect for these rights and freedoms and by progressive measures, national and international, to secure their universal and effective recognition and observance, both among the peoples of Member States themselves and among the peoples of territories under their jurisdiction.

Article 1

All human beings are born free and equal in dignity and rights. They are endowed with reason and conscience and should act towards one another in a spirit of brotherhood.

Article 2

Everyone is entitled to all the rights and freedoms set forth in this Declaration, without distinction of any kind, such as race, colour, sex, language, religion, political or other opinion, national or social origin, property, birth or other status.

Furthermore, no distinction shall be made on the basis of the political, jurisdictional or international status of the country or territory to which a person belongs, whether it be independent, trust, non-self-governing or under any other limitation of sovereignty.

Article 3

Everyone has the right to life, liberty and security of person.

Article 4

No one shall be held in slavery or servitude; slavery and the slave trade shall be prohibited in all their forms.

Article 5

No one shall be subjected to torture or to cruel, inhuman or degrading treatment or punishment.

Article 6

Everyone has the right to recognition everywhere as a person before the law.

Article 7

All are equal before the law and are entitled without any discrimination to equal protection of the law. All are entitled to equal protection against any discrimination in violation of this Declaration and against any incitement to such discrimination.

Article 8

Everyone has the right to an effective remedy by the competent national tribunals for acts violating the fundamental rights granted him by the constitution or by law.

Article 9

No one shall be subjected to arbitrary arrest, detention or exile.

Article 10

Everyone is entitled in full equality to a fair and public hearing by an independent and impartial tribunal, in the determination of his rights and obligations and of any criminal charge against him.

Article 11

1 Everyone charged with a penal offence has the right to be presumed innocent until proved guilty according to law in a public trial at which he has had all the guarantees necessary for his defence.
2 No one shall be held guilty of any penal offence on account of any act or omission which did not constitute a penal offence, under national or international law, at the time when it was committed. Nor shall a heavier penalty be imposed than the one that was applicable at the time the penal offence was committed.

Article 12

No one shall be subjected to arbitrary interference with his privacy, family, home or correspondence, nor to attacks upon his honour and reputation. Everyone has the right to the protection of the law against such interference or attacks.

Article 13

1 Everyone has the right to freedom of movement and residence within the borders of each State.
2 Everyone has the right to leave any country, including his own, and to return to his country.

Article 14

1 Everyone has the right to seek and to enjoy in other countries asylum from persecution.
2 This right may not be invoked in the case of prosecutions genuinely arising from non-political crimes or from acts contrary to the purposes and principles of the United Nations.

Article 15

1 Everyone has the right to a nationality.
2 No one shall be arbitrarily deprived of his nationality nor denied the right to change his nationality.

Article 16

1 Men and women of full age, without any limitation due to race, nationality or religion, have the right to marry and to found a family. They are entitled to equal rights as to marriage, during marriage and at its dissolution.
2 Marriage shall be entered into only with the free and full consent of the intending spouses.
3 The family is the natural and fundamental group unit of society and is entitled to protection by society and the State.

Article 17

1 Everyone has the right to own property alone as well as in association with others.
2 No one shall be arbitrarily deprived of his property.

Article 18

Everyone has the right to freedom of thought, conscience and religion; this right includes freedom to change his religion or belief, and freedom, either alone or in community with others and in public or private, to manifest his religion or belief in teaching, practice, worship and observance.

Article 19

Everyone has the right to freedom of opinion and expression; this right includes freedom to hold opinions without interference and to seek, receive and impart information and ideas through any media and regardless of frontiers.

Article 20

1 Everyone has the right to freedom of peaceful assembly and association.
2 No one may be compelled to belong to an association.

Article 21

1 Everyone has the right to take part in the government of his country, directly or through freely chosen representatives.
2 Everyone has the right to equal access to public service in his country.
3 The will of the people shall be the basis of the authority of government; this will shall be expressed in periodic and genuine elections which shall be by universal and equal suffrage and shall be held by secret vote or by equivalent free voting procedures.

Article 22

Everyone, as a member of society, has the right to social security and is entitled to real-ization, through national effort and international co-operation and in accordance with the organization and resources of each State, of the economic, social and cultural rights indispensable for his dignity and the free development of his personality.

Article 23

1 Everyone has the right to work, to free choice of employment, to just and favour-able conditions of work and to protection against unemployment.
2 Everyone, without any discrimination, has the right to equal pay for equal work.
3 Everyone who works has the right to just and favourable remuneration ensuring for himself and his family an existence worthy of human dignity, and supplemented, if necessary, by other means of social protection.
4 Everyone has the right to form and to join trade unions for the protection of his interests.

Article 24

Everyone has the right to rest and leisure, including reasonable limitation of working hours and periodic holidays with pay.

Article 25

1 Everyone has the right to a standard of living adequate for the health and well-being of himself and of his family, including food, clothing, housing and medical care and necessary social services, and the right to security in the event of unem-ployment, sickness, disability, widowhood, old age or other lack of livelihood in circumstances beyond his control.
2 Motherhood and childhood are entitled to special care and assistance. All children, whether born in or out of wedlock, shall enjoy the same social protection.

Article 26

1 Everyone has the right to education. Education shall be free, at least in the elementary and fundamental stages. Elementary education shall be compulsory. Technical and professional education shall be made generally available and higher education shall be equally accessible to all on the basis of merit.

2 Education shall be directed to the full development of the human personality and to the strengthening of respect for human rights and fundamental freedoms. It shall promote understanding, tolerance and friendship among all nations, racial or religious groups, and shall further the activities of the United Nations for the maintenance of peace.

3 Parents have a prior right to choose the kind of education that shall be given to their children.

Article 27

1 Everyone has the right freely to participate in the cultural life of the community, to enjoy the arts and to share in scientific advancement and its benefits.

2 Everyone has the right to the protection of the moral and material interests resulting from any scientific, literary or artistic production of which he is the author.

Article 28

Everyone is entitled to a social and international order in which the rights and freedoms set forth in this Declaration can be fully realized.

Article 29

1 Everyone has duties to the community in which alone the free and full development of his personality is possible.

2 In the exercise of his rights and freedoms, everyone shall be subject only to such limitations as are determined by law solely for the purpose of securing due recognition and respect for the rights and freedoms of others and of meeting the just requirements of morality, public order and the general welfare in a democratic society.

3 These rights and freedoms may in no case be exercised contrary to the purposes and principles of the United Nations.

Article 30

Nothing in this Declaration may be interpreted as implying for any State, group or person any right to engage in any activity or to perform any act aimed at the destruction of any of the rights and freedoms set forth herein.

FURTHER READING

We have avoided citations of the academic literature in the text because this is designed as an introductory text to the rights and the law on them, rather than to the academic discussion concerning them. However, there is a great deal of material available for those who wish to learn more about any particular area covered. Thus we include some suggestions for further reading.

General texts on the Act

There are a very large number of other books and articles on the Act and the Convention. The following are some of the leading general textbooks.

Starmer, *European Human Rights Law* (Legal Action Group, 1999)

Lester & Pannick, *Human Rights Law and Practice* (Butterworths, 1999)

Grosz, Beatson & Duffy, *Human Rights: the 1998 Act and the European Convention* (Sweet & Maxwell, 2000)

Simor and Emmerson, *Human Rights Practice* (Sweet & Maxwell, 2002)

Some useful digests of European Court case law are:

Starmer, *Blackstone's Human Rights Digest* (Blackstone Press, 2001)

Nash & Furse, *Essential Human Rights Cases* (Jordans, 2002)

Lawson & Schermers, *Leading Cases of the European Court* (1994)

There have also been a host of articles, collections of essays and case notes on various aspects of the Act. The following are some of those which are more general in their discussion:

Beatson & Smith (eds), *The Human Rights Act and the Criminal Justice and Regulatory Process* (Hart, 1999)

Campbell, Ewing and Tomkins (eds), *Sceptical Essays on Human Rights* (Oxford University Press, 2001)

Craig, *The Courts, The Human Rights Act and Judicial Review* (2001) 117 Law Quarterly Review 589

Ashworth, *Criminal Proceedings after the Human Rights Act: The First Year* [2001] Criminal Law Review 855

Beyleveld, Kirkham & Townend, *Which Presumption? A critique of the House of Lords' reasoning on retrospectivity and the Human Rights Act* (2002) 22 Legal Studies 185

Morgan, *Questioning the 'true effect' of the Human Rights Act* (2002) 22 Legal Studies 259

The Law Commission, the government's law review and reform body, has published a number of reports which are relevant to this area, most especially Report 266, *Damages under the Human Rights Act 1998*, which is a comprehensive survey of this topic. Reports 267, *Double Jeopardy and Prosecution Appeals*, and 269, *Bail and the Human Rights Act 1998*, raise specific human rights issues. These, and their other reports, can be found online at http://www.lawcom.gov.uk/

Theory of rights

There is, of course, a vast literature on the nature of rights within the disciplines of legal and political theory, Some of the key writers in the development of modern views of rights and their place in our law and constitution are mentioned in Chapter 3, such as Locke, Blackstone, Paine, Wollstonecraft, Dicey, etc. All we can really do here is acknowledge the main modern jurisprudential texts which underlie the discussion in Chapter 2 (and elsewhere). These are:

Hohfeld, *Fundamental Legal Conceptions as Applied in Judicial Reasoning* (Yale University Press, 1923), an influential analysis of rights.

Fuller, *The Morality of Law* (Yale University Press, 1964), is an important analysis of the rule of law; and one significant response was that of: Hart (1965) 78 Harvard Law Review 1281, reprinted in Hart, *Essays in Jurisprudence and Philosophy* (Oxford University Press, 1983).

Hart, *The Concept of Law* (Oxford University Press, 1961, re-issued 1997)

Finnis, *Natural law and Natural Rights* (Oxford University Press, 1980)

A useful introductory selection of material on the subject of rights, including some of the above, can be found in: Davies & Holdcroft, *Jurisprudence, Text and Materials* (Butterworths, 1991).

History of rights

For those interested in the history of rights in general, we recommend: Kelly, *A Short History of Western Legal Theory* (Oxford University Press, 1992). For the history of the precedents to, and genesis of, the Convention itself, we highly recommend: Simpson, *Human Rights and the End of Empire* (Oxford University Press, 2001); this was an invaluable source for our substantially more summary survey in Chapter 3.

For a more general history of English law, a good overview is: Baker, *An Introduction to English Legal History* (Butterworths, 1990); or there are more substantial works such as Holdsworth's *A History of English Law*.

Constitutional and administrative law

Our discussion of the United Kingdom constitution, of the field of administrative law, which is primarily the law of judicial review, and of the relationship between Parliament and the courts, is necessarily limited. For more detail in these areas, some leading textbooks are:

Craig, *Administrative Law* (Sweet & Maxwell, 1999)

Wade & Forsyth, *Administrative Law* (Oxford University Press, 2000)

De Smith & Brazier, *Constitutional and Administrative Law* (Penguin, 1998)

Forsyth (ed), *Judicial Review and the Constitution* (Hart, 2000)

Heuston, *Essays in Constitutional Law* (Stevens, 1964)

Some useful websites

References to debates in Parliament are references to volumes of *Hansard*, the official record of Parliamentary proceedings, which are either HC (House of Commons) or HL (House of Lords). These can be found online at http://www.parliament.the-stationery-office.co.uk This includes House of Lords' judicial decisions. Privy Council decisions can be found at http://www.privy-council.org.uk

Some other decisions can be found online at the Court Service website, http://www.courtservice.gov.uk, which also contains information should you wish to bring a claim under the Act.

More recent Acts of Parliament and Statutory Instruments (SI) can be found online at http://www.legislation.hmso.gov.uk The government's website, for other governmental information, which includes proposals for legislation, is http://www.ukonline.gov.uk

The Council of Europe has a very full website at http://www.coe.int In particular, it contains the full series of Council treaties, including the Convention, with the status of the various protocols, etc. at http://conventions.coe.int The European Court's site can be found at: http://www.echr.coe.int

If you are interested more generally in human rights treaties, the most relevant website is the United Nations website: http://www.un.org/ which contains all the UN treaties.

Case references

The following abbreviations used in the text refer to series of law reports. The leading series of reports referred to are:

EHRR	European Human Rights Reports: European Court cases
DR, CD	European Commission decisions
AC	Appeal Cases (House of Lords and Privy Council decisions)
QB/KB	Queen's Bench/King's Bench Reports
Ch	Chancery Division Reports
Fam	Family Division Reports
All ER	All England Law Reports
WLR	Weekly Law Reports

QB/KB, Ch, Fam: } Reports of Court of Appeal and High Court decisions

Other general series of law reports cited are:

BHRC	Butterworths Human Rights Cases
CAR	Criminal Appeal Reports
Crim LR	Criminal Law Review
EHRLR	European Human Rights Law Review
FCR	Family Court Reporter
FLR	Family Law Reports
FSR	Fleet Street Reports
IRLR	Industrial Relations Law Reports
LGR	Local Government Reports
LTL	Lawtel Law Reports (online at http://www.lawtel.co.uk)
RTR	Road Traffic Reports
Times	The Times Law Reports
UKHRR	United Kingdom Human Rights Reports
US	United States report

INDEX